A CALL TO ASSEMBLY

WILLIE RUFF

VIKING

A Call to Assembly

THE AUTOBIOGRAPHY OF A MUSICAL STORYTELLER

VIKING
Published by the Penguin Group
Viking Penguin, a division of Penguin Books USA Inc.,
375 Hudson Street, New York, New York 10014, U.S.A.
Penguin Books Ltd, 27 Wrights Lane,
London W8 5TZ, England
Penguin Books Australia Ltd, Ringwood,
Victoria, Australia
Penguin Books Canada Ltd, 2801 John Street,
Markham, Ontario, Canada L3R 1B4
Penguin Books (N.Z.) Ltd, 182–190 Wairau Road,
Auckland 10, New Zealand

Penguin Books Ltd, Registered Offices:
Harmondsworth, Middlesex, England

First published in 1991 by Viking Penguin,
a division of Penguin Books USA Inc.

10 9 8 7 6 5 4 3 2 1

Photograph credits appear on pages xv and xvi.

LIBRARY OF CONGRESS CATALOGING IN PUBLICATION DATA
Ruff, Willie.
    A call to assembly : the autobiography of a musical storyteller /
Willie Ruff.
        p.   cm.
    ISBN 0–670–83800–4
    1. Ruff, Willie. 2. Jazz musicians—United States—Biography.
I. Title.
ML419.R84A3   1991
788.9'4165'092—dc20
[B]   90–50514

Printed in the United States of America
Set in Electra
Designed by Kate Nichols

This book is dedicated to Mama, who taught me to read between the lines. It is also for my many students; they showed me how to teach.

"Hambone, hambone, where you bin?
Been around the world and I'm back agin."

A catalogue of recordings by Willie Ruff and the Mitchell-Ruff Duo is available from The Kepler Label, P.O. Box 1779, New Haven, Connecticut 06507, or from Dargason Music, P.O. Box 189, Burbank, California 91503.

Acknowledgments

I am grateful to Bill Zinsser who, after writing a book and two *New Yorker* pieces about me, my music, and the Mitchell-Ruff Duo, went one better: he told me what a great editor and music lover Al Silverman is, and he put us together. Al, as my editor-in-chief, shepherded me and my ideas through this writing, took my story to heart, taught me much, and together with his warm and wonderful bride, Rosa, fed me fabulous home cooking and became my trusted friend.

No author should expect the good luck of having both Al and Beena Kamlani edit them; I was that lucky.

I also thank the gifted young writer, Cheryl Cavitt, my former UCLA student and friend, who read my manuscript and gave me the benefit of her wisdom and good taste.

The photographs of the 1972 Duke Ellington Convocation at Yale were taken by the ex-drummer and former Tuskegee flight cadet, Reggie Jackson of New Haven. Cal Stoner, while stationed at Tuskegee during World War II as official photographer, took the pictures of Lena Horne, Joe Louis, and General B. O. Davis, Sr., and his son, Colonel B. O. Davis, Jr.

Contents

PART ONE
Home

PART TWO
Army

PART THREE
New Haven

PART FOUR
Performing

PART FIVE
International Relations

Illustrations

Lionel Hampton, Billy Brooks and Eddie Preston (AP/Wide World Photos)

The duo in Yale's Sprague Hall

Michele Ruff, at age 14

Kenny Clarke (Reggie Jackson)

Willie "The Lion" Smith and Duke Ellington (Reggie Jackson)

Mary Lou Williams (Reggie Jackson)

Joe Williams (Reggie Jackson)

Charlie Mingus (Reggie Jackson)

The author with Dwike Mitchell, Max Roach, Clark Terry and Sonny Stitt (Reggie Jackson)

William Warfield (Reggie Jackson)

Cootie Williams (Reggie Jackson)

Kingman Brewster and Duke Ellington (Reggie Jackson)

Benny Carter (Reggie Jackson)

Odetta and others (Reggie Jackson)

Eubie Blake and Noble Sissle (Reggie Jackson)

Dizzy Gillespie (Reggie Jackson)

Jo Jones (Reggie Jackson)

The Mitchell-Ruff Duo in China, 1981

Major General Joseph Wheeler

Grover Ruff at age 90

The duo today

Unless otherwise indicated, all the photographs in this book are from the author's collection.

PROLOGUE

ONE NIGHT IN 1967, my musical partner, Dwike Mitchell, and I were in New York, playing at a jazz emporium called the Hickory House, when Duke Ellington and Billy Strayhorn came in together. John Popkin, the proprietor, loved feeding stars, and Ellington, a friend of Popkin's who was devoted to the Hickory House menu, was never allowed to pay for a meal there. To return the kindness, Duke advised Popkin on jazz groups he felt would be good for business. In fact, he had suggested the Mitchell-Ruff Duo, Mitchell's piano and my French horn and bass, for the job we were playing that night.

I knew Ellington was then between tours. I also knew he was there that night on a diplomatic mission: he'd called me very early one morning a few days earlier from somewhere on the road. He did all his social calling (often to the consternation of his friends) after a night's work, generally in the predawn hours. When the sound of the hotel phone jolted me out of a deep sleep, Ellington began cooing into my ear the sugary platitudes he loved using when jiving his friends.

"One hopes not to disturb the sweet repose of the Muses' favorite French horn and bass man at this uncivilized hour," he began in his characteristic fashion. "And please believe that this humble working slob prays forgiveness. But ahh me, how one envies the exalted who've already achieved beyond measure, and whose riches and fame afford, such luxurious leisure as yours. [Pause for breath.] *"We* want you to know that when *we* grow up, *we* want to be exactly like *you."*

Then I knew why Duke was calling. Two nights earlier, Popkin and I had had a noisy spat when I told him the duo was ready for a rest and would be leaving in two weeks. He went through the roof—but hard. Business was good, and he'd hoped we would stay right through the summer. And there he stood in front of a packed house of diners, his face gone purple, shaking his raised fists and screaming at me:

"Whaddya mean, Ruff, giving notice, for Chrissakes? You can't do this to me. Don't we treat you good? Duke Ellington said you were good people. He likes you fellows. He went to the trouble to recommend you, didn't he? I'm going to call Duke tonight and tell him what you're doing to me!" So here was Ambassador Ellington on the phone, sweet-talking me in the line of duty.

I said, "OK, Maestro, when did Popkin call, and just what did he say?"

Switching gears out of the jive mode, Duke said, "Aw, come on, where's your charity, Willie? John Popkin's just a little guy running a good place to eat steaks and good Chinese food. How is it going to hurt you and Mitchell to stick with him awhile longer? If business is as good as he says it is, ask him for a raise. Haven't you learned how to handle white folk yet?" I said that we needed a rest, not a raise; to which he remarked—back in the jive mode—"You're tired? You need a rest? Ohhh, poor lamb . . . poor baby . . . Hold the phone while I borrow Ray Nance's violin and improvise an appropriately sad and pitying air for the working class."

I tried not to laugh too long and went on to explain that after my recent divorce, I was moving to Los Angeles and had promised to spend some undivided time during the summer with my ten-year-old daughter, Michele. At that, Ellington stopped kidding around.

"Go back to sleep," he said. "I'll fall by to see you kitties in a couple of days. Sweet dreams."

Over the years, I had come to enjoy a congenial friendship with Ellington. I was always welcome backstage whenever I turned up in cities around the world where Duke and his musicians were working. I loved to listen to the band and visit with my idols, Harry Carney, Johnny Hodges, Ray Nance, Lawrence Brown, Cootie Williams, and others among his distinguished sidemen. Put simply, Dwike Mitchell and I worshiped Ellington, both the legend and the man.

So here were Duke and Strayhorn at Popkin's joint inviting Mitchell and me to sit with them and share the Chinese meal. The talk predictably turned to our "problem" with the boss. Ellington was expansive, felt good, and was visibly making the most of his role of peacemaker.

He had good news. He'd already talked to Popkin, told him of my promise to my daughter, soothed him, and found him a replacement for the Mitchell-Ruff Duo, an English piano trio. There was, however, one minor hitch: the Englishmen were in London, still on another job.

"Would you gents consider staying on an extra week or so, until the Brits arrive?" Mitchell said he'd enjoy helping me entertain Michele in New York that extra week, and Popkin was satisfied. Duke, leveling his most self-satisfied smirk at us, tossed off this improvisation on one of his favorite biblical pronouncements:

"You see, baby," he said as he took up a Hickory House napkin and flicked a grain of shrimp fried rice from his mustache, "bread cast upon the water comes back buttered on *both* sides."

A few nights later, when the Ellington orchestra had taken off on a string of cross-country one-nighters, Strayhorn was back at the Hickory House, alone. We knew he'd had surgery weeks before he came in with Duke, but was on the mend. He ate dinner while we played. I noticed him writing something on paper as I played the horn. He stayed on late into the night. The next night, he was back again, and over a drink during intermission he put a few technical questions to me about the French horn's range, its loudness, bent notes, and the use of the mute. A couple of nights later he showed up once more, this time with a message:

"Willie," Billy Strayhorn said, "can you come over to my apartment sometime soon and play something I've written for you and the French horn?"

I was startled. Strayhorn had written something for me? "Is this afternoon soon enough?" I asked.

That afternoon, horn in hand, I called on the master composer, songwriter, and arranger. Strayhorn was seated at the Steinway. He still looked slightly frail from his operation, but he went right to work accompanying me as I played a passage of his new composition. It was a heavy work of dark sonorities, laden with surprising melodic turns that seemed to leap through daring rhythmic configurations into totally unexplored crevasses of the diatonic scale. No light musical entertainment, this, and like his thoughtful "Lush Life," the composition was extremely hard to play but overwhelmingly rewarding and masterful.

He led me through the first movement of what he intended as a suite, taking it section by section until he was sure of what was needed. Then he used his eraser, tore away pages, resketched, and played through the new materials with me until he was nearly satisfied. I was in heaven. How did I get lucky enough to attract the notice of the composer of "Take the A Train" and "Passion Flower"? Nobody this important had ever written an original work for me or the duo before.

Then more work with the manuscript, and we took a break for the dinner working on the stove; Strayhorn cooked as imaginatively as he wrote music. During the main course of lamb chops, fried corn, new peas, and yams, the phone rang. Ellington was calling from Omaha.

"Listen, Edward," his arranger said, "you called at a good time. I want you to hear something new. Gotta minute?" Strayhorn poured a generous slug of wine into my glass and signaled me to wash away the lamb chop and take up the horn. Performing an unfinished work long-distance for Duke Ellington with the grease of a lamb chop still on my embouchure made my blood rush. But I did as I was told.

When we had played all he'd written, Billy took up the phone and accepted Ellington's compliments graciously. More talk followed. Words like "transition," "modulation," "bridge," "coda," and "diminuendo" flew back and forth to Omaha. More scribbling. Then came the signal to rinse again, and Strayhorn sat down to repeat with me the middle section. After we'd played a few bars of it through twice, there was further talk on the phone, and out came the eraser. Strayhorn expanded parts and added dynamics, while the receiver rested on the

Steinway. There was no apparent rush and scurry. We played the new and very much improved version again and again. By then it was time for me to rush out to the Hickory House. I shudder to think how much that phone call cost the Ellington-Strayhorn duo. But that's the way we did it for the rest of the week, my horn and I at Strayhorn's, playing for Ellington somewhere out on the distant prairie.

Days later, when he had the suite set down in its final manuscript form, Strayhorn said, "Now I want to hear it with a *real* pianist. Call Mitchell!"

For the next several days, Mitchell and I came together to Strayhorn's apartment and worked at learning the suite. On the first day, Strayhorn sat beside Mitchell on the piano bench, propped the new manuscript on the music rack of his Steinway and turned to sections he wanted to discuss. With his elegant finger, he pointed to places in the score.

"What I've written here," he said to Mitchell, "is quite complete in the compositional sense. But I want this first meeting to feel to you like a fitting, as in 'fit' a custom-made suit. The compositional elements should fit *your* hands, which are so much larger and more powerful than mine. . . . You know how to make sections like these on this page as big and as rich in sonority as you can. But here in this interlude, let the horn ring through. . . . Let Willie's sound kind of hover over it all, right there. And pause here, but only slightly. . . . Over in this middle part, your line and the horn line are of equal importance. Balance is the key word; but that's the kind of thing you two do naturally anyway. I have left you space and, at the same time, given indications of essential details. . . ."

By now Mitchell was alive with excitement. His large fingers trembled as he carefully shaped them to fit the powerful, two-fisted chords Stray had written to underscore the horn theme. And *wham!* Stray was up off the piano bench at the huge sound Mitchell made. He stomped the floor and beamed at Mitchell. "Hell yes!" he hollered. "That's what I had in mind; I just don't have the hands and strength to make it sound *that* way."

Mitchell's reaction to the compliment was almost sheepish. "Ohhh, I see more clearly now what Ruff has been trying to describe these past two weeks. It's a very beautiful and powerful piece, Billy."

When Ellington called later that afternoon, Strayhorn put the receiver close to the piano strings.

"Now, Edward, you'll hear the final setting, with Dwike Mitchell at the Steinway." And at last Billy Strayhorn's Suite for Horn and Piano took its place in our permanent repertoire.

Several months later, while I was living in Los Angeles and teaching at UCLA, my phone rang and Ellington's voice surprised me; it was afternoon, the wrong time for him to call. But Strayhorn had died a few weeks before, and Ellington's life and most of his old habits had changed. Nobody among his friends could have guessed how much the loss of Strayhorn, his greatest artistic ally, would cost him. Still, his voice that day sounded the same as ever, only better, more enthusiastic than I'd heard him in a long time.

"Strayhorn had such an extraordinary musical life in New York," Ellington began; he was in no mood for small talk. "He should have a fitting memorial here. He was a New York composer; I mean, what other New Yorker wrote 'Take the A Train' and 'Upper Manhattan Medical Group'? I'm establishing a Billy Strayhorn Memorial Scholarship at the Juilliard School, and we're going to kick it off with a gala: the *dream* concert, man.

"Imagine a program with Stray's friends: Lena Horne, Tony Bennett, Willie 'The Lion' Smith, Joe Williams, Clarke Terry, Lou Rawls, Carmen DeLavallade, Geoffrey Holder, and of course all his many friends in my band—"

I interrupted, "That sounds like a concert I don't want to miss. Count me in for a ticket."

"Oh, no," said Ellington, "that's not what we had in mind. I want you and your partner on the stage to play that fabulous suite Strayhorn wrote for you two. I still hear that music coming from Stray's apartment on the phone.

"The concert will be at Lincoln Center on Sunday, October 6. I'll get back to you later about a rehearsal time."

On the day of the performance, at Philharmonic Hall, Ellington's rehearsal plans were still sketchy; there was only enough time for the singers and dancers to do a quick run-through with the orchestra. Mitchell and I made ourselves comfortable backstage, cooled our heels and "visited" with the stars. Carmen DeLavallade and Miss Horne charmed us all with their beauty, and Geoffrey Holder, with his deep voice and towering frame, gave us individual lessons in the side-to-side neck-stretching head dance of Thai dancers.

Ellington, rehearsing the band onstage, led Tony Bennett through his set, called Lena for a run-through, and Joe Williams sang "Come Sunday." Willie "The Lion" Smith, the old piano patriarch, just directed traffic and told us all how much the "kid" (Ellington), along with Fats Waller, had learned from him since he, Smith, had become Duke's adviser in Harlem in the 1920s, how he had taught him the ropes—on and off the keyboard—and watched him grow into his artistic maturity. It was clear, too, that Ellington valued the Lion's presence. They acted like father and son.

By showtime, everything was in readiness, and the program began with Duke and the orchestra onstage. The artists waiting backstage could hear that the band sounded great. Lena Horne said, "Listen to them! They're playing their hearts out for Strayhorn."

But none of us knew beforehand when Duke wanted the next act onstage, or who it would be. We all just had to wait and wonder when Ellington would call on us.

During an extended trombone solo by Lawrence Brown, or a Jimmy Hamilton clarinet solo, Duke would sidle to the wings to chat with Lena Horne, laugh with the Lion, Tony Bennett, Lou Rawls, and jive around with Joe Williams and me. He was comfortable now, in his element, working his magic. But we, his anxious pool of performers, waiting to be told when we would go on, were pacing nervously. He gazed casually into our expectant faces like a seasoned gourmet considering a dream menu.

Smiling at Miss Horne, he said, "I think your public is properly primed and ready for you now, darling. Ready?" Then he suddenly scooted back to the front of the orchestra, cut off their large resonant chord, and went to the microphone. When he announced Lena Horne, the audience roared. Willie the Lion snatched off his derby hat, slapped his thigh, and exploded out of his chair.

"You can't beat him! That guy just can't be beat. I don't care *how* you cut it. My Gawd! You see what he just did? He's got a dozen world-class artists, a *million dollars'* worth a talent waiting right here in this wing, and he hasn't said a word to anybody about the order of this program. Only *he* knows who's on next; he's making it up as he goes along, I tell ya. You can't beat experience, man. You know what I call him? 'The Master of Situations'!"

For more than two and a half hours we all watched as Ellington mastered the situation: playing out his dream concert, dishing up his musical feast with the flair of the consummate host-presenter. One surprising delicacy after another showed his practiced attention to texture, color, and, above all, timing. The dancing was tastefully placed and balanced, and there was proportion to the singing and the instrumental performances.

Then Ellington pointed at Mitchell and me in the wings at the side of the stage and went to the microphone to share with his audience just how it was that he'd been the first person to hear Strayhorn's new suite, long-distance. Willie the Lion eased up to my ear and whispered:

"Now go out there and kill 'em for Strayhorn."

The suite we were about to play was written during Strayhorn's short but stunningly introspective final creative outburst. Another of his most serious compositions, "Blood Count," was also a product of that period, and like "Blood Count," the suite thunders with highly autobiographical overtones; the moods of a vibrant musical career, shutting down.

As Mitchell and I began to play, I was oblivious to our Lincoln Center surroundings. I was hearing Strayhorn in his apartment, leading us through the music; talking us through the transitions; showing me when to bring out a counterline, when to make my horn's voice match Mitchell's heavy piano sonorities. Strayhorn's powerful presence was there on the stage with us, giving directions and sounding his music through us and making us play better than we knew we could. The spell was broken for me only as the last note lingered and died and Joe Williams and Tony Bennett led the applause there among the performers in the wings.

As soon as we left the stage, Dizzy Gillespie, who had been down in the audience, burst through the dressing room door. "Mitchell and

Ruff! Man! I didn't even know Stray had written that music for you guys. What a compliment to you. He sure as hell *wrote* it, didn't he? And you two played it so fabulously. The three of us have to make a record together some time soon, you hear?"

Ellington ended the concert with a sensational string of selections by the orchestra. Then all the artists assembled to link hands in a long line across the stage and bow long and low with Ellington.

Afterward, in a moment of quiet, Duke gave a wise wink to us all.

"Strayhorn," he said, "smiled tonight."

I write this years later, remembering it as if I had just stepped out of Strayhorn's apartment or slipped into the wings at Lincoln Center, with Ellington's voice shivering me in the heart. It was indeed a landmark, a transition for a still young artist who had come from what seemed like nowhere, had arrived somewhere, and was going he knew not where.

The one thing I do know about that magical evening—about the totality of that experience with those creators and ambassadors of the music that was born and bred nowhere else but in America—is that it seemed to represent to me a calling: "a call to assembly" was the phrase they used when I was a young army private. I knew I was on notice, and I had to heed the call.

So my life in music did become what one of my mentors, an old army musician, once hung on me as I was learning to play the horn. "Junior," he said, "always remember that music don't mean a thing unless it tells a story. You've got a story to tell, and don't you ever let nothing or nobody make you ashamed to tell it in music."

I hope you will hear the music behind the words, the good "re-members" of one American musician.

PART ONE

Home

CHAPTER ONE

Daddy Long

THE BANKS OF THE WINDING TENNESSEE RIVER in northwest Alabama encompassed the whole world for me from the time I can remember what music sounded like until I grew into my rambling shoes. My hometown, Sheffield, is the heart of Muscle Shoals, a cluster of small towns named for two prominent local features: the freshwater mussels we spell "muscle," and the great and treacherous rocky shoals scattered about the bustling waterway. Sheffield sits on the south bank of the river. A mile-long bridge connects us with the town of Florence, where high atop a scenic bluff sits the birthplace of W. C. Handy, the "Father of the Blues."

By the time of my birth, Labor Day, 1931, Mr. Handy had long gone, first to Memphis and later to New York, where he prospered as a celebrated composer and music publisher. He enjoyed the distinction of being the first black composer of a major hit song to publish his own music. His "St. Louis Blues" had made his name a household word on the levees of the rivers of the world.

To the south, two miles in the opposite direction from the Handy home, is Tuscumbia, the hometown of Helen Keller. Of the two celebrities of our world, it was the musician who attracted my notice first, for I began at the age of two and a half to sing in local grocery stores

15

for candy. Mr. Handy's "St. Louis Blues" was one of the songs in my repertoire. The other was "There's an old spinning wheel in the parlor."

Miss Keller was more mythical for me and the other children of the Sheffield School for Colored. Our teachers always hoped that pressing her remarkable book-learning example on us might motivate us to learn. Book learning was on everybody's mind.

The strongest learning advocate to touch my life, besides my mother, was Daddy Long, a slim man who was then about seventy-five. Daddy Long had smooth mocha-colored skin and white hair that shimmered in the sun. His carriage was that of a Watusi king. The kingliness remained with him even after his forced retirement from his work as headwaiter at the Sheffield Hotel. The swollen ankles that accompany dropsy slowed him down before he came to finish out his days with a widowed niece, Mrs. Minnie Fort, just two houses from ours.

Mrs. Minnie kept the most interesting house on the street. Her grown sons all lived at home. Isaiah, the oldest and a college graduate, was alternately a professor and a burial society salesman. Joel, her second son, worked with Daddy Long at the hotel. Red was just quiet. Then there was their "special" boy, Henry, whom I admired for his music, his dancing, and his cunning enterprise. Henry was said to be retarded, but he was nobody's fool. On Saturday market-day mornings, he transformed himself completely and set up shop on the busiest street corner in town, to do what Sheffield's grown folk said was undoable: he mixed business with pleasure. Crowds pressed in close to watch him buckdance his own special, breathtaking bucking, full of slick moves and gravity-defying choreographic feints. Henry buckdanced like one overtaken by a delicately controlled rhythm spasm, and he needed no outside accompaniment to attract his audience. When the crowd was warmed up enough to offer him the encouragement of their hand-clapping to go with the music in his feet, he would grin slyly and float over the sidewalk as he pulled his fans along on the rhythmical free ride of their lives. At just the right moment in the performance, Henry would deftly flick open the top of an "out of the way" lard can so that the mouth-watering aroma of hot roasted peanuts could rise up and brighten the morning. Then a very special brand of commerce sprang to life: the dancing man peddled his goobers, made change, held several conversations at once, and never missed a step in his ingenious choreography. But Monday mornings, like clockwork, he went back to being what Sheffield called retarded.

Henry's mama's house was an open haven for any of her extended family in trouble or in need of solace. They came to her in all shades and conditions. She took in the two children of a niece, Mrs. Pearl Hill, who was sent to the pen for blowing out the brains of Mr. Levi Goldman, a too-slick gambler and bootlegger recently moved to town. Periodically, Doc Long, Mrs. Minnie's youngest brother and a real Columbia University–educated and Meharry Medical School–trained M.D., moved in and added his learned presence to that household's social soup.

Daddy Long brought his teenaged daughter, Dorothy Lee, with him to Mrs. Minnie's house after his wife died. They joined the moiling household, which was, for yet another reason, a thundering paradox among colored families of the South back then—Mrs. Minnie's crowd *all* slept late. Daddy Long, as a hotel headwaiter, had been accustomed to rising early for his sumptuous southern-style breakfasts in the kitchen at the hotel.

That is how Daddy Long came to our house. While Mrs. Minnie's household was always still aslumber as the rooster crowed, ours was fully astir, with six children busy at chores before school, while Mama boiled coffee and fried meat. This caught Daddy Long's attention and his sense of smell, and brought him to our house early mornings. Mama knew what was on his mind and welcomed him, coffee cup in his jumper pocket, to share our fare, which was a great deal more modest than Daddy Long's customary hotel breakfasts. He never took any of the offered protein, seeing that there was really not enough for the "pickaninnies," his affectionate name for the children of the house. He asked only for coffee in his cup and, "if you can spare one, please, ma'am, one of them pretty biscuits." Mama always stuffed his steaming biscuit full of homemade preserves or, at least, Karo syrup, and he'd take it back to Mrs. Minnie's house and sit in the rocker with it on the front porch. I was drawn to him even then, before I was two years old, because of his gentle nature and elegant manners. Soon after learning to walk, I began following him on back to Mrs. Minnie's porch, clutching my own cup of java, much diluted from the Pet Milk can, and my own sticky stuffed biscuit.

Only I called him "Daddy Long." He was "Uncle Henry" or "Mister Long" to others. I don't remember when I adopted him or named him "Daddy." It all must have come from my need to put a paternal tag on some grown man, for my own father had left Sheffield a year after I was born. But for me, Daddy Long constituted everything I thought a father could be. The only difference to me was that he didn't live in my house. I even tried to remedy that with a strong suggestion to Mama that he could fit in the bed next to me, where I slept with my three older brothers, George Fred, Dave, and Eddie, in the back room.

From my perch in Daddy Long's lap on Mrs. Minnie's porch, I heard stories of slavery time, told him by his parents, who had lived through it. They were funny stories, sad stories, ghost stories, romances, and riddles. He started me off early on simple animal rhymes:

Little fishes in the brook,
Baby catch em widda hook,
Mama fry em inna pan,
Papa eat em lak a man.

Straddling his knee, my back and head leaning on his resonant chest, I felt his calm and well-modulated voice recount for me the wonders of the St. Louis 1904 World's Fair. The big fair convinced Daddy Long for all time that humankind's greatest achievements were the result of its "book learning," and he said I should get all I could of it.

"Boy, that's the onliest thing white folks can't take away from you. Can't *nobody* take nothin from outta your head."

His descriptions of the engineering feats exhibited at the fair were full of fantastic speculations as to just how whoever thought up those ideas ever got them in the first place. Offering his own guesses at the genesis of a great idea, he'd put his face close to mine, open his laughing eyes wide, and quickly say to me, "What you reckon bout that?" When I ventured to reckon on a possibility more farfetched than his, he'd explode with laughter, grab me up in a big squeeze, and roar, "Boy, you sho nuff got your thinkin cap on. When you get your book learning, you might think up you a gret *big* world's fair idea all by yoursef."

A deep yearning for at least one genuine world's fair–sized idea of my own began to grow in me very early in life. Daddy Long said, "Man, one is all it takes! Look at the man what invented the safety pin. A simple thing like that, I bet that booger's at least a billionaire by now."

It was Daddy Long who introduced me to horehound candy, of which he partook whenever it was available from Karg's store. Horehound was more like a cough drop than a candy: I never cared for its smell, which was like strong liniment mixed with coal oil; good, they said, for a host of ailments in grown people and a natural purge for worms in children. Yet on my singing trips to the store, I would offer an encore for a piece of horehound to take home to Daddy Long. "Jesus wants me for a sunbeam" was "in progress" in my repertoire, but it was more than Mr. Karg could bear after my candy sack was loaded to capacity from my already completed renditions of "Old Spinning Wheel" and "St. Louis Blues." After a few bars of "Jesus Wants," Mr. Karg would hold up his hand, pitch me the horehound, and show me the door.

Memory, so prized by the unlettered, was the mark of gumption and aptness with Daddy Long's crowd. And while he was a stickler for book learning, he thought every man ought to have good "remembers." He admitted to short schooling but came close to being vain about his memory. I learned from him how to remember long lists of items, names, dates, and places. "So*say*shun" (association was what he meant) was his name for the memory hook he'd learned along the way, and it was a word he swore by and dearly loved saying. He made me say it over and over, and when he was satisfied that my pronunciation was as perfect as his own, he put his face close to mine and confided its meaning to me as if it were a secret to be protected from thieves in the night. "So*say*shun means connek-up-wif," he whispered at me, and stuck out his strong pointing finger, forming it into a hook.

"Hook your pointing finger right here onto mine," he said. "Now hold on tight. You see," he said, as he tugged on our hook, "we got us a connekshun now; we bound up together. A man can keep his good remembers if he conneks one thing with another in his head. I like to make pretty poems and sayings to connek up particulars for my remembers."

One day he showed me how, back at the hotel, he could take a whole dining room full of dinner orders, write nothing down, and never serve anybody English peas who had ordered slaw, or cross up a lemonade with a tea order. His trick rhymes went something like:

Cornbread
for that knucklehead,
slaw for his paw.
Butter beans,
ain't never seen
her tell no taters,
naw.

When he and Mama were satisfied that I'd caught on to the "remembers" knack, Daddy Long would take me by the hand and trot me off to Karg's store, wait until the store filled up with white folk, then nudge me, my signal to go into my recitation and spout off the long list of Mama's grocery order. After we'd dazzled the clerks and patrons and got outside, Daddy Long would give me a big wink and tap his skull lightly with that pointing finger and say, "I told you, ain't nothing like good remembers to impress white folk; how you spect I got to be a *head*waiter?"

Most of Daddy Long's crowd signed their names with an "X," yet many could recite the entire New Testament from memory. Folktales, African animal stories, and made-up verses were favorites too. Even young children in their prereading years recited impressively long Paul Laurence Dunbar poems and "pieces." Just about any occurrence in daily life was liable to set off "ol heads" to recollect a piece. The sight of me, motley-mouthed, all sticky, clutching my little candy sack, often brought on this one from Daddy Long:

Little Brown Baby wif sparklin eyes,
Come to your Pappy and set on his knee.
What you been doin, suh—makin sand pies?
Look at dat bib, you as durty as me!
Look at dat mouf, dem's merlasses, I bet.
Come here, Maria, and wipe off his hans!
Bees gwine ketch you an eat you up yet.
Bein so sticky and sweet, goodness lans!
Little Brown Baby wif sparklin eyes,
Who's Pappy's darlin and who's Pappy's chile?

CHAPTER TWO

Mama

MAMA WAS a quietly self-possessed woman and was considered something of a beauty around town. At home she was as generous with her time as she was with her affection, unless any of her children failed to shoulder their share of the struggle to maintain the household with the meager resources at hand. The five dollars a week she earned as a maid required cunning and careful management to sustain us all.

Though her eight children were born of four different fathers, she was, for us all, our blood link and the centerpiece of our world.

I gathered from overheard conversations between her and other grown folk—certainly not intended for my ears—that she'd arrived in Sheffield six years before I was born. She had slipped off from a south Alabama town with her four young children to escape a brutalizing, hard-drinking husband, who'd fathered her first child when she was still sixteen.

Once she had settled in Sheffield, Mr. Autry Broaden, her second husband, the man Mama always called the best of them, came into her life. He, she said, was a good provider and a balm for the scars of her earlier married hell. But a year after their marriage and shortly after the birth of their baby girl, Mary Louise, Mr. Broaden was shot to death by Sheffield's police. It was, the police said, a case of mistaken identity.

Back then, in 1926, the police and the municipalities of our South were routinely not required to make restitution or assume liabilities for Negroes killed under those conditions. So, with one more infant to raise, Mama pressed on, alone and in worse straits than before.

Whatever the drawbacks and hardships my mother, Manie Carolyn Broaden, found in Sheffield, it was, she said, a step up the ladder from what she'd known in south Alabama during her first marriage. "The Lord will make a way somehow" was an old hymn she kept humming. After her workdays—cleaning, cooking, and doing laundry at the white folks' house—sundown found her at home, squinting by the poor light of a kerosene lamp, helping the children with schoolwork. Although she had no schooling beyond the early grades, she nursed a mild vanity about her knack with numbers. She relished her role as tutor to my older sisters and brothers in high school algebra.

No profession enjoyed her admiration as much as schoolteaching. She often said she wished she could have stayed in school and trained as a teacher. "That was my calling, I do believe," she would say. Her passion for it stemmed from an early encounter with a very special teacher, a Miss Mallory, who stepped into her life shortly after it became apparent that Mama's own fourteen-year-old unmarried mother was unprepared to raise her. Miss Mallory became Mama's surrogate mother until her own young mother, after several years of live-in-maid work, came back to claim her daughter. When the two got reunited, it was for life.

Mama's mother, Minnie Smith, was "Mama Minnie" to her grandchildren, and she was part of our household for most of my life in Sheffield.

Our small four-room house was rented for eight dollars a month from the Largomosino family, the land barons of our world, who also owned the ice plant down by the river. I thought the ice plant, a huge building into which piped water and ammonia flowed and out of which huge blocks of smoking cold ice rumbled and slid onto Rufus Rand's and Tab's delivery trucks, was the most captivating miracle on the planet.

The little two-bedroom house Mama rented didn't have electricity, but that didn't stop our family from listening to every detail of all the Joe Louis fights on the radio. Whenever Joe fought, my big brothers salvaged a car radio from a wrecked car headed for the junkyard. A neighbor procured an old battery from someplace. The afternoons before any Joe Louis fights were filled with getting the front porch ready. By dark, our porch was craftily wired with coat hangers and clotheslines for antennae, and our makeshift radio squawked lustily. Burning rags smoldered and smoked under the chinaberry tree and under the house: our trusty mosquito repellent. Although a few neighbors had electricity and radios, our house was more congenial as a listening post. My pretty sisters interested the boys. Grown people came for the libations that were available in the kitchen or on the back porch between rounds, and the improvised radio's static and faulty reception added to the drama. Somehow, over the years, we all managed to hear Joe knock out Hitler's darling, Max Schmeling, in one round and, later, Joe's tough thirteenth-round victory over Billy Conn. There was no doubt about it: those radio broadcasts were a call to assembly for "the folk" all over our world. It was always a race fight, plain and simple.

I always associate the earliest Joe Louis fight I can remember with the arrival in town of my one and only uncle, whom I had seen so rarely I'd nearly forgotten him. My father's only brother, Uncle Grover, drove an automobile into Sheffield from Evansville, Indiana, one day and flabbergasted us all: he had a radio in his car! When the fight was about to begin, he inched the automobile over the curb and carefully brought it to rest just at the edge of the porch so we could hear Joe whip his man right from the comfort of our own "fresh-air parlor."

Uncle Grover was only passing through, and during his short stay I couldn't get enough of him. My father was not with him, but looking at my uncle's face was almost like looking at my father's, or looking in the mirror at myself as I expected to be when I got grown. But I always thought Uncle Grover's copper-colored skin, from our Mississippi Choctaw Indian blood heritage, and his sandy hair showed to greater advantage on him.

I always remembered that when Joe knocked out whoever his white opponent was that night, grown folk on the porch admired the neatness of the victory. They said that knocking his man out was what Joe had to do to win; he couldn't get a fair shake if the white judges had to decide or vote on a winner.

"Yeah, chile," one elderly neighbor lady pronounced. "Joe Louis don't leave dem jedges no doubt; he jes leaves dat udder man flat on de flo!" Uncle Grover held forth on how courage and backbone and a fighting spirit were the last things white folks were willing to give our race credit for; we would always have to prove what we're made of the hard way. He offered his wartime example and told us that as a soldier in the First World War in Europe, he and his fellow American black combat troops had to serve under the command of French officers, a ploy Washington contrived to keep white American officers from having to command them. Uncle Grover said that when his compatriots fought so well the French Army decorated them with the Croix de Guerre, but Washington still tried to ignore them.

After Joe's fight, we all felt triumphant, and my exotic uncle sped out of Sheffield, as I stood on the curb squalling my eyes out to follow him and that car radio and his stories.

In those times of discovery, I was listening to more than the radio. I was discovering my ears. Besides music, it was the magic in grown women's language I most loved listening to. I began mastering the art of eavesdropping on women's talk while still a small boy, and in the bargain I glimpsed some of the real powers operating in our world. I didn't have to be told that what shaped and ruled our South seemed best understood by those of our women who—in the course of their work as maids—saw into the hearts of the families in whose houses they toiled and whose children they raised, nursed, and very often deeply loved. With Mama and Mama Minnie both following that line of work, I came very early in life to sense something special and powerful about what such women knew. I also enjoyed being around, though out of sight, when their colleagues gathered on our front porch at the end of their workday. Theirs was a close sorority, galvanized by their common and insatiable need to share "news" from the society they served.

Mama Minnie, the consummate porch hostess, was generally not a woman of excess, but she was wild for gossip and had a special talent for it. Other women loved telling her things. She was a rapt listener, which seemed to inspire in her informants that rare trust which encourages the "discreetest" sharing of unimaginable secrets. No part of her day delighted her as much as when it was time for the ladies to mount the porch.

She was aware of my appreciation for the wisdom of mature woman-talk and contrived several tactics to get me from underfoot and out of earshot. None worked completely. If I lingered on the porch after the ladies arrived, I was first sent to the kitchen to fetch them all a cool drink in the gourd dipper. After I'd watered each one and still tarried, Mama Minnie ran her hand down into her apron pocket, handed me her penknife, and pointed to the hedge bush, which meant: Go cut toothbrushes. I'd choose several tender shoots from the green hedge, skin off the bark with the knife, and pass the twigs out to the ladies, who chewed the ends of them until they were brushy. The brushy ends they then dipped into their snuff cans to catch a mound of the dusty elixir, which they brushed onto their gums and teeth; they claimed it made talking easier—an old African habit. After they'd loaded the lower lip with a fat wad of brown dust poured straight from the can, their speech became stylishly distinctive. Understanding snuff dippers' speech requires a good ear for language and much concentrated practice. I was used to it, because both Mama Minnie and Mama dipped.

Somewhere along the way, Mama Minnie must have tipped the sisterhood off about the size of my ears. "Mind your tongues in front of you-know-who," she'd say. I was expected to leave in due time, but as long as I stuck around, they would limit their talk to such trivia as: "Child, didn't Celie Appleton sing that song at Sis Abernathy's funeral?" or "Didn't Brother Brackett pray that prayer at prayer meetin las night?" But when, at last, the small talk and niceties were finished, and all were comfortable and ready, Mama Minnie would lower her head, peer over her specs, point a stiff finger hard at me, and say sharply, "You, suh—scat!"

With a faked show of hurt and a dejected "yessum," I ambled off the porch and down the street, kicking a rock or a tin can all the way past Mrs. Minnie Fort's house, where I turned and doubled back in front of the Sanctified church, cut into our backyard, and quietly crawled to my listening spot under the house. From there I shamelessly stole my education. I thought the accounts of the strength, the dreams, and the deep faith and heart of the sorority sitting not two feet above my head were the most inspirational things in the world. From there the richest of matriarchal mysteries unfolded for me and the drama of a day in Sheffield's "society" unfolded. The sisters brought out the white folks' dirty linen, aired and examined it, and flung it with gusto right into the street.

Miss Mabel might be the one leading off. "Honey! Let me tell y'all something. I jes got to find me another job. Y'all know I can't stand trashy ways. I done worked for 'quality' white folk all my life, and sich mess as *these* folks spect outta me I jes ain't gonna stan for. Talking bout *nasty!* Child! That deblish woman tol me jes yestiddy, 'Mabel, you *too* clean,' jes cause she caught me washing that chicken with Oxydol befo I cooked it. Sez I'd wash all the taste outta it. I tol her as long as I eats what I cooks in dis house, I washes it to *my* satisfaction, and ef she ain't satisfied, I *knows* my way home." I would hear Miss Della's rocking chair slow down, then she would skeet a brown stream of snuff juice with the force of a rifle shot, which raised a puff of dust in the yard. To Miss Mabel she would say, "You sho tol her right, sister. These deblish folk'll put *any*thing in they moufs dese days, honey. Stan yo groun!"

Food, during these Depression days, and tactics for acquiring a superior quality of it at a cost unheard of outside their own society, often came up with the guest ladies on the porch.

One Monday afternoon, Miss Sally opened the proceedings with a story based on a rump roast she'd cooked for a dinner party her boss lady threw on Saturday two nights past.

"Luveenya, I tried and tried to get aholt a you Saturday, girl. Didn't Ida Mabel tell you? First I tried to call you up on your boss lady's telefoam, then I sent Leroy by your house. But I reckon you was off somewhere 'visiting.' Honey, you missed it!"

Miss Luveenya snorted, and skeeted her brown stream into the yard, saying, "Unnh huh, I know. Bless your heart for trying. I'm sure sorry I missed that call too, child. That rump roast y'all had sounded like mighty good eating—specially when it didn't cost y'all half a what I paid for my chicken."

It was an old story. On Saturday, Miss Sally had bought the dinner roast for her boss lady at midday, noting its exquisite quality as the merchant cut her portion from a nearly full side of beef. Miss Sally had a good eye for food portioning, and by her estimate, the number of Sheffield's beef eaters that weekend was liable to fall short of the merchant's expectation; she was ready to bet he'd bought a little too much. On her way home, she slyly checked back at the store just before closing. There, still hanging on the hook, was plenty of prime meat, which in those days before walk-in coolers would surely spoil if left in the store over Sunday. Miss Sally struck up a bargain, got herself a roast for pennies, trotted by our house so Mama could do likewise, and thanks to the vitality of their grapevine, the families of every lady on the porch had prime roasts on their Sunday table—all except Miss Luveenya.

From my perch under the porch I gathered that to make extra coin, Miss Luveenya sometimes took in washing as a sideline to her maid's job. And from time to time, some white lady or other drove to our house to deliver a basket of laundry to Mama Minnie and Mama, who was also "moonlighting." I would never have guessed at the subtle overtones and the social complexities of doing Sheffield's white folk's laundry. The first thing I learned was: the porch ladies did not take in just anybody's wash. With this crowd, interviews were necessary. There were important questions to consider. Firstly, one should know in advance the makeup of the client family by gender. How many of the men in the family wore ties in their work? Their shirts had to be starched and ironed. How many males in the house wore work clothes? Those were ironed, but no starch. How many beds in the house? Sheets and pillowcases needed bluing and ironing. Did the women of the house fancy cotton blouses? How about female under-items? Was the family "quality," or did the household have "common" women who sent along princess slips, step-ins, and worse? But above all other considerations, according to Miss Luveenya, especially in summer, one must avoid clients with young girls owning pleated sunsuits with ruffles all over them (that year, the trend in sunsuits had gone scandalously outlandish with ruffles), the most hellish of all God's damnations to iron, so said Miss Luveenya.

My eavesdropping uncovered yet another wonder about the politics of the services these ladies rendered. It came from Miss Luveenya, with her mental data bank on local laundering.

"Mattie," she said one day to Mrs. MacCray, "you oughta think about washing for the Fitzgerald family after Lucy Belle gets married next week and moves back to the country. That's a easy one, honey. No li'l gals, just Sunday shirts to starch for the ol man. Not much boiling in the whole batch. And it's a quality family too."

Mama, having serviced the Fitzgerald account in the past, confirmed Miss Luveenya's estimate; it was, she said, indeed a quality family. But Mrs. Mattie, a relatively recent entrant to the trade, asked Mama, "Well, I wanna know why you give it up if it was so good." "It's like this, baby," Mama said. "Mrs. Fitzgerald put on a lot of weight here lately. She ain't my size anymore." "Yeah," Miss Luveenya cut in, "and that's a shame too, honey, cause you sho looked 'uptown' in them expensive lace blouses that woman used to order outta Memphis. Girl, I believe you got more wear outta them blouses than she did. But you must have had your hands full washing and ironing them clothes before you wore em, then washing em again before Mrs. Fitzgerald came back to pick em up. I'm mighty glad that white woman never caught you struttin round town all dolled out in her satin and lace."

Miss Sally said, "Oh, child, no danger bout that. This gal had that thang all figgered out. Her and Mrs. Fitzgerald don't move in eksakly the same circles, doncha see?"

CHAPTER THREE

"God Has Given You Gumption, Fool"

WHEN I WAS NEARLY FOUR, my nine-year-old sister, Mary Louise, working on secret orders from Mama, sat with me on the curb in front of the house and began teaching me to read and write. She, Mama, and Daddy Long bragged of my progress just enough to encourage me to keep at it so I could begin first grade at five years old.

The work was apparently something more than an idle academic exercise for show. Mama had put my accelerated education in motion to serve a practical purpose in the household: everybody at home had a job or was in school, and there was nobody left behind to look after me. If I could show that I had as much sense as a six-year-old, Mama would lie about my age and pass me off as old enough to be in the first grade. There was no kindergarten at our school, though the white school had it, and the Depression was heating up every day. Even I felt the heat when Mama told me in no uncertain terms, "God has given you gumption, fool, and you had better use it." It was up to me to help her resolve the problem of day care. I *had* to be let into that school.

Mary Louise did her curbside teacher's work well, for by the time I turned five, I was considered school material. I trudged along behind her—she was already a fifth grader—to the schoolhouse. Our big sister Velma, Mama's firstborn, whom we all called Sister, was in the upper grades and doing maid work every day before and after classes. The three older boys, Eddie, George Fred, and Dave, had already dropped out and taken jobs to help Mama.

I thought the brick schoolhouse sitting in Baptist Bottom beyond the railroad tracks, a half mile south of our house, was a magical place. All my life I'd heard the grown folk brag that our teachers, though paid far less than the teachers at the white school, were the best-educated teachers, white or black, in Colbert County. During my time there, all of our teachers were women, except young Professor Tyler, who himself had been a pupil of those same women. Professor Matthews, the principal at our school before my time, had always put great stock in teachers trained at Talladega College. And in our world, Talladega was called the "Harvard of the South." Like Professor Matthews, black principals from all over the South coveted Talladega's graduates as teachers.

Even before I ever crossed the tracks to our Baptist Bottom schoolhouse, I'd heard about Mrs. Coker, our town's learned Talladega-trained teacher. She was a stunning beauty, had taught all my older brothers and sisters before me, read to her pupils in French, loved teaching literature and poetry, and was married to Baptist Bottom's only dentist, Dr. M. P. Coker.

After I was enrolled at school, but a full two years before I was old enough for Mrs. Coker's fourth-grade classroom, she and Dr. Coker did something special for my ears, and something very special for the student body's pride of race: they brought a legend to school. Dr. Coker had been a student at Alabama Agriculture and Mechanical College in Huntsville years earlier, when W. C. Handy, as a young man, had been the music teacher there and had conducted the A & M band.

It was while I was in the second grade that the Cokers persuaded the famous "father of the blues," on one of his frequent trips from New York back to his hometown across the river, to bring his trumpet to our school to play and talk to us children.

Although his eyesight was nearly gone by 1937, Mr. Handy's eyes danced and sparkled with enthusiasm for his subject—"the music of the Negro race." I remember the sound of his trumpet, which he played for us with a mute in the bell to make it sound like a sweet singing soprano. He stood alone on the stage of our little auditorium. Of course, he played "St. Louis Blues" and "Memphis Blues," songs that had made him famous. But he was far from content to leave us with the impression that the blues and the jazz we loved so much were the sum total of our musical story. I was six years old and hung on his every word.

"It is from the spiritual," he said, "that all else in our musical story in America took root." He demonstrated "Go Down Moses" and "Swing Low, Sweet Chariot" on his trumpet and showed us those qualities that our sacred music shares with the blues and jazz. His musical examples were so clear and easy to follow, and his words were so strong, that I knew I was on the receiving end of a precious gift. He was passionate about the music's worth and admonished us children to always value *all* the rich legacy of our musical ancestry, the secular and the sacred alike.

"Be proud of it and hold it up," he said. "Sing it with thanksgiving in your hearts, and with pride and dignity in your voices."

I felt as if his words were aimed directly at me, and I knew they would stay with me always.

CHAPTER FOUR

The Family Grows

SOMEWHERE AROUND THAT TIME, a new visitor, a fat and jovial man, Mr. Will Pruitt, starting coming often to our house, wearing a seersucker suit, a dress shirt and tie, and a straw hat. A country man in late middle age, Mr. Pruitt met Mama while selling fruit and vegetables he grew on his farm to the family Mama worked for and their neighbors. Now he was coming to our house courting. He drove an A-model Ford and peddled his produce from its back seat and trunk. A man with a farm and an A-model Ford, to us, was a gentleman of consequence. The management of the farm he left to his children; he did all the selling of his produce. His oldest son, Buddy Boy, the first of his family that we in Sheffield met, and whom I adored, was an enterprising hard worker who ran the farm operation together with the help of a houseful of sisters and another brother.

Occasionally, Mr. Pruitt took a carload of our clan out to the farm. The mules and cows and the wholesome country food were all novel and wonderful stuff for me. Farm life was a fascinating discovery. But there never was anything on the farm that sent electricity through me like the household's musical instrument, an old Civil War blowing bugle. The bugle had belonged to Mr. Pruitt's uncle Henry Green, who'd been a star bugler in that war, fighting for the Union Army.

Mr. Pruitt could blow the army calls pretty well, and he even knew the words to "Taps" and "There's a Soldier in the Grass." On my first visit to the farm he shoved the horn in my face and said, "Go ahead and see if you can blow it." I'd noticed that his own blowing pucker was strange and off to the side of his mouth. But at school, when Mr. Handy had played the spirituals and "St. Louis Blues" on his trumpet, he'd made his lips smile a little as he set the horn straight onto his mouth.

When I took up Mr. Pruitt's challenge with the bugle, I made my pucker the way Mr. Handy had. With all my might, I swelled up and blew like a hurricane. A deafening bleat that nearly scared me to death shot out of the thing. The sound scattered the livestock and shook the barnyard. I was in love.

My fascination with that bugle made Mr. Pruitt laugh and shake like jelly, and he was unable to wrench the thing from me for the rest of my stay. I tried with all that was in me to make that bugle play "St. Louis Blues" and one of the spirituals Mr. Handy had played on his trumpet at school, but all it knew was government songs. I gave it a fit anyway, until the Pruitt children got tired of it and sent me with it to the woods. "Boy," scolded Bea, the youngest daughter, "that racket gonna dry up the milk cows and scare the hens outta laying."

Even on his visits back in Sheffield, Mr. Pruitt seemed to go out of his way to indulge me. That made Mama Minnie suspicious. Since I was the baby of the family, she was certain Mama's new suitor was trying to make points by paying a lot of attention to me. He would take me up on his knee and tell me menfolk stories. Most of his stories were about wars: the Civil War, the Revolutionary War, the Spanish-American War, and some of the famous battles from the Bible. The moral examples that grew out of the great battles in Scripture and in mankind's history were great teachers, he said. All of us in the house could tell by his stories that this was a bookish man. It had to have been a bookish black man, back then, who could sing solfeggio scales like opera singers. He could put the do-re-mi-fa-sol sounds to any melody in the Baptist hymnbook—a skill he said he'd learned as a youth when missionaries from the national Baptist Convention—white people—came through the South to spread religious instruction. Mama

Minnie, a true stomp-down Baptist, went soft and fell for that one herself. Soon the big man visiting Mama was starting to make a lot of points at our house, and especially with me. By the time he and Mama were married, in 1937, I knew my new stepfather's affection for me was genuine.

He moved into the house with us. The first thing we had to do was change the sleeping arrangements. Before he came, Mama had a bed in the room off the kitchen, and there was another bed in that room for Mama Minnie and Mary Louise. Sister slept in the parlor on a divan, and we boys had two beds in the other bedroom, in the back of the house. The new arrangement moved Mary in with Velma. Mama Minnie's bed got squeezed into the back room with the boys. Living was tight until the marriage produced two babies, Jessie Yvonne and little Nathaniel; then it was kinfolk cozy.

By the time Mr. Pruitt moved in with us, Daddy Long's health was slowing him down, but he still liked to be kept up to date on my book learning. He'd come and sit on the porch with me, and we'd listen to Mr. Pruitt's bookish stories. Mr. Pruitt impressed Daddy Long mightily, and that egged my stepfather on.

Bookish though his stories and speech were, the only book he brought with him to our house was his big Bible. But even his non-religious stories seemed to ring with biblical authority.

There was one special local character who'd captured Mr. Pruitt's fertile imagination. His name was Joe Wheeler—"Fightin Joe"—the ex–Confederate general who'd lived just upriver, near the Pruitt farm. After the Civil War, Wheeler had become a planter, a lawyer, then a U.S. congressman from our district. In 1898, he was a general again, in the war with Spain in Cuba. It impressed Mr. Pruitt that Wheeler had been one of only two Confederate generals whom President McKinley would recommission in the Army of the United States. This honor was an acknowledgment of Wheeler's sincere efforts to weld the torn relations between the North and the South after the Civil War.

A federal project to honor the old general got under way on the river. As a young man, Mr. Pruitt was hired as a laborer on this hydroelectric generating plant and navigation lock on our Tennessee River. It was one of the great events of my stepfather's youth, and he became a walking statistics book on data and facts of the dam's construction. We heard how many cubic yards of concrete went into the construction; how many tons of steel, gravel, and sand; how many dozens of men got entombed in the concrete forms when accidents happened. Mr. Pruitt could transfix me, Daddy Long, and our whole household by simply drawing on his limitless storehouse of stories about the Joe Wheeler Dam and the local lore surrounding the general.

My stepfather's presence in the house was great entertainment for me, but he also heightened the focus on my book learning. First, he began taking me up in his lap in the evenings and opening the Bible, for me to read certain passages aloud to him. His interest included my school lessons, even though Mama, Sister, and Mary Louise gave me all the help I needed on that score. Mr. Pruitt was too much the diplomat to try to butt in on the help I was getting from the women of the house. But when I started taking geography at school, he went to work pointing out facts the textbooks had left out: the biblical names of countries and regions; who, way back in history, had outfoxed who in some political swap of land or of rights. Life at home was coming alive in a new way with the presence of this new father figure. And then he really scored heavily with me: he took Mama and me all the way to Florence for my first store-bought wool suit, with two pair of long pants, $7.50 at Rogers's store. I was his boy, sure enough, from then on.

CHAPTER FIVE

"Hi Do, I Play the Drums Too"

AFTER MR. HANDY'S VISIT to our school, my musical horizons broadened, from singing at the grocery store for candy, to ownership of a snare drum and a pair of drumsticks. Mama Minnie considered the contraption a tool of the devil and was certain that I would beat myself straight into hell. The drum, the sticks, and my first music lessons were gifts from a white boy, Mutt McCord, my neighbor and major early musical influence. A warm lifelong friendship developed from those lessons. About ten years younger than Mutt, I idolized him, and he liked teaching me about drumming and making slingshots. I lived to watch him practice his drums, and to listen to the records he played on the lawn in his front yard, just across the street from our house. Benny Goodman's drummer, Gene Krupa, was one of Mutt's heroes. From time to time, Mutt would bring home records of Count Basie's band and try to decipher the new and dazzling cymbal work of Basie's flashy drummer, Jo Jones.

In the 1930s, the jazz drummers of the world were wild about the sock cymbal, a new invention that allowed the player, seated at his kit, to use a foot pedal to operate a set of crashing cymbals on a metal stand. Jo Jones, and big Sid Catlett, a stated favorite of Louis Armstrong's, were masters of the innovation.

Mutt was eager to teach me to read drum music correctly, for he took a manly pride in his art. Even as a high school student, he was considered a semiprofessional musician in our circle; for he was earning money playing in bands in the little white joints all around the Muscle Shoals area. When he thought I was ready for it, he began trying to explain to me the intricacies of ensemble work in big-band drumming (listening with a careful ear to the harmony, melodies, and counter-melodies around you) and why it was important for the drummer to be able to read the music and know what all the instruments in the orchestra were playing at all times. Ellington, Basie, Goodman, and Jimmie Lunceford furnished models for our examination.

Mutt often took me along with him to the football field at the white school so I could watch him play the bass drum at their marching-band rehearsals. It was a compensating gesture, for it saddened him deeply that my schoolmates and I had few of the advantages he and Sheffield's other white students enjoyed—especially in music.

During the years of my apprenticeship with Mutt, our school never had a band, which is not to say we didn't have music. We had choral music of exceptional quality, and several performing glee clubs and choruses. Every morning began with all classes singing "devotion." We enjoyed several assemblies in our auditorium each week, and the entire student body, all twelve grades, marched in as our fifth-grade teacher, Mrs. Minor, played the spirited marches of Sousa and W. C. Handy on the piano. Mrs. Minor had strong rhythm and could look out the window while playing. Nothing was as fascinating to me as a good piano player who could negotiate the music while watching traffic. Her piano playing whipped up the anticipation we all felt each time all twelve grades—more than two hundred voices—got a chance to sing together in chapel. We knew about the magic in the sound of small boy sopranos, and how they differed from the sopranos of near-grown robust country girls, and what beauty there was in the mixture of the two when we opened our mouths for "Listen to the Lamb." We knew, too, about the transforming power of inner-part movement of alto and middle voices, moving parallel and counter to the small boys' and near-grown girls' soprano mixture, all firmly supported by the thundering bass voices of a squad of aspiring Paul Robesons. Our musical assemblies at school were unmatched for their inspirational power, and I noticed that all souls at the Sheffield School for Colored, teachers and pupils alike, always left the auditorium with their faces brightened up and shining with optimistic anticipation of the promises of life. Our exits from these assemblies always turned to grand marches, full of triumph. We loved to sing, and above all, we loved to hear it while we sang. In chapel, if nowhere else in our world, we had power.

There was always great music to be heard on the Tennessee River stern-wheel paddleboats, which carried fat bales of cotton and assorted freight. Some even hauled passengers and a noisy steam-driven calliope, which could be heard for miles along the river. The river ran around a dog-leg bend coming from Tuscumbia into Sheffield, and we could hear the calliope playing a half hour before the boat hit the Sheffield dock. Sometimes the man playing the calliope would start somewhere around Tuscumbia with light classics, or "Beer Barrel Polka," or maybe even a rag. If I was out on my paper route, or selling bottles, it was an easy stroll down the Montgomery Avenue hill to the river for the free concert while the crew unloaded cargo and took on wood and water at Sheffield's dock. Once in a while, a boat would pull in with a jazz calliope player, who would start at the trestle playing W. C. Handy. He'd segue from "Memphis Blues" to "Aunt Hagar," cut into a bluesy long modulation as if to flex his fingers in preparation to take flight into "St. Louis Blues," which he would make last until the boat glided home, practically in sight of Mr. Handy's homeplace, high up on the Florence bluff. Icemen, shoeshine boys, maids, and hoboes, all friends of mine, lined the levee to listen to the jazzman "play that thing till it rained on him." The "rain" was just condensed steam from the calliope, falling back to soak the player's straw hat, his red-and-white-striped shirt with fancy sleeve garters. I often wondered what Mrs. Minor would sound like playing that little steam piano.

The most memorable and, by far, the most enjoyable music-making experiences Mutt and I shared were the traveling carnival and minstrel shows that covered the South of our childhood. Several of these tent shows came to Sheffield each year and provided the only opportunity we had to participate and get a good look at professional bands playing jazz. Their drummers were outstanding. They also played for the parade before the show, the way the great circus bands do, and later they would set up in front of the show tent to draw a crowd. Inside, of course, was the real show: vaudeville routines and high-kicking dancing girls moving feverishly to hot jazz.

One day on my way to school, I saw trucks pulling into town with the tents, rides, and games that are part of traveling carnivals. I was torn between a burning need to see a show being mounted and my terror of being reported to Mama for playing hooky. That day, her threat bested my curiosity for tent shows, and I went to school and sat through the morning with my mind nowhere close to the schoolhouse or the teachers. As soon as the bell rang for recess, I streaked to the show lot on Jackson Highway and visited.

"Visiting" in our world was a high art. When visiting strangers, the visitor usually arrives at a pace that is at once easy but with purpose. While one must not appear aggressive, like a bill collector, one's tempo mustn't betray, at all costs, the shiftlessness of a hobo. I had watched expert visitors—snake-oil peddlers, burial-policy agents, and tramps—come to our house for years. Mama regarded them with great disdain and enjoyed pointing out the flaws in their technique. "Hi do," "Ev-enin," or "Mornin" were good openers only if well modulated with regard to pitch, and the rhythm had to be just right. If the visitor didn't wait for the reply before proceeding, Mama knew he was in too much of a hurry to be credible. She said she could tell, even with strangers, what they wanted before they got as far as the yard.

At the show site, I found the band swinging sledgehammers and hustling heavy tent ropes. I put on my best visiting face and asked who was the drummer. A middle-aged man with a shovel said "Heah!" while keeping a watchful eye on a little boy playing in a nearby sawdust pile. As soon as I said, "Hi do, I play the drums too," the boy hit me square in the face with a fistful of pine shavings and said, "You git away from my daddy!" I was momentarily blinded, but between swipes at my eyes with my shirttail, I could make out that the father had thrown down his shovel and snatched the boy several inches up off the ground to work on his rump. Then I got an apology and the instructions to go wash the sawdust out of my eyes and come back. "I'll show you my drums," the drummer said.

The boy was still pouting when I returned, but his daddy made him shake my hand and apologize. Then the drummer showed me his arsenal of gadgets: exotic gear that drummers use to give life to fast-moving dancing. He had sirens, rattles, razzes, whistles, woodblocks, Chinese tom-toms, and various cymbals that he played with a reshaped wire coat hanger. I told him about the set of drums Mutt owned, with an electric light in the bass drum that flashed on and off. I told him I knew a couple of Gene Krupa licks that Mutt was helping me with. The carnival man encouraged me to demonstrate something on his drums. I nervously beat out my "Sing Sing Sing" solo on his tom-toms, and he applauded and said it was just fine and for me to bring Mutt to the show that night. "I'll show you both how to play for dancers; how to keep them on their toes and give them 'inspiration,' " he promised.

That evening, Mama said that as long as I stayed with Mutt I could stay up late enough to go to the show. We got dressed up and found the show in full swing when we hit the lot. The band and dancers were at work in front of the tent and already drawing a good-sized crowd. A barker using a megaphone hollered at the top of his lungs: "Step right up, step right up, and see the hottest band in the land, and this land is hot tonight . . . look at that gal shake that thang." Then he ran out next to the girl and cried, "Shake it, baby, but don't break it!"

Periodically, the barker rested, and the dancing girls carried on the show, propelled by the drummer doing his specialty. He spotted me in the crowd and put in a trick that was new to me: he juggled his sticks! While his foot drove a steady beat on his bass drum, he tossed first one stick, then another, in the air, caught them, and hit a gong right on the downbeat, which sent Mutt and me to heaven. When the crowd grew large enough to block my view, Mutt hauled me up on his shoulder, where I kicked, hollered, and applauded.

After the show we went backstage to talk shop and get pointers on stick twirling. It wasn't long after the show left town that I noticed a difference in Mutt's music. His drumming showed a new drive, and in time he started expanding his horizon with the tricks he'd picked up from the carnival drummer.

W e had a local drumming idol too. Mrs. Nance was the drummer for the only Sanctified church in town. She was a solo bass drummer: just her drum and the singing congregation. Mrs. Nance had a most extraordinary gift, and her reputation for inciting dance riots in the church was famous all over the Tennessee Valley. Yet her single drum was ordinary—no pedals, levers, cymbals, or gadgets—and she played it with a large long-handled wooden cooking spoon, its business end wrapped tightly with a gray-and-red boot sock. She could coax out of that single drum all of the complex combinations of sounds and rhythms I've ever heard coming from great jazz drummers using a full set. Mutt and I would bet on Mrs. Nance for plain, raw, stomping African-flavored timekeeping and emotional excitement.

Summer nights in our South were made for Sanctified church music. Mutt and I sometimes waited on the steps of the church for Mrs. Nance's arrival before the night services.

Sitting on the grass outside the church, we had a full view of the pulpit and our drum hero, whose beat gave her right arm the churning motion of a set of steam locomotive wheels. Her movements, all circles and arcs, made figure eights in the air before the boot sock kissed the drumskin. Never were her strokes straight out and into the drum. To make a smooth drum roll, she used both ends of the spoon, with a rapid pivot of the wrist. With the flat palm of the empty hand, she muffled the drumhead, and at appropriate moments in the sermon, or a song, she made her instrument speak a clear and discernible "Amen" or "Hallelujah" or "Thank you, Jesus." These short statements she played with eyes closed, lips pursed, head thrown back, and the look of pure rapture on her face, as if she were already reaping her heavenly reward.

Mrs. Nance was such an inspiration for Mutt and me that we'd wait on the church steps just to talk to her as she came or went. We could be said to be the original Sanctified groupies. Mrs. Nance liked us but had no enthusiasm for our music.

"You chillun oughta be drumming for the Lord," she would always say, shaking her head sadly. "That ol devil don't deserve such sweet young-uns!"

The Sanctified church is, at least in name, a relatively new denomination of black Protestants whose style of worship maintains much of the richness of West African religious practices. The church was founded in Memphis in 1898, and what characterized its services and separated them from those of the other Christian sects of our South was their animated drumming, spirit possessions, and the free expression of totally unbridled joy through dancing. It was, in part, because of their preference for these ancestral African characteristics that the "Saints" left the more conservative southern sects and formed their own Church Of God In Christ.

Until the middle of this century, the membership tended to come from the ranks of the southern poor and uneducated, and they were not highly regarded by the other black Christians, who called them Holy Rollers. "Them Sanctified people must think God is deef!" said the conservatives. "Listen to all the racket they make with that ol holy rolling and dancing and beating them ol drums." But the more they rolled and danced, and the louder and hotter they drummed, the more Mutt and I loved them. And Mrs. Nance and her drum could sure enough inspire them to roll and brighten up our summer nights. Sanctified church music coming from the building not fifty yards out of our back door provided my nightly summertime lullabies.

That little sanctuary, about the size of our house, was built about the time of my birth and entirely by a small, mild-mannered, and very kindly man we called Brother Suggs. Brother Suggs was as enterprising as he was neat and religious. He kept the church spotless and always freshly painted. He even hired an itinerant Depression hobo artist to paint a panel over the front door, a full-color pastoral scene that illustrated the Bible verse "Suffer the little children to come unto me."

Brother Suggs never married. His main job was as a janitor at the only synagogue in the Muscle Shoals area. The Jewish congregation contributed Old Testament literature they no longer needed to his church. Brother Suggs of course severely scrutinized the gifts and made certain that Jewish pronouncements were consonant with what Sanctified folk believed. Judging from the abundance of Old Testament material we used, it was my guess that compatibility was never a problem.

Even the poor white children from neighboring streets, our everyday playmates, came to Brother Suggs's Sunday school. Virgil Tidwell, a fat, asthmatic white boy on our street, grew up to be a preacher himself and never stopped giving credit to Brother Suggs's little Sunday school, which in 1936 was the only racially mixed Christian children's meeting in our world. And to make our Sunday mornings even sweeter, Brother Suggs stood at the church door as we entered and handed out the most scrumptious hard candy a young sinner ever stuffed in his jaw.

Many in his congregation were in their nineties, and having been born during slavery, very few of them could read. Readers and teachers in that church were in such short supply that my sister Mary Louise was recruited to teach Sunday school when she was about ten years old. After only a year in school, while I was still five, I was put on as a teacher. The classes were divided into four or five small groups scattered about the little church, with five or six students clustered around their teacher. Young children just learning to read sat among bent and white-headed pupils. On my first day of teaching, Brother Suggs showed me what to do and where to read from in the lesson of the day. It was very simple, the kind of text any first grader could handle. When I read aloud from a small picture card, "God is Love," my whole group of elders jumped up from the benches, led by Albert Hogan, a pupil in his sixties, who shouted, "Listen at him go. Gonna be a sho *nuff* scholar, doncha reckon!"

Each year after Labor Day, when school started and we all had new school clothes and shoes, our family spent Sundays at the First Baptist Church, across town in Baptist Bottom. Here was altogether another world of music-making. Whereas the Sanctified Church's music was all congregational singing with drum accompaniment, the Baptist Church had a piano and a polished choir, well rehearsed and trained to the teeth. Our Baptist choir was hot on dramatic effect. Mrs. Winston, the pianist and choir director, ruled supreme. Herself a virtuoso pianist, she taught fifty-cent piano lessons on the side. Mama Minnie bought a few of Mrs. Winston's lessons for me, but it was money wasted; drumming was already too hot in my blood. But I admired the great power in Mrs. Winston's piano playing.

The spirited piano introductions she fashioned for choir numbers were inspired and entirely improvised. Her hands and the fertility of her imagination mesmerized her choir, and the congregation couldn't get enough of her. When she was fully wound up in an introduction, there was no telling how long she was going to work it through. She also had the instinct and the ear of a great silent-film piano player. Reverend J. C. Yarborough was a stickler for style, and when he and Mrs. Winston were teamed, they were a matched pair. She would work him the way the carnival trap drummer worked his shake dancers; she knew when to introduce music in the middle of his sermon, when to build tension with her piano, and when to help him bring the house down.

There were two star soloists in her choir, whom she featured each Sunday immediately after the production number, which always came just before the preaching—Reverend Yarborough detested preaching to a cold congregation.

Mr. Buddy Jenkins, a skinny little dried-up man about the size of a twelve-year-old boy, was one of the soloists Mrs. Winston relished featuring each week. His bass voice was deep as an organ pipe, its tone warm and dark as his glowing face, resonant and smooth; and he lived to sing in church.

Miss Celia Appleton was our other star. She was a low soprano, whose voice was to the high and middle range what Mr. Buddy's was in the bass register.

When the spirits were generous to Sheffield's Baptists, Mr. Buddy and Miss Celia would sing a duet, and that was like being sent to glory. Around 1936, Sister Celia saw her billing change in the church: she came to be known as a contralto. Few of Sheffield's citizens knew exactly what "contralto" meant, but it had to be good, since Marian Anderson was said to be about the best in the world at it.

That year, Miss Anderson was big news in Washington, D.C., because the Daughters of the American Revolution, the owners of the famous landmark Constitution Hall, flatly refused to allow any Negro to perform on their stage. The refusal so enraged the First Lady, Eleanor Roosevelt, herself a member of the DAR, that she resigned her membership in protest and arranged for Miss Anderson to sing outdoors. She chose the perfect alternative spot: the base of the Lincoln Memorial. No white Washington public figure had ever gone so far with a human rights issue. The world press picked up the story. Spirited accounts of the DAR's refusal erupted all through the black press, and before long a powerful photograph of Mrs. Roosevelt and Miss Anderson with old Abe Lincoln looming large before the massive audience became one of the major symbols for human rights in our world. At school, our teachers clipped the photograph and the accompanying article and tacked them to our classroom walls.

Then, when President Roosevelt came to Muscle Shoals to visit the Tennessee Valley Authority, the rural electrification project his administration fostered, our churches turned out in force just for a look at the white man whose wife stood up for the great young black contralto. I didn't get to see the President, but I always remembered that his wife had fought a righteous battle that was, like Mr. Pruitt's warrior examples, loaded with moral significance. It was a story that carried added weight with me because music was at the center of it.

At the First Baptist Church, from then on, it was hard to listen to Miss Celia's rich and fervent contralto voice without thinking of Marian Anderson.

Midsummer was big revival time at home, and these were musical occasions. Several of the Colbert County Baptist churches consolidated their baptizing, usually on the last Sunday in June. It was a show as spectacular as the tent shows.

The mile-long procession, everyone draped in white, snaked through town and down Montgomery Avenue Hill. The mood of the singing matched that of the preludes to New Orleans funerals: dirgelike and expectant. Once arrived at the river, where each town's church took to the water in turn, the singing shifted to a mood of impending glory, as candidates for baptism went into the water. The preacher would chant, "I baptize you in the name of the Father and the Son and the Holy Ghost," and *Kaloosha* went the water as the new Christian was submerged. Washed clean of their sins, people came up screaming and slobbering: "So glad, so glad."

At church I was always slow to warm up to just straight preaching. The best of it put me to sleep unless it had music. Even Reverend Yarborough couldn't hold my attention without Mrs. Winston's contributions.

Everybody in our crowd was expected to go to the mourners' bench while young. Anyone holding back until he was twelve years old was suspect. The mourners' bench, those seats in front of the church reserved for candidates for salvation, was holy ground. Aspirants had to pass through a period of "mourning" for past sins during their candidacy.

I was around nine when I volunteered for my first pass at the mourners' bench, mostly to please Mama Minnie because she'd wasted her money on those piano lessons for me from Mrs. Winston. She'd had her heart set so hard on having a church pianist in the family, and she'd washed and ironed a lot of white folks' clothes for the little coin she'd spent on me in vain. I'd disappointed her by preferring the drums. The least I could do for her, I thought, was to get saved.

My first night as a candidate for my salvation was full of expectation, though I don't know what I expected. There were three long benches filled with children about my size and a few adults: repeaters, backsliders, and those who wanted to try again. A few were even crossovers who'd left other denominations. As ever, the music was the show. Nobody jumped up to shout that first night except a middle-aged Methodist gone straight. The revival preacher, a visitor whose fame rested on fast conversions, was distressed with such a slow beginning.

Adults took off from work during their days on the mourners' bench, and children, as a rule, were not allowed to play. "This is a time," according to Mama Minnie, my self-appointed guide to redemption, "when you s'pose to be on your knees beggin the Lord to forgive your sins. Then you meditate, and be still and don't talk. Be quiet!" Shut away in the house while my friends were fishing at the river or playing baseball or jumping on and off freight trains brought me no joy. To ease the tedious hours, I sang a lot and made up my own Christian meditation songs. At first, the little original tunes were without words, but after a few run-throughs, words would start to come to me.

One afternoon as I was singing a new song I'd made, I heard running on the porch. The screen door swished open and strained the hinges. Into the room shot Mama Minnie, outraged and aghast. She stood over me breathing fire.

"You low-down little rascal you. You s'posed to be on the mourners' bench, a candidate for redemption. All the way to the yard I can hear you in here howling them ol nasty blues."

There was no explaining to her that my song wasn't blues; any attempt to explain would have been sassing her. She heard in my song too much of what was associated with sin, dancing, and chitlin struts. But I couldn't just let it go at that. After all, had I not heard the great W. C. Handy discuss the subject in my presence and not in hers? "Mama Minnie," I politely protested, "I was making me up a church song. Can't you hear the difference?" She snatched off her glasses and shook her head like I'd gone crazy.

"If you call that a church song," she said, "Lord help you if you took a notion to sing one a them ol barrelhouse 'Midnight Ramble' blues."

I spent the rest of the week with a diminished interest in the mourners' bench. I didn't get baptized, for I was convinced that trusting my spirit to a denomination where the lines between God's and the devil's music were so blurred was not a good idea at all.

CHAPTER SIX

My Disagreement with
the Divinity

ONE DAY WHEN I WAS STILL NINE, I came home from play in high anticipation of some private time with Mama and found the entire block locked in an eerie hush. The sidewalk was empty as I walked past the row of houses on my way to our front porch, where Mama sat quietly rocking and patching school clothes. As I approached the porch she spoke quietly, using a pet name she always reserved for the baby of the house. "Step here, Pigmeat." I noticed an extra and unusual warmth in her voice. "I have some bad news to give you," she said, hugging me close. "Baby, while you were playing, your Daddy Long passed away." I bristled, then went into a running fit. I ran toward Mrs. Minnie's house, screaming, "I want my Daddy Long—I want my Daddy Long!" Mama climbed off the porch and followed me. Mrs. Minnie's daughter-in-law, Christine, met me at their door and told me they had taken Daddy Long away. She said about the last words he said were: "You all watch out for my boy." I just dissolved on the floor and tried to die too. Mama lifted me up and, taking me by the hand, led me home to our porch. I was too big for lap sitting anymore, but she took me up anyhow, and I cried myself limp in her lap, clinging to her neck, for a long time. But after a while I let her go, and alive again with anger, I declared that I hated God. "Why did he have to kill my Daddy Long, Mama?"

I remembered a favorite plaything I kept under the house, a hefty steel railroad spike I'd picked up from the tracks and brought home to sharpen with a file so I could dig little play canals in the dirt under the house. In my fury, I scrambled down out of Mama's lap and crawled under the house, whimpering like a hurt dog, then came out tear-blinded, clutching my spike as my weapon. I was ready to spill God's blood. I ran to the open yard and shouted defiantly up to heaven. "God!" I cried out at the top of my lungs. "You so big and bad; let me see you come down here and fight *me!* I'll kill you dead for killing my Daddy Long. I dare you, I double-dog dare you, to come down here and fight me!" It took but a moment for me to catch myself with spike and fist raised high; I'd gone too far, and I fully expected to be jolted back to my senses—not by the fist of God: by Mama's. I'd felt that Baptist woman's severe hand and scalding wrath for lesser transgressions than standing in her yard cussing out the Almighty. I just knew I had a killing coming now. But no. There sat Mama on the porch, stone-still in the rocker, looking down at me with the most quietly compassionate expression on her face. That look, and the understanding implicit in her silence, sent an uplifting rush of emotion thrilling through me, for I realized how lucky I was to have a mama smart enough to understand my special need and to keep still and allow the nine-year-old me the liberty of a private disagreement with the Divinity.

It was an unforgettable moment, and it marked in me the beginning of a new and larger appreciation of my mama. I sensed from then on that she was looking at me with fresh eyes too. Something definitely deep and large had begun for us.

When she stretched out her arms for me to climb into her lap again, I went back full of the knowledge that at least some of the void left by my Daddy Long's death was being filled with the warming assurance that my mama knew how to love me so intelligently. There in her lap, I clung to her neck again, sobbing as she held me close and rocked us gently to her soft song—"Blessed Assurance, Jesus Is Mine." By and by, I'd cried myself dry.

CHAPTER SEVEN

"Read Between the Lines, Boy!"

IN ORDER TO HELP MAMA put food on the table, our big sister Velma quit high school in her second year to go to work at the white high school cafeteria, a job recommended by one of the porch ladies. Our school didn't have a cafeteria; my crowd came to associate book learning with a gnawing emptiness in the gut. Mama had hoped Sister would be the first in the family to represent our family one day wearing the high school graduate's cap and gown. Only an opportunity as promising as working for Mrs. Solomon, a fair-minded white woman who ran the school cafeteria for white children, could entice Mama to interrupt Sister's education. When Sister quit school to go to work for Mrs. Solomon full time, I heard from under the porch, "The good Lord shur blessed that gal with more'n a pretty face, bless his Name!"

Besides the small wage, the cafeteria staff was allowed to take home left-over food from the white children's meals: a windfall for us. No matter how bland or uninteresting the food was when it left the cafeteria with Sister, by the time it appeared on our table, Mama Minnie, whose culinary talents matched her gift for "news," had doctored and transformed it into fare fit for the most discriminating gourmet.

Sister never gave up on getting her diploma, and after several years of both full-time and part-time labor for Mrs. Solomon, she graduated

51

from high school at age twenty-one. She was the most poised and sophisticated graduate in the procession that year.

Graduation presents flooded our house, especially from the porch ladies, who'd come to regard Sister as one of their own. Stockings, dress gloves, fountain pens, pocketbooks, and cards with cash money enclosed all weighted down the divan in the front room, where the graduate slept.

On Sister's graduation day, while I was still in the low grades, I sat with the porch ladies, crowded into the front-row seats at our school auditorium. Mrs. Minor hit the downbeat of a march I loved; I was grown before I learned it was called "Pomp and Circumstance." The procession marched into the auditorium and filled it with sedate and scholarly dignity. Our faculty was at the front of the line, then came the graduates, gliding gloriously.

On her big day, Sister wore beneath her flowing black graduation gown at least one of every item the ladies had given her. When she mounted the stage at her most dignified gait, her elegantly gloved left hand, which clutched a new linen hankie, flicked an acknowledgment to the front row. Miss Della, encouraged by the sight of the gloves she'd given, lost control and shouted, "Walk it, gal!" This encouraged Sister to add the faintest hint of a strut to her pomp and her circumstance, and that encouraged Miss Luveenya, donor of the lace hankie, to cry out, "Feel just like I'm up dere right along wid her. Thank you, sweet Jesus!"

As much as Mama loved education, she lost no time in letting us know: "You won't find everything in books, sugar. You got to learn to read *between* the lines."

For her, the key to her children's surviving the brutal segregation of our South was understanding the sinister and well-hidden motives lurking behind the Jim Crow laws. She saw cloaked in the South's laws an even greater and more crippling danger than the physical inconvenience they imposed. And she never tired of pointing out that the law's real purpose was to diminish our people's spirit and sense of self. Thus, if you stomped into the house complaining too long and too loud of having to stand up in the back of the bus while seats were empty in front, where white folk sat, she'd chase after you and instruct you.

"You can survive the back of the bus, Jim Crow schools, and the color bar," she'd hammer away at us, "but you just make *very* sure that you *never* let the white man's law convince you that you're not as good as any of God's children. Can't you see that *that* is just what they intend for those laws to do to you? Use your head for something beside a hatrack, fool. It's their law that puts you in the back of the bus, along with all the other Jim Crow laws they make up to try to make you bow down and slouch around and feel like nothing. God's own hand put a light in your soul. There is no Dixiecrat law greater than God's own light. Do you understand me, mister?"

"Yessum," I would say wearily.

"Well, don't you come waltzing your little narrow hind parts into this house whining about *that!* The next time you ride the bus, don't you dare slouch. You throw your chest out and *march* back there to your seat, holding your head up *high*, and strut just like you own that whole dadblamed bus *and* the ground it rolls on. You gotta look beyond your nose, Willie Henry. Learn to read between the lines, boy!"

If you lived in Mama's house, these lessons went with the territory. But she could reach you far beyond the boundaries of home should you show her you needed it. I did once.

Just when I'd finally learned to accept that visits and even mail from my father would always be rare, short, and entirely impromptu, out of the blue and from somewhere up north, a letter arrived from him addressed to me. I got so excited I sat right down and answered it, expressing myself in greatest detail, with news of my life at school and at church. I especially asked for news of my Uncle Grover, whose visit in that car with the Joe Louis fight on the radio I'd never stopped thinking about. It was a pretty good letter for a boy my size, as I remember it. Very soon another letter arrived from my father, saying he'd shared my reply with Uncle Grover, who lived somewhere near my father. Before too long, a special delivery letter from Detroit arrived for me: Uncle Grover was writing to say he had a fine job at the Packard motorcar company. Could I come to Detroit to visit him and his wife for a week or two that summer? I was beside myself and wore the letter out, opening and reading it over and over for days.

Mama had always liked Uncle Grover, who had recently remarried but was still childless. He'd often said he wished he had a boy like me. Mama appreciated his affection for me and felt I shouldn't miss a good chance to see a big place like Detroit. "It will be nice for you to see other places and have some contact with your daddy's people," she encouraged. I couldn't wait for summer.

In due course my train tickets arrived, in another special delivery letter. When I got to Detroit, Uncle Grover and his new wife, Seculia, began making my vacation everything I thought a big-city experience ought to be: cowboy movies, amusement parks, integrated seating on buses, in theaters and restaurants. But it was hearing the neighborhood kids my age describe their well-equipped, integrated schools, and all the things they did in them, that set my imagination aflame.

Uncle Grover seemed to enjoy showing me Detroit's barbershops, the barbecue joints, and even a real Chinese restaurant he frequented in one thriving black neighborhood. On the bus home from Hudson's department store downtown, where he'd bought me a snazzy new outfit one day, my generous uncle said, "Willie Henry, if you like this place and think you would like to go to school here and be my boy, why don't you write to your mama and see if she'll let you stay." I could hardly believe what I was hearing. I sent off my best letter ever, I thought, telling Mama how exciting a place Detroit was, listing in lavish detail all its obvious up-north advantages. Most of all, I knew that elaborating on those descriptions of the schools I'd heard about and Uncle Grover's good job would convince her that Detroit's progressive environment was just the thing for me. Certainly she'd let me stay after reading a letter with such a logical argument from her boy.

I got a letter right back, in Mama's neat and classy handwriting, addressed to Master Willie Henry Ruff, and it read:

My Dear Son, Willie Henry:

I am so happy you are having a good time with Uncle Grover and your aunt Seculia, and it makes me feel good that they think enough of you to want you to be their boy. I can see how going to school in Detroit could be a great advantage for you. I know too that with the fine job Uncle Grover has, he can give you things I cannot provide for you. But, Son, I am your mother, and in the eyes of the Lord, I, and nobody else in this world am responsible for your up-bringing. That is a mother's lot and duty. It is a duty I will never turn my back on where any of my children are concerned.

When you come of age, you will be free to do what you will or may. Until then, that responsibility is mine. I am sorry to disappoint you. We all miss you here in the house and I expect you home on the date we already agreed on.

Your Loving Mother,
Manie C. Pruitt

CHAPTER EIGHT

Chitlin Struts

THE STORY OF "strong drink and the law" had no rival as a socializing factor in the north Alabama of my time. From as far back as I can remember, our little river towns were called "dry." But "dry" was only a legal description, never our world's true condition. Bootlegging was the center of Muscle Shoals's social commerce, and in some way, it touched the lives of all our citizens, regardless of class, color, or their "wet" or "dry" persuasions.

The enormous appeal "leggin" enjoyed in our world, I always suspected, was rooted in the fact that it was so deliciously outside the law and so universally admired.

No social institution complemented bootlegging like the chitlin strut, the most dynamic form of functional home entertainment ever devised in the "dry" South of my childhood. A chitlin strut was a musical frolic with dancing, distinctive food, and the kind of freewheeling entertainment that made Alabama's Saturday nights the best night of the week. Stylish poor people mastered the chitlin strut as a contrivance to help pay the rent. Harlem imported them and called them, with misplaced dignity, "rent parties."

A plate of chitlins and fresh slaw with a shot of corn liquor was thirty-five cents, twenty-five cents for just the chitlin dinner. Musicians from all over the county came and played for the corn liquor and all the chitlins they could eat. A good player or singer might drop in at three or four struts in different neighborhoods during the course of an active Saturday night. Our house, where Mama occasionally plied a discreet commerce in white lightnin, attracted good banjo players, guitarists, washboard pickers, and jug blowers. I would sometimes join them, blowing on a bass jug when I could pull it away from Mama, who had a deep love for low-pitched music.

The struts at our house took place in the boys' room, in the back of the house. On a strut day, we set the two iron beds out in the backyard, and it was my job to sprinkle cornmeal on the freshly scrubbed floor to make "gliding" easy for the dancing.

All of us in our house, including Mama Minnie, who by then had put the dancing of sinners aside, were hot dancers. Sister was a marvel, our handsome big brother Eddie was great too, but Mama was the best. After I was grown, some thirty years after Mama died, Mrs. Sally Sledge told me that Mama and my father were celebrated rug cutters, in high demand as "bait dancers" at struts all over town; they put on a little warm-up show that "baited" the shy folk onto the floor to make a better party and promote a finer commerce. "Those two could take over a dance floor and make a mop handle wanta dance," Mrs. Sally said.

When chitlin strut music got fully cranked up at our house, I watched in rapt amazement as the otherwise lumbering and awkward-looking country men suddenly became graceful on the dance floor. Animal imitations—the "buzzard lope," "snake hips," and "ride the mule"—were all favorites. Mr. J. W. Mays, who lived on our street, could dance a "mule ride" on a rolling washboard-and-jug rhythm with such realism I could smell the barn.

But I found the nonmusical preludes to the evenings' festivities nearly as much to my liking as the music that followed. "Liars' contests" sprang to life, and the most outrageous and exaggerated boastfulness flew back and forth between contestants. Good liars pridefully practiced the improviser's art as they spun stylish lies about the fierceness of favorite heroes, villains, or dangerous animals. These contests made good party entertainment and properly set the stage, ensuring a chitlin strut's conviviality. Old Ice-Truck Tab, who had the loudest mouth of all the Largomosinos' truckdrivers on the ice route, often warmed the gathering up with something like:

"Y'all hear about the storm over in Lawrence County last week? Well, they said it blowed so hard and so bad it blowed four wells up outta the ground and plumb outta sight, and blowed on and on till it blowed two crooked roads straight. And it jes keppa huffing and keppa puffing till it scattered up the days of the week so messy that Sunday didn't come around till Tuesday, way over late in the next evening."

Rosebud Rump, Mr. Will Rump's party-loving daughter, said, "Yeah, Tab, you lying hound you. I hear they got bad ol snakes over in that county too."

"Aw, girl, don't mention them mean rascals! They told me one of them long Lawrence County No-Shoulders got so mad las week, he ran out and bit the L and N railroad track and killed three inbound freight trains."

And then the lying and "woofing" would be cut short by the electrifying rhythm of a man with a fistful of sewing thimbled fingers snapping against the tin washboard: our chitlin strut drummer. The zumming roar of a lard-can gutbucket thumped like a store-bought bass fiddle and brought dancers gliding onto the floor just to warm up and shake the kinks out.

Unhappily for me, after one set of the music and before the late-evening woofing degenerated to language not fit for the ears of fans my size, I had to make the long walk all the way to Mrs. Lizzy Rick's house in Baptist Bottom, to spend the night. I dearly loved Mrs. Lizzy, the sweetest and gentlest and tallest—well over six feet—fat lady in town, who had the face of an angel and the hospitality to match it; and the feeling was mutual. She'd cook up the best pot of turnip greens in Sheffield just to get me to come and spend the night with her, and I loved doing it. But to be sent to her on chitlin strut night meant missing that colorful back-room language and the music, and I always cried to have to leave it.

In those preadolescent days, the delicious pleasures of my ear—the music and the stylish spoken language of our world—got out of hand and developed into serious distractions that caused me no end of problems at home. For a time, Mama Minnie insisted I was close to being retarded and a little "off." I was too much a listener. Impossible for me to concentrate on anything else if there was an ear diversion close by. I'd get stuck, for instance, at the barbershop for hours, listening to Doc Long and Wonderful C. Hill and Bitsy Pillar weaving the most colorful and engrossing stories. And when Tab and Ice-Truck Raymond came in, woofing with their boastful lying, I'd totally forget myself and linger for hours. Then suddenly I would realize I had a country skinning coming when I got back home, because Mama Minnie had ordered, "You get that head cut and get yourself back home and scrub that kitchen floor and sweep the front yard." It would be worse if I'd pass the railroad tracks and the hobo jungle on an errand and be pulled into it by the soulful strains of a traveling tramp's fiddle, or a mouth organ and a banjo, and forget the errand. Music and the spoken language of our world, which sounded like music, were taking over my life.

I was a slave to my ear and in love with my shackles.

But then I had a chance encounter with an altogether different kind of language, full of another kind of color, and it sucked me into its sphere and turned my impressionable ten-year-old mind completely upside down: it was sign language—talking with hands—the language of the deaf.

It happened when I went to work in a shoe repair shop, replacing a young black man who'd decided to go on to better things. This was a job that Mama Minnie was enthusiastic about, because it was an opportunity to learn a good trade while earning a little coin. The work was not hard to learn, and Mr. Steele, the owner, was a good teacher even though he could be touchy and sharp.

He started me off on the basics of nailing and gluing leather and rubber soles and heels, polishing and dyeing shoes, and making deliveries on the shop's nearly new Elgin bicycle—the absolute best part of the job for me. He kept me away from the big sewing machines, power cutters, and polishers, saying that when I got bigger he would teach me to use them safely. His wife worked the cash register. Mrs. Steele was a kind, quiet woman, whose presence in the shop took the edge off the old man's occasional abrasiveness. If, for instance, she went out to get him and herself a Coca-Cola, she'd bring me one, and she was polite enough to call me by my name and not "boy" all the time, as Mr. Steele did.

One day a man came into the shop and started rattling off talk on his hands with Mr. Steele. I was amazed that the boss could give it right back to this deaf fellow. Such expressive agility in his big shoe-maker's dirty fingers made me wonder. He looked perfectly at home signing and even laughed out loud a couple of times with the deaf man before he left. Then I asked Mr. Steele, "Where did you learn to talk on your hands?"

"I was raised and taught my trade by my older brother," he said. "He was deaf, and he taught me shoemaking and the sign language. It ain't hard." After that, I kind of regarded the boss as a man of some mysterious inner substance, for I'd never heard or seen a real conversation in a foreign language before. This shoemaker speaking that silent secret code was an intoxicatingly exotic curiosity: "a white man with a language mojo," I told myself.

A few days later, Mr. Steele called me over to his workbench and said, "You remember that deaf man who was in here? Well, in a couple of weeks we're going to have company in the shop; a deaf boy is coming from the Talladega School for the Deaf and Blind to apprentice with me." He added a warning: "You got to learn how to talk to him. It'll be for your own good. You have to be careful working around deaf people, because they can sometimes be dangerous." I was confused. "Why are they dangerous?" I asked. Mr. Steele said, "Well, it's aggravating for them if they can't make you understand them or if they can't understand you. Then they're liable to hurt you. But I can teach you to talk on your hands in no time." That news provoked mixed feelings; I wanted desperately to learn to talk on my hands, but I wasn't looking forward to courting danger in the bargain.

We began my lessons that same day. In slack moments in the shop or during our rest breaks, he'd show me finger spelling. He'd been right about the ease of it; and it got to be fun saying the ABCs on my fingers. In a couple of days I could form all twenty-six letters without mistakes, and we began spelling out most of our conversation. Then, because I'd practiced at home and got pretty good showing off for Mama and the neighborhood, Mr. Steele said we'd not talk anymore at all, just spell. But I had trouble figuring out where one word ended and the next began, he spelled so quickly; I got better when he slowed down. Then he started teaching me real signs.

"Look here, boy," he said. "You can say a lotta things with one or two motions of your hands. You can do it real quick and with practically no fuss." He held up one hand and, with the middle finger of the other hand, touched the first palm and then reversed the process, with motions that were quick as a snake. "Bet you can guess what that means, can't you?" No, I really couldn't. "Come on! Wake up, boy. Ain't you a Christian? That means Jesus Christ. Didn't you just see me point to the nails in Jesus' hands? Get it?" It was, I thought, a gruesome association to start me off with, but I had to admit it was interesting and efficient. Mr. Steele made me imitate the nails-in-the-hands sign until I got it down pat and with nearly the speed of a copperhead. Then I asked for more.

With his right hand, thumb extended, going up to touch his forehead, he said, "This means mother." Then, moving the same shape of the hand down so the thumb touched his chin, he said, "This means father." Then, back up with the same configuration, he thumbed his big nose and wiggled the other four fingers and said with an irreverent guffaw, "This means mother-in-law!" His wife cringed. Even Mr. Steele's cold crudeness and bad jokes couldn't dull my appetite for this powerful new magic. I was hooked.

When he told me that much of the sign language we use came from the American Indians, I felt proud of the Choctaw and Cherokee blood Mama said I had in me.

This, my very first foreign language, was starting to absorb me in its nonverbalness and its direct reference to thought and explicit meanings. I was falling in love with the magic of the live symbols shaped in the air between people doing all that communicating. Not suddenly, but gradually, I started to appreciate that these expressive hand shapes represented concepts that seemed bigger than just words to me, and I couldn't wait to learn as many as I could take in.

I went home one night after the lessons had progressed from the simple finger spelling to real signs and showed Mama some of what I was learning. I signed "love" for her, and she looked at my fists drawn in and folded across my chest and gave me an admiring smile. Then I showed her the thumb and forefinger of both hands opening both eyelids, and she hollered, "Wake up!" She said, "Why, baby, those are mind pictures you're making." She was just as proud as I'd been when I told her about the Indian origins of many signs. Every night when I brought her more new mind pictures, she'd guess at their meanings and marvel—at least she made me think it was marvelous—at my growing repertoire.

Then Smitty, the deaf boy from Talladega, joined us at the shoeshop. Smitty was about eighteen, a big, beefy blond with an appealing gentleness. It would have been hard not to like him. He was amused that I could even finger spell. That I also had learned quite a few signs from Mr. Steele really knocked him out. When I finger-spelled "Welcome," he shook my hand and with his opened right hand covered his mouth and moved the hand smartly away and down from his mouth, like a salute—the sign for "Thank you." I couldn't wait to get home that evening to lay that one on Mama. Smitty then signed for me to keep my face in his line of vision when addressing him and asked me not to pull on his clothes to get his attention unless it was an emergency, saying that was all I had to remember for us to get along just fine. Those were reasonable precautions, I thought, and with a combination of finger spelling and signing, I told him, "I hate people pulling on my clothes too." He lit up and shook with laughter, and my fears for all those dangers of the deaf Mr. Steele had warned me about flew right out the window.

By the time Smitty had been there a few weeks, I was getting better at signing and he and I were setting up routines to make our shopwork easier and more efficient. He told me about his school in Talladega and the trades—auto bodywork, piano tuning, shoe repair—it offered. He said one blind boy at the school was a wizard at auto body and fender work. He could feel the wrinkle in a fender with his hands and hammer it out with amazing precision.

I was soon overtaken by a sudden Helen Keller obsession. Until then, I'd not given Miss Keller's abilities at communicating as much thought as I had her prodigious book learning. Grown folk had said that when, as a little girl, she'd learned to read braille, she'd stayed with it so long and with such fierce tenacity that her fingers would bleed. Now I couldn't wait until "colored school day" rolled around at the Keller homeplace and museum in Tuscumbia. State law required the absolute racial separation of schoolchildren, and our school had to wait to visit the museum on a day when white children would not be there. I tried to picture in my mind what it would be like living in Miss Keller's dark and silent world. And when I asked myself, "What must it be like to never know music?" I shuddered at the horror of it. Now, for the first time, my Tuscumbia neighbor who'd moved on to world fame for her brilliance was coming into sharp focus in my imagination.

In an effort to better understand what it would be like to be Helen Keller, I clamped my eyes shut tight as if blind, and I stuffed cotton from one of Mr. Jim Clerk's cotton patches in my ears to make me close to deaf. I fumbled all over the house and in the yard. After practicing at home for a while, I left one day for work in that condition, trying—as Daddy Long used to say—to "rememberize" my route: the curbs, the traffic patterns, the trees that could bust your brains out if you were careless, and where the bad dogs were to be dodged along the way. Amazingly, I made it to work unscathed. Before long, with my eyes closed, I could negotiate downtown Sheffield pretty well. I was finding my way in my ersatz deaf-blind Helen Keller state until the day Ice-Truck Raymond sped across town with an overloaded truck and nearly ran me over as I crossed Second Street. He slammed on his brakes and hollered.

"Hey, fool, you think you was born with bumpers on your ass? You better open them damn eyes!" But I kept right on courting death as I practiced and explored Miss Keller's world, right up to the day when I got one of Mama Minnie's bad switch-whippings for not speaking back to Miss Callie, who'd spoken to me first and wondered why she'd had to. Mama Minnie wasn't ready to believe I'd not heard Miss Callie's greeting because I had cotton in my ears and missed seeing her because I was playing being blind. She'd preached my funeral after whipping me that day: "You are getting more foolish with every day the good Lord sends here, boy! You better throw away that dadblamed cotton, mister, and use them good eyes God done give you if you don't want some more of my hickory!" Mama Minnie with her quick and ready hickory was hard to reason with. I threw up my hands and promised to give up being Helen Keller on the streets of Sheffield.

One day at the shoeshop, I was in a conversation with Smitty and he was having trouble reading one of my signs. Though I thought I had it right, I obviously was faltering somewhere with a sign involving a complicated movement of the right fist. Mr. Steele, seeing my meaning and my problem right away, interrupted. "Naw, boy!" he said. "Your problem is you got to hold that fist up like this." I held it up. "No! Hold it like this: just like you gonna hit a nigger."

I went cold. The color of deep red began crowding my vision, and an anger welled up in me that choked off my breath. I wanted to rage and strike out at him, but I was so stunned I just went weak. All I could think to do when I recovered a bit was to rip my apron off, make a fist with my right hand with the little finger up and move it toward my chest—the sign for "I"—then, placing the first two fingers of my right hand in my left hand immediately snatching the two fingers out again. I'd signed: "I quit!" and was out the door.

I spent the next few days missing Smitty and the work. I couldn't have guessed that I'd miss sign language as much as I did. Most painful of all was my loss of respect for Mr. Steele. I couldn't bring myself to even mention having quit the job to Mama or Mama Minnie. I would just stay out of the house during regular work hours. I'd walk over to Tuscumbia and circle Helen Keller's homeplace and come back to tour Baptist Bottom. But then one day during the shop's regular lunch hour, Mama Minnie and my little sister and brother and I were in the front yard, when Mr. Steele's car pulled up. He called Mama Minnie out to the car and they talked for a while and he drove off. Mama Minnie came back and asked me what had happened at the shop to make me sass a grown person. I said I hadn't sassed anybody, I hadn't even said a word. "Don't you dast get smart with me, young-un! I know y'all talk on y'all's hands down there. Just tell me what did you say to the man when you quit that good job?"

"I quit because Mr. Steele said 'nigger,' " I said.

"Did he call you a nigger?"

"No, ma'am," I said, "but he used the word to me."

"*To you?*" she shot back, with strong emphasis on the "to." "Well, let me tell you something, child: this ol world is hard. And as long as your hind parts point to the ground, you're gonna hear white folk use that word *and* a whole lot worse ones. Don't you know that?" I said I guess I did.

"Well, boy," she went on, "you can't get along in this here world if every time you hear somebody say 'nigger,' or something else you don't like, you gotta jump mad and swell up and quit your job and want to go to war. Willie Henry, let me tell you something. Sometimes you got to stoop to conquer, honey. I *know* what I'm talkin bout. Now, just as long as that white man in that shoeshop don't call *you* a nigger or hit you, it's foolish for you to quit—specially when you learning a good trade and making a little money." Mama Minnie completely missed the fact that I had no interest in the shoemaker's trade and that the dollar and a half a week I earned was nothing compared to the sign language I was learning.

"Well, suh," she said, "Mr. Steele said you're a good worker and a right apt learner. He'll take you back if you come on back after you eat. So you just cool off, and after you eat some of the dinner I got cooking on the stove, you go along on back to work and try to overlook whatever white folk say in front of you. As long as he ain't calling *you* names, pay it no mind." My spirit sank, but Mama was away at work, and my grandmother's word was law in the house until Mama came home. I was stuck.

Everybody knew Mama Minnie was one of the best cooks in Sheffield, but the meal she set before me that day tasted like gall. I felt like a condemned man swallowing his last meal, with all the taste drawn out of it.

When I stepped into the shoeshop, Smitty's face gleamed, and he happily whapped the workbench with his hammer to signal Mr. Steele I was back. As I went for my work apron, hanging on the nail on the wall near Mr. Steele's last, I could see him gloating and silently asserting his supremacy over me. He was flushed with the victory he'd gained through Mama Minnie, and it was absolute. Suddenly my hand froze midair; it wouldn't move. I knew if I touched that apron something within me would die. My thoughts flashed back to that first sign he'd taught me—the gruesome "nails in the hands of Jesus"—and I knew my nailing days were done. A voice within me seemed to say, "There is nothing more for you in this place. Leave it. You're free!" I turned hard around and walked out of the shop toward Baptist Bottom and on to Tuscumbia, not caring what Mama Minnie was going to say or do to me when I got home.

I knew I'd lost my chance for learning more in my beloved sign language, but in the bargain I'd got in touch with a part of myself I'd not known before: the part I could always rely on to let me know just how far I was willing to stoop to conquer just to "get along" in Mama Minnie's hard ol world.

CHAPTER NINE

A Staggering Discovery

A T OUR HOUSE, newspapers were the most important bridge to the world outside Sheffield. We couldn't afford to buy them, but Mama's boss lady, Mrs. Gault, let her bring their *Memphis Commercial Appeal* home to us when it was a day old. The paper was one of the fringe benefits the Gaults threw in. Leftover food, clothing, and "cake privileges" were also windfalls. None of us children ever had a birthday go by without a cake Mama baked in the Gaults' kitchen, complete with a shiny coin (boiled sterile) stuck flat in the center of the icing.

Mama brought the newspaper home and sectioned it out to us according to reading ability and interest. I cut my reading teeth on the funnies about the time I started teaching Sunday school in the Sanctified church; year by year, I worked up to world events and finally to the editorials.

Early on, soon after I had mastered the funnies, I made a staggering discovery in Mr. Sam Hill's barbershop. A new man hit town, selling a newspaper I'd never seen before, never known existed. The stranger stood up in the middle of the little barbershop and pulled from his canvas sack a paper whose large heading read *Pittsburgh Courier*. He held it up and turned himself around for all to see. With the paper displayed flat across his chest, he recited the headlines. Inside the front sheet were big pictures of Joe Louis, Satchel Paige, Josh Gibson, and the black baseball teams—the Kansas City Clowns and the Birmingham Black Barons.

The stranger licked his thumb, still turning himself around, reached up with it, and turned the page again. I moved from the corner where I sat, so as to keep the stranger's front in view, and right then I knew that paper was talking my language. There were pictures and stories about Mr. Handy, Lena Horne, and Count Basie. I'd never seen Count Basie's picture, but I'd already "performed" as drummer with his band in Mutt's front yard. I kept walking around the revolving stranger, getting in his way and blocking the view of his audience, until Mr. Sam snatched me back by my shirttail, pointing to my seat in the corner. The stranger handed the paper to his first customer, pocketed a nickel, and pulled out another paper.

This one was different. Across the top, it read: *Chicago Defender*, and on its first page was a picture of General B. O. Davis, the first and only black general of the U.S. Army. Every time the stranger licked his thumb and flipped, he revealed more news of prominent black folk: Dr. George Washington Carver, other famous chemists and medical men, insurance company owners, and operators of chains of funeral homes in Birmingham, Atlanta, Memphis, and New Orleans.

I asked the stranger from my seat, where Mr. Sam had admonished me to stay put, "Mister, that paper got musicianers in it?" Without breaking his pitch about the men of science in his marvelous paper, he turned in my direction, passed his thumb across his damp forehead, reserving his tongue for selling, and flipped the page to a picture of Jimmie Lunceford's entire band. Facing it, on the opposite page, was a picture story of Ethel Waters, whose movie *Cabin in the Sky* we'd seen the week before from the "colored section" in the balcony of the Ritz picture show on Third Street. That did it! I said, "Gimme one." Mr. Sam looked at me and frowned, knowing that I had gone too far. I had only the fifteen cents from Mama for my haircut, but I didn't give that a second thought while I read about jazz music and Ethel Waters.

The stranger, without a pause in his presentation, shot his hand down into the sack again and came out with still another paper, whose top read: *Amsterdam News*. He ran his finger under the letters, reciting "Amsterdam News" aloud. Mr. Vincent Perkins, sitting near the electric fan, was amazed.

"Say, buddy," he said. "You mean to tell us country people that they got colored folks enough to put em in a paper way over yonder across the water in Amsterdam?"

"No, sir," answered the stranger. "It was people from across the water who settled *New York* and called it New Amsterdam, which is where the heavenly land of Harlem is situated, and that's where this here newspaper is from. . . . A-hem," said the paper man.

Let me school you,
brother, so the white man can't fool you—
I'm selling you history,
which ain't no mystery.
For just one buffalo nickel,
look at what you get.

"Looka here, young man," he said, turning to me.

Since he hadn't stopped for breath for a while, he paused just long enough to gulp air, which allowed him time to lick his thumb again, and he flipped to the entertainment section. There was a picture story of Duke Ellington playing at the Savoy Ballroom in Harlem. I couldn't stand it. Losing all reason, I handed him the last haircut dime, and he gave me back a nickel change and my *Amsterdam News*. He said, "You all don't mean to tell me this boy's got more gumption and curiosity about what's going on in the world of colored people than you old heads?"

"His mama's going to fix his gumption," Mr. Sam said, "*and* his curiosity, too, when he gits home without a haircut." Nodding in my direction, he asked me, "You got fifteen cents left?" I heard him, but I was reading.

Mr. Vincent Perkins, noticing that I was too busy to answer Mr. Sam, said, "He shur *nuff* crazy bout that music."

"Well, if he likes it that much, I'm going to throw in the *Pittsburgh Courier* with Count Basie's picture in it for him." The stranger laid

Count Basie in my lap, and I left for a quiet place under a shade tree. Mama was sitting on the front porch when I got home, and as soon as she looked up and saw me coming into the yard, she said, "Didn't you get to that barbershop yet, fool?"

"Yessum. But, Mama, look at these papers I bought with a dime of the money. They're about colored people."

"You what?" she said.

"I bought them for a dime; the man gave me one too."

"Well, how in the world are you going to walk into the First Baptist Church tomorrow with that head looking like cats been sucking on it? I ought to tan your narrow butt, boy." I said I could get one of Mr. John Green Simpson's back-porch haircuts for the nickel I had left.

"I thought you said his clippers smell too much like coal oil and they pull," she said. "Besides, you know he can't cut it so it looks even." I said I could always just go to the Sanctified church till it grew out again. After a while, she cooled down, and the two of us sat on the porch and read stories in a newspaper written for black folk by black folk. She appreciated the windfall. We had Dick Tracy and Andy Gump all the time, but papers with Duke and Ethel Waters seldom reached Sheffield. This inspired Mama to fetch her good sewing scissors and strut back to the porch to help me cut out the pictures of the drummer Jo Jones and Count Basie to save for Mutt.

Early in 1941, I went into business for myself. I felt old enough to relieve Mama of the burden of buying my clothes and schoolbooks. Selling was easy for me; I had already gained experience at "benefit" enterprises for school, especially the turkey raffles each Thanksgiving. The raffles were organized to raise money to supplement our teachers' salaries and narrow the gap between their earnings and that of white teachers. Turkey raffles made the difference. All of Sheffield's black schoolchildren were challenged to sell the raffle tickets as if their lives depended on it. I always won one of the offered prizes for my "significant" sales. Storekeepers, Sanctified church members, icemen, hustlers at the poolroom, and any citizen walking the street—white or black—were my prospects.

But my new for-profit business was selling the black weekly newspapers. The stranger I'd met at Mr. Sam Hill's barbershop earlier became my regional wholesaler, and the Sheffield monopoly was mine. I picked up my load every Friday night and was ready to hit the street with it early Saturday morning. Friday nights were spent reading the papers and sharpening my pitch. After reading the extra copy of each paper, I cut out the pictures of bands whose drummers Mutt and I admired and added them to my collection. Mutt owes much of his musical education to the *Pittsburgh Courier* and the *Chicago Defender*.

I made a point of calling on every black family in town; I often made as much as forty cents a week. Some of the old folks I had taught in the Sanctified Sunday school bought the papers only if I sat and read aloud to them the way I'd read them the Scriptures at Brother Suggs's church. They always showed genuine interest in what I read, but I knew they were spending their scarce coin mostly to help me out and encourage me, the little Sanctified scholar, to "hustle."

CHAPTER TEN

A Yearning to March

SOLDIER SUITS CAPTURED MY ATTENTION in a strong way early in my life. I was not the only one at home or around town smitten by the looks and the near-mythic significance of a uniform. Only the women of our South, the maids and church mothers in the Baptist, Methodist, and Sanctified churches, ever wore uniforms. Our environment was so completely devoid of uniformed male authority figures—no Negro policemen, no Negro firemen, and certainly no Negro militia—that a suit on a soldier was something to make folk sit up and take notice.

Thus, when President Roosevelt's Civilian Conservation Corps was introduced in the Tennessee Valley, our boys took to the uniformed service with the vigor of a forest fire. In the lean and idle Depression days and beyond, the CCC camps were a windfall for the hungry. The eager recruits planted trees, fought forest fires, dug drainage ditches, and built roads. My big brother George Fred enlisted in the CCC for that snappy forest-green woolen uniform with big shiny brass buttons, the cocky little cap, the sturdy brogans, and, of course, the hearty food. Then, after a few months, he decided to take the next step and join the real army. Soon other young black Sheffield men followed his lead.

Shortly after I got my paper route, George Fred came home from the army camp; he looked beautiful in his uniform. He taught me my first GI word, "furlough," and said that was why he was home right then: he was on furlough. His former schoolmates, along with my fourth-grade gang, crowded our front yard to admire the soldier suit. Neighbors pressed in close to examine George's brass, to finger his PFC stripe, and then someone turned him around slowly, like a mannequin. The attention he was receiving excited him and made him swell up and swagger. He threw his chest forward and made a show of flicking the ashes from his ready-roll cigarettes, while spouting other big army words, like "nomenclature." Little Mutt Johnson, my main sidekick, declared, "Sure be glad when I git big enough to fit in one of them sharp soldier suits so I kin come back on me a nice furlough like ol George doing!"

We fashioned mock rifles from broomsticks, stole cook pots out of the house to cram down on our skulls to look like war helmets, then pestered George until he taught us how to march, strutlike, with his brand of swagger. George barked his orders to us boys so professionally that Hattie and Lucille, two curvy, sloe-eyed morsels at the edge of the crowd, were convinced that my GI big brother was at least a colonel. The women customers on my paper route pressed perfumed notes on me to take home to him. That soldier suit did wonders for George.

He had been in the army more than a year when Pearl Harbor was bombed. By then, B. O. Davis, Jr., the son of the famous Negro general, was a cadet at West Point. His tortured experiences at the academy were widely reported in the black press of the day, which I continued to read avidly. Photos showed Davis staring out at eternity, supreme self-confidence packed into every inch of his six-foot-two frame. Handsome and majestic in his uniform, our man carried himself as if his brown presence had been imposed on the U.S. Military Academy by direct order from Hannibal.

A Negro officer in America's armed services was at that time an exotic oddity. In all of America's wars, white officers had commanded black troops. It was not uncommon for white officers to be assigned to command a black unit as punishment for some serious military crime or transgression. Young Davis at West Point would take getting used to. His unusual ability to maintain a stoic military deportment in the face of abuse and racial slurs set him apart. The West Point faculty and his peers would not speak to him or otherwise acknowledge his presence, assuming that denying his existence would surely break his spirit. But they had misjudged Davis. Not only did he refuse to break; the attempts to cripple him psychologically served rather to feed his determination and inspired him to excel at all he touched.

War fever filled every corner of our world. At churches, preachers prayed for the "boys across the water"; at school, the entire student body filled the auditorium daily for morning devotion, and Mrs. Minor taught us new patriotic songs.

At the peak of the war bond drive, the children at our school went selling bonds door to door. The white students across town were also out on the hustle for Uncle Sam. Hitler and Tojo had to be kept out of Alabama. Grown people declared, "Ef y'all think ol Mississippi Bilbo is bad on black asses, wait till Hitler git here." Bilbo, the worst Dixiecrat racist in the U.S. Senate, had seemed our folk's biggest enemy until Hitler and Tojo surfaced.

One Saturday while I was out on my paper route, I found Miss Lulla, a quiet but testy old lady, who made her living washing and ironing, in her usual spot in her backyard, with a vigorous fire working under her old black iron washpot. She stirred the pot with a long-handled paddle, boiled white from long years of stirring the wash of others. "Morning, Miss Lulla," I said.

"Morning, boy," she said, and in the same breath added, "Naw, I don't want to buy no paper. You know I kaint read."

"Yessum, but I wondered if you heard about war bonds and stamps to help Uncle Sam fight Hitler and Tojo."

She stopped stirring, left the paddle to float in the bubbling washpot, dug both hands into her ample hips, and squinted her eyes, saying, "That Hitler! Sho I heard uh him, the dirty little hound. I saw what he did when Jesse Owens winned that footrace over yonder across the water. Saw it at the picture show. . . . Saw how he called Jesse a nigger and got up and walked his little narrow ass out the place. Naw, child, he don't mean no colored folks no good, the little pop-eyed buzzard. How much you say it cost to fight him?"

I never could sell Miss Lulla a paper, but she turned into a regular for my war bonds and savings stamps.

All over America the war bond drives picked up steam. During a bond rally in Sheffield, a prize was created for the school with the best bond sales. Our school came up against the children at the white school. We figured out a way to compete with them.

At the start of the war, young black men, like their white counterparts, volunteered for pilot training. But the Army Air Corps insisted that flying was a complex skill, manageable only by white men. Not only was the rejection of Negroes absolute, it was rude and mean. Some of the more determined black men left the country and ultimately wore the uniforms of the Royal Canadian and the British air forces as fliers.

But Allied air losses both in the Pacific and in Europe rapidly escalated, and young American fliers were being shot down faster than they could be trained. In desperation and against the advice of the Dixiecrats, President Roosevelt ordered the Air Corps to begin training Negroes to fly. But where? Most Air Corps flying schools were in Texas or other southern facilities. Strict segregation was the law, and Roosevelt's staff was convinced that America's elite Air Corps would never stand for our men integrating the nation's pilot-training facilities.

Then someone remembered that Alabama's Tuskegee Institute had vast land holdings, with an airstrip and instructional facilities for pilots, and the government began trying to attract those black applicants who'd earlier been turned away.

"Hitler must be winning the war!" said Doc Long one day there in the barbershop, as he read in the Negro papers I sold him that Tuskegee's first group of aviators was going into training. Doc was quick to point out that our men had to be better by far than their white counterparts going into training.

"You see what it says here." He pointed to the *Pittsburgh Courier*. "That entire group of our men going into pilot training are *all* college graduates, and one of them, B. O. Davis, Jr., is already a captain and a graduate of West Point. The white boys who want to fly are accepted for training at eighteen years old, with no more than high school educations! Now, what does *that* tell you? It tells you that this government has always preferred that our people not wear the uniform at all! And except in desperation, they have always resisted our assuming the role of heroic defenders. The white military bosses have suppressed all accounts of our patriotism and the excellence of our men on the battlefield, so that the world will look on us as cowards, unfit to lead and to fight. Why has the black race been deprived of its Sergeant York? You mark my words: it will take a long time for America to accept the black man as a war hero. I won't live to see it, but it will happen."

Once Tuskegee started training our fliers, the up-north presses couldn't run fast enough to produce the black newspapers I sold. I begged my distributor for more papers, but New York, Chicago, Atlanta, and other big-city readers beat us out of the short supply. With the help of the black press spreading the word, Tuskegee soon had all the volunteers it could accommodate—and more.

We had an older Tuskegee graduate in Sheffield, Mr. Paris B. Swoopes, a fine tailor who'd worked his way through the institute in the service of the science wizard Dr. George Washington Carver. Young Swoopes's job at Tuskegee had been to gather discarded banana stalks from the town's markets. Dr. Carver transformed these and other waste products into valuable commodities and research materials.

One Sunday morning in church during our biggest war bond drive ever, Mr. Swoopes stood before the congregation and announced a plan to help our Baptist Bottom school come out on top. Working quietly with the authorities of Tuskegee, he had arranged for a squadron of the celebrated airmen to fly their fighter planes up to Sheffield for an air show. From the front of the church, he said, "If we want to win that bond-selling prize and do something special, we've got to show the world that our people can do anything anybody else can do. Flying airplanes is an admirable skill, but God has not ordained it the white man's *private* work. We have it within ourselves to show the world something special about our race, and we can do it right here and right *now*, in Sheffield!" The worshipers clapped like thunder and came off the benches shouting, "Amen, brother, let's show em we're special!"

Standing next to the collection table, Mr. Swoopes waited for the congregation to quiet down, then he said, "You will see with your own eyes a whole squadron of black men flying U.S. Air Corps fighter planes through the air over Sheffield." I gasped so hard at that news I thought I'd swallowed my tongue.

This news sped up and down both sides of the river. Assemblies in our school auditorium turned into pep rallies for war bonds. Conversations on Sheffield's porches, in the barbershop and the poolroom, centered around "the airplane drivers from the Tuskegee war camp." During the bond drive, our teachers swelled our national pride with accounts of feats of patriotism and courage by black people all through our nation's history. We were admonished to remember Crispus Attucks, a black American fighting the British in the Revolutionary War in Boston, the first American to die in that war; and the courageous fighters of our race in the Civil War. Professor Tyler got drafted into the army, and back home on furlough in his uniform, he visited the school to remind us that "not only have the members of our race distinguished themselves in all of America's wars: no Negro has ever been convicted of treason against the United States." All that Doc Long had said in the barbershop, Professor Tyler repeated and expanded upon, standing there in his soldier suit in the schoolyard, just as sharp as he could be.

New American flags began to appear in our classrooms and auditorium. Small boys started wearing their brothers' stripes and soldier caps, and every Sunday at church, Reverend Yarborough made the mothers and fathers of boys in the "war camp" stand up. At the movie houses, the "March of Time" news films showed that "four-star" mothers were the mothers closest to America's heart. The Ritz Theater flashed a news clip of Joe Louis, in the army then, fighting one of a series of exhibition fights and donating the entire purse to his government; that fight brought the total of the champion's donations to more than three million dollars. I heard the Brown Bomber say in an on-camera interview, "We gonna win the war cause God's on our side." As the air show day drew near, Mr. Swoopes ordered and paid for advertising posters to tack up all over town. When the printer had them ready and delivered to the tailor shop, I volunteered to nail them up on trees, barns, telephone poles—anyplace that was easy to see. The afternoon I went to the tailor shop for my posters, Mr. Swoopes said he had a surprise for me. He hadn't mentioned it at church because it had just been confirmed. Coolly and without looking in my direction, he reached under the counter and handed me a poster that made me quiver. It read:

AIR SHOW and PARADE featuring
THE TUSKEGEE FIGHTER PILOTS
and the
TUSKEGEE AIR BASE MARCHING BAND

When at last the big day arrived, I took a seat on the curb in front of the tailor shop hours before parade time to wait for the band bus to pull up from Tuskegee. Every few minutes, I peeped inside the door to ask Mr. Swoopes, "Isn't it time that band got here?" He said calmly, "They'll be along. There is plenty of time." Mr. Swoopes had explained in church that because of the limited flying range of the fighter planes, they wouldn't be able to land and talk to us. They would fly up to Sheffield from Tuskegee, do their air show over the town, then fly back to the home base before their fuel ran out. But the parade, with the Tuskegee band, was going to be right down on the ground with me, and I was going to be the first man to greet them when the bus pulled in. I was on special lookout for the bass drummer, because Mutt, who was in the army by then, had once told me that the bass drummer is the most important man in a marching band, the man who "sets the measure." "Hell, boy, John Philip Sousa's highest-paid musician is his bass drummer. The rest of the musicians work to his beat. He's got the big 'papa drum.' "

Finally, two army buses pulled up; we had expected only one. Mr. Swoopes came out of the shop and took his place by the door of the first bus and shook hands with all the men as they got off. I scurried to the door of the second bus, wearing my own sharp Eisenhower-style jacket, which Miss Lyda Mae had cut down from a wool GI shirt George Fred had given me. My GI cap Mutt had given me the last time he was home on furlough, before he went overseas and was taken prisoner in Germany. I wore it tilted far over to the side of my bean, the way Mutt had put it there. I felt grown up in my GI stuff and almost like a Tuskegee war camp man myself as I took my place at the door of the second bus to proudly pump the bandsmen's hands and welcome them to Sheffield, just as Mr. Swoopes was doing up ahead.

The parade was more than two hours away, and the musicians wanted to get some home cooking and see something of the town. I took several in tow and lit out for Baptist Bottom. By parade time, the bass drummer and I had become pals, and he took me aboard the bus to see the papa drum. We had to snake our way through the aisle and around men with horns of every size and sound. Hunkered down in their seats, the musicians coaxed out of the cold instruments brief Sousa march phrases. A hidden slide-trombone man crooned his slippery blues from the rear of the bus. My drummer friend gathered up the papa drum and strapped it to his chest, and he picked up *two* serious-looking bass-drum beaters. Gazing longingly at it all, I got goose bumps. "Whap it one time, please," I asked of the drummer. "Naw, naw, man. Not yet; let the horns get warmed up good. Besides, this big baby would tear your eardrums out in this closed-up bus. When we get outside you'll hear me whap it."

Out of the buses, the men gathered around the bandmaster, a sophisticated older officer, who, like a football coach, laid out his game plan. At the signal from the grand marshal, Mr. Swoopes, the parade began. I marched in lockstep with the bass drummer in the last row. Even though I was behind the band, and the horns were all pointing away from me, the power and volume of the music was overwhelming. They played "Colonel Bogey" with such breathtaking precision that when they jazzed it, it sounded as if it been written that way. Their six tubas were something to rival Mr. Buddy Jenkins's voice, especially on their virtuoso number, "Them Basses." The papa drummer filled the music's open spaces, and with his two mighty mallets, one in each fist, he doubled up the meter on the end of phrases, whapping cadences that jarred my stomach and thrilled me all the way down to my toes. I suspected he was Sanctified, because he did all the things Mrs. Nance did with her drum and stirring spoon. Every time he executed his two-mallet licks and cadences, he'd snatch his head high in the air and his strut went into overdrive, making him swagger as if he was the boss of the world and Adolf Hitler could kiss where the sun don't shine.

The distance from Mr. Swoopes's shop to the city hall, where the parade would end, was only three blocks, and that left the musicians enough time for just two marches. When we reached the city hall, the mayor and several local dignitaries were already assembled, high up on a flag-draped reviewing stand. The mayor spoke to the massive crowd, preachers prayed prayers of thanksgiving for the Air Corps, and Mr. Swoopes welcomed the band and said they would play a group of W. C. Handy selections.

Right in the middle of "Aunt Hagar's Blues," we heard the screaming fighter squadron, in tight formation, coming at us just over the rooftops. Their deafening sound sent dogs and babies into howling fits. Dipping their wings in a salute to the crowd, they rolled over several times and climbed steeply above the river, turned back around at Mr. Handy's homeplace, and shot back in the direction of Helen Keller's house, to do it all over again. The crowd screamed and waved things. When the squadron came back across the river, the Tuskegee Band struck up the "Air Corps Song," and everybody started singing "Off we go into the wild blue yonder." Girls waved and cried, "Oh, fly, fly, fly, fly!" As they came back again and again over the crowd, flying lower with every pass, we could see that the pilots had taken off their goggles and leather helmets to give us a clear view of their handsome brown faces beaming down on us as they tilted their planes sideways, then upside down, to show themselves to us. Hattie Pearl cupped her hands and hollered up to the formation, "Sweet Jesus, y'all sure are pretty!" They made their last pass and headed south, still saluting Sheffield with their dipping wings until the machines became sparkling specks in the distant clouds, then vanished, as the hot band played on.

Nothing had ever made me prouder than the brown pilots in the air and the musicians leading that parade in my hometown that day. My only problem was that I wanted to be like them all, the pilots flying and the musicians playing.

Back at the tailor shop, the musicians were putting down their instruments in a hurry. I noticed a drummer and a clarinet player shifting from one foot to the other in front of Mr. Swoopes's already occupied toilet. A line formed that reached all the way out to the alley. Mr. Swoopes took off, on the double, for permission for some of the men to use the toilets of one or another of his neighboring white merchants (his was the only nonwhite business downtown). In just a couple of minutes, Mr. Swoopes was back in the shop. His jaws were as tight as a vise. We all knew his requests had been refused. Close to tears, he said, "They are just ignorant to behave that way in spite of what they just witnessed."

One of the musicians said, "Sir, they're behaving this way *because* of what they've witnessed. We see that sort of thing all the time." For the first time in my life, I wasn't proud of my hometown.

In spite of the toilet unpleasantness, the Tuskegee bandsmen and the air show brought our school the inspiration that put us over the top in the bond-selling contest, and Baptist Bottom won the prize handsomely.

When the papa-drum man waved goodbye to me as the buses pulled out of town, I rushed home and wrote a letter to Mutt in that prisoner-of-war camp in Germany. The Tuskegee band and the bass drummer were his kind of musicians, and he would have been thrilled by the parade.

Mama looked over my letter and insisted I not even mention the toilet affair. "Poor Mutt," she said sadly, "away off from home in God knows what kind of condition for food and medicine; he probably got all the aggravation he can stand without us making him mad at that Montgomery Avenue trash back here with their low-down common ways."

The Tuskegee air show and the parade musicians ignited a mighty spark in our musical consciousness around Sheffield. My own musical horizons expanded; Mama got me a piano of my own in spite of the earlier failure with Mrs. Winston's lessons. Mama's boss lady knew someone who was selling an old fifteen-dollar upright piano, which Mama paid Mr. Elmo Appleton two dollars to haul home in his old coal truck.

Even at school, our music-making took on a new tone. A new principal came to us, who loved music and formed our first band. Professor Richard Stewart, already solidly trained as a teacher-administrator, also started a male chorus. He got a lot of help from his beautiful young wife, herself an excellent elementary school teacher, who played the piano quite well. And on occasion, the professor played his trombone along with the baritones in our choir.

Then he approached the Sheffield city school board for a music program and a band teacher, such as the white school had. The board said, "We'll see." Nothing happened. Reverend Michael, a well-educated local preacher, wrote letters to the board, listing the advantages music brought to young students and using Sheffield's white school as an example. "We'll see," the all-white education board members kept telling them. Finally, a compromise was struck. We got a part-time band teacher from Montgomery, a man who would visit our school one afternoon every third week as he traveled a circuit of small-town Negro schools all over the state.

Our maestro, Mr. Duncan, was a marvel as a bandmaster and a tireless servant of the muse. Everything about him suggested that he was where he wanted to be, doing precisely what he was born to do. He radiated warm satisfaction whenever he walked into a roomful of children holding musical instruments.

His own instrument was the piccolo. On his first day, Professor Stewart introduced him to us and Mr. Duncan stood before our small aspiring band, speaking eloquently about the nobility of a musical calling and of his hopes for us. He then volunteered a solo on the spot and took a little case, about the size of his hand, out of his book satchel; opening it, he prepared his tiny piccolo. None of us children could believe that something so small could be a legitimate musical instrument. But then Mr. Duncan tucked the silver pipe firmly under his bottom lip, gasped a great waft of air, and threw himself like a cyclone into the jagged melody I later came to know as "Stars and Stripes Forever." His performance on the little silver contraption was a sight to hear.

His solo finished, he wasted no time showing us that he was a teacher who believed in setting examples. Before our first lesson was over, he had puckered up his ample round lips, with both fleshy jaws puffed out, his barrel chest swelling, and made a trombone, a tuba, a trumpet, and the various saxophones talk. Our dream of a band in Baptist Bottom grew a little with each demonstration the marvelous Mr. Duncan gave us.

Professor Stewart and Mr. Duncan couldn't have come to Sheffield at a better time for us. In the relative prosperity of wartime, parents were better able than ever before to buy instruments for their children. Black Sheffield went music wild. With Mr. Duncan's every visit up from Montgomery, he found our little band progressing. Even in his absence, we met several times each week. Professor Stewart brought his trombone to our rehearsals, Mrs. Minor worked from her piano, and our marches began to take on tone. Our rhythm steadied.

More confidence.

We were on our way.

CHAPTER ELEVEN

Home to Die

I CAME HOME from school one day in the early spring of 1944 and found Mama alone in the house, resting in bed. She'd sent the babies to spend the night with J. W. and Mamie Mays, our neighbors. "I've been feeling very tired lately, sugar. Dr. Littlepage wants me to rest in bed a few days."

The news stopped me. Mama'd never slowed down enough to be sick. The minute I caught her dozing, I tore off across town to give the news to Sister, who by then was married and keeping house in Baptist Bottom. Sister dropped all the ladylike pretensions of a married woman and outran me getting back home to grill the patient:

"Are you in pain, Mama? Do you have fever?"

Mama just shook her head no, not saying much: a sure sign she was holding something back. Sister kept pressing. Mama got testy, but Sister, closing in like a tenacious bulldog, was her match.

Finally, Mama allowed, "Dr. Littlepage said it was a spot on the lungs."

In 1944, a "spot on the lungs" was TB—the kiss of death for fifteen out of every thousand southern blacks; and it was killing seven in a thousand whites. Dr. Littlepage advised a trip to Meharry Medical College in Nashville, the South's only training hospital for Negro doctors. If an operation was possible, they would have to do it at the Meharry clinic. Our Colbert County Hospital, across town, wouldn't touch a Negro in Mama's condition.

Sister moved back home to take charge until the Meharry details could be worked out, and the first thing we did was turn the entire household upside down and reorganize it. Mama needed a private room. The children had to be isolated from her and the danger of spreading the disease. That meant moving Mama into the room I shared with David. He and I moved our bed to the room where Mr. Pruitt and the two babies would sleep.

After we got Mama settled into the sickroom, Sister called me to the kitchen for a conference. In a voice both sad and determined, she said, "Now listen to me, boy, and you listen good. Mama and I both need you now. You're thirteen years old, and that's old enough to take on some responsibility. With Mr. Pruitt and Dave working, you're the only one I have to help me take care of Mama. I'm sorry you have to grow up so fast, but that's just the way it is."

My sister Mary Louise had married Samuel Bonds, and she had moved with him to New Haven, Connecticut, where he had a good job at the Winchester Repeating Arms Company. Our brothers George Fred and Eddie were soldiers in the war camp. So at home now there were just my big brother David, Mr. Pruitt, the two new babies, and me. I took the responsibility Sister was thrusting on me as an empowerment to help Mama. I felt proud to have a chance to make a difference.

Sister had me throwing out items we suspected were contaminated. We opened and adjusted windows in the house for the best cross-ventilation; TB patients need fresh air. We found special cooking utensils and dishes for Mama's exclusive use. "Remember not to mix up Mama's dishes with those of the rest of the family; wash and dry everything separately. Everything has its place in this house from now on and must be kept in its place."

As we flew through the house, altering everything in our path, my admiration for my big sister swelled, and I thought: I know this girl is smart, but where in the world did she learn all *this?*

Hours later, as I began to sag, bone-tired, from the heavy drudgery, Sister never slackened. She stiffened her back and said, "Go to the backyard and get Mama Minnie's old washpot full of water and start up a good hot fire under it."

The old iron washpot had sat unused since our grandmother, Mama Minnie, died two years before. Her long illness and death from cancer had taken a heavy toll on Mama's spirits and energy. I could see something in Mama whenever our family went with her across the bridge to Florence to see her mother dying in the dark basement ward where Coffee Hospital consigned its black patients. Our grandmother's death was the first in our family, but before her mother died, Mama must have had a strong premonition, for she scrimped further to make the small weekly installment payments on cemetery plots for her mother, her children, and herself.

When I got the water boiling in the old iron pot, Sister sent me running to the store to buy Oxydol, Lysol, bleach, and lye. We boiled, bleached, and sterilized sheets, blankets, and quilts late into the night. Our backyard became an antiseptic fog bottom. Long past my bedtime, our work still unfinished, we stood resting by the glowing light of the washpot fire. Sister's tired face showed the sooty stains of tears as she stared into the boiling pot and whispered to me. "People will start to treat you differently now that there is TB in our house. Some folks won't let their children play with you or give you a drink of water in their homes. Consumption is a terrible thing. You will have to learn to live with it until we can get Mama to our own people's doctors at Meharry."

I hugged her hard around the waist. "Why can't Mama go to Colbert County Hospital, Sister? Aren't the white doctors smart enough to help her?"

A fleeting smile erased a shadow in her face, and in the flickering light of the washpot fire, I watched her shake her head. "No, baby, I guess they aren't."

Mama's cough worsened, keeping her and the entire household awake through the long nights. She was wasting away, vanishing day by day before our eyes. Sometimes Sister sent me in with Mama's meals on a tray.

"Take this in to her, and don't you tarry."

When I needed to talk to Mama, I had to speak from the doorway.

I missed telling her about school and sharing the letters I got from Mutt, away in the war, and telling her all the things I wanted to be when I got to be a man—all of them musical.

"Don't cross that doorframe line," Sister repeated.

Still, I contrived tactics to get close. I kept Mama's water jar over-filled; cut too many toothbrushes from the hedge bush in the yard; read aloud to her too often and too long from the *Chicago Defender*. Her eyes said, "Not bad for somebody your size, buddy," but she gave me a tired smile and, in a voice hoarse from coughing, whispered, "Go and read to me from the door, sugar—don't get too close."

The worst part of my job was guarding the door to keep the babies out of the room. Nobody could explain to little Nathaniel why his mama was suddenly off-limits.

One morning, Sister told me not to come straight home from school that day; I was to go to the county health department over near Helen Keller's home in Tuscumbia and get a chest X-ray and a skin-patch test for TB. She then said, "Those damned people will ask you a million questions. You know how they love to get in colored people's business. Don't you tell them anything more than that. You want a chest X-ray and a skin-patch test for tu-ber-cu-lo-sis. Don't say TB; they'll think you're ignorant. That's all you say, you hear me? If they press you and ask you why, tell them you've been exposed. Ex-posed. Got it? Say nothing about where, when, or how. The next thing you know, they will be snooping around here trying to take the babies off somewhere. Just say what I told you. That's it, *period!* And if they ask you who sent you, say *Missus* Velma Lucille Harden."

I followed Sister's instructions to the letter when I got to the clerk and technician at the health department. A week later, a card with the results from the skin patch and the X-rays was mailed to the school, giving me a clean bill of health.

Still no word from Meharry. Out on the newspaper job, too many of my customers asked about Mama's condition. I grew tired of giving uninformed or untruthful answers and quit the job for another, in Mr. John's shoeshine parlor. Happily, the shoeshine job brought me much better pay, as well as a bonus in rhythm: I learned to play the shoeshine rag from a teacher who had no rivals.

Mr. John was a world-class rhythm-rag virtuoso, who enjoyed his custodial role as preserver of fine footery. He taught me the trade from the bottom up, paying special attention to the prestigious "quality" brands: the handwork and superior design of Edmund Clapp, Stacy-Adams, Nunn-Bush, and Florsheim. He himself was partial to Stacy-Adams and owned several pairs, in all colors. A customer walking in with a tan pair of kidskin Stacies was all it took to put a whistle on Mr. John's lips and brighten our world.

When we were alone in the shop, we spent our time cleaning the marble floor and the solid-brass footrests high up on the stand. We shined the large mirrors on the walls and washed our finishing rags and cleaned the fine English bristle brushes. Mr. John's shop looked and smelled like the "place of bidniz" he loved to tell folks he ran. When he saw how his ragwork mesmerized me, he promised to make of me a first-class practitioner, like himself.

To show me how it was done, he sat me in one of the chairs and went to work on my Buster Browns, saying it was important for the learner to feel the rhythm of the rag in his own feet. He demonstrated three or four different tap dance–like patterns on my shoes. The brush-work prior to the rag is "the heart of a good shine," Mr. John insisted. The vigorous brushing works the polish into the leather, warms it, and lets it breathe, so that a thin cushion of air "floats" the finish rag. Mr. John was famous for his fluid body English during the brushwork; it allowed him to apply the same meticulous attention to the backs and heels as to the toes. The body English, he pointed out, was also essential to accuracy with the brush—a missed stroke could smudge a white sock and reduce, even wipe out, one's tip.

No part of the shine was as important as the rag for tips. The proud owner of a pair of Stacy-Adamses got a whistled accompaniment to Mr. John's ragwork. "Sweet Georgia Brown" and "Tea for Two" were specialty numbers. He sometimes got enthusiastic enough while he brushed to hum a few bars of something I didn't recognize. The tune was fuzzy but bursting with rhythm.

There never was a craftsman as fanatical about his equipment as

Mr. John. He said, "If a man can't run a place where quality ladies and gents can get service, he may as well shine shoes on a box in the damned street." And about nothing was he so protective, picky, and close to the chest as his "music" rags. He explained to me the first day I was on the job that a fine pop rag is as important to a master shineman as a fine violin is to a musician. He liked the analogy, he said, for the rag and the fiddle shared still another quality: the older they were, the better they sounded. Only a well-broken-in (thin) finish rag had the proper timbre for a good performance; it had to be kept meticulously clean, and each color shoe had its own separate rag. Mr. John would sooner lend out his toothbrush than his finish rag.

One Saturday morning during my apprenticeship, the local Oldsmobile dealer came into the shop, en route to a district meeting. He wore a pair of Stacies, which Mr. John had cared for for years (good Stacies have been known to last generations). Mr. John had just begun to saddle soap a pair of Florsheim high-top oxfords on the feet of the chief of police. Apologizing to the Olds dealer for being tied up, Mr. John said his assistant had a fine education on, and an appreciation for Stacies. Guaranteed to do a good job. Pointing to his own Stacies as an example of my work, he bragged on my rhythm-rag work.

The Olds man said he'd give me a try, and I went to work, making certain to keep my body English fluid during the brushing. I found myself humming the fuzzy tune that was Mr. John's. For the first time, I understood that the humming made no claims to being music; rather, it served as a kind of anticipatory throat-clearing, the vocal musings of a craftsman anxious to lay the rhythm rag to a properly prepared piece of leather.

Just as I reached to my back pocket for my best pop rag, Mr. John glided noiselessly over from the police chief's Florsheims and laid his best oxblood finisher on the toe of the Stacies. He winked at me, looked up, and told the Olds man, "Can't let him touch Stacy-Adams with nothing less than the best." I puckered and blew a couple of choruses of "Sweet Georgia Brown" and jazzed the rag, until the Olds man said I had done almost as good as Mr. John. When finished, I grabbed the whisk broom from the rack next to the mirror, as Mr. John always did, and worked on the jacket shoulders and back of the pants, while the

Olds man dug in his pocket for two bits, which he flipped high in the air for me to catch. Mr. John didn't see the size of the coin, and when the chief left he asked, "What he give you?"

I opened out my palm. "That's what I always get from him. You a sho-nuff shineman now!"

Proud and flattered, I said, "Well, thanks, Mr. John."

He cocked his head and quickly added, "But you gotta gimme back my oxblood finish rag. You a competitor now!"

Word finally came for Mama to come to Meharry. All our hopes rode with her, as Sister held her hand in the ambulance the whole hundred and thirty miles north to Nashville. Late that night, Sister returned home, full of praise for the doctors. "There will have to be tests," she cautioned, "then they will decide if it's too late for surgery."

With that good news, I set up and played my trap drums again. Then I played all the boogie-woogie piano tunes I knew.

Sister returned to Nashville to try to sort out Mama's treatment. There were more delays. More indecision. Her waiting dragged on into days, and to save room rent, she slept in a chair by Mama's bed.

One morning a few days later, Mr. Wilbur McLane's empty ambulance rolled up out front, and Ozzie Newsome, our town's best driver, got out. "Velma called Mr. Wilbur on the telephone from Nashville," Ozzie said. "She said for me to come up there and get her and y'all's mama."

When my brother Dave came home from work, I met him at the door with the news. "What'd I tell you," Dave boasted. "I told you those Meharry doctors could cure her. To hell with that damn peckerwood Colbert County Hospital. You can't beat the Meharry doctors, man!"

I stayed home from the shine parlor and Dave put off his nighttime entertainment to welcome Mama home. I rechecked the sickroom, filled the water pitcher, and cut toothbrushes. Dave and little Nat and Yvonne and I entertained ourselves in the front yard while we waited. Mr. Pruitt had been quiet and subdued since Mama's illness. Now he sat on the porch, looking crushed as he read the Bible.

Shortly past dark, two headlights floated slowly toward the house, and the family gathered expectantly at the curb. Dave and Ozzie carried Mama gingerly into the house on the stretcher. She looked weaker than ever, but she smiled and waved individual little greetings to each of us. Sister motioned to me to hold the babies back; the no-contact rule still held.

"How was your operation, Mama?" Dave asked.

Too weak to answer, she shook her head. Sister said, "There was no operation; we'll talk about it later. We're very tired."

Little Nathaniel, anxious for the hugs he'd missed for months, stretched his little arms wide and whined, "Is Mama well now?"

Nobody ever said it, but I knew Mama had come home to die. The household fell back into its earlier hush. I draped a bed sheet over the trap-drum set and closed the lid of the piano. Sister, worn out, kept her soldierly vigil, refusing to trust her patient to anyone else. In the sickroom, the two of them talked more than ever before. In one whispered conversation, I overheard Sister ask Mama if she should send for George Fred. A few days later he arrived. On most of my trips to the room, I found Mama asleep and no longer strong enough to care about my reading the paper to her from the door.

One Saturday, after a business rush at the shine parlor, I went to Collins's store to buy sardines and crackers for my lunch. A deliveryman brought in several cartons for the store. One of them contained Kleenex, which was, along with other paper products, sugar, and gasoline, a painfully scarce wartime item. TB patients use mountains of tissues, and Mama never had enough.

I asked Mr. Collins if he would sell me the large carton of Kleenex. He said, "All of em?"

I said, "Every last one of em!"

He said, "A lot of my customers is waiting on em."

I asked if they were credit customers or cash.

"Some of both, but mostly credit, I reckon. Why?"

I ran my hand into my pocket for the wad I'd made shining shoes and said, "I'll pay you cash for the whole bunch right now. Cash money! How much you take for the whole box?"

"Seven thirty-five," he said.

The box was too large for me to get my arms around. I had to slide it on the sidewalk all the way home.

Mama was asleep. I unpacked the big carton in the hallway and tiptoed into the sickroom with an armful of the smaller boxes. Coming awake, Mama brightened and said, "Man, what store did you rob?" Her first joke in weeks.

Easing the boxes onto the bed, I said, "Just wait a minute, Mama," and went back for a bigger armful. When, after several trips, I was through, Mama was covered with treasure, and for the first time since her illness, I felt I'd contributed something tangible to her comfort.

After more quiet talking in the sickroom, Sister sent wires to Eddie and Mary Louise.

Superstition was a part of our world that nobody took lightly. Even small boys playing leapfrog would snap, "Hey, fool, you stepped on my heel. Pat me on the back three times." No smoker ever accepted the third light from a match. A borrowed pocketknife must be returned blade open if borrowed that way. A lone dog howling past midnight meant death close by and soon. There came such a dog howling from somewhere near the Sanctified church. Nobody seemed to know whose dog it was, but its meaning, no secret to anyone, unnerved the neighborhood. Then out of the predawn silence came the high-pitched, tortured shriek of a female voice, whose terrifying shrillness startled the household awake. The voice, sharp like a trumpet blast, could only be Sister, and I whispered into my pillow even before opening my eyes, "Mama's gone." In my grief I knew that manhood was being thrust upon me. But was I ready? Excused from school for the first time ever, I walked for miles back and forth along the railroad tracks, trying to guess what would become of me without my mama.

Passing the hobo jungle by the tracks outside Baptist Bottom, I learned that the hoboes, too, were in mourning: President Roosevelt had died that same morning. It was April 12, 1945. Mama was forty-five, I was thirteen.

CHAPTER TWELVE

A Stay with Red Ruff

SISTER'S NEW AUTHORITY and responsibility grew at home. I was lost for weeks. I spent more time than usual at the shoeshine parlor. If there was no business, I came home and tried to liven up the mood of the house with my drumming and boogie-woogie piano playing.

My father was living in Evansville, Indiana. I thought of asking Sister if I could go there to finish school, but our school in Baptist Bottom was becoming an exciting place. The black citizens had got together and changed the name, from Sheffield High School for Colored, to Sterling High School—period—in honor of the late and distinguished Professor Sterling, a teacher there before my time. Our faculty had now moved even further ahead of their counterparts at the white school: new teachers had more graduate degrees and classroom experience. There was renewed promise for us all, and for me, our growing music program at Sterling High meant everything. I wasn't sure whether to go north to live with my father or stay in Sheffield to finish school.

One day as I was pacing about, wrestling privately with my choices, Sister surprised me with a call to the kitchen for a conference. She said the whisperings I'd overheard between her and our dying mama had been Mama instructing her on how to carry on after her death. "Whatever you do," Mama said to her, "keep all my children together if you possibly can; especially the babies: they'll need one another. You don't have to worry too much about Willie Henry. He'll find his way one way or another, with the Lord's help."

Then Sister said to me, "Bill, I don't have to tell you Mama had a lot of confidence in you. But it's still a fact that Negroes have a much better chance away from the South. Mama wanted you not to have to quit school to go to work the way we older ones had to do. I think you should look into going to live with your daddy in Evansville. Maybe you can get the kind of education Mama wanted for you up there."

I liked the thought of the North, but I didn't really know my father all that well. The most I could really remember of him was that in my preschool years, he occasionally came riding into Sheffield on freight trains late at night to visit me. But he never stayed more than a day or two. The only time I stayed with him was the first half of a school year, after Mama married Mr. Pruitt. Mama was pregnant, and I was a third grader. The understanding was that I would return home to my own school after the baby was born. So I joined my father and his new wife over in Tupelo, Mississippi, about a hundred miles from Sheffield.

When the baby—Jessie Yvonne—came, Mama wrote us that it was time for me to come back home. But my father didn't respond. Then our Mississippi household got a surprise. One afternoon, I was sitting alone in the yard in Tupelo, when I saw a familiar figure approaching. When I recognized Mama, I jumped for joy and dashed excitedly out of the yard to meet her. But there was something about the tempo of her greeting that was out of tune; her hugs and kisses were hurried and cold, and they didn't quite fit. I recognized that certain set of her jaw, which said, Business now, loving later. "Where's your daddy, baby?" she asked abruptly, not even giving me news of my Alabama. "Take me to your daddy and get all your things. We're going home." Even in that distant tone of voice, those words thrilled me. My father was inside, washing up from his workday at the cottonseed-oil mill, while my stepmother cooked supper.

Mama walked into the house ahead of me and gave a short, two-word greeting: "Good evening." Then she laid on the table her opened purse, in which, right out in plain view, lay our old Sheffield household's mean-looking Colt .41 pistol. The sight of the old Colt in that purse was so comforting I could have hugged it. Now I knew I was sho nuff going home!

My father had been good to me there in Tupelo. He had tried hard to make a good home for me with my new stepmother. But I hadn't fully realized just how much I had needed to be back in my Sheffield until I saw Mama marching up that hill. Mama, her pistol, and her boy were on the next train headed for Alabama.

Now my father was agreeing to let me come to Evansville to finish high school. By this time he was a bachelor again, making rooming houses a way of life. He came to Sheffield in his coal truck to haul me, my piano, and my drums up north. "We got us a nice room in a place close to the school," he said.

In my new home, I was expected to learn the ropes quickly and look after myself while he did his work. He left each morning before sunup, giving me a dollar for meals. In the beginning, eating in restaurants every day was a big adventure, but I overdid the hot dogs and barbecue pork sandwiches, the candy and sweet drinks. And the dollar-a-day food allowance was not enough. I was nearly always hungry and, used to Mama's and Sister's wholesome table, was dogged by digestive complaints from the Evansville fare. My dad and I seldom had meals together because of his work hours. He made his living by driving his truck to a coal mine across the Kentucky state line, where he bought a truckload of coal to sell by the bushel basket back in Evansville. Hefting the hundred-pound weight onto his shoulder and climbing torturous stairs was bone-crushing work; also it was profitable only seasonally. But he did it "because it's my own business, and I don't have to be beholden to no white man."

Though I was nearly always hungry, I don't think I ever asked for more than the dollar to buy more or better food. Perhaps my dad spent no more than that for his own food and gauged it adequate for a boy my size. It was clear that if I was to eat better, I would have to have a job. I hit the streets, looking for work, but soon learned that a thirteen-year-old new boy in town had no chance. Newspaper routes were already taken, and all the stores and shops I applied to just shook their heads.

One day I told my father that as a shoeshine man, I felt I could compete with the best anywhere. He was not encouraging. "Naw, man, this ain't like Alabama; grown men got that hustle up here." I got huffy and said that if there was a grown man in Evansville who could put a better shine on a piece of leather than I could, and match my rhythm rag, I'd give him a free shine. Never did I say that I wanted the work because I was hungry. But one Saturday morning soon after our talk, we went to a shoe repair shop where a man called Bad Luck, an old friend of my father's, ran a shoeshine stand.

Mr. Bad Luck wore two artificial legs, yet he was a carouser of great fame around town. His stumps gave him trouble whenever he overdid his sinning, and several times a year he went down. During one of his spells, my father suggested to Mr. Bad Luck that I take over the shine stand while he recuperated. My rhythm rag and I were back in business again, and my gut was happy.

The owner of the shop was ecstatic about my work. Mr. Bad Luck wasn't in my league as a shineman. Without the owner having to tell me, I kept the whole place swept clean, and I hosed down the sidewalk out front several times a day—things Mr. Bad Luck never did or perhaps couldn't manage with no real legs. But then word got back to him that I was making something out of his shine business, and he cut his convalescence short and sent me packing.

With time on my hands, and a little money hidden away, I was able to throw myself into music again. I had stored the piano Mama had bought me in the landlady's parlor at the rooming house, and she encouraged me to play whenever I felt like it. I played my boogie-woogie every day until school started in September.

Evansville's Lincoln High School was an imposing edifice with a music program that was, for me, its strong feature. But in spite of its up-northness, the school was not integrated and lacked many of the advantages the bigger and better-funded white schools in town enjoyed.

The band director, Mr. Porter, was a virtuoso solo cornet player and all-around musician, who'd already heard about the new boy in town who could play a little piano and read drum music. A nice Mississippi lady, Miss Crawford, was the choir director, and a great pianist too. She went out of her way to make me welcome, for she knew how hard it was for a real Southerner to adjust to Evansville. I signed up for every music activity at the school, I became the choir's first tenor, I played snare drum in the marching band, and at recess every day I dashed to the music room to play my boogies and blues on the piano. That always attracted a crowd of girls.

My dad's musical enthusiasm easily matched my own. In fact, music was our strongest common interest. He had been a clarinetist and guitar player before an accident in a Mississippi cottonseed-oil press severely mangled eight of his fingers and ended his music-making.

Ignoring convention and the law, he took me to Evansville's nightspots some weekends to hear professional bands, and we stayed late into the night. One night in a crowded dance hall near the river, we heard an out-of-town dance band of sixteen players rumble the foundation. Even at the chitlin struts in Sheffield, I had never seen such inspired dancing. The solo trumpeter made his horn growl through a derby hat, while a skinny slide-trombone player answered him note for note, pulling the sounds out of the bell of the horn with a plumber's rubber toilet plunger. It was music that made my father throw back his head and holler:

"Play it till the cows come home!"

An older boy at school, Milton Lambert, two grades ahead of me, played the piano like nobody I'd ever heard in person. His father, a federal postal worker, paid a white man to come to his house every Tuesday before school to teach Milton classical music. Having begun the lessons while still a toddler, Milton could read piano music like a professional, and he played every piece of sheet music he could find by Duke Ellington and Fats Waller. Art Tatum was his god. Even though I was eaten up with envy, Milton and I became good friends, and we played boogie-woogie duets for kicks. We went at it daily. I played the bass end of the keyboard, leaving precocious Milton free to rip out complex, jagged melodies and syncopated chords at blistering speed. I didn't know it then, but right there with Milton, I was cutting my teeth as a bassist. The two of us together could make the piano sound like a full orchestra. We began giving little four-hand performances at school during recess. We played for parties, then we decided to form a band, with him as leader and his older brother, Robert, as our clarinetist. We enlisted a trumpet player and a trombonist from school, and all of us chipped in to buy the music to a seventy-five-cent arrangement of Artie Shaw's "Blue Flame."

Our little band couldn't practice at Milton's house because his mother was delicate and often had migraine headaches and what white ladies called the vapors, so my dad persuaded our landlady to let us practice in her living room, using my piano.

Our rehearsals were tentative at first, but after a few meetings, neighbors began to gather. My dad said privately to Milton and me, "Don't you two worry too much if the other boys are slow catching on. With a good piano man and a strong drummer, you'll be able to make it work. Be patient."

A couple of Evansville's serious adult musicians took an interest in us and offered us the use of their own arrangements, along with coaching. It was not unusual to find professionals, home from bandwork on the road, sitting in with our little group to help us along. My father and Mr. Bad Luck's crowd bragged on us in all the joints around town, and it was not long before the crowds at our rooming house rehearsals began to grow.

My dad had an inspired idea, which had worked for a jazz group he'd played with down south. He said he would clean up the coal truck, mount a platform bandstand on the back, drive us downtown, and park at a busy corner. All we had to do was play hot music, and he would pass the hat. He began planning a little bandstand for the truck. Meanwhile, our reputation had spread enough to attract a couple of invitations to play for big school dances and parties.

One of the dance hall owners, in a weak moment, let my dad talk him into hiring us as the intermission band one Saturday night. The owner said he couldn't afford two bands, which was exactly what Dad wanted to hear: my old man wanted to pass the hat. The emcee at the dance hall, Mr. Coolbreeze, a faded blues singer unable to get show business out of his blood, was another of my father's drinking buddies.

Mr. Coolbreeze, who thought nothing in the world was as inspiring as youngsters playing jazz music, volunteered to give us a big plug on the microphone at the dance hall. "We oughta encourage these boys. I'll take care of everything," he assured my father.

The night of the dance rolled around, and our little band played during the adult band's intermission. The crowd, recognizing several of us as their neighbors and kin, was warm and friendly with its applause. When we went into our theme song, "Blue Flame," Mr. Coolbreeze jumped up on the bandstand and motioned to us all to play quietly.

"Hey, everybody!" he screamed into the microphone. "Listen to these boys. Hear what they doing. Let's give em a big hand." The applause and shouts completely extinguished "Blue Flame." "Y'all ain't never heard no kids play no music like that. Let's have another big hand for these here fine little musicians. They ain't nothing but babies!"

Again, "Blue Flame" went out.

"Y'all never know," he said, shaking his head slowly to dramatize the warning. "Right here in Evansville, these children from our own Lincoln High School just might develop into new Duke Ellingtons someday. That's right, I said Duke Ellington! Now y'all put down them damn bottles and glasses, and put some *folding* money in that man's hat," he said, pointing to my dad, who snake-hipped through the crowd to the swelling drone of my drums, pumping rhythm. We finished the song and bolted outdoors to split the hatful of greenbacks, a sum that dwarfed the paid band's earnings for the whole night. Even after we'd given my dad a down payment for lumber, nails, and red paint for our proposed truck bandstand, we were still rich.

But trouble awaited us at Milton's house. His mother's mother, Mrs. Edmunds, a fierce churchwoman, put no stock in nonreligious music. She wasn't even enthusiastic when Milton played "Clair de lune" on the piano, and she looked on jazz with a searing hatred. A member of Grandmother Edmunds's church told her that Red Ruff—the name folks called my dad because of his sandy hair—had her grandsons playing in a "likker sink." She threw a fit. Milton's father, a meek, henpecked man, loved the band and what we were trying to do, but he was no match for his mother-in-law. It broke his heart that his boys had to quit playing jazz just to please their grandmama. But my father wasn't just brokenhearted, he was mad as hell, and he cussed for days at Mrs. Edmunds's interference.

For me, our band had fed more than my spirit. Since we got busy, I had come to enjoy using the little money we made playing to become friends again with my stomach.

With the return of hungry days and the loss of the joys I'd known in the band, I began lagging in school; even the music classes at Lincoln no longer interested me much. Though I would not then admit it, I wanted terribly to be back in Alabama. Troubling thoughts of my little brother and sister nagged me, though I knew they still had Sister and their father with them. Sister's reassuring letters didn't help much. I was getting in the habit of going off by myself and crying every day; my father's work was slow, and we had to eat more often on credit in the various greasy joints around town, to my humiliation. Worst of all, I began imagining that Mama could see my condition, and I became even sicker with self-pity.

One night, a small group of men, including Mr. Coolbreeze and Mr. Bad Luck, came to the parlor at the rooming house, bringing with them the smell of the tavern. Bottles bulged from hip pockets, and the talk was of hard times, faded dreams, and that "goddamned fat-ass hypocrite churchwoman"—Milton's grandmother. Mr. Coolbreeze felt the blues come on him and started singing: "Trouble in mind and I'm blue, But I won't be blue always, Cause the sun's gon shine in my back door someday." I loved the song and was tempted to join Mr. C. at the piano, but I smelled trouble in the air and went upstairs to bed. It wasn't long before my dad yelled up to the room:

"Come on and play the piano for Breeze to sing that song."

I refused. He asked again. Again I said I just didn't feel like it. Embarrassed and angry at my refusal, he said, "OK, I'm not gonna make you play, but I am gonna whip your butt for disobeying me."

He had never had to whip me before, and to his credit, he wouldn't do it while mad or drinking. After the crowd left and before we went to sleep later that night, I told him I felt his buddies spelled trouble; I was sure of it.

I stayed out of his way for a day or two, just to dodge the whipping he'd promised. But the trouble I'd foreseen came knocking on my door one morning before daybreak. An urgent female voice on the other side of the door whispered, "Willie junior, don't get excited, now. Your daddy just got hurt in a battle up on Lincoln Avenue. He's OK, though. He told me to tell you to come over to Miss Smith's Rest Home bout six in the morning."

At six I was at Mrs. Smith's, which was a combination rooming house and convalescent home. Sitting there on the front porch, smoking his cigar, was my daddy, with his head in a huge bandage. "Aw, I'm all right," he said sheepishly, eyes downcast. "I lost a right smart of blood, but I'll be fine soon as they build me up in here."

He complained of having to eat Cream of Wheat, liver, and other iron-building foods and told me to just carry on as usual. "I won't be here but four or five days. You take this wallet and the fifty-six dollars for what you need. It's all I got, but I'll be on my feet soon."

I knew he expected me to treat the money as a windfall and spend it on hotdogs, movies, and playthings by the time he recovered. Even though I walked the streets richer than I'd ever been, I was reluctant to buy food for myself for fear that there wouldn't be enough to take care of my daddy when he came home to get well. So instead of splurging on food, I cut back and spent less than half the dollar a day I was accustomed to. After a few of these hungrier than usual days, my dad came home and I proudly presented him with his wallet, containing $52.65, and a sparkling-clean room to rest in. I never got that promised whipping.

While my father was still recuperating at home, my Uncle Grover breezed into town one day, driving a surplus army truck he'd just bought in Detroit. He was taking a week's vacation, he said, because his job at Packard had played out at the end of the war; he was planning to go into the hauling business when he returned to Detroit. My father convinced him to stay the week with us there in our rented room, in which three was a large crowd. Though the quarters were cramped, I loved having us three Ruff men there together, all looking like one another. It gave me a chance to learn something new about our side of my family. Even though my father had talked readily enough to me about his early life whenever I asked, having Uncle Grover there to jog his memory and remind him of our kinfolk and some of the tantalizing incidents back in their Mississippi childhood was fabulous.

They were the only children of Mary and Will Ruff senior. My father was Will junior, and he and Uncle Grover were too young when their father died to remember him well. They did know that he had a reputation around Mississippi as quite a fiddle player.

The most exciting thing I learned about my kinfolk from Uncle Grover and my father was that we had a deaf, mute Mississippi great-uncle, who, according to them, was the smartest member of our clan: a man with a trade, who'd raised a big family. That news gave me a chance to surprise my father and uncle with the sign language I knew. Uncle Grover said it was too bad I couldn't have met the great-uncle and signed with him, but they were sure he was dead.

There was a bonus of another sort in having Uncle Grover there visiting us: he bought me some badly needed shoes and school clothes, and he took me with him to restaurants, where I always had enough to eat.

As I was coming in from school one day, I overheard a conversation between my father and Uncle Grover. My uncle was giving my dad "down the country" for not seeing to my needs better than he'd been doing. "It would be a little different if that boy hadn't had the kind of mama he had, Willie. A child that age needs good regular meals and a clean bed, and better clothes and care than I see him with." Uncle Grover was as forceful as he dared to be; he respected his brother's short fuse and wanted none of it, but he did talk him into letting me go to Detroit to see if I could get in school there in the middle of the year. I thought that at last I'd be escaping the Evansville gloom that had begun to crowd out much of the bright hope I'd arrived there with.

But it didn't work. My overgenerous uncle had not bothered to discuss my rescue from Evansville with his wife, Aunt Seculia, and the school in their Detroit neighborhood was not encouraging in the talk we had with them about my moving to town midyear. Uncle Grover looked so dejected when he put me on the bus back to Evansville that I cried more for him than for myself. I felt like a displaced orphan.

Shortly after my return to Evansville, my father came home one day full of enthusiasm after he had talked himself into a fifty-dollar contract for sodding a lawn for a white family in the suburbs. With help, it took only the better part of a day. A neighbor admired the work and asked for an estimate on several truckloads of loam and some sodding work. The man wanted a per-cubic-yard estimate on the loam, and my dad knew only how to figure square yards. He gave the man the sod estimate but stalled him on the loam.

I found him in our room after school the next day, still worrying the problem of cubic yardage. As I walked in the door, he said to me, "You got the education in the family, son. What the hell is a *cubic yard*?" I was no help, and with embarrassment said that we hadn't studied that far into practical math at school. In our ignorance of dictionaries and libraries, my father and I guessed and speculated for hours without the solution. Finally, we decided to try a "dead reckoning" solution. We measured a bushel of coal against a store-bought cubic yard of peat moss. Guessing that a bushel was roughly a cubic yard, we multiplied it by the number of bushels of coal we knew the truck held. The customer never knew he was getting a guesswork calculation when he wrote our check for the job.

My father, to the end of his life, was convinced that cubic volume and other such "systems" were nothing but stumbling blocks white folk invented to trip up Negroes with scant book learning.

CHAPTER THIRTEEN

On the Front
of the Bus

EARLY ONE MORNING in Evansville, soon after the cubic-volume epi-sode, I noticed a large crowd in the schoolyard, gathered around a tall and dapper young soldier. As I got closer, I saw that he was Arthur Rucker, the younger brother of Uncle Grover's wife, Seculia. I'd gotten to know Rucker when I first came to Evansville. My dad took me to visit their family, and I'd played their piano while Arthur, a lanky, loose-jointed, dance-crazy kid, twisted his snaky frame around my music. Now Rucker was back: a big-time soldier in the schoolyard, charming the lads with his tales of the big time.

Having enlisted in a special army program for seventeen-year-olds, Rucker described the fun he'd sampled already and speculated teasingly about the delicious joys that awaited him "across the water, in Germany—way over yonder." For three solid days he was the main attraction there at the school. Girls who wouldn't have given him a second look before he enlisted now threw themselves at that uniform. But his new success with women didn't seem to bring him as much joy as chiding and taunting his old buddies for wasting their time in high school.

"The army," he boasted at me, "got better schools, offers travel and career training that will make your country head swim."

He had me convinced in about five minutes that if I signed up and went into his army, I could learn to be a great drummer like the cat who "blows" drums with Charlie Parker. He'd already met another cat, he said, who used to be in Duke's band. Evansville and other country towns just couldn't stand up to what Uncle Sam was putting down. "I'm just laying this on you cause you kin to me and I like you, but look at yourself. You raggedy as a ten-cent can of kraut! And I know you hungry too. The U.S. Army provides these sharp threads to its men—dig me!" He strutted splendidly in a small circle. "We get the best of food, a chance to finish school and even go to college on the GI Bill. Now, let me see you beat that in this jive-assed burg, sucker!"

Rucker was so right it hurt me to hear him. But my problem, I kept telling him, would be to convince the recruiting man that I was seventeen. I was only fourteen and looked it, and I knew my dad would think I was crazy for asking him to sign anything for me to go into the army. Rucker said, "Damn it, boy, you shore are country! Ain't you got *no* damned sense? If you can't bluff a recruiter bout your age, you ought to be ashamed to call yourself a man! Hell, if your old man won't sign the permission slip, then sign the sommich yourself. Who's gonna know the difference? Do I have to tell you *everything*, fool? For a musician, you shore are dumb. Damn!"

I picked up my parental permission form from the recruiter at the post office that same afternoon and kept it hidden until the end of the school year, about a month away. It would have to be notarized after I'd forged my dad's name. When the time came, I took it to a neighborhood grocer, who would affirm and affix his notary stamp on anything for twenty-five cents, no questions asked. He signed and stamped my forgery while weighing a sack of onions, with never a glance at what the paper said.

The last day of school found me at the recruitment office with a crowd of older boys. We were given seventy-two hours to put our affairs in order before reporting back for induction. The man said the bus would take us to Camp Atterbury, Indiana, near Indianapolis.

During the three days before the trip to Camp Atterbury, I avoided my dad as much as possible, staying out late each night and managing not to be home when he was there during the day. My conscience was uneasy about running away from home. I wondered: What will he think has happened to me? Will he get in touch with my sisters and brothers in Alabama and worry them? The night before the bus left for Camp Atterbury, I heard my dad's truck pull up in the yard, and I went out to meet him. He was weary from hunting landscaping work. While we climbed the creaking stairs to our room, I told him I'd made some plans for a job away from home where I could continue my schooling. I mentioned what the pay was, the music training I could get, pouring it on as Arthur Rucker had.

"Bands have men in them that have already played with Duke and Count Basie and Lionel Hampton. The government will send me to college for free."

This point I saved for last. He asked who was giving me this job. Finally, I said, "The army."

Surprised anger flashed across his face. He said, "Since when is the army hard up enough to take fourteen-year-old boys?"

"I told them I was seventeen and had your permission."

"But you don't."

I mentioned the alternatives, such as getting in trouble, like Otis down the street, who was sent up for robbery and rape during the first school semester, and Lester Jones, who was serving time for bike theft, even though it was his cousin who had snatched the wheel. I wasn't actually lying when I told him I saw a great big reform school, or worse, in my future if I stayed in Evansville.

"Arthur Rucker is making it in the army, and if he can, so can I."

"That may be, but your mama wanted me to see that you finished school. I'd feel like hell if you didn't."

I promised him that I would make finishing school my first business, because I, too, didn't want to let Mama and Sister down. He sagged under the weight of the heavy decision and said he'd have to sleep on the matter.

That night when I went to sleep, I'd already made up my mind to be on that bus, with or without my father's consent. But in the middle of the night, he came awake and lit his cigar stub and quietly paced the floor in the darkness. When he'd smoked the stub down to nothing, he got back in bed and called out to me. "Well, I reckon you can take care of yourself good enough to be a soldier boy. I'm thinkin to let you go."

"Yessuh," I said, happy enough to shout out loud.

"When you have to leave?"

"At seven this morning."

He said, "Well, I'll be damned," and he turned over and laughed himself back to sleep.

With my burden of guilt gone, the sleep of the dead fell on me until 5:30 A.M., when my father bent over my cot, giggling quietly and calling into my ear, "Some soldier you are, boy! I hear they shoot late sleepers in the war camp—heh heh. Come on, son, grab up your stuff. I'll drive you to the bus in the truck."

I reached under the cot and pulled out a paper sack into which I had stuffed a change of underwear, socks, and a T-shirt. Looking at my sack, my old man joked, "Man, you sho as hell ready to travel. You pack like a hobo!"

We searched the room for items he thought I should take along. I rejected everything he came up with, including my favorite red sweater. I said, "Naw, man, Uncle Sam furnishes soldier suits." He picked up my silver-colored whistling yo-yo, thought a moment, shook his head, and giggled. "Naw, I reckon soldiers don't play with these—heh heh."

Wrapping the wet business end of my toothbrush in toilet paper and stuffing it into the sack along with my comb, I was ready to roll. He was taking longer because he would stay out and look for work after dropping me off at the bus. When he emerged from the room and closed the door, I felt sure that the door of my childhood was being locked forever. I was a genuinely happy boy.

Listening to me whistle a glad tune as the old coal truck rattled its way downtown, my father smiled and said, "You mighty happy, ain't you, son? Well, I can see it. You're right to get the hell away from here. This place ain't nothin but a dead end for colored people. I ain't never been able to get my head above water here."

At the bus station, the recruiting man who'd signed us all up was grinning and milling through the crowd, congratulating parents who had approved early enlistment for their seventeen-year-olds. We watched as he approached a white father and his young son and vigorously pumped the father's hand. "Mr. Walters, you're doing a mighty smart thing for Lenny. These early enlistments allow the fellows a real chance to get a good start on several of the army's training programs. Fine thing, mighty fine."

Then he came up to my dad. "Mr. Ruff, you should be very proud of what you're doing for this young man. His early enlistment will mean a lot to him in the programs that interest him, and especially the fine training he'll get in one of the army bands. Yes, sir, he can have a fine career if he measures up. Smart thing you're doing." It was time to leave.

Fighting back tears with an effort that made his whole body tremble, my father said, in a low voice that was new to me, "Keep yourself clean, be a good boy, and don't let your mama down."

I couldn't wait for the bus door to open. When it did, I charged on and resolutely planted myself in the first seat behind the driver, asserting my up-north legal right to the bus seat of my choice. Outside the window, my old man gave my seat choice a wink of his approval through a teary eye.

"Look out, army," I was saying to myself. "Here I come on the *first* seat on the bus!"

PART TWO

Army

Fourteen-Year-Old Private

CAMP ATTERBURY, INDIANA, a couple of hours' ride from Evansville, had the look of a military movie set. Our bus eased through the imposing sentry gate, and two MPs packing .45s saluted. We rolled past a commissary, a PX, a movie theater, a bowling alley, a swimming pool, and a jailhouse. Our first stop was the mess hall, a brightly lit and spotlessly scrubbed building. Glittering stainless-steel steam vats were loaded with several kinds of meats, surrounded by squash, peas, slaw, prunes, mashed potatoes, and spinach; there were salads of fruits, salads of vegetables, and a separate dessert table.

I went to work on the chow line, trying to gain enough weight to tip the scales at 118 pounds, the required minimum for army service. I'd confirmed my 115 pounds on the penny scale in front of the ten-cent store the day before.

After lunch we were all assembled in ragged formation in front of the mess hall, where the white sergeant who had accompanied us from Evansville said, "The men whose names I call will step out of rank and form a new formation over here." After he'd read a few names, it was clear that he was separating out the white boys. Then he pointed to a building where the rest of us would live.

I was the first to dash for our barracks, which was by far the most imposing building I had ever lived in. Nothing at the camp thrilled me as much as our barracks showers. Back in Evansville, the bathroom my dad and I used had been a boxed-in flusher in the corner of an unused kitchen. The landlady's downstairs bathtub was grudgingly available to us a few times a week.

"She keeps count," my dad had warned.

Now I couldn't stand the sight of all those GI showers going to waste. I peeled off, turned all ten gushers full steam, and sprinted around the duckboards, sampling them all. In the mess hall that night, I sat next to an athlete, a burly hulk who impressed me by the size of his appetite. He observed that I was mighty trim for a man who ate as much as I was putting away. I said I was worried about making the 118-pound weight limit. He had a suggestion. He'd heard from a boxer who'd worked in Joe Louis's training camp that one could put on several pounds before weigh-in simply by eating heaps of bananas and drinking lots of water. He urged me to give it a try, and when I left the mess hall, my pockets were loaded with bananas. The athlete said for me to hold off on the bananas and water until it was time to get on the scales. The trick worked; I passed the physical. On June 17, 1946, I was a proud fourteen-year-old private in Uncle Sam's army.

The next day, our group of two dozen new recruits, still in our civilian clothes, boarded a train headed south on a two-day ride to Fort McClellan, Alabama.

When we crossed the Mason-Dixon line that afternoon, a porter came into our car to announce that at dinnertime we were to go to the dining car in groups of eight. At five o'clock, the first eight men lined up in the aisle and left for dinner. Only a minute later, Roosevelt Allen, a Chicagoan, returned to the car, cussing at the top of his voice.

"Hell, I'm a United States soldier. It ain't dignified eating at a table behind a goddamned curtain in a car full of white people who sit anywhere they damned please. If I can't eat in dignity, I ain't eating at all."

It was Lester Bodie who put everything in perspective. "Well, Allen, you heading south, my man, and your body will look like the great Gandhi's before you'll find dignity in the laws of Dixie. Dignity is what you carry into the dining room with you and take with you when you leave. Didn't anybody up in Chicago ever tell you that dignity is a quality, not a thing? It shines above segregated seating, and no dining car curtain can hide it. Now move out of the aisle, man. I'm taking my dignity to supper."

The Alabama night at Fort McClellan was as black as pitch when we arrived. We fumbled around in the heavy darkness, trying to find our way to the supply room for bedding. "Ain't this hell," hollered Theodore McBain. "Will you look at them raggedy-assed barracks? Looks more like a hog farm than a war camp."

From out of the darkness strode a large, broad-framed master sergeant, with the face of bulldog and eyes that looked like walnuts set in oversized sockets. He barked out at us, "Gentlemen, I'm Sergeant Gleason. I hear you don't appreciate the accommodations here. Well, don't let the condition of these barracks disturb you. You are here to be made into soldiers, and soldiers ain't made in barracks. You'll work so hard, and see so little of these little huts, that when you *do* get a chance to rest in them, they'll look to you like the Waldorf-Astoria."

The bugler was still asleep when our hut was jarred astir by the screaming wail of Corporal Conyers's police whistle. He was loud and brash and carried a mean-looking billy club. Going from bed to bed, pounding on the metal bars next to the sleepers' heads with his terrible club, he screamed, "Off and on, off and on—off your asses and on your feet. Drop them cocks, and grab your socks. Look like soldiers, goddamn it. When you hear this whistle, you better stop *whatever* you doing and run toward me. I'm going outside, and when I blow this whistle, you better tear this place down getting into formation. You have ten seconds!"

Not happy with our get-outside time, he said, "All of you can't get through the door at the same time. Next time I blow this whistle, you'd better tear the goddamn hinges off the doors, jump out the windows, and make me some new doors. You have ten seconds!" Off in the dark distance, while we tried to please Conyers, we heard the sound of rhythmic drilling and singing, and even that early in the morning it sounded like good music.

Hot Huu A-Rhee A-Hoar, Hot A-Hoar
Had a good home and you lef
[Troops] You're right
Wanna go back but you can't
[Troops] You're right
Jody's in bed with your wife
[Troops] You're right
Eatin your steak with your knife
[Troops] You're right

Corporal Conyers turned us over to Platoon Sergeant Marion Barber, who introduced himself in a musical southern drawl. With the large feet of a Georgia farmer accustomed to following the plow, Sergeant Barber wore his cartridge belt low on his broad, mulelike rump. He had a mouthful of country-folk gold teeth, which flashed in the morning light and reflected a smile as friendly as a letter from home. I was glad to hear him say that he was the real boss and that we were to bring all our problems to him. "After breakfast," he said, "you will be issued uniforms and rifles, and we can get on with the business of soldiering."

The mess hall was the one bright spot in our little ghetto, a clean and comfortable building where excellent cooks served outstanding southern food that my Mama Minnie would have applauded.

On my first trip through the breakfast line that morning, one of the cooks noticed my size and said out loud, "Lord, looka here! Good thing we won that war already. They're lettin titty-sucking babies in the damn army!"

I knew I would have to get used to remarks about my size and age. I heard it all the time. At the mess hall, the cooks all insisted my five-foot-seven frame was too frail. "Now, you eat all these turnip greens and corn bread, Junior, and take another helping of okra. We got to build you up strong so you can kick ol Jody"—the mythical civilian wife-stealer—"smack in the ass when you go home on furlough."

The military wardrobe was, for me, unimaginably exciting, and the sheer quantity of the haul was astounding. We got summer clothes and winter woolens, complete with heavy overcoat and several pairs of shoes and boots all at once. I couldn't carry it all in one trip. From the moment I got into my first pair of khakis, I was a new boy, and one thought consumed me: Find an officer to salute!

Years of long, hard practice back home in Sheffield had perfected my salute. My brother George, a virtuoso saluter, had coached me so that my delivery had the smart crackle and snap of his own. I checked myself out in the full-length mirror in the latrine, adjusted and buffed the brass on my collar and hat, and ran off in search of an officer to receive my first official salute—any officer would do.

Out near the flagpole in front of post headquarters, I confronted three or four captains and a major in a space of no more than a minute. Each officer thrilled me with the return of my salute, and I marveled that a fourteen-year-old from Sheffield could make a colonel salute back. I felt incredibly empowered. I couldn't keep from running rapturously around the camp, crisply saluting all the officers in sight and accepting theirs in return.

My enthusiasm for soldiering was boundless. Even during rest breaks, some of the men in my squad and I practiced drilling, with me imitating Sergeant Barber right down to his drawling Georgia voice and his gestures. Barber was one of the best on the post as a drillmaster. His rhythm was strong and steady, and he could improvise his syncopated marching orders as if he'd swallowed a Sanctified metronome.

The young recruits were passionate for a new form of drilling called Jitterbug Marching, a flashy thing close to dancing. Sergeant Barber and his assistants detested the outrageously exaggerated antics of jitterbugging in ranks and punished those of us who tried it even before we'd mastered the fundamentals of simple regulation drilling.

On a scorching-hot day just before noon chow, our squad took a few minutes' rest break, and Sergeant Barber went off to his own hut to rest. The men wanted to practice marching. Would I play the sergeant? I was in rare vocal form, sounding out the orders just like our Barber. My pals, McKinley, McBain, and Pettifield, hucklebucked as I called the orders, giving the smart "left flank" the special attention it deserved. All jitterbuggers love the left-flank maneuver. In it lies the essence of the jitterbug art. It begins with a loud stomp on the ground with the right foot while simultaneously lifting the left knee shoulder-high. The torso leans severely to the right as the hip and pelvis float smoothly to the left, transferring the body weight onto the left foot again. The squad then glides off in a nasty and outrageously irreverent pimp strut. When executed well, the "left flank" has the high-toned look of choreography. I was calling out a long series of left-flank commands when Sergeant Barber's voice shattered our ecstasy. *"Freeze!"* The whole squad hung on its just-stomped right foot, left knee raised against chest, while leaning way back for the angled pivot. We waited— and waited some more. A few men, weakening under the strain, visibly trembled.

Sergeant Barber came into view. "I said, Freeze, goddamn it, and that means *'don't* a swinging dick move.' Y'all like to jitterbug, I see. Well, you hepcats can just stand there in your cute little jitterbug pose and enjoy yourselves until the rest of the company is finished with chow." I had not taken the pose myself and tried to avoid his eyes.

"You there, Private Ruff," he said. "Take your place in ranks with the rest of the hepcats." I complied sheepishly, and we all stood there trembling in the broiling sun, fighting for our balance on one leg, with the other screaming from cramps. Sergeant Barber walked up and down in front of us, preaching.

"You damn smart-assed young fuck-ups got a lot to learn. Why the hell do you think you haven't seen a Negro officer since you been on this post? Answer me, Pettifield!"

Milford Pettifield, a Memphis left-flank freak, replied, "I reckon cause they don't like colored folks, Sarge."

Sergeant Barber, now silent, contemplated Pettifield's response while moving through the ranks, pushing drooping knees back up to chests and helping the victims lean back at their proper jitterbug angle. " 'At's right, Pettifield, they don't like niggers, but you tell me why."

Pettifield groaned, "I don't know, Sarge."

"Well, I'll tell you why: it's cause smart-ass fuck-ups like you can't wait to learn a thing the right way before you go and try to get cute with it. That makes the white man say you're dumb and not fit to learn. Every colored company in this regiment got a misfit white officer commanding it, and not one of them is as good a soldier as Sergeant Gleason and a half-dozen other noncoms right here in this company."

A man in the back fell to the ground—fainted from the heat. To another soldier, who tried to help him back to his feet, Barber barked, "Don't you move a goddamn muscle there, boy!"

He walked about and continued tidying up our trembling ranks even as he stepped over the downed recruit.

"They put fuck-up white officers in charge of fuck-up fools like you, Pettifield—and you, Ruff—because they don't *respect* you. You, also, can't learn a thing right before you go and fuck it up!"

Sergeant Barber's lecture left an impression, but the lunch I'd missed while posing statuelike in the sun really focused my attention. I made up my mind then and there to get truly serious about soldiering. And though I didn't give up jitterbug completely, I waited until I'd learned the regular basics of marching before giving myself up completely to dancing in rank.

One afternoon, during a training session with the automatic rifle, Corporal Conyers sent me to the noncommissioned officers' hut for a technical manual. Sergeant Barber, resting on his bunk, pointed to a table stacked with manuals. I took in all the extra appointments in the open room—the record player, the chairs, a reading lamp, and curtains. I had no idea the huts could be so comfortable. In my fascination with the place and the books, I nearly forgot my mission. But Sergeant Barber caught me.

"Hey, boy," he said, "get that book and get the hell outta here. If you're interested in books, come back later when you're not on duty. You got sent in here for something. When you gonna learn not to fuck around all the time?"

I went again after supper and found some of the men listening to records, some writing letters, still others drinking beer and talking in an atmosphere I imagined a college dormitory would resemble.

In one corner a small cluster of men were poring over a notebook, locked in a discussion of "quadratic equations." Others debated politics. Now I could see that along with the technical manuals scattered about the room, there were novels, books on mathematics and physics, and several college texts. My eyes fell on a stack of books the color of my khaki clothes. I asked Corporal Conyers about them. "They are published just for GIs. We get them free from the U.S. Armed Forces Institute, or USAFI."

One could finish high school and even earn college credits by taking the USAFI correspondence courses. So Rucker had been right with his boasting about all the education Uncle Sam offered his men, along with the threads and the chow.

Conyers pointed to a PFC right there in the hut. "He knows USAFI's programs better than anybody. He's taken damn near everything they offer."

I never knew his proper name; everyone called him F.C., short for Private First Class. F.C. had a reputation for brilliance. His encyclopedic mind and memory were rumored to have taken him through the ranks several times. However, his short fuse was also famous and had gotten him busted back to buck private just as often. Along with his intellectual accomplishments, F.C. had a lot of the teacher in him. The lowest-ranking man among our trainers, with a mere one stripe, was the most approachable and the least intimidating of them all. He read constantly, memorized volumes of army regulations, all the articles of war, and weapons manuals. He was preparing to take the examination for officer training school. Conyers said F.C. also tutored some of the sergeants there who were preparing for officer training. When I asked if I could sign up to finish high school, he said, "There's not enough time during basic training for you to get involved with USAFI, but make it your business to look into it as soon as you get to your next station."

CHAPTER FIFTEEN

The Display Soldier

A BIG, RUGGEDLY HANDSOME MASTER SERGEANT, famous throughout the Twenty-fourth Infantry as a gunnery champion and hand-to-hand-combat expert, came to our company temporarily as a special training instructor. He was a "display soldier," whom the army treated as a showpiece. He traveled to infantry training posts all over the country, whipping recruits into condition for combat, no matter that the war was behind us.

He arrived among us wearing the first custom-tailored uniform we'd laid eyes on. And on his first day on the training field, he challenged any man among us to try to bayonet him while he stood unarmed. Of course, there were no takers. None of us was willing to turn up with lost teeth or a missing eye. Who hadn't heard about such tricks?

It came out that the display sergeant and F.C. had known each other in college, years earlier. I even detected some of the same teacherly qualities in Display that I saw in F.C. But he struck me as a man living in a divided self and seemed driven by some mysterious energy, some deep anger. Sometimes he seemed to need to teach with a big stick, yet the teacher in him surfaced easily and effectively. In a classroom lecture or a field demonstration, he would deftly weave into his presentation some educational aside, some little-known fact about the history of the

Negro in the military. His first historical aside—and it was a staggering one—came in the middle of a lecture on the Browning automatic rifle. He was wrapping up a technical review of the nomenclature of the gas-powered mechanism of the gun, when suddenly he fell silent and halted midstride. His back to the chalkboard, he faced his audience, standing in his custom-made kidskin combat boots, arms folded over his barrel chest, full of medals. He looked mean as a coiled rattlesnake as he stared out at us, seething as he roared:

"You are—by far—the most ignorant—country—stupid-looking bunch of lazy bastards I've ever laid eyes on. What makes me despise you is not your inexperience—the cure for that can only come with experience and time. I detest in you the look that I see on your dumb animal faces, which says to me that you have become convinced that you cannot learn, or, what is worse, that you *need* not learn, complex things. You who believe that are wrong—every last son-of-a-bitching one of you who believes that is as wrong as two left shoes!

"I am sure nobody has bothered to tell you what I am about to say, and frankly, I don't know why I should waste my breath. But Negro soldiers who ran away from slavery to fight the Civil War in order for you to be free did not think that way. You didn't know that it was a regiment of our people who, in Missouri at the end of the Civil War, contributed most of their pitiful mustering-out pay to establish one of the first colleges in this nation for colored people. These men were former slaves. They—unlike you—had the courage and backbone to provide a start for our race to pull themselves up, and to show self-determination and commitment to being free and responsible people. Lincoln University is a monument to their dreams for you. Did I say dream? You sons of bitches are nightmares!

"Now, dammit to hell, on your feet! We are going for a five-mile run at *my* goddamned pace. When we return to this lecture area, the first Uncle Tom–looking son of a bitch I find looking sleepy is going to feel my combat boot in his ass, and I dare even a single mother's son among you to fall behind my pace."

Whenever Sergeant Display was on the podium from then on, I paid strict attention and tried with all my might to look alert and intelligent.

F.C. spent more time with the youngsters in the squad with education on our minds. Sometimes he and Sergeant Barber invited me to their hut to borrow books, but when Display was around I kept my distance; his meanness always made me nervous. F.C. knew what I was thinking.

"Oh, man," he said, "Display is harmless enough. He's just complicated, and angry. And let me tell you, that cat's got a right to his anger. He is definitely officer material. Back when the war started, he was passed over time after time. He was among the first of the young Negroes to try to enlist for flight training while he was a student at Lincoln University. The recruiting officer insulted them, telling them that flying was too complicated for Negroes to learn: he should leave that part of the war effort to white men and think about cooking school or truckdriving. Display just stewed for a while, then came into the infantry. He's been one bad-assed mean fucker since."

Our whole company groaned at the news that it would be Sergeant Display running us through bayonet training. I shuddered at the thought of winding up on the ground under his boot, with the feel of cold steel at my throat. No matter that the exercises were supposed to be only simulated fighting; that mean bastard could disarm and seriously bleed any four men in the company if he chose to. I figured he wanted us frozen in fear of him with his bayoneted rifle.

Poor Pettifield, a slow learner at best, took the sharp edge of Display's attack one morning just by being himself.

"Damn your Stepin Fetchit slouching ass, Pettifield," Display bellowed. "Look smart! Don't you know that you're here to be trained as a part of the old and heroic Twenty-fourth Infantry?"

We all knew that. But Pettifield said, "Yassuh, Sergeant." Display bristled at the crudeness of Pettifield's language.

"Well, country boy, do you also know that the Twenty-fourth Infantry was founded in 1868, three years after the Civil War? That it is famous for its role in the war in Cuba, that war they called the Spanish-American War?"

None of us knew that.

"Answer me this, plowboy: did you ever hear of Teddy Roosevelt?"

"I don't know for sure, Sergeant. Is he President Roosevelt's little boy?"

"Hell no, turd-lips. He was a lieutenant colonel who led the New York Rough Riders. Do you know who the Rough Riders were, Pettifield?"

"Naw, Sergeant."

"Can you guess?"

"Could they be some of Willie Ruff's kin people?"

"Hell no! The Rough Riders were a group of white New York State volunteers who were credited with capturing San Juan Hill in Cuba. That was nearly fifty years ago, Pettifield. Teddy Roosevelt made his reputation on that battle, became President of the United States, and never credited the black U.S. Tenth Cavalry, who actually took San Juan Hill, on *foot*, before Roosevelt even reached the scene! Using the tactics they'd perfected earlier when they fought out on the western plains as the 'Buffalo Soldiers,' they took San Juan Hill, and Roosevelt took the fucking credit and left them out! The Twenty-fourth Infantry fought in that same battle, Pettifield. Did you know that the outfit you're in is that same Twenty-fourth Infantry, Pettifield?" Poor Pettifield nodded, and Display went on:

"Both the Twenty-fourth Infantry and the U.S. Tenth Cavalry got fucked, and Roosevelt got the credit. Now, you'd better look like you're proud to be a part of this outfit, and neaten up that fucked-up uniform."

By the time we'd become passable bayonet men, our sense of history was sharpened and we'd all learned from Display, with examples to illustrate it, that we were part of a proud tradition.

Army food, wholesome, plentiful, and regular, triggered a growth spurt in me that made F.C. ask if I had changed my khakis for a better fit. Corporal Talley, a fatherly and gentle man of middle age, noticed my changed physique and made a special trip to my barracks to double-check my shoe size. "Ruff, you're growing like a young mule; growing right outta everything. An infantryman got to wear shoes that fit his feet, son."

He led me to the supply room for larger combat boots. The added weight and strength bolstered my confidence in my ability to stand up to the hardest part of basic training, which was yet to come. I already knew what that meant in an Alabama summer. At first, I had wondered: Can I, the youngest and smallest man in my outfit, even hope to keep up? What about those brutal twenty-mile hikes coming up? Can I make it carrying a ninety-pound field pack? If I failed to measure up, I was sunk: somebody would think to check my age, and I would certainly be sent home; wherever that was.

In the end, my unbridled adolescent energy and my enthusiasm for soldiering carried me through the grueling exercises with energy to spare. Furthermore, another kind of growth was taking control of me; a mysterious and powerfully supportive something in my midst was getting bigger and nourishing parts of me I hadn't felt before. Etched in the combined personalities and examples of F.C., Corporal Talley, Sergeant Barber, and especially the display soldier, was an uplifting quality that seemed to make me feel a lot like I had when Mama was there keeping on my case and preaching at me: "Read between the lines, boy!"

It was a baffling enigma, but there it was: the army, for all its "strictly business" GI fierceness and blatant segregation, suddenly was my deliverance, and I knew it would be my new home for quite a while. I was starting to see my future growing into real possibilities. I no longer felt envy for other boys my age, such as Milton Lambert, even with his loving and supporting father. Unfolding before me daily were opportunities to grow into a healthy maturity, with as good an education and a profession as Milton, or any boy anywhere. These were the possibilities I'd left Evansville for. If they'd been there for me, I would probably have stayed and maybe lost my future.

CHAPTER SIXTEEN

Learning to Tell a Story

WHEN I LEFT FORT MCCLELLAN as a basic training graduate, Sergeant Barber handed me a large packet containing train tickets and traveling orders and wished me good luck. I was to report in thirty days to Camp Stoneman, California, for reassignment as an infantryman somewhere in the Pacific. I stopped off first in Sheffield and found our house standing empty and ghostly, with every trace of the years of my family's occupancy now only a haunting memory. Sister, now divorced, was in Detroit, looking for work, seeking to fulfill her promise to Mama to make a home for Yvonne, now eight years old, and Nathaniel, five, and keep them together. Meanwhile, the two youngsters were living with Mr. Pruitt's grown children out in the country. In the few days we had together, I bought them as many clothes, pencils, and tablets for school as I had money for. Then, deeply depressed, I went to spend the rest of my furlough in Evansville with my father. I got on the train crying for my little sister and brother, back there without Mama or any of us from her side of the family.

Evansville was the same dead end. My father had no work and no prospects until cold weather brought back his basket-coal business. Several times each day, he and I sat in his truck and fingered through the bulging envelope of train tickets and dining car vouchers Sergeant Barber had given me for my trip to California. Nothing seemed as magical to my father, the old hobo, as those train tickets.

Savoring the exotic names stamped on them, he would say, "Ogden, Utah. Um *um!* I bet that's a pretty place." He kept repeating the names of the station stops in Wyoming and Nevada.

"Damn," he said at last. "You're just fourteen years old and going places no freight trains ever took me. Must be nice riding five days in a soft seat on a passenger train, and Uncle Sam feeding you too."

After a few days, with another two weeks of furlough to go, my money had run out. My father and I had been eating in joints around town, and I refused to see him humiliate himself further to feed me on credit, as he'd done before I enlisted. I mustered up the courage to tell him it would be best for me just to go on to the California army camp, where my food was free.

Emotionally whipped, I boarded the California-bound train and counted on the five-day ride across the continent on a full stomach, hoping that would improve my mood. Somewhere west of Chicago, my sadness began to recede and I lost myself in days of deep daydreaming, watching America roll past my window seat and thinking about my life. I knew that the first thing I had to do for myself and Mama was to start getting myself educated. At fourteen, I couldn't help trying to make comparisons between myself and other men in uniform on that train. I was one of the few black soldiers aboard. As I rolled across the vast continent, my thoughts went back again and again to the war bond parade years earlier, back in Sheffield, and the good times with Daddy Long and Mama. And even after the train arrived on the West Coast—where I was stunned by the sight of the sunny shimmering Pacific Ocean—I was still trying to decide which I really wanted to be: a flying officer in the Ninety-ninth Fighter Squadron or a musician on the ground.

Camp Stoneman, about an hour north of San Francisco, served as a way station for troops about to be shipped overseas. A section of the camp housed the various all-black units in transit. I found Company C and was told that when my Fort McClellan pals finished their furloughs, we would be headed for either Japan or Korea. Without them, I felt like the original unknown soldier; I had no duties, no identity, and a lot of time on my hands.

I had so much free time that I decided to go to work in the camp's bowling alley as a pin-setter. I wanted to earn enough money to buy my little brother, back in Alabama, a special present. Little Nat needed cheering up. I'd found out after I left Sheffield on my furlough that one of Mr. Pruitt's sisters had taken little Yvonne with her to Chicago. The perfect gift for Nat was sitting in the Stoneman PX—a gorgeous big red scooter with rubber balloon tires.

When I'd earned twelve dollars at the bowling alley, I went to the PX to make my purchase and was waited on by a very classy-looking black saleslady. She said she had noticed me in the PX before and wondered if I was really a soldier or some serviceman's kid who'd swiped a uniform. She asked me, kiddingly, if the vehicle I was eyeing was for myself. But when I told her it was for my little brother and explained why he needed to be cheered up, I thought the lady was going to cry. She said that she and her husband, who'd recently retired from the service, had children too, and they lived in the little town of Pittsburgh, just outside the gates of our camp. "Why don't you apply for the army's dependency allotments for your little brother and your sister too?" she asked. "The government will more than match your monthly contribution. That should help some." I did apply, and the kids began to get their small check monthly.

Somehow, my service records were lost at Camp Stoneman, and the men I'd known at Fort McClellan came through and went on to the Pacific as replacements for the Twenty-fourth Infantry. I was stuck for months, working in the bowling alley at Stoneman and taking trips to San Francisco, until orders came from Washington to send all unassigned Negro soldiers to a quartermaster post, Fort Francis E. Warren, in Cheyenne, Wyoming. I was to be moved in with the 3480th Truck Company to wait for the snow to let up long enough so I could begin driver training. Having some structure in my life again wasn't hard to take—I hadn't joined the army to work in a bowling alley. A few days after I arrived in Cheyenne, I ambled into the recreation room in the imposing brick barracks, sat down at the piano, and played some boogie-woogie and blues. I didn't know the first sergeant was listening. After a few minutes, he came over to me.

"You ought to be in the band, kid," he said. "We have too many truckdrivers already." I told him I wasn't good enough to play piano with a real band, but I would love to join as their drummer. He called the bandmaster, Warrant Officer Frank Ruffin, and got me an audition, and though I didn't play very well for the test, I was accepted as a snare drummer with the 353rd Army Band. The unit was understrength and not that good—they needed even me.

Pat Patterson, a masterful jazz drummer, was one of our better players and a specialist in the new bebop. He was also a fabulous sight reader and could play all the percussion instruments. Pat was very generous about helping me learn to read drum music more accurately. He listened politely as I played my Gene Krupa and Jo Jones swing licks for him, but he said I had to get modern and pick up on the modern jazz masters such as Max Roach, Kenny Clarke, and Art Blakey, names that were all new to me. Pat demonstrated bebop and tried to teach me how to "drop bombs": "Play melodies with your right foot on the bass drum and make your accents with your left hand on the snare drum and cymbals." But the rhythms and the style of playing he pressed on me were complex and so disjointed they seemed to make little sense to my crude ears without accompanying instruments. This new rhythmic engine of modern jazz passed right over my head. Pat helped me out of my square habits by playing me lots of his Charlie Parker and Dizzy Gillespie records. The records didn't change my habits right away, but a whole new world of music burst into full blossom for me during those snowy Wyoming days. Hearing Charlie Parker and all those young masters play such sophisticated music set my soul afire, and the point of modern jazz, even if I couldn't play it yet, was suddenly obvious to me. I heard in Charlie Parker's ideas, and Dizzy's too, that they were deeply rooted in the blues and the earlier forms of our music. They seemed, as Mr. Handy had advocated, to be taking all the traditional music they'd already absorbed as points of departure on which to create a thoroughly modern music for a modern America. One thing was abundantly plain: this was no fool's music; I knew I'd have to do a lot of growing just to understand its complexities.

One day at morning marching band rehearsal, our bandleader made an announcement. "I've just got a letter from Washington saying that the band from Fort Lee, Virginia, has been deactivated and reassigned here." The Fort Lee band combined with ours would make us the largest Negro band of the army's ground forces. The guild of master military career musicians of our race was small; many of the men had been colleagues for more than thirty years and could trace a direct line to their musical predecessors all the way back to the Civil War. Mr. Ruffin himself had been in the Ninth Cavalry before and during the First World War, and the prospect of being reunited with his old friends from that unit seemed to brighten his whole outlook and to ease his frustration with his own band's mediocrity.

While fussing at the trombone and baritone horn players one day, he said, "You brass instrument players just wait till old Pete Lewis gets here from Fort Lee. I've known him for thirty years. His tone and technique will make your hair stand up on your head." "Pete the poet" was all we kept hearing about. When the Virginia musicians arrived, I could see that Mr. Ruffin had been right about Pete Lewis; he was a master, with a gift for stating a melody that was all his own. But all the musicians who came were good, the drummers especially, and I knew I was outclassed. I had a feeling my army career in music was about to end.

We began planning a formal symphonic concert in the post theater to show off our new band. Rumor had it that all the big wheels from military bases for miles around were coming to hear what the Negroes could do with classical music. Mr. Ruffin chose his repertoire carefully; Pete would be our soloist, our ace in the hole. We began to sound almost professional. There were a few obvious weak spots, such as the French horn section, which had no real French horns. The men all played mellophones, which are also called "peck horns." (The peck horns, a poor substitute for the French horn in bands, is an alto horn that typically plays simple repeated notes that sound like "peck, pecka, peck, peck, peck, peck.") Real French horns were said to be too difficult for any of us to learn.

Mr. Ruffin called me into his office one morning. "I'm sorry, young fellow," he said, "but we have too many men on the drums now. You just don't have the experience to keep up with these players. I have to send you back to the truck company." My heart traveled to my shoes.

"But, sir, I could learn how to play another instrument. There're no French horn players among all those Virginia musicians, and the peck horn players here are awful. You're always saying that yourself."

Mr. Ruffin stared at me for a time; he seemed put off by my aggressiveness.

"Well, you're right about them peck horn players. I ought to be shipping their asses out too."

I pressed on. "Sir, if you give me a chance to learn the French horn, I promise I will practice, and before you know it, I'll be in the band."

He shook his head. "Ignorance is bliss. I don't think you know what you're asking for. It takes years to do anything worth a damn with the French horn."

"All I ask is a chance, sir. If I don't make it, you can put me back in the truck company."

"Aw, hell, you're as bad as my wife about talking. Dry up and come on with me to the supply room."

That basement room was the prettiest thing in the world to me. Every kind of wind instrument and drum was there. Mr. Ruffin pulled a case from one of the higher shelves. Inside was nestled a silver-plated French horn. It was gorgeous. From another shelf he took a new practice book, still in its wrapping paper. Then he led the way to the boiler room. He pointed to a spot next to the coal pile. "This is your new place of business," he said. "Keep the door shut so we won't hear you upstairs. I'll look in on you every once in a while. Now, you have to understand, boy, we can't waste a whole lot of time fooling around with you. . . . If you are not serious about this thing, we just can't use you. Understand?"

I went to work. Mr. Ruffin had been right about the horn's problems. The small mouthpiece and the hellish frustration of learning to control the instrument's tone and pitch were nerve-racking. The few notes I could manage sounded vile. I saw right away that I couldn't bully the instrument as I had that bugle back at Mr. Pruitt's place. Everything I tried seemed to want to go the other way, but I kept reminding myself of the below-zero winter outside and what it would be like to have to drive a big-assed trailer truck in Wyoming's snow and ice.

The instruction book had English and German on facing pages, and its author, Oscar Franz, had included, along with the exercises and instructions, a lavish pictorial history of the horn, which was fascinating. The instrument's ancestors were the actual horns of rams and other animals. Then there were pictures of gracefully curved horns made of wood and covered over with fine leather. These had been played by robed men in cathedrals and in the royal courts of Europe in the Middle Ages. There was even a picture of an elegant glass horn. Such engrossing history convinced me I was joining an old and distinguished guild. My determination mounted. But still the sound I made was pathetic, unruly, and entirely unmusical.

It was my habit to take a few minutes' break after each hour's practice at the horn; I'd heard experienced wind instrument players say the blood needs to flow back into the lips. The famous trumpeter and bandleader Harry James had recently developed a cancer of the lip, which everyone said came from excessive blowing, and lip strain was on everybody's mind after that. Several times each morning, during these rest breaks, I would ease into the rehearsal room to hear the band; my way of judging my own progress. Fortunately for me, the peck horns sounded nearly as bad as I did, and that gave me heart.

While the Oscar Franz horn book was interesting and full of in-spiration, it was obviously a manual to be used with a teacher; there were no indications of which valves to use for the notes printed there, nor were there fingering charts. I learned from bitter experience that each note on the instrument has several possible fingering patterns, and only an experienced horn player or teacher could have saved me the torture of learning through trial and error the patterns that sounded best to my as yet untrained ear.

One night after supper, I was on my way to the boiler room when Pete "the poet" Lewis, the lean, fifty-five-year-old virtuoso, with his warm, steady eyes, stopped me. He was annoyed. He began by using the nickname "Peewee" for me, because of my evident youth. (It was not long before I got promoted to "Junior.") "Peewee," he said that night, "you see those old no-account peck horn players? They're the same ones who messed up the music so bad at the rehearsal this morning. Every damn one of them is on his way to the PX to swill on them beer bottles instead of parking his ass in a practice room like you an' me."

I was naturally encouraged that my diligence was noticed, but I was unprepared for what he next said to me. "You bring your horn and come on back upstairs to the practice room with me. Old Pete's going to show you the difference between C major and C minor."

I'd gained an ally without even asking, and that night was the beginning of our official teacher-pupil relationship.

The song Pete chose to illustrate his first lesson was "Annie Laurie," the old Scottish air. All my life I'd noticed that a physique sometimes telegraphs the lifework of its owner: Joe Louis was built to box, Joe DiMaggio to stroke homers. Pete Lewis's lips puckered and became part of his sculptured, gold-plated euphonium with a naturalness that seemed divine. I'd already noticed his mild resemblance to Daddy Long, with his deep, dark, rich brown color and his enveloping smile. I'd also tried to imitate the elegant way he held his horn and his way of moving the valves with his shapely fingers. Pete sounded pretty before he played the first note! When he took up the horn that night and rested it on his lips and breathed into "Annie Laurie," I was amazed that such a simple tune could swell out into the air sounding like Marian Anderson's contralto, only deeper and with nuances and feelings that took my breath away. Pete played the last note and let it die into a whisper, then modestly rested the instrument in his lap as if nothing special at all had taken place all day. "Now, Peewee," he said, "let me hear you play that."

"Aw, come on, Pete," I protested. "I can't make all those notes. How you expect me to play *that* when I don't even know the fingerings for this thing yet?"

"Hold up there!" he interjected, a startling sharpness in his voice. "That is an *instrument*, not a *thing*. Don't you ever treat it, or even *think* of it, as a thing. It could make a bigger difference in your life than you ever dreamed about. Understand?" I understood and said I was sorry.

"Now, you asked how I expect you to play that song. I don't expect you to play it the first time, but I do expect you to at least try. With me helping you, maybe you can. Now come on, boy"—I hated "boy" even more than "Peewee"—"the good Lord gave you ears, and you can use em to pick out that song just like you pick out those scales in the boiler room every day. Come on, try it!"

I did as I was told, fumbled nervously with the tune, and while I protested that I couldn't get it, Pete pushed me hard, taking up his horn again to play a fragment for me to match. I plodded on, painfully reconstructing little snips of his melody; trying one fingering, then moving on to search for another if the first was too flat or too sharp. I was playing in the cracks. If I occasionally lucked up on a single genuine note of "Annie Laurie," it startled me but brought a nod and a grin to Pete's face. He was the model of patience and encouragement. He talked and blew and persisted with gentle firmness. Sooner than expected, my pitiful bleating began to take on some crude semblance of what I'd heard him play—at least the notes, Lord knows, if not the feeling. Once or twice, when I made it to the end of any consecutive three- or four-note phrase with the right fingering, Pete's eyes would dance and he'd shout out encouragingly, "Hell yes, Junior, you almost got it, boy, don't give up yet!" Then he'd pause and draw in a deep breath while I sputtered on. "Now you take a big breath before you start this next passage. Breathe in a *big ball* of air, but gently blow out a long, long *thread*." He was hurling these instructions at me, his right arm stretched out near my face, the open upturned palm moving energetically up and down as if hefting a huge invisible weight.

"Hold on to that note," he hollered. "Support it from your diaphragm. Swell on it! Make that phrase bigger, bigger!" I reached the tune's end spent and panting and amazed at what he'd made me do. Pete said, "Now, Junior, that's what you call telling a story. Always remember that music don't mean a thing unless it tells a story. It's got to say something. Now, you got a story to tell, and don't you ever let nothing or nobody make you ashamed to tell it in music. You understand what I'm telling you, son? Well, I want you to understand that you can tell a story with just one single note! Listen to this E flat." He blew a long soft and resonant E flat with a little vibrato in it, which gave me chills.

The rest of that evening was devoted to showing me the enormous difference between stories told on his euphonium in major keys and those told soulfully in the minor.

Another night while the peck horn players were at the beer hall, I swiped their music folder to try to see what the music to the hellish "Ballet Égyptienne" really looked like. I shouldn't have looked. It was a frightening mess of notes; the page was black with them, and I wondered if I'd ever learn to decipher so complicated a mess. I had already begun to pick out the tune on my horn in the boiler room, relying solely on my ear. When I'd learned what sounded to me like the right melody, I asked Pete to come down and check me for accuracy. By bedtime, we were blowing the solo in unison. When he was satisfied that I could negotiate the notes, never mind that they sounded weak and thin on my horn, he said, "Now match me, play along with me, and pay attention to your tone quality."

I was a parrot. But surely enough, as I blew into my horn, with Pete's big round warm tone right there next to me to mimic, my puny tone grew gradually to approximate the rich singing sound of his euphonium. Sleep that night was impossible for me in my excited state, and several times before dawn I crawled out of bed in the cold darkness and crept down to my warm boiler room to work at my storytelling.

In the rehearsal hall the next morning, the peck horns again murdered "Ballet Égyptienne." One of the clarinet players had shamed a couple of peck horn players into the practice room. Still, they kept flubbing. None of them, I was certain, would have humbled himself enough to ask Pete or Mr. Ruffin for help. Furthermore, they had by then become psychologically conditioned to falter.

I worked all morning in the boiler room, playing the passage slowly as Pete had admonished, and quit only when my lips began to swell.

A few days after Pete had certified that I could manage "Ballet Égyptienne," I attended a band rehearsal to listen as Mr. Ruffin put the new full band through its paces. Victor Herbert took on an astonishing majesty. But then came the "Ballet," with its terrible peck horn challenge. I tensed as the entire section splattered their cacophony and flubbed over and over. Mr. Ruffin threw down his baton, stomped his heavy foot in rage, and stopped the band.

He glared at the peck horners. I was standing just inside the door, and Mr. Ruffin turned in my direction. "Private Ruff," he said, "are you prepared to try this piece? . . . Well, speak up—yes or no?" I looked over at Pete for a sign. His eyes held mine for the briefest moment, then his sly and passive gaze shifted to the vast prairie beyond the window.

"Yessir, I think I could try it," I said.

When I returned from the boiler room with the horn, a fourth chair had been added to the peck horn line. Mr. Ruffin would test us individually. At the downbeat, the first-chair peck horn man began "Ballet Égyptienne." He lost his place, missed the trills, and played several wrong notes. The other two broke down—defeated before they'd gotten out three notes. Then it was my turn. I ached for a clue from Pete, some sign: a nod, maybe a wink for good luck. But his rheumy soft eyes still swept the lonesome prairie. Mr. Ruffin's downbeat started me blowing, nervous and terrified. When I came to the end of the first phrase unscathed, someone in the clarinet section said, "Well, all right, then!" The fuss nearly broke my concentration, but the nasty trills and tricky passages came off well enough. Pete's coaching had been so intense that I knew myself to be operating entirely on muscle memory. I was still holding out the last note of the cadence when Mr. Ruffin held up his hand to quiet the applause.

"All right," he said. "The whole band at the French horn solo." At our conductor's downbeat, I experienced the thrill of hearing, for the first time, my own horn sound accompanied by the full and glorious lushness of sixty-seven musicians. Mr. Ruffin stopped the band. He looked at me and said, "You are the new first-horn player. Change seats with Corporal Sleepy." Only then did Pete draw his gaze back indoors. He wore that same big grin Daddy Long had flashed whenever he thought I'd hit on something like a world's fair idea.

The new job brought an immediate promotion to Private First Class. Now I was in the band again, but I never slacked up on the practicing, for I was painfully aware that my getting to sit in that first-horn chair was a fluke, a wild stroke of luck. Both Mr. Ruffin and Pete would stop in the boiler room from time to time to check up on me as I practiced and offer help if I needed it. Mr. Ruffin coached me when he was on duty in the building during the day, but Pete lived there, and it was he who sat with me most often.

"Now, boy," he'd say to me, "with any wind instrument, it's the *breath* that makes the music. That's why the wind instruments are said to be the ones that produce 'living' sounds. They say that because, just like in singing, the human breath is the note's engine. See what I'm saying?" He went on to lay out for me the practice routine all players of wind instruments must work at in order to develop tone, control, and the physical foundation that had made him the master he was. "To a musician playing a wind instrument, long tones are money in the bank," he said. The unexciting practice of blowing single long notes— the musical equivalent to the athlete's push-ups—which builds lip muscles and promotes control, solid intonation, and endurance, is no fun at all for any beginner. But even Pete at his advanced stage seemed never to miss a day in the practice room, making deposits in his musical bank account with copious long-tone practice. His habit became mine.

Even though I'd lost my heart to the horn, I wasn't spending all my off-duty time in the practice room, with the long tones and scales. My favorite fun hangout was the lavish brick service club, which was complete with game rooms, a movie theater, a ballroom, a music room with records and a great radio, and a reading room with desks for letter writing. The club also boasted a modern gymnasium, with a basketball court and every sort of professional sports equipment. I decided to work at building up my string-bean physique so Pete and others would leave off the Peewee, Junior, and "boy" tags.

Fort Warren had a championship boxing team that enjoyed all sorts of special privileges and "light duty" on the post, which meant they did no other work. The weekly fights were major attractions. Golden Gloves champs from all over the country were on the bill regularly. On my trips to the gym I hefted weights—with no result—and then I began checking out the speed bag, because at the movies I'd always loved watching Sugar Ray Robinson make the bag sound like drumming. An easygoing West Indian, Sergeant Dexter Maynard, a man whose distinctive accent and figures of speech I loved listening to, was in charge of the boxing team and served as its trainer. Maynard was about my size but a good fifteen years or more older. He was always in the training area, helping fighters and matching them up with different sparring partners. Size meant nothing. He'd put a bantamweight in the ring to spar with a middleweight, or jump in there himself with a heavyweight and give him pointers and sometimes even a good licking. I'd noticed that everybody looked up to Maynard, whom they called Coach, and often sought his advice. I had no interest in fighting; I just wanted to train and get bigger and play with the speed bag, but Maynard seemed to like interrupting my little routines and giving me pointers on moving smoother and with more rhythm. He improved my stance at the bag, corrected my footwork, and before long offered me general encouragement.

"Mon," he said, smiling, "you got quick honds, but de feet—dey all lead!" He'd give me a demonstration of moving lightly like a dancer. Maynard was a storehouse of scientific knowledge of the mechanics and physics of boxing. One day, he prescribed a complex series of neck- and head-rolling exercises that would build up resistance to a "glass jaw" for me, even though he'd never seen me box. Another of his obsessions was the fighter's diet, and he never stopped talking about ring discipline and sportsmanship. Watching him work drew me more and more into his game, but strictly as an appreciative spectator; I didn't even want to fool around sparring with anybody, for fear of a blow to the chops that would spoil my horn playing.

I liked best of all watching fighters on the team who looked to be near my age. There were several my own size too—flyweights—and almost without exception, they were Mexicans who prided themselves on their toughness and guts. They had plenty of both. Blood meant nothing to them, and it flowed often in the real fights. But as I stood on the sidelines watching the Mexican lads training and sparring with Maynard, I found their speech even more intoxicating than their fighting. I'd never heard Spanish before, and suddenly something of the old language love I thought I'd left behind when my sign language lessons came to a halt back in Sheffield was surfacing again. Maynard could talk Spanish to the Mexicans, and something about that was encouraging. I told myself that if he could learn it, I could too, and I determined to speak Spanish.

I found as much time as I could to go to the gym at night. There was a Mexican flyweight, Angel Coronado, about my size but three years older, who was a holy terror in the ring, fast and smart. Angel was a gentle soul outside the ring, and he always smiled and nodded his greeting whenever he came to the equipment area and found me there. If I got a good rhythm going on the speed bag, he'd say, "Nice moves, champ. You looking good." After I'd seen Angel win a few fights, and he had noticed me marching in the band with my horn, we struck up a friendship. I mentioned my fascination with Spanish and asked if it was hard to learn.

"I never thought about hard or nothing for Spanish, man. It was the only thing we talked at home in Texas. Me and my brothers and sisters learned Spanish from our mother and father before we learned English." I said I sure would like to learn it and offered to teach Angel some sign language if he showed me a few things in Spanish.

"Naahh, champ. Who am I gonna talk it to in the army? No deaf people here." But then he said, "Don't worry about showing me that. I'll teach you some words anyway." I asked if he'd start off by clearing up for me some of the words I'd heard so often around the gym when he and his friends were boxing or rooting for one of their teammates; words that sounded like *coño, chingal,* and *cabrone.* Angel held up his hand and said, "Naahh, those are not nice words. They just mean 'fucking' and 'son of a bitch'—you know, all that shit. I'll teach you clean Spanish. Hey," he said, bright with a new idea. "I'll take you to mass Sunday here on the post, and you can hear some Latin too. That sounds a lot like Spanish; the Catholic chaplain is a nice guy." I took Angel up on all offers that might give me a chance to learn Spanish, even if the stations of the cross and the office of the mass escaped my Baptist comprehension.

Once I got started with Spanish, the Mexican boxers were great about encouraging me and egging me on to try to talk more. I began sitting with them at the real fights and added my voice to the cussings they gave the other team's fighters. Listening hard and aping them gave me pretty good pronunciation and inflection, with the slang at least. In time, I'd picked up a pretty colorful arsenal of fighter talk—good and dirty.

The army's method of segregation by nationality was always a mystery to me; they must have done it all by eye, for the separation seemed to be done by color rather than by blood. Dark-skinned Puerto Ricans, like Chico the clarinet player in our band, were always housed with blacks. Those who looked white, as did some of Chico's relatives, lived in white barracks. But all of Fort Warren's Mexicans were housed with white troops. However, for hanging out, the hip ones always found us. This was especially true at the weekly dances at the service club, where our jazz band played and the Mexican boxers came in droves to dance. They were among the best jitterbug rug cutters on the post, and that was saying a lot.

Two of the musicians who'd come to us from Virginia, Sonny Wilson, a great trombone man, and Phil Wilmot, a strong and likable hot trumpeter, added pepper to the jazz band and lightness to the boxers' feet. The black ladies from Cheyenne were favorite dance partners of the Mexican guys at the dances. Angel was all over the dance floor, boogying like a stylish little demon and twirling the ladies fast and furiously. For the slow drags, he expertly bent them back in their rubber-spined dips, to the applause of his fighter friends. Never any problem between the Mexicans and our guys over the ladies at the dances; it was all friendly and civil, a multinational celebration of good jazz music and the human need to move to it.

One night while Angel and I were hurling the medicine ball back and forth to each other's midsections, Maynard came up to me and said, "Champ, we need a flyweight for de fight coming up Friday night; our best guy is having his appendix out. Real bad luck, mon! Why don't you take his place on de card. You can handle dot guy he is supposed to fight." Angel liked the idea and said, "Yeah, Guillermo! You can take that chump. I saw him fight. No power, no speed, no legs, slow hands, and he's dumb. Come on!" I flat out refused, citing my embouchure. But I learned later that Angel had gone back and told Maynard to put my name on the placard and he would take care of changing my mind.

After a few days the card did appear, and Leonard Perry, one of our musicians, came into the band room and congratulated me. The place broke up; some guys laughed at the thought of me in the ring, and some encouraged me. Everybody was excited. Everybody, that is, but Pete Lewis. Pete had been sitting in the corner, reading a newspaper. Hearing Perry's congratulations, he threw it to the floor and signaled for me to come out in the hall for a private talk. Pete, I could see, was hotter than a two-dollar pistol. I'd seen a touch of his ire only once, when he drew me up short for referring to the horn as a thing, but I'd never seen him really angry, the way he was that day. He pointed his big finger hard in my face, and I knew I was in for it when he called me by my last name.

"Ruff, I thought you were smarter than to do a fool thing like that. Do you want to be Sugar Ray Robinson or a musician? All those hours of long tones, scales, and studies you've worked so hard at could be destroyed—thrown away—with one lick in the mouth! That's foolish, Ruff!" Before I could explain the mix-up, Pete was tuning up for a second chorus. "I been wasting my time trying to show you what an opportunity you have to make a first-class musician out of yourself. Looks like everything I tried to tell you went in one ear and out the other. Doggone it! I swear I thought you were smart enough to see what you can do with yourself. You're no doggone boxer, boy! Can't you see that?"

"Pete," I pleaded, "that fight card has it all wrong. I'm not fighting anybody. Sure, I go to the gym all the time, but that's just to build myself up so people will stop calling me Peewee and Junior and Young-blood and all that childish shit." He shot me a warning look about the *s* word. I apologized and went on to explain that I didn't know yet how my name got on that card and that I thought it was a joke. But when I told him my other reason for spending so much time at the gym— the opportunity to learn and practice Spanish—he let up a bit. "Go get your coat and hat," he said, "and meet me back here in five minutes. If you want to learn Spanish that bad, I'll fix that." We took off in the snow, headed for the Office of Information and Education. Though I knew that Fort Warren, like every other army post, had such an edu-cation facility, I'd not yet found time to use it. Teaching myself the

French horn had left me too little opportunity to work on my book learning. Pete changed that.

I followed him into the office, and we found a schedule of dozens of night classes. The first-level Spanish class had begun a few weeks earlier, but I signed up anyway and checked out the books to take home, figuring my head start with the Mexican boxers would help me catch up and even it all out. Pete was satisfied but ordered me to keep away from the boxing ring. Hitting the speed bag receded as my Wyoming evening diversion; I began hitting the Spanish books instead. But I kept on sitting with the Mexicans at the fights even after I cancelled my advertised ring debut.

Pete came to the boiler room one night with a book and his horn and took a chair beside mine at the music stand. "Go wash your hands," he said. "You doing all right with the books, but I want to show you a sho-nuff book." I looked at my hands and saw they weren't dirty. "Pete," I said, "my hands are clean."

"Not clean enough for you to handle *this* book." When I returned from the sink, Pete had the book opened to a page showing a picture of a military band of black men in uniforms that looked strangely exotic—certainly not World War I uniforms.

"Junior," he said, "I want you to know that as a musician here, you are a part of a special Negro military family. We got us a glorious history, boy. This book is about our cavalrymen, and they were mighty special. You already know that many of us old soldiers—Mr. Ruffin, Sergeant Sloan, Sergeant Parker, and others—were in the Ninth and Tenth Cavalry. Well, this book was written by Negroes, and some of them were in the Tenth, and it shows for the first time the truth of what our men did not just in the Spanish-American War but in all this nation's wars. Here, look at these fellows and read to me aloud what it says on the page back of this picture of the band, then I'll tell you a story."

I took his treasured book, and I read the account of the bandsmen's bravery in Cuba under fire and learned that they were in the battle for San Juan Hill. There was a moving account of the musicians rescuing wounded soldiers, white and black, and carrying them to safety behind the battle lines while under fire and up against incredible odds. Pete was so proud of the band it made me proud too. When I finished reading, he took back the book as if were a fragile golden egg and said, "Now, some of these musicians in this picture were not just my friends: they were my teachers years and years ago, when I was a youngster like you. They taught me like I'm teaching you. Maybe later on, you might be able to teach somebody else." Little could I know that Pete Lewis was speaking prophetically. Forty years later, as I was stretching my memories for this book, I was to come across *that* sacred book again, and in a way that would help round out not only my book but my life too.

After thirty-five years as an army musician, Pete was gathering up his vast accumulation of musical mementos for his retirement, that year of 1947. It didn't take much persuading for Mr. Ruffin to get him to stay several weeks past his retirement date to be the soloist for our expanded band's debut symphonic concert. Pete was our ace in the hole, and Mr. Ruffin carefully programmed several virtuoso selections to feature Pete's last "solo appearance" as a government man.

We played to a packed house, the first audience I'd ever seen where the races were mixed. Pete, decked out in his ribbons and stripes, was the picture of the veteran. Pat Patterson, the drummer, said, "We could take that sommich to Carnegie Hall!"

With the calm assurance of the seasoned artist in complete command, Pete, more poetic than I'd ever heard him, played like an angel. Mr. Ruffin led us through his accompaniment with prideful sensitivity; even the peck horn players came through without flawed entrances. We knew that very few of our listeners had ever heard a classical music program before. All the men I'd been with in the truck company came because word had spread that Pete Lewis was indeed a world-class artist, respected in military music circles all over the world. When Mr. Ruffin announced to the crowd that they were hearing Pete's last army performance, they gave him a standing ovation. He made me so proud, I carried his horn back to the barracks for him. I felt he'd done all this,

his superb performance that night and all the earlier lessons and advice, to inspire me to go on and take it upon myself to be the best musician I could become. He certainly had charted my future, and even if the usual racial barriers got in my way, I, like my old soldier teacher, would never stop trying. In spite of everything, Pete's musical life just seemed to me to be more stimulating and satisfying than anybody else's on that post, and I thought if I could ever become half the artist he was, I'd settle for that—it would be more than worthwhile. At least I knew that playing the horn, and learning all the different kinds of music I could, would be my life's goal.

CHAPTER SEVENTEEN

Found Out

A FTER PETE'S RETIREMENT I was like a cork on water, floundering and lost. I missed him a lot, of course, and to take up the slack time in the rehearsal room, I started toying with other instruments. I'd inherited Mama's deep passion for bass music, whether sung, plucked, bowed, or blown, and had always looked on the bass fiddle as a melody-making drum combining something of Mutt McCord and Mr. Buddy Jenkins, our Baptist Bottom bass singer. I started amusing myself by plucking a shuffling bass line on a GI plywood bass fiddle. I would fool around with it every chance I got. I was at it one morning when I was summoned to the orderly room. I found Mr. Ruffin sitting at his desk, looking unhappy. He nodded in the direction of a chair and told me to take a seat. I didn't know what was up, but I sensed I was in trouble.

"Tell me the truth about your age, Ruff," he said.

"I'm seventeen, sir, like it says on my service record. I signed up with my dad's permission."

"I've been all through your service record. Then I sent away and got this." He shoved a paper at me that had "Colbert County, Alabama" printed across the top. It was my birth certificate. I can tell you that looking at Mr. Ruffin, I was feeling a lot older than my fifteen years. Though certain that the game was finally over, I tried to bluff.

"That paper," I said with as much conviction as I could muster, "must have the wrong Willie Ruff on it."

Reaching for the telephone, he said, "Then let's call that Alabama courthouse and make sure." He sat with his hand on the phone for a moment, all the while watching my face and eyes, with the look of someone wise to a lie. I fought to maintain control, but when a welling tear fell, Mr. Ruffin put the phone down and walked around to my side of the desk.

"I know this paper is right, Ruff. You better tell me the truth now. Why aren't you at home, where you belong? Does your mother know where you are?"

In as steady a voice as I could muster, I said, "My mama is dead."

"How about your father—does he know where you are?"

"He knows where I am. He's not working enough to give me the kind of home I had when my mama was living. He knows I'm better off here." There followed a very, very long silence. I smelled doom. Finally, and with some resignation, Mr. Ruffin sighed and pulled himself up.

"Well, you can relax now. I sent away for this birth certificate just to check up on you because of a certain suspicion." He sat on the edge of the desk. "I'm going to tell you one of my secrets. When I was about your age, I did the same damn thing you did." Then he laughed. "Except I was sixteen when I joined up.

"You know," Mr. Ruffin continued, "before Pete Lewis left, he and I had a long talk about you. Pete and I both knew you could only be fourteen or fifteen. He had too much respect for what you were trying to do for yourself to ask you straight out how old you were. But he wanted to be sure that you had the chance to make it as a musician.

"And you know, Ruff, as good as Pete Lewis was, he never had the opportunity to show what a musician he really is, because of his color. There isn't a baritone horn soloist in any of the all-white service bands in Washington that can touch that man as an artist; and I mean the army band, the navy band, and the marine band. Those doors are closed to our people. No Washington band for us. This is as far as any of us can go. Pete is a sensitive person, and it hurt his soul that the color of his face kept him from the artistic recognition he deserved. He was more than good enough to play in Sousa's band; but you know how that is. He wants you and other youngsters like you to get the chances he never had. I promised him I'd keep my eye on you."

I was relieved by what Mr. Ruffin was telling me. Relieved? I was ecstatic! He was telling me I could stay in the army.

"Here is something I want you to sign," he said. "Read it."

"What is it?"

"It's an agreement for you to have all of your pay, minus a small monthly allowance, go into Soldiers Deposit. That's a high-interest savings plan for servicemen. Sign it." I asked how much allowance I would get each month.

"Five dollars. . . . Now, about your schooling. Are you aware of the army's many educational programs?" I recited all the programs I'd looked up at the I and E office, adding that I was already enrolled in Spanish class three nights a week.

"Well," Mr. Ruffin said, "you're going to need to know more than Spanish to graduate from high school. I want you to get the high school equivalency out of the way as soon as you can. I will help you if you need it." Pete Lewis had left me with an able surrogate who had a solid self-development plan all worked out for me.

M y elevated sense of security was short-lived. When the year 1947 rolled in, it had found the Pentagon still reeling from a staggering confrontation that had occurred between the races in uniform more than a year earlier in Indiana, not far from Evansville. It was a conflict that could not have been more crucially timed, and it had threatened to explode into a national crisis. No boy in America of my age and of my race could have identified more strongly than I with the event and its outcome, for at its center were the same Tuskegee flying officers who'd flown over my Alabama hometown for our war bond drive.

The *Indianapolis Recorder*, a black newspaper, printed the first account of the affair, which the white press would all but totally ignore. Even the date of the article had meaning for me, for it was published on the very day of the death of President Roosevelt—the unforgettable day, also, of my mother's death. The news article as it appeared:

SIXTY OFFICERS ARRESTED
FOR CRASHING WHITE CLUB

Freeman Field, Seymour, Ind. (ANP) Sixty Negro Officers were placed under arrest at this field Friday for defying a ban on colored officers at the swanky officers' club at this post, by order of Col. Robert Selway, jr. The mass arrest, which is believed unprecedented in the history of the Army, has this post in an uproar and has disrupted the Bombardment group, the first Negro bomb unit.

All of those arrested are members of the 118th Base unit which is a replacement group for the 477th now in the final stages of its overseas training. Their names are not available at this time. However, they include captains, lieutenants and flight officers, several of them overseas veterans and proud wearers of the Distinguished Flying Cross.

Col. Selway's move in setting up a separate officers' club and denying admittance to Negro officers is termed a direct violation of Army Regulations 210-10, Par. 19, which specifically states that membership shall not be denied to any officer on any Army post. This regulation is further substantiated by Executive Order of President Roosevelt on July 6, 1944, banning any such discrimination.

Further reporting by the nation's black press kept its readers at least partially informed about the officers and the progression of the army's case against them. Intervention by the NAACP followed the arrest, and that organization stepped forward with legal defense when a larger contingent, 103 officers, was arrested for refusing to sign an agreement with the base commander, Colonel Selway, that would have required their promise to refrain from any further confrontation. At their refusal, Selway shipped the officers to Godman Field in Kentucky, a post that had been abandoned since the First World War. Upon arrival, the men were arrested again and held until the government's case against them was ready for court.

In the interim, the national black press and influential black politicians across the country pushed so hard for justice, the army saw that their no-win flimsy case against so large a group of warriors acting within their legal rights could only be an embarrassment. But there had to be a trial to save face for the army. Three of the men, the "ringleaders" of the defiance, Lieutenants Marsden Thompson, Shirley Clinton, and Roger Perry, were court-martialed on lesser charges. These men ultimately came to be regarded as heroes to men and women of color in uniform all over America.

Months after the Freeman Field mass arrest, even in Cheyenne's small black community, one still occasionally heard the question: "What ever happened to them Tuskegee Air Corps guys?" What had happened following the court-martial was still unclear. And by 1947, even the black press that reached us in remote Cheyenne made no mention of a permanent resolution to the problem.

Only the Negro press of the time reported the true story. Such a precedent-setting mass defiance of unjust authority—a precursor of the civil rights cases a full decade later—was not the kind of news the major American press wanted to present. Except for a War Department propaganda documentary narrated by the young actor Ronald Reagan (how do you like that for irony?), no one had even reported the existence of such a unit and its feats of heroism against the Nazis in Europe. Black males as war heroes had never been an acceptable image in America.

One day about a month after Mr. Ruffin agreed to let me stay in the army, a musician from the Fort Lee band threw out his chest in a rehearsal and complimented us all.

"This band is sounding better all the time. We must be as good as that band old Warrant Officer Brice has back in Ohio." Sergeant Sloan, an old cavalry vet and our drum major, came to life. "What's that you said about Brice and a band, young fellow?"

"Damn, man! Don't you guys get news at all out here in the wild west? Don't tell me you haven't heard about that air base in Ohio where the Tuskegee pilots are! I got my scrapbook filled up with clippings of that whole story all the way from the mutiny in Indiana right through Godman Field."

"Wait a minute," another Fort Lee musician said. "I read in the *Pittsburgh Courier* that after their court-martial, Washington gave them their own air base at Godman Field, Kentucky, for a while. But the whole unit moved to Columbus, Ohio, to a base called Lockbourne. Shit, baby, all the Negro fliers, engineers, doctors, nurses, and lawyers, all the women in the Air Corps and the famous John Brice and his musicians, too, are all together there. B. O. Davis, Jr., is a full colonel now, and he's the base commander. Hell, man, where have all you people been?"

For the next several days, the legend of John Brice and the new air base expanded in the band barracks, and when we went among the men in the truck companies, we asked for information about Lockbourne and learned more with nearly every query. If such a place was to have a band, according to several old vets among us, Brice was the man to give it the class and distinction of the other units there.

Not many days after the Lockbourne story began among us, Mr. Ruffin called a special meeting in the large rehearsal hall. Another document had arrived from Washington. Mr. Ruffin quieted our nervous murmurings.

"Men, I have news that I would rather not have to share with you, but I have to. I was informed this morning that in thirty days, this band will be broken up." A long groan followed. Mr. Ruffin held up his hand for quiet.

"Just when it seemed like we would have the best band in the army, they decide to break it up. It's rough on your families, being transferred all over the place every few weeks like Gypsies. But the orders I got just said that reassignment orders will follow. As for myself, I will be going to Ohio as assistant bandmaster to Chief Warrant Officer John Brice. Many of you know who he is."

Within a week we all knew where we were being sent. Some men, the best of our musicians who had at least two years of their enlistments to serve, would be going along with Mr. Ruffin to Ohio. Brice was interested only in players who had time to become part of a growing performance unit. That left me out. My original enlistment had been for only eighteen months; I had already served one year.

Again, Mr. Ruffin called me to the office, and he fidgeted for a while before breaking the news to me that I would have to turn in my horn. Terrible news. I asked him if he had any idea how good the French horn players in Mr. Brice's band were.

"Well, you know I haven't heard any of them yet, but there are never enough good French horn players in any band in the army. Maybe we can figure out a way to get you in that band. After you serve out your six months, you might think about reenlisting at Lockbourne."

I was among the last group leaving our post. About twenty-five of us who didn't make it to Ohio headed for Oakland Army Base in California. I boarded the train with no horn and not much hope for a future in a musical world I was quickly learning not to trust.

CHAPTER EIGHTEEN

"Take a Chance, for Heffen's Sake"

THE DREGS OF THE CHEYENNE BAND straggled onto Oakland Army Base, a camp consisting of a few dozen wooden barracks and endless acres of cavernous warehouses and heavy ship-loading equipment. We were to be trained as dockworkers and stevedores, and it took no time at all for me to learn that I was no good at any of it. Even as we did the mindless dockwork, we musicians fought hard to keep our identity. We flaunted the band insignia on our uniforms, refused to replace them with Quartermaster emblems, and talked to one another only in the hip jargon of jazz. Those among us with instruments organized daily jam sessions. I went back to drumming, thumping out shuffling noises on a rolled-up GI mattress with sticks made from a sawed-off mop handle. Besides my mop handles and mattress, the only other rhythm instrument we had to propel our trombone, trumpet, and alto sax was an electric guitar. We all noticed that our guitarist, Howard Lewis, had begun turning belligerent and pushy there in California. A large man, brutish in stature, he hadn't seemed so aggressive back in Cheyenne. But bitterly disappointed that Mr. Brice had not invited him to Lock-bourne, Lewis grew sour. He'd get drunk in the middle of the day and desert his work on the docks, stealing back to the barracks to plug in his guitar amplifier and vent his spleen with raw low-down gutbucket blues playing. We could hear him picking and stomping at top volume from halfway across the base. Crowds followed their ears to our barracks. Word spread that there was a wild go-to-hell guitar man on the base, with a band, and someone organized Saturday night dances. I found an old snare drum and a battered cymbal to play. Loose, easy Oakland women came in droves to our dances, and we musicians felt rich on the twelve dollars we each were paid for a Saturday night. Then we spent the rest of the week at our jam sessions learning repertoire, including all the current Louis Jordan and Nat King Cole songs.

The postwar traffic to and from the Pacific slackened, and we bandsmen ended up working as GI redcaps; we carried the baggage for the GI wives and dependents returning home. After helping the passengers off the ships, we scrubbed the cabins from top to bottom, then painted them. I hated the work and felt certain that music had left my life forever. For the first time since my enlistment, I couldn't wait to get out of the army. I was so miserable I came close to admitting my age and asking for my discharge.

The only other good part of Oakland Army Base was the Information and Education office, with its supply of books. All the subjects I needed to complete high school were there. After duty each day and on weekends, I went to the office to study and, sometimes, just to kill time.

Just a year and a half after V-J Day, the poignant remnants of the war had returned. The army was turning its attention to the dead. Thousands of burial boxes were dug up from cemeteries in the Pacific area and brought back to Oakland Army Base for shipment home.

Forklifts and hand trucks, manipulated by experts, worked on into the stillness of the night, plucking stacked burial boxes from the rail cars that rolled like clockwork from the morgue ships docked in San Francisco Bay. This ghoulish ballet played nightly for months, just yards from our front door. Sleep became difficult, and our men grew baggy-eyed and short-tempered under the strain. Some of the timid among us stopped using the door on the warehouse side of the barracks after dark. We were so close to the dead that conversation softened; cussing nearly died out. Beboppers played in whispers, Lewis's raging blues faded into snide whimpers, and the regular jammers felt like playing only after a drunken run on the town. Even then, the music rang false.

Veteran crane operators assigned to work on the morgue detail ended up deserting the army. MPs brought two of them back in chains. Our guitarist got in trouble in town and became a jailhouse regular.

One Sunday morning after a night in the Oakland pokey, Lewis staggered back to the barracks still in his cups and raring to get at his guitar. A staff sergeant we'd never seen before, nattily tailored and polished, stepped into our living space and made himself at home. He had simply followed the roar of Lewis's amplifier to our door. Lewis, still loaded and heedless of the nearby dead, rocked and raged. The visitor, we noticed, patted his foot with a practiced correctness, and he smiled with quiet appreciation whenever Lewis let something nice peek out from under his anger. When Lewis was finished, the visitor said coolly, "Nice, man. Real wild." Then, to nobody in particular, he asked, "You cats heard about the rerelease of the big Walt Disney flick just out?"

Lewis said, "Hell, man, we're musicians here. We don't want to hear about no fucking Mickey Mouse."

The stranger smiled and said, "This, my man, isn't your usual Mickey Mouse. I found the whole idea very hip. You got to give the white boys credit on this one. 'Progressive' musicians will dig it!"

Turning to leave, he said to Lewis, "*Fantasia* is the name of the flick. Dig it, champ; you might learn something."

Nobody among us was interested in spending another evening listening to the mournful arrival of more burial boxes. A small group of us crossed the Bay Bridge and found *Fantasia* at a San Francisco theater. When we heard Stravinsky's ballet *Rite of Spring*, a work we all knew from a recorded version that had been a favorite on our band's record player back in Cheyenne, we realized that the strange sergeant knew about "progressive." Leopold Stokowski and his Philadelphia Orchestra were a revelation. Each man among us busied himself fingering his own imaginary instrument along with the Philadelphia Orchestra.

Fantasia and its power lasted for weeks. Stravinsky's name was on everybody's lips in the barracks, and most of us saw the film several times. Another of Stravinsky's ballets, *The Firebird*, alternated with the music of Dizzy Gillespie and Charlie Parker on the record player some-one had bought in a pawnshop.

Meanwhile, I wrote to Mr. Ruffin at Lockbourne to ask about the French horn players there. My dream to play the horn was growing with each new day, and I would have done anything to be a musician again and to be at Lockbourne with Mr. Ruffin. A letter from him came back almost immediately, saying how great the band was. There were too many horn players, he said, but none were really outstanding. He urged me to try to find a horn and practice. I could come out there for an audition after my discharge in a few months. He promised to write me again and reminded me to study the USAFI high school corre-spondence courses.

I didn't have nearly enough money saved to buy an instrument to practice on, so I spent my weekends blowing all the horns in the music stores of Oakland and San Francisco, until the owners and clerks got wise that I was a blower, not a buyer. When they threw me out, I moved on and blew horns in stores in other nearby Bay Area towns. I covered them all as far south as San Jose.

Two weeks before Christmas, 1947, my eighteen-month army en-listment was over and I headed for New Haven to be with my sisters and brothers. Sister had moved there to get a job as a maid at Yale, and brought our baby sister, Yvonne, from Chicago to live with her. I moved in with them. Our baby brother, Nathaniel, was with Mary Louise and living just down the street from us. Our oldest brother, Eddie, after his army discharge, settled in an apartment across the street from Mary Louise. It felt like home again.

Sister rented one of the rooms in her apartment to Dinky Robinson, an amiable small man I liked immediately. Dinky was a Yale Medical School worker, and he got me a job as an animal caretaker at Yale's cancer research facility. They were desperate for somebody to take the job: the previous man had run off with a couple of monkeys and peddled them to a pet shop.

My boss on the new job, whose last name I never heard, was Emil. Emil was an unforgettable and totally unexpected musical windfall for me. Like Dinky, he was small, and he looked to be in his sixties. He had come from Russia and made a new home in New Haven's bustling Jewish district on Oak Street, just down the street from the medical school. As soon as he finished showing me my job—cleaning monkey, mouse, and rabbit cages—he escorted me to his little basement office so we could get acquainted. He poured me a cup of coffee from a pot on a hot plate and asked me where I'd worked before.

"I just got out of the army," I told him. He did a double take. "So young? So what job you do in army?"

"I'm a musician."

"Oh, what instrument?"

"French horn."

His face lit up, then a sly smile overtook him and he said, "OK, Mister Horn Player. You know this melody?" He puckered up and whistled a horn theme that Pete Lewis and I had listened to often on records: the "Pilgrims' Chorus" from Wagner's *Tannhäuser*. I named it, and Emil slapped his hands together rapidly two or three times in applause.

"Bravo." He was enjoying himself, and I was in no rush to start scooping up monkey shit. Before I knew it, Emil was already halfway into his rendition of Strauss's *Till Eulenspiegel*. This time I applauded him and said I wished I could play *Till* as well as that on the horn. (I couldn't.) I asked him, "How do you know all those horn solos?"

"Well, long time ago, I was horn player too—in Russian Army."

On into the week, as I went about my job feeding the animals and cleaning the cages, Emil whistled and hummed musical quizzes at me. If, over the din of monkey chatter, I'd hear a melody I didn't know, he'd shake his head and say, "Tsk tsk, you must learn that music, boychik—that composition is so-o beautiful!"

Emil was a daily reminder of just how much I would have to do to get a real music education. I couldn't put conservatories out of my mind. On my first Saturday off from work, I took the train to New York's 125th Street station in Harlem and walked over to visit the famous Juilliard conservatory at its old uptown campus. I stood around in the halls watching students carrying instruments I had never seen before and stopped outside practice rooms and eavesdropped on the strange and alluring sounds. I saw no classes on Saturday, so whatever it was that professors and students did in the conservatory classrooms remained a mystery.

Back at work, I told Emil what I'd done at Juilliard, and he grew serious. "Vasily"—Willie, in Russian—"what you plan to do with horn? You have time for practice?" I told him I had no instrument and hadn't played regularly in six months, since leaving Wyoming back when I was fifteen (letting the cat out of the bag about my true age).

I must have spoken so pridefully, and perhaps longingly, of Lockbourne and what it would mean to me to be there, that Emil said:

"Ah, it must be wun-der-ful place for colored people. But listen, sixteen years old, what's to lose if you go to your friends in Ohio? Who wants to schlepp monkey dreck when you can play beautiful music? Life is short; you should get out of here. Take a chance, for heffen's sake!" Emil's urging was music to my ears, and I decided, then and there, to take a chance.

The next morning, I was on the first bus to Columbus, dressed in my uniform, which I was entitled to wear for up to thirty days after my discharge. If I was going to reenlist and keep the corporal stripes I'd earned in Wyoming, I would have to do it within that same thirty days. I had two weeks left to play my audition and get sworn back into the army—if I could play well enough.

The Greyhound bus station in Columbus served as terminal for the military buses between town and Lockbourne. I shouldered my duffel bag and got in line with a waiting group of uniformed black men and women. Our driver, a black corporal, talked about the base with the enthusiasm of a tour guide. Since I was his only passenger carrying baggage, he pegged me as a newcomer.

"This is the Lockbourne bus, Ace. You coming with us?"

I said, "All the way, Corporal." I took a seat right behind him.

"What's your specialty, Ace?"

"Music," I said.

"Well, if old man Brice sent for you, you must be hell. He's getting the best musicians in the country here."

I said, "He didn't exactly send for me, but that's where I'm going."

"Well, you can take it from me: I heard a lot of music in my life, but Lockbourne's musicians are in the big league. Those guys got the sweet life too."

"How d'you mean?"

"They do nothing but play music all day and fly all over the country playing concerts and parades."

"Sounds about right to me," I said as complacently as a sixteen-year-old veteran two-striper could.

As we rolled through the front gate, I was struck by how spotlessly kept and immaculately landscaped the small base was. I knew I was riding on unusual real estate. Straight ahead of us was a parade field, with the soft glitter of brass tubas and trombones and silver cornets moving in neat formation but making no sound. The drone of P-47 fighter engines overhead mixed with the din of engine sounds coming from the direction of a row of airplane hangars still ahead. A commanding bass drum and the crisp rolling snap of snare drums and cymbals brought the bus passengers smilingly to life. The closer the bus got to the parade field, the stronger the pull of the drums.

"How you like em, Ace?" asked the driver as he cruised slowly up to the parade field. "You want to get off here?"

I was on the ground with my duffel bag before the bus stopped.

I immediately spotted several of my old Wyoming buddies marching by: first Sonny Wilson, the trombonist, then Leonard Perry, and—my oh my—Mr. Ruffin. He walked right past me, glanced in my direction without recognition, did a double take, then came at me running. I had to fight back my unsoldierly urge to hug him, even if he was an officer. But we had us one big long warm laugh-like-hell handshake.

"Boy, I sure am glad to see you," he said. "I wrote to you in California, saying for you to come on here for an audition, and my letter came back stamped 'Discharged.' I didn't know where to find you."

I was grinning from ear to ear. "I took a chance because I figured you all could use another rusty and out-of-practice horn player."

"Do we need horn players! Some of these guys are getting discharged soon, and what's left ain't too hot." He excused himself to trot back onto the parade field and tell Mr. Brice that he was returning to band headquarters to settle me in with a horn and a bunk. Then something happened on the playing field that I'd never seen before. As the band marched neatly in formation, rehearsing a march, the drum major blew his shrill whistle and gave the signal with his baton for the musicians to turn left to avoid a deep ditch of muddy drain water directly in front of them. Marching and playing furiously in the front row was a skinny glockenspiel player. He was playing so loud he drowned out the sound of the drum major's turn signal. Suddenly he vanished into the ditch, headfirst.

The bandleader, the famous Mr. Brice, grabbed the long, heavy marching baton out of the drum major's hand and ran for the wet GI in the ditch, swinging the baton like a club.

"Mr. Brice, please," the lad pleaded. "I didn't fall in the damn ditch on purpose!"

"Dammit, you little devil. Don't you cuss at me; I'll have you shot! Humiliating my band out here in public." The kid pulled himself out of the ditch and sprinted off.

Mr. Ruffin doubled up. The men in the band stopped playing and sat down with their instruments to laugh and watch their dignified conductor chase the glockenspielist.

"Who in the world is that crazy guy?" I asked Mr. Ruffin.

"That's Ivory Mitchell, our best piano player. And that's Warrant Officer Brice trying to catch him." Mr. Ruffin said, "Mr. Brice is crazy about that guy. But Mitchell has no discipline; he's just too plain lazy to care anything about soldiering and military deportment. He's all artist. Period. Mr. Brice says he's going to make him work and live up to his natural potential as a musician, even if he has to hang him."

How could I know at that instant that the ungainly piano player and the irate old bandleader would not only shape my own musical potential but affect my future?

Mr. Ruffin walked on with me, telling me about the base: what a special place it was and the high quality of its officers, doctors, nurses, engineers, and pilots. "Some of the most accomplished people in all of America are right here on this base. This is certainly a great place for you to spend some time, Ruff."

At the supply room door, Mr. Ruffin grinned at me and said, "Seems like we've been through this somewhere before." This wasn't Wyoming, that's for sure. The room looked like a music store. There were enough instruments in there to outfit another band, larger than the one I'd just heard.

Seeing how thrilled I was, Mr. Ruffin said, "You know this is the only band in the whole Air Corps for Negroes, don't you, son? Warrant Officer Brice knows how to get the men he wants, and here we have the best of everything."

I had heard about Mr. Brice's easy access to influential ears in Washington—ears he'd spent thirty-five years cultivating. "Yeah," Mr. Ruffin added, "I knew him back in Washington when he taught military science and history in the ROTC program at Howard University. He spent a lot of those years playing society balls and birthday concerts for the Washington big shots and especially generals and their wives. I bet he has memorized every general's wife's birthday, from Mark Clark and Omar Bradley on down. He played for them all and made lasting friendships, not just with them but with presidents too. He can call his chickens home to roost now. That's how he's been able to equip his band with the best instruments and supplies that government money can buy." He handed me a horn crafted like a piece of finely worked jewelry.

"Here, take this one. It's never been out of the case." I took the beautiful new horn, hugged it, and headed for the most remote boiler room. I wanted to be out of everybody's earshot, even Mr. Ruffin's.

The lip muscles I'd worked so hard to train in Cheyenne had lost their strength and sensitivity. Though the horn was the best I'd ever played, what tones I managed to squeeze out were puny and off key.

Mr. Ruffin stuck his head in the door a couple of times that first day. "Go at it slowly," he said to me. "Build your lip back up gradually. Remember Pete Lewis and those long tones."

I played every day, working for as long as I could stand it. While resting, I would take exploratory walks about the base and along the flight line, where I could get a close-up look at the airplanes landing and taking off. There seemed to be no hour of the day or night when the skies were empty of Lockbourne's pilots. Mechanics and engineers worked in shifts, on into the night. The lights in the pilots' lounge burned around the clock, and all along the flight line I found officers coming and going. Saluting black officers was a thrilling new experience for me; I had never seen more than a handful before Lockbourne.

As my lip grew stronger, I needed less time to rest between sessions. Instead of the walks to the airplanes, I began listening in on the band's rehearsal, next door. Seen on the podium wielding his conductor's baton in a rehearsal of symphonic music, rather than chasing after his errant pianist-glockenspielist, Mr. Brice seemed a different man. At one point he held the slim white conductor's baton with both hands, drew himself up, hurled his tall, slim frame onto an undulating rhythm, and rode the jagged syncopation like a rodeo rider. He was masterful.

A few days after my first visit to the rehearsal hall, I saw Mr. Brice lose patience with a young tuba player and yell, "Give me that damn tuba, son. For God's sake *blow* into it, don't suck on it! I can fart louder and more in tune than *that*." He played the passage on the young man's instrument. The youngster got the point and reproduced what he'd heard, matching the master perfectly. It was easy to see that Mr. Brice loved what he'd done and enjoyed his reputation for his uncanny ability to do the same with most of the other instruments in the band—except for the French horn.

After a few days, my scales and long tones started paying off. Lip muscles firmed, and the feel of the horn slowly returned. Mr. Ruffin brought music to the boiler room.

Then, on my first Sunday afternoon on the base, came the thrill of hearing the band play a concert. The hundred and twenty musicians crowded the stage of the base theater. Mr. Ruffin told me before the performance, "If you want a good seat for the concert, you better come in early, with the band. Folks can't get enough of these Sunday performances, and they fill the theater. Wait till you see that crowd." Mr. Ruffin had been right. The place was packed: families with lots of children, plenty of officers and WACs and nurses.

The audience settled down, and a pleasant, smiling captain appeared on the stage to introduce the band and boast of their credentials. Then Mr. Brice charged out, wearing his elegant full-dress conducting regalia and affecting the air of a lion tamer. With one large energetic swoop of his baton, he pulled from the band a gigantic chord that was dramatically underscored by the timpani, rolling like approaching thunder from a great distance. With small finger movements, he coaxed the rumble nearer, and with a beseeching gaze he led Elvin Jones, the timpanist, into his gradual but assertive increase. This same Elvin Jones would later join John Coltrane, to blaze trails with his drums. Then a blazing crash of lightning—the work of a man with cymbals the size of manhole covers—cleared the air and brought sunshine and the majestic and uplifting theme of the overture. Hope, optimism, and torrents of Mr. Brice's great theatrical magnetism wafted out across the footlights, and Lockbourne's proud audience glowed with pride. They had a right to be proud of their band, and I knew I'd done right to follow Emil's advice to take a chance and come to Lockbourne.

As Mr. Brice and the band worked on into the drama of the overture, I sensed a quiet movement in the theater. A tall and regal officer led a beautiful lady royally down the aisle. I'd not grown up reading the *Pittsburgh Courier* for nothing: I recognized the base commander, Colonel Benjamin O. Davis, Jr., with his bride. Maybe it was coincidence, but their entrance timed perfectly with the overture's shift to a noble theme.

The high spot of the whole concert was Tchaikovsky's First Piano Concerto, and it featured Ivory Mitchell, the ditch man. Mr. Ruffin had been right; the boy played the piano so sensationally, it was hard to believe he was the same person I'd seen on the parade field.

After the concert I went back to the boiler room, heartened by what I had witnessed and more certain than ever that I was where I belonged. I hoped with everything in me I would be good enough to stay there.

On the day of my audition, I sat nervously alone in the rehearsal hall, practicing and waiting for Mr. Brice to come from lunch to listen to me.

He stole into the hall punctually, went immediately for a chair, and said to me, "Bring your music stand and chair over here, son. I have to sit down; I've got pain in my privates." He asked me a few questions about myself, what I had done since the Wyoming band had broken up. Then he said, "Mr. Ruffin has told me about how well you did in such a short time, teaching yourself to play the horn. I commend you for sticking to it."

"I have Pete Lewis to thank for helping me along," I said.

"You couldn't have had a finer artist working with you. I wish we could have had Pete here before he retired. It's a shame he never had a chance to show what he could do. Opportunities for the musicians of our race will come someday, son, but it will only be there for those of us who are ready. You just keep getting yourself ready." He asked me to play something of my own choosing. I said I wanted to play through the major and minor scales. I had guessed right; Mr. Brice loved to see youngsters work on scales.

When I finished he said, "Pretty good, considering how long you've been off the instrument." Then he had me play several short sections of horn music from the band's regular repertoire, works I'd heard them play at the theater and in rehearsals.

Then suddenly, after I'd played for only seven or eight minutes, the audition was over. "That's enough, son. You know what you have to do. I don't have a lot of time. But as you already heard, I need French horn players. They are the weakest section in my band, and they frustrate the hell out of me. I'm going to give you a chance. But if you're lazy and don't work at it, I'm going to kick your little ass out of here. I'll be keeping my eye on you."

Somehow, it had been too simple; the most important test of my life was over, and it seemed anticlimactic. Had Mr. Ruffin told the old man our secret about my age? Was I in the band because those two old soldiers felt sorry for me? I must have sat there for a long time, fretting, before it came to me that the important thing was that I was where I wanted to be.

Mr. Ruffin drove me to headquarters in his car, got me sworn back into the army, and we were comrades again. I knew nothing could ever match the pride I had in having become a Lockbourne musician.

I've valued the teachings of my elders all my life—nobody ever had to teach me that; it came naturally. But at Lockbourne, I noticed that some of the musicians closest to my age were among the best-trained players there. I was fascinated to learn that they were all, without exception, from the North, where public schools had outstanding music programs, skilled teachers, and good instruments. Pennsylvania led the states that turned out these polished and precocious youngsters I knew.

The Lockbourne musician closest to my age was Gilbert Upshur, an eighteen-year-old trumpeter from Philadelphia. Upshur's history sounded like something out of a storybook, and Mr. Brice was so impressed with the boy that he made him the associate solo cornetist, a post he shared with a veteran musician twice Upshur's age. The solo cornetist in a military band is the equivalent of the concertmaster, the first violinist in a symphony orchestra, and he is often a "prima donna," overproud of his abilities and brimming with self-importance and arrogance. Not so with Upshur.

Gilbert Upshur . . . I envied him even the ring of his name, for who in the South is named Gilbert? Our man was all discipline and dedication. He lived for his craft, was a flawless player, cool under public scrutiny, and quietly self-assured. I admired above all the way he went about his practice. I had never heard anyone get so much from a practice book.

His daily musical calisthenics began early, and his was the first clarion to sound before breakfast each morning. While his barracks mates, still beneath the covers, fought to come awake, Upshur was up, washed, and already busy at his workouts. It was not unpleasant to lie abed a few extra moments in the dawn to listen to him begin his morning service to the trumpet.

Mr. Brice could burst with pride just hearing a finely turned Upshur solo. The old man was known to choose concert-pieces that would show off all his outstanding soloists in public. But he clearly favored Upshur in "Carnival of Venice," in which the trumpet soars through the syrupy melody before flying through a series of variations, tossed off by our man at blistering speed.

Our other virtuoso was a clarinetist, Henry Mitchell, a heavyset middle-aged man. Henry Mitchell lived off the base in Columbus with his wife. It was Upshur's success that made Henry decide to seek out the solo clarinetist in the Columbus Philharmonic Orchestra for private lessons. Once Henry's lessons began, his progress astounded even Mr. Brice. Almost every day in rehearsals, the old man found some reason to brag on Henry. He gave him extra solos in the concerts and held him up to us all as an example.

As one of seven or eight French hornists in the band, I found myself part of the weakest section there. In order to sound the least bit decent, we had to double up on each of the four parts. Even so, we were tentative and shaky. Not one of us could produce a tone on his instrument that could even blend well with the full-bodied and mature tone in Upshur's trumpet section. Mr. Brice, Henry Mitchell, and Upshur let us know that we were holding back not just the whole band but the reputation for all-around excellence that was Lockbourne's. It was frustrating for me not to have the skill to make a difference. I felt sick, and my earlier pride slowly turned to shame. I began looking around, probing for a way—any way—to improve my musicianship and my horn playing. Then all of a sudden, I got lucky.

CHAPTER NINETEEN

I Find a New Teacher

ONE NIGHT, a group of us gathered in the dayroom to listen to the Columbus Philharmonic Orchestra, whose concerts were broadcast on a local radio station. The first work on the program was the famous horn showpiece *Till Eulenspiegel*. The French hornist played the solo with verve and poetry, his tone full and secure. He was superb. All the musicians in the dayroom stopped in their tracks, checking around the room to make certain that any French horn player within earshot would take the hint and go hang himself. I didn't do that, but I got little sleep that night for thinking about the great horn playing I'd heard.

The next morning, Mr. Ruffin came into the rehearsal hall, to find me already practicing. "Ruff, did you hear that French horn player last night on the radio? Now, if we had someone like him and three or four more, we could really sound like something." Mr. Brice came in the door bragging on the horn player too; he kissed the tips of his fingers the way French people do when something is delicious. I couldn't stand it, but suddenly I knew what I had to do.

On my first payday at Lockbourne, I picked up my money and took the bus to Columbus. At concert time, I was sitting in the audience at Memorial Hall as Izler Solomon led the Columbus orchestra through a Rossini overture, a serenade for strings by Tchaikovsky, and Beethoven's Third Symphony. When the last note on the program faded out, I rushed backstage and asked the first musician I saw to point out the principal horn player.

"You want Abe Kniaz. There he is, over there."

I had been sitting in a cheap seat and was unable to see the French hornists. Now I was stunned to find a man so young in such a position. I approached him hesitatingly and said I was a horn player in the band out on the air base. We shook hands, and I asked if he would teach me. He said he would need to hear me play first, then, if he decided to take me on, we could discuss his fee. He invited me to come to his home on Saturday with my horn.

I went about my usual Lockbourne routine, saying nothing about my resolve to really become a horn player. I couldn't wait for Saturday to come.

When it finally did and I arrived for my lesson, Mr. Kniaz greeted me warmly and immediately put me at ease. He asked for details of my musical life, and in turn, I learned that he was twenty-six years old, came from Chicago, had studied at the Curtis Institute of Music in Philadelphia, and had a master's degree in music from Michigan State University. Already, he had played in symphony orchestras in Pittsburgh and Dallas.

The background briefing over, Kniaz said, "Play something you play with the band at the air base." So I played from music I had in my horn case. Then he asked me to play just any solo for the horn I liked. I ripped into the "Sam Spade" theme from a radio detective story. He laughed.

"I like that 'Sam Spade' theme a lot," he said. "It's not something I would have thought of playing for an audition—which this isn't, of course. But it is characteristic of the horn, and you played it quite well. Not a bad choice. Not bad at all."

Next he gave me music to sight-read, and as I played, he stood smiling from across the room. Then, staring at my left hand, he stopped me. "Play that again!"

I was puzzled. I knew the notes were right. I began to play.

He wrinkled his brow. "Play that phrase again."

Still confused, I played it again.

"Hold on a moment," he said. "Who told you to use those fingerings?"

"Nobody told me anything at all about the horn. I've never had a teacher, so I had to try to figure it all out for myself."

He shook his head. "My God! It's a wonder you can play anything at all like that. I've got great news for you, Willie. It really is simpler than you know."

He dragged a chair next to mine. "You do the blowing, and leave the fingering to me for now." With his fingers working my horn as I blew, my notes were suddenly and miraculously more in tune and far clearer in tone than ever before. In just a few minutes I was breaking free from the finger combinations that had shackled me since Wyoming. He then took a sheet of music paper from his desk and wrote down the proper fingerings for every note on the horn. And he went on to explain in simple and clear language, and also without making me feel like a fool, just why my own imperfect discoveries had been holding me back.

"What you've figured out for yourself is remarkable," he said, "but it's also impractical and needlessly complicated. You can't possibly play in tune that way. Acoustically impossible!"

After about an hour, he told me what I desperately wanted to hear. "OK, I'll take you on as a student. It will mean starting from the beginning, obviously." I said I was prepared for that.

He thought a moment. "Tell me, are the other French hornists in your air base band better than you are?"

"Yessir," I said. "That's why I'm here."

"So you want to get better. Is that right?"

"Just as good as I can get."

"OK, you've come to the right place. I charge my students five dollars for lessons. If that suits you, you can come back next Saturday at the same time." Then he wrote down the name of a book of horn studies for me to buy at a downtown music store. I took out my wallet to pay him his five dollars, but he stopped me and said the first lesson was on the house. "You can start paying next week." I was certain that the help I was going to get with the symphony man each week was going to be worth every bit of the cost, even if it was twenty percent of my monthly GI salary.

As the weeks passed, lessons with Mr. Kniaz grew longer. I was paying for an hour's lesson, but he usually kept me there more than two hours. We worked through the book of studies he'd prescribed, spending a lot of time on technical problems of range, breathing, the proper use of the diaphragm, and tone.

"In your private practice at the air base, work on these little things," he said. "Be aware of them, no matter how small. They add up quickly." Every Saturday I returned to Lockbourne a much improved horn player and a prouder musician.

Mr. Ruffin, the only one who knew I was taking lessons, tracked my progress in the practice room. One day he found me playing from the first-horn part of our band music, and he seated himself to help me through the tricky passages. "You ought to take this music to your lessons, so your teacher can coach you. That's the way to make real progress and make those lessons pay off. Before you know it, you'll be good enough to sit in that first chair."

After I had been studying with Abe Kniaz a couple of months, he suggested that I begin to come later in the afternoon. That would make me the last of the several students he taught each week. I was happy to do that. After we finished the lesson, Abe's wife, Judy, prepared snacks (Chicago-style delicatessen!), and the three of us sat and ate and exchanged stories. But the real reason he had asked me to stay longer into the afternoon soon became obvious. At an earlier lesson, I had made reference to a problem I was having with homework for my night school English class on the base. And even before that, he had sometimes tactfully corrected an error in my grammar. Sitting around that afternoon, munching on sandwiches and cookies, Mr. Kniaz talked about the need for professional musicians to make a good impression wherever they might find themselves. And as a professional, I would certainly find myself in educated company.

"Are you not out of your league, educationally, at Lockbourne?" he suddenly asked me. I had to admit that I was.

"Well, along with learning your craft and becoming a first-rate musical artist, Willie, you need to get as much education as possible. Above all, learn to speak correctly. I hope you won't mind my offering to correct your speech during our time here in the lessons." He had my solid assurance that all corrections and suggestions were invited and welcome.

Until they met me, the Kniazes, like most of the other citizens of Columbus, had not known how and why an all-black military facility had become their neighbor. That Lockbourne was America's only all-black military post was news to them. Segregation was a fact of life in America and taken for granted in most facets of life. Certainly the army never made a public announcement that Lockbourne had been created to accommodate the most accomplished, best-educated community of Negroes in America because normal military society couldn't assimilate them.

The more the Kniazes and I got to know one another, the more we talked about the "race problem" as it affected me as a Negro and them as Jews. The challenge and response to being an underdog in our society seldom receded from its central place in our conversations. And when eventually they learned how old I was, about my family situation and how proudly placed I was at Lockbourne, the young couple doubled their efforts in helping me get the education they knew I needed and wanted so badly.

CHAPTER TWENTY

Becoming a Duo

IN 1948, a few months into my Lockbourne tutorials and my Saturday mealtime quizzes with the Kniazes, I took and passed all the tests for the high school equivalency diploma. That June, Lincoln High School in Evansville printed my name on the graduating-class list. My very first diploma came to me in the mail at Lockbourne.

Proud to be a high school graduate, I put in more practice time in the boiler room and intensified my efforts to become a professional French horn player.

One evening, while working on the horn in the main rehearsal hall, I looked up from the music stand, and there stood Ivory Mitchell, listening to my playing. But most of his attention was fastened on the way I was tapping my right foot to keep time. With some amusement in his southern voice, he said, "How would you like to learn to play the bass?" Perhaps he had seen me fooling around with one of the bass fiddles lying around the practice room.

"Sure," I said, wondering how he knew how to play the bass.

"I noticed you've got good time by the way you pat your foot."

"You play bass too?" I asked.

"I'm not a bass player, if that's what you mean. But Boswell, our best bass player, got discharged just before you came to the band. We used to play together a lot, and I learned where the notes are on the instrument by watching him and Proctor, our other good bassist. I can show you if you're interested."

I'd already heard Ivory play jazz piano, and it was clear that his real musical enthusiasm was rooted in that music. Naturally, I jumped at the chance to learn to play with the young genius giving out the invitation. We took a bass and went to the piano. He found a piece of blackboard chalk and marked the strings and fingerboard as guides to the notes I would have to find. When I'd fooled around by myself with the bass, I'd not played long enough to hurt my fingers. But now, plucking along through his long lessons was painful and made my fingers swell. Still, he taught me the B-flat-major, the C-major, and the F-major scales by having me match my swelling fingers to the appropriate chalk marks.

My fingers were on fire, but I could find something close to scales and had memorized the chalk marks, so we rubbed them off the instrument. Then he said, "OK now, let's play the blues."

"Are you crazy?"

"Don't get excited, now. I'll call out the notes, and you just listen carefully to me and play what I tell you." At first, I was so badly out of tune that my notes didn't fit what he played. We both cringed a lot, and every chance I got, I shook my fingers in the air to cool them down. Then some real notes began to come through my pitiful thumping, and a new world of music slowly came into focus.

The next day, when I'd finished my work on the horn, Ivory and I went back to duo practice. He was getting more daring with the notes he wanted me to play on the bass, notes that sounded strangely modern along with the thick harmonies he constructed on the piano. Somebody in the band came to listen to us one day and said we were playing "progressive" jazz. I knew I'd never heard any of the other bass players produce notes like those Mitchell had dreamed up to make our two instruments sound like a complete band. Ivory had a natural and sophisticated harmonic sense, and we put it to good use.

As we ended our session late on the second night, he said to me, "Meet me here tomorrow evening after chow, and I'll show you how to play 'All the Things You Are.'" Charlie Parker's version of the song was so popular among modern-jazz fans that no band went on the stage without it in their repertoire.

"Oh, yes," Mitchell added from the door. "I forgot to tell you. Mr. Brice and the concert band is featured on a weekly radio show in Columbus. Colonel Davis likes the band having that kind of exposure in the community. Next Saturday, you and I are going to play on the show. We'll play 'All the Things You Are' and learn a couple other things." Half of me felt like jumping for joy, but the half with the blistered fingers, facing the terrible task of learning all that music on a new instrument, panicked. Before I could protest, Mitchell was out the door.

In the days we had left to work up the numbers in our radio show, the two of us spent all our free time working together. I took his orders as cheerfully as I could, listened carefully, and it began to work. We soon decided that we liked each other enough to build up a repertoire and we kept working beyond the radio show. We were typical sixteen- and nineteen-year-old boys, dying to clown, run foot races, stage water fights, and box each other. We developed the idiotic game of "sneak the bolo": one man would sneak up behind the other to slam an overhand jolt to the shoulder—blows into which we threw all our weight and power. I should have known better. I was outweighed and outpowered and could only stay in the game by treading quietly to sneak up behind him and gain the advantage of surprise.

Even though I made a mistake in "All the Things" on the radio, for which I got a paralyzing shoulder bolo plus a choking, the radio people invited us back as regulars. And though Mr. Kniaz's homework for the horn lessons took most of my time, I *made* time to rehearse the new duo material with Mitchell every day and most nights. Soon we were playing jobs for money. That felt so good and sounded so classy we vowed that someday, as civilians, we would become a professional duo.

I learned that one of the things Ivory Mitchell held back about himself— and he was secretive—was that he didn't use Junior after his name. His father had given him his own proud moniker. But Mitchell said he dropped the tag because, "People are always telling me, 'Ivory isn't your real name. You just call yourself that because you play the piano. It's a stage name, like Ivory Joe Hunter.' " He said, "Hell, I don't even like Ivory-damn-Joe Hunter's piano playing, so why would I want his fucking name?"

Having grown up in Dunedin, on the west coast of Florida, Mitchell had a small-town southernness that was similar to mine. The Baptist Church had shaped us, we'd both been taught mostly by proud and accomplished black women schoolteachers in small segregated schools and raised on good southern cooking in one-parent households during most of childhood. But there the similarities ended; the home lives that had developed and dictated who we had become were light-years apart. He'd been raised by his divorced father, a model provider with a steady job driving the city garbage truck. As an only child, he had all his father's attention and concern, but he complained of the senior Ivory's domineering personality and unbending demands, delivered to the boy at volumes that drove him stone-deaf at six or seven. No physical damage to the ears; he simply switched them off.

Another glaring difference between us showed itself in the nature of our musical gifts. He was the textbook example of the naturally gifted music child: the savant. He said he'd played on his baby chair as if it were a piano, even before he learned to walk. Soon after he could steady himself on his baby pins, he'd simply pull himself off the floor, walk to the piano, and play it. Period. His was a musical childhood un-cluttered by the tedium of penitential instruction at the hands of tyran-nical piano teachers: no scales, finger drills, or the other musical exercises children love to hate. All these dreary services to the Muses he'd ignored.

Mr. Brice couldn't stand the fact that of all the men in his 766th Air Corps Band, it was his piano soloist who had the largest gift yet was the most difficult to inspire to a seriousness toward the musical studies the old soldier thought such a gift demanded. There was a running battle between the two. Mitchell fell in ditches, wore the sloppiest uniform in the band, saluted as if he were swatting flies, would run off to avoid taking GI shots with the rest of us. What was worse, he seemed never to give music a second thought, until he sat down at the piano and played the keys off it. These quirks and lapses sent Mr. Brice into fits, and he punished my friend with sentences of backbreaking hours on the coal pile, firing the barracks furnaces; KP duty washing pots and pans; and the mindless drudgery of picking up trash outside the barracks. None of it did any good.

Mr. Brice, no doubt about it, was a hater: he detested anything that smacked of a musical standard less than the perfection of the professional.

Every Thursday night was Lockbourne Amateur Night at the base theater. Good comedians, dancers who could burn up a stage, a magician, an unbelievable acrobat, and a number of girl singers from the WAC unit always packed the house. Somehow, word of the Thursday night shows reached Washington, and a group of show business colonels got the idea that such a show would be a sensation on a national tour of military posts.

That was an idea Mr. Brice hated with gusto. He'd taken it as his mission to build a symphonic ensemble to rival the prestigious all-white Army Air Corps Band in Washington. "Those damn lowbrow Washington trashy-assed colonels can't stand the idea of a black symphonic band here. No, you're not supposed to be getting too uppity and playing 'white folks' music.' They want to keep the big official service bands in Washington lily white. That's 'cultural' as long as we can't get in it. You black boys are just supposed to sing and buckdance and crack jokes and slap your goddamn thighs and bust out laughing all over the stage. Hell no, I won't have my musicians playing in anybody's GI minstrel show."

Our bandleader, much like Sergeant Display back at Fort Mc-Clellan, was constantly pulling our coats to the way things stacked up in our world. He lost no opportunity to instruct us on the state of our art by tossing us startling bombshells from his rich teacher's arsenal.

One morning we were working hard at a rehearsal for an upcoming concert, the centerpiece of which was Dvořák's famous Symphony no. 9, "From the New World." I was having the time of my life sitting smack in the midst of all that sound, listening to all those sensational down home themes rebounding around the room and all over the ensemble. Mr. Brice conducted with a firm hand, correcting us where we needed it and coaching the ensemble through the heavy spots with his characteristically thorough rehearsal style. Then we came to the symphony's mournful Adagio movement, the famous "Going Home" melody, which we played right up to the movement's most poignant climax. At that point Mr. Brice dramatically cut us off midphrase, sat himself down on the stool on the podium, and said:

"Now, gentlemen, every person in this room has a close connection with this symphony. But this movement's main theme is something you feel in a special way because it goes to the heart of something deep within you that you cannot deny. You couldn't keep yourselves from feeling it even if you tried. Such is the power of music to express the true soul of a people. But feeling it is not enough. I programmed this symphony to play at our next concert here on the base because our audience—every man, woman, and child in it—has the same close connection with the music, and will feel it the way you do.

"I insist that you know and understand why this Adagio sounds the way it does, because it is important not only to the way you play the music; it is important to who you are.

"In 1893, Dvořák came to New York to head the National School of Music, and among his most gifted composition students was a Negro musician, Will Vodrey, a first-class composer and arranger, who could do it all. Another of Dvořák's black musical colleagues, Henry T. Burleigh, was a prominent organist and a specialist in the performance of the great spirituals. Burleigh became Dvořák's close friend, and he helped educate the Czech master on the subject of Negro music and introduced him to the wealth of musical material that grew out of our people's story in America. This movement is a distillation of the essence of the great Negro spiritual. Now that you have some idea of the origins of the notes on the paper before you, let's play this movement once again from the top. Watch your intonation, and listen always to your neighbor." Coming to his feet again, he rapped his baton on his music stand and gave us the grave downbeat, and the "New World" Symphony became a different composition for every musician in the room.

When it was time to perform the symphony on that Sunday's afternoon concert in Lockbourne's theater, our audience read in the program notes, which Mr. Brice had written himself, all the things he'd told us in rehearsal. That classical music would have the power to go straight to the spirit and heart of Lockbourne's population, reflecting the strength of our culture, was for me a strong reaffirmation that I had chosen a discipline with real meaning and importance.

Music was filling my days from early-morning bugle call to past taps late at night. I was busy with Mr. Brice and classical music; there were the lessons in town with Mr. Kniaz and the copious hours of practice to prepare the studies he assigned me each week; then at night, Mitchell and I worked on duo material. Even that was not enough—I longed for more.

A t about this time, everybody in the band noticed Mr. Brice getting more testy than usual. He complained more often of gnawing pains. "Hand me a stool, son," he'd say at a rehearsal as he rubbed between his legs. "I'll have to sit down and conduct. My nuts hurt."

But the distraction of the Washington brass pushing for their national variety show gave the old musician more pain than his physical complaints. A flamboyant Broadway-type officer, a Colonel Goetz, head of Air Corps special services and entertainment in Washington, was Mr. Brice's chief worry. Goetz was always underfoot, pretending to understand the conservatory Mr. Brice ran for his youngsters—his desire to project serious music as a calling that young Negroes might aspire to. Mr. Brice felt certain that Lockbourne and his band could be a beginning. All the while, Goetz had a whole stage production planned in his head for the dancing girls, musicians, and comedians. But in order to really pull it off, he needed an orchestra, an orchestra that could play jazz.

Mr. Brice went on with his symphonic music-making while hating everything Colonel Goetz stood for. But suddenly his illness worsened, and Major Marchbanks, our excellent flight surgeon, told us that the gnawing at Mr. Brice's privates was leukemia.

Mr. Ruffin and Proctor, the best-educated musician we had, took over the conducting duties, while Mr. Brice was hospitalized; they organized classes and consulted with Mr. Brice daily on how to keep us busy. We worked in classes on ear training and were assigned more detailed section rehearsals. We learned new and more challenging music. Mr. Ruffin said that his instructions from Mr. Brice were to "work hell out of those boys at the music and keep that tight-assed Washington trash away from them. When I get out of this damn hospital I'm going to take my concert band to Washington to show them what we can do, and I don't want all my first-chair men, my best piss-cutters, Upshur and Henry Mitchell, going off playing with some goddamn coon show."

One Saturday while Mr. Brice was still in the hospital, I was in town for a lesson with Mr. Kniaz. As I unpacked the horn, he said, "Willie, do you remember that when we first began, I asked you about the horn players in the air base band? You said they all played better than you and that was why you wanted to study and get better."

I said, "I remember."

"Are they still better than you are?"

"No."

"Then our work is done. You don't need me anymore."

The remark startled me, and I said, "I intend to go on getting better. I may be as good as the others in *that* band, but someday I intend to play in a symphony orchestra, like you." The sound of what I'd said shocked me so much that I wanted to take it back. When had I decided on that course? Did taking on a white symphony man as my music teacher mean imitation to *that* extent? Then I got angry at myself for feeling embarrassed.

"I have to tell you, Willie," Mr. Kniaz went on in a very serious tone, "playing in a symphony orchestra is not a realistic ambition for any Negro in America yet. No professional symphony orchestra in this country has a musician of your race. You and I both know the tragedy and the shame of that. Who can say if it will ever change during our lives?"

"I understand what you're saying. Everybody at Lockbourne is aware of it too. The color bar exists for musicians just like it does for everybody else in the military; otherwise our special air base wouldn't even be there. I live with men every day who've suffered through long careers without advancement because of it. I really appreciate what you're saying to me, but music is all I have. I will not be run off from it. I want to

LEFT: Mama at age 26, before I was born.

BELOW: Willie Henry, eight years old.

ABOVE: A 1936 school picture of the elementary grades of the Sheffield High School for Colored. I'm front row center, wearing a sweater.

LEFT: Mama at age 43, the way I remember her to this day.

FACING PAGE: My Alabama "neighbors"—Helen Keller (ABOVE), and W. C. Handy (BELOW).

FACING PAGE, ABOVE: Lieutenant Colonel Benjamin Davis, Jr., on the wing of a fighter plane, with another pilot in 1943. Davis, the son of the army's first black general, later commanded Lockbourne Air Base, where I, at age 16, became a proud member of the 766th Air Force Band.

FACING PAGE, BELOW: Self-portrait of a grinning 16-year-old corporal, who snapped the picture, developed, and printed it in the recreation center darkroom at Oakland Army Base, California.

ABOVE: Lena Horne, surrounded by black flight cadets at Tuskegee in 1943.

LEFT: 353rd Army Band in Fort Francis E. Warren, Wyoming, my first military band experience. At the far left is Warrant Officer Frank Ruffin, bless him, who gave me my chance to learn the French horn.

ABOVE: The cast and band of Operation Happiness, an air force variety show commanded by Lieutenant Daniel "Chappie" James, at the far right. Chappie later became a four-star general and commander of S.A.C. I'm in the third row, third from the left. The kid who taught me to play the bass, Private Ivory Mitchell, is standing in the top row, eighth airman from the left.

RIGHT: Mutt "The Drummer" McCord, my Alabama neighbor and my first music teacher, shown here in his lieutenant's suit. We are still best buddies today.

LEFT: Another of my boyhood heroes, Joe Louis, in his wartime habit, at the Tuskegee airfield, where he was on a tour of exhibition fights to boost troop morale.

BELOW: Chief Warrant Officer John Brice, the 766th Band's taskmaster, conductor, and perfectionist, who ruled our lives with an iron hand cloaked in the gloves of an artist. One of the greatest teachers and musicians I ever knew.

ABOVE: In 1949 I was supposed to play the bass at a picnic in Peekskill, N.Y., where Paul Robeson was to be the main attraction. The picnic turned into a riot, and I was lucky to get out of there alive.

LEFT: Playing at the Playback, a club I owned in New Haven in the 1960s.

get as good as I can get now, and I'm prepared to take my chances with the future."

"All right," he said. "I just want you to understand clearly just what you are up against. And I'm going to keep reminding you. Now let's go to work."

From that day forward, I could count on all my lessons starting with that caring reminder or some variation on its theme.

Early one spring morning in 1948, word came to the band that Mr. Brice had died in his sleep. And though I sensed that an era had ended with him, it was only in the days following his death that I started to learn from the talk of the old vets in our midst just what a powerful and vital part of the generations-old khaki conservatory for black musicians he had been. I started to understand why he was so rough on Ivory Mitchell for not studying harder and refusing to take his gift more seriously, and why, one day, as punishment for crossing my legs in his rehearsal, he had snapped angrily at me. "Son," he had bellowed, "in my band I don't tolerate slouching around and leg-crossing: it looks unprofessional, and it's disrespectful to the music. You just pack your horn away and report to the mess officer. Tell him I sent you there to scrub pots and pans for two days. When you return to the band, bring a more professional attitude toward the music back with you. If you can't manage that, we can do without you."

It wasn't long after Mr. Brice's death that Colonel Goetz came back from Washington and started all over again with his plans to mount his variety show for a national tour. With Mr. Brice gone, Goetz's was the only music game in town.

Washington was solidly behind Goetz's "Operation Happiness" idea. The budget seemed unlimited, and the touring itinerary included every military installation in the U.S. that had an airstrip large enough for passenger and cargo planes to land on. Not only did the show now have a jazz orchestra; that orchestra was expanded to include a French horn—mine.

Shortly before we began our national tour, the Army Air Corps was renamed the U.S. Air Force. Then the new Air Force changed its uniforms from khaki to sky blue. Colonel Goetz persuaded the authorities to have Operation Happiness premiere the new blue uniform onstage. Though Goetz was the show's producer, the unit was put under the command of our amiable master of ceremonies, Daniel "Chappy" James, a Florida native and one of our most accomplished pilots, later to become a four-star general.

The line of chorus girls was a dozen strong, and Colonel Goetz spared none of the government's money when he ordered costumes and equipment. Our comedians got laughs with clean material, and our magician could charm the world. Suddenly we were a road show, and a damn good one.

For all of Mr. Brice's fears, Colonel Goetz presented a "family" show with a surprisingly high level of sophistication.

For me, the worst part of touring was missing a few of my lessons with Mr. Kniaz. The best part was sending postcards and letters from all over the country to my dad and to my New Haven sisters and brothers. In the year it took us to cover all the air bases, Operation Happiness represented the best-spent money the military ever put into public relations. Colonel Goetz got a promotion and the show personnel were given citations along with promotions. I, on my seventeenth birthday, became a sergeant.

During the spring of 1949, about six months after my seventeenth birthday, we were on a week-long run of Operation Happiness at air bases near San Francisco, when Ivory Mitchell's three-year enlistment came to an end. It was a moment I had dreaded for months. We all knew he would go on to great things, but I would be losing my main musical ally and bass-line inventor. Mitchell got all togged up in the new civilian clothes he'd bought, and was saying goodbye to a large crowd of well-wishers, with a taxi waiting outside. I held back from the group, to be the last one to send him off. We'd already memorized each other's family's addresses, so we could contact one another after our real formal musical training.

I saw him craning his neck around the barracks, looking for me, and I was tempted to lay my best bolo on him as a goodbye, and would have, but he caught me and threw up his dukes.

"Don't you dare! I see your little sneaking ass. Keep practicing and learn to play that bass in tune, boy. We'll surely make us a duo when we finish our conservatory training."

We touched dukes, hugged, and he was gone.

CHAPTER TWENTY-ONE

A Transfer to University

A T ABOUT THE TIME of Mitchell's discharge, President Truman made
his electrifying announcement: the United States armed services
would be integrated. We felt great about that and what it would mean
to black people everywhere in the country. At the same time, we all
knew Lockbourne was doomed, and that was heartbreaking. In a few
months, our people would be sent out to join white units, and there
would be nobody at Lockbourne whose life would not be touched in
some way by the impending move.

Those of us with military-career leanings braced ourselves for the
unknown. Reassignment to mixed units would inevitably have its problems. Some of our people had never, in their entire lives, lived, worked,
gone to school, or worshiped with white people. I was one of them,
and we were probably in the majority. What about Colonel Davis?
Would he be given another base to command? Our extremely gifted
medical staff faced untold uncertainties. Our own sergeant, Mal Whit-
field, had the year before won a gold medal in the Olympics for the
800-meter race. What would happen to him?

A number of our officers began resigning their commissions, to pick up where they had left off during the war. Some went to law schools, others to medical, dental, and business schools. Enlisted men and women, however, could not resign. For us it meant serving the remainder of our time wherever the Air Force chose to send us.

Mr. Ruffin called me into his office one day. "Ruff," he said, "have you ever thought about becoming a career officer?" I had once expressed such an interest, but now I wasn't so sure. Events had moved awfully fast, and I was confused.

"It's now possible," he went on, "for enlisted men whose IQ scores are high enough to be appointed directly to West Point, providing they have a recommendation from their commanding officer. You can qualify, and as the commander of this band, I can write a letter for you."

I knew I was not ready for West Point, and I knew it would be years before I could get enough musical education to ever consider being a warrant officer and bandmaster. I thanked Mr. Ruffin and said I would like to keep his offer in mind while I considered other, civilian schools. When I had talked about my future to Mr. Kniaz, he had mentioned the Curtis Institute in Philadelphia. Some of the men on the base suggested applying to the Paris Conservatory. I still thought about Juilliard.

One day at a lesson, Mr. Kniaz showed me the horn part of a composition by a German composer, Paul Hindemith. Kniaz had become a devotee of Hindemith's music while a student at Curtis. A few days later, browsing through a jazz magazine, I saw an interview in which the king of modern jazz, Charlie Parker, also praised Paul Hindemith and his music. Parker, in response to the question "How would you like most to spend the next few years?" had said he would like to drop everything and enroll at Yale University to study composition with this little German cat, Hindemith. Mr. Kniaz hadn't mentioned that Yale and Hindemith were connected. At my next lesson, I told him what I had read.

"It's true," Mr. Kniaz said. He thought a moment, then said, "Maybe we should consider Yale as a possibility for you. I know another composer there, Alvin Etler, who also directs Yale's band. I'll write you a letter of recommendation." The more I thought of going to college while living at home with my sisters and visiting my friend and former boss, Emil, the better I liked the idea. I wrote for the Yale School of Music catalogue.

M eanwhile, everything was breaking up at Lockbourne. Sometimes literally. Late one night, past midnight, a thunderous explosion hit the flight line a hundred yards from the band barracks, jarring the entire base awake. A searing hot light lit up the night, and screaming fire trucks raced to the shimmering glow. One of our pilots had landed his P-47 on top of another plane on the runway, and both planes exploded, killing their pilots.

Fatal plane crashes had not been rare at Lockbourne during my two years there. The band kept a special version of Chopin's Funeral March on the shelf. We had marched to its somber chords from the chapel to the main gate behind more hearses than I like to remember. But during those difficult last months before the base closed, crashes seemed like one more manifestation of our end. Our comfortable segregated little world was dissolving. Stress was in the streets. Men fought each other for little or no reason. Wives of prominent officers showed up in public carrying the scars of home battles. I swore that if another pilot drilled a hole in the sod, or burned his plane on the runway, I was going AWOL. I couldn't take another Chopin Funeral March.

Mr. Ruffin soon got his moving orders and left Lockbourne for Alaska, along with twenty-eight men to make a band. My real life with the horn had begun with him. He'd given me my chance to make a career for myself, and seeing him leave made me feel as if my last real father figure was vanishing.

Other players joined white bands all over the country. What was left of our band was pitiful. We all assembled on our own one day just to play a little music for the fun of it. It was one of the saddest sounds I ever heard. Too many of Mr. Brice's leading protégés were gone. It could have been a band of junior high school beginners.

One day, orders came for us to vacate the buildings the band had occupied since the base was formed. We were assigned space in cramped quarters on the other side of the field. All the equipment Mr. Brice had fought for for his musicians was padlocked. After days of watching our musical world crumble, I told myself, "To hell with hanging around a sinking ship," and decided right then to get out of the service. The challenge would be to leave legally and preserve my educational benefits under the GI Bill.

I wrote to Yale for an application, and after a few days a letter arrived with instructions for me to come to New Haven for written tests and an audition. I dared not make any mention of my plans to anyone but Mr. Kniaz. Several months earlier, he had sold me a nearly new horn for $225, the largest purchase of my life. I played it for a few days, then sent it home to my sister Velma for safekeeping. Now, for the Yale audition, I had my own horn.

I still hadn't learned about getting used to an unfamiliar instrument before attempting to play an important audition, and my playing at Yale wasn't great. I was lucky to have a good examiner in Keith Wilson, a thirty-two-year-old professor and, I was later to learn, one of the world's truly great clarinetists. He made allowances for my shaky audition and saw something in me he felt he should encourage. Thanks to his effectiveness in convincing a reluctant faculty at the School of Music that I deserved a chance, I was admitted.

Though I returned to Lockbourne with an official letter of acceptance from Yale, the road back to New Haven was uncertain. Officially, I had another year left of my three-year enlistment in the Air Force. My only chance of getting out was to prove a hardship at home. Hardship discharges were not too uncommon. On the books, I did quite legitimately have two dependents: Nathaniel and Yvonne had been my dependents since my first enlistment, when I claimed them in Camp Stoneman. Part of my pay was deducted each month, and all during my service days the children got a small allotment check. Now I would have to show the Air Force that they needed me at home.

Although it was always available, I had never had reason to call on the chaplain's office for help of any sort. But if ever I needed a man of the cloth, it was now. The morning after I got back from New Haven, I made an appointment with our chaplain, a new major on the base. I had admired the new man's services for their brevity, but never did I expect to see his office.

The major was an easygoing gentleman, whose friendly manner helped to put me at ease. Business in his office had picked up for him since the integration order came. I explained about my young siblings and their need to have a big brother around. He listened well, but it was clear that I didn't have all his attention.

"Sir," I said, now feeling a little panicky, "in addition to needing to be with those children, I need to get me an education, and I've already been accepted to college."

"Oh? What college?" he asked.

"Yale's School of Music."

He came to his feet, flashing a very unpreacherly grin, whacked his desktop with his fist, and said, "No shit, son?"

A little taken aback, I said, "Uh, no shit, sir!" and went into my shirt pocket and showed him my acceptance letter on the Yale letterhead. He took it and read it through.

Still chuckling, he handed back the letter and said, "Well, this is a coincidence. I graduated from the Yale Divinity School."

When he'd finished questioning me about my plans, he told me how much he had admired Mr. Brice and said he could imagine what it must be like for all the young fellows Mr. Brice had trained, now that the old man was gone. Then he looked hard at me. "Take some advice from an old dog, young fellow. You are very fortunate to have been a part of this whole Lockbourne experience. What you take from this base and its story, and from Mr. Brice, should have made you stronger. Our people are standing at a crossroads right now. We're going to need that strength, all of us. Use what you've learned at Lockbourne, take it with you to New Haven. You will damn sure need it.

"Remember," he went on. "Take advantage of as much as you can *outside* of music at Yale. It would be a sin to learn just one thing in so rich an intellectual environment. Music is fickle, you know, and Jim Crow ain't going to lay down and die because Mr. Brice taught you a thing or two and you bought an instrument and got yourself into an Ivy League school. Bless your heart, son, my hat is off to you. When do you want to leave for New Haven?"

"Whenever it can be arranged, sir."

The chaplain picked up the telephone, called the base adjutant, and explained my situation. "When can we ship him out?" There was a pause. "Hold on and I'll ask him." He put his hand over the mouthpiece.

"Is three o'clock soon enough for you to get out of here?"

"Today?" I gasped.

"Hell yes, man. Time waits for no one. Good luck, God bless you, son, and give em hell in New Haven!"

PART THREE

New Haven

CHAPTER TWENTY-TWO

At the Robeson Riot

NEW HAVEN SEEMED a different place now that I was there as a civilian with a purpose. I moved in again with Sister. Once I got settled, one of my first visits in town was with my old boss Emil, still with the monkeys at the medical school. He was really happy that things were turning out well for me after I'd followed his advice and gone on to Lockbourne.

Sister, Mary, and her kids, along with our little sister and brother and our oldest brother, Eddie Howard, all lived in the same block. They made me feel so much at home that it seemed like Alabama again in some ways. Nathaniel and Yvonne, healthy and happy children, were students at the Hamilton Street School, a neighborhood public school situated behind a huge Catholic church just across the street from Sister's apartment. It had been a parochial school until a few years earlier, and when the city took it over, the nuns who'd taught there were asked to stay on. We never imagined Mama's babies thriving on the teaching of nuns, whom they both adored.

I was wondering if I would thrive on what awaited me, a few blocks away at Yale, in three months. Even with that much lead time, I had my work cut out for me. There was daily practicing to do, along with the academic catching up that was heavy on my mind: I had nightmares about having to compete with Yale's prep school crowd, who would be miles ahead of me. Still, I found time to listen to world-class jazz stars who played in New Haven. Billie Holiday, Miles Davis, and Erroll Garner all came to Lillian's Paradise, a local nightspot close to Sister's apartment. New Haven also had its own outstanding jazz players, and as soon as I started going to jam sessions I found ready work among them. Bass players who could sight-read show music and play in tune, with a strong, steady beat, could keep busy around town. I was getting bass jobs playing floor shows, dances, and stag parties even before I had time to buy an instrument.

All the musicians I met said I should buy a bass from Frank DiLeone, a bass-maker who had a shop in the Italian neighborhood where we lived. It was said that nothing pleased him more than helping bass students choose an affordable instrument.

His shop was a crazy but congenial place, crammed full of brand-new bass fiddles he'd built, along with several fine old ones made centuries ago by earlier Italian masters. I listened to this man covered with sawdust; he was talking in Italian with several other musicians while he worked. I then introduced myself as a new student at Yale's School of Music, a bassist and horn player, and watched the warm glow come into his eyes. I picked up a nearby bass and tried it out. I played "All the Things You Are" the way Mitchell had taught it to me.

"Nice bass; you play nice too," he said graciously. Then he showed me the instrument I ought to have. "I make him myself. He's a strong, and a loud like a sonovabeech!" he boasted. It also had a gorgeous varnish finish. For seventy-five bucks (with student discount), I was in business with the newest ax in town, making the rounds of the gin mills of New Haven.

One day not long after I had acquired my bass, I got a call from a drummer I had played with at a jam session. "Look, man, my group has this little gig, and my bass player's ax ain't too hip, dig? The gig pays thirty-five clams. All the cats're talking about the new ax you copped from DiLeone. They say it's nice, man, real *nice*, dig? You want to rent my bassman your ax for twelve clams?" I liked this drummer, especially his bebop vernacular, because it was current with the way Lockbourne's and New York's hipsters talked. "Gig," the modern jazz-man's linguistic invention for "paid engagement," later filtered down to the symphony crowd. Now the term is standard usage far beyond the music world, even among the Harvard Business School set.

That drummer's offer sounded reasonable, and I said he could pick up the bass in an hour. But I didn't know Sister had overheard the phone conversation. I took one look at her after I'd put down the phone and knew there was going to be trouble.

"Why can't they hire *you* to play the bass," she said, "instead of renting it to some tramp-assed bum that's too trifling to own his own?" Sister had got wise to up-north slick ways. She went on and on about how I should know enough to be careful about that sort of thing and not get taken in by "sharks." She made a convincing case, but I said I didn't have the drummer's phone number to call him back to get out of the deal. "To hell with him and his sorry-assed bass player too! Just tell him *no* when he gets here." I said I would be too embarrassed to back out on my word.

"Well, it sure as hell won't embarrass me. I'll tell him myself!" I took a walk. I had no stomach for what that poor unsuspecting bebopper was walking into.

A week or so later, I saw the drummer at another jam session, and instead of being angry with me, he was full of smiles and praise for my sister. "Man, I sure did dig your sister. She is right on your case, baby. The way she was looking out for you knocked me out! Damn, man, our people oughta look out for each other like that more often. She said, 'That bass is not leaving this house unless my brother is playing it.' Then she put her hand on her hip, and she looked me in the eye and said, 'I'm sorry, mister, but that's the way it is!' Oh, wow!" the drummer exclaimed. "That *gassed* me, man."

Another time, later that summer, Sister relented on a particular bass rental. I convinced her this transaction was special. And it was. Slam Stewart, one of my idols (he'd played with the Benny Goodman Trio and made some great records with Goodman, Gene Krupa, and Teddy Wilson and later with Charlie Parker and Dizzy Gillespie), had a Sunday night off from a Boston club, and he was coming to play at Lillian's

Paradise. The club's owner, Mrs. Lillian Lumpkin, had heard of my new DiLeone, which was getting a good name in the jazz joints around town. Would I rent the ax to Slam? When I told Sister who Slam was and that he'd written a song Mama had loved to dance to, "Flat Foot Floogee with the Floy, Floy," she softened but offered a condition: Slam could use my bass if I went to the gig and stood bodyguard. "You can't be too careful, Willie Henry." Sister was even starting to look like Mama.

It was like being in bass heaven, just listening to the great Slam Stewart bowing my own loud, strong, seventy-five-dollar DiLeone plywood bass.

The best jazz jobs in town for us locals were at the Monterey, on Dixwell Avenue, in the heart of New Haven's black business and entertainment district. The owner was a retired dancer, Mr. Rufus Greenlee. A natty, sophisticated man who always dressed like the artist he was, Mr. Greenlee had danced all over the world in a team known as Greenlee and Drayton, a suave and serious act. Their team had been the first black vaudeville stars not required to perform as "tramp acts" on the American stage: that is, to dress in the degrading attire of shiftless hobo "darkies." Mr. Greenlee stuck out his chest and pointed his chin toward the ceiling when he spoke of those days. "We had a *class act*, and we *always* worked in white tie and tails on *all* the stages, at home and abroad!" The two men's pictures appear now in all the good books on the history of black theatrical greats. And he could still dance that summer of 1949, when I was his main man on bass. Often, I'd go to the club early to practice a few minutes and warm up before the rest of the band got there. He liked seeing me come early: "a true sign of the professional," he would say, with a wink and a nod. But he would always stand around and listen to me play the bass, and he'd watch my hands as I played. If I got a nice beat going, Mr. Greenlee would move a table or two to make room and join me for a duet, with him performing a dance number he called "walking." He'd start moving with elegant steps, the simplest rhythmic flow coursing through his dancing frame, as he swore out loud that all he was doing was "walking, man, just walking." I loved it when he danced along with my bass. Mr. G. must have been about seventy-five then, but he could do any kind of dance, even the rock-and-roll dances that were just emerging.

Other things going on that summer were not as lighthearted as the walking dance. It was the beginning of the Joe McCarthy era, and New Haven literally buzzed with Communist Party recruiting activities. Few in our crowd could tell a Communist from an Episcopalian. I was astounded to see Yankee versions of Alabama chitlin struts, run by party members. Many of their "affairs," organized on the order of rent parties, were put on after hours, when the regular drinking establishments were closed.

One Saturday night while I was on the bandstand at the Monterey, the same drummer Sister had laid out about renting my bass hired me to play for a picnic in Peekskill, New York, the next afternoon. He didn't mention who the sponsor was; transactions for jazz work are seldom cluttered with such nonessentials. Time, place, and pay covers it. Our quartet would travel in the drummer's car to this park where the picnic was to be held.

Some picnic it turned out to be! We rolled into the park, and the first thing I noticed was that the state police outnumbered the civilians. A trooper at the main gate looked into our car, saw the bass, and waved us on to the bandstand, in an open area. By the time we started playing the first number, a distracting noise from the direction of the entry gate drowned us out. We heard rumbles and roars from a crowd far away. At first we couldn't make out the sounds. Then it began to hit us: "Send Robeson back to Russia! Send Paul Robeson back to Russia! No nigger Reds in Peekskill! Get the kikes out too!" The sound grew louder and more menacing. We stopped playing. Nobody in the band had known that Paul Robeson was on the bill with us.

A cruising state trooper came to the bandstand and told us that Robeson had been stopped by a veterans group and prevented from entering the park.

The noise from that unruly mob kept coming closer. A bunch of them, thinking Robeson had already entered and was on the bandstand, approached us from the opposite direction. These citizens charged our perch, shouting and cussing, their eyes blazing. I saw a rock go through the bass drum. A hurled metal trash can knocked several keys from under the piano player's fingers. I grabbed my bass and streaked off the bandstand at a speed Jesse Owens would have envied. I headed for the woods, using Mr. DiLeone's instrument as my shield. Rocks and flying bottles bouncing off the bass's sides and back made a terrible racket. I added speed and dived with the big bass fiddle into a lush thicket, out of harm's way. I never did see Paul Robeson, or the thirty-five dollars I was promised for the job.

On the evening radio news the next day, I learned that the Peekskill riot had had greater significance than was apparent. Robeson, whose passport was under suspension by the State Department, said in press interviews that he would make the riot a rallying point for him and his fight for his freedom to travel and for the freedom of all his people: "I will go back to Peekskill." And he did, later, under the watchful protection of bodyguards from several New York trade unions, but without our little band.

An exhaustive check by Mr. DiLeone revealed that only the varnish and a couple of rock dents needed touching up. "See, I told you," he said. "I make him strong! You tell a that goddamn communista drummer, go scratch his ass!" And with a wagging finger pointed at me, he offered one last piece of wisdom:

"And you keep away from the wrong crowd!" The repair and the advice were on the house.

CHAPTER TWENTY-THREE

"Dress British, Think Yiddish"

AFTER LABOR DAY, the sleepy Yale campus, situated in the heart of New Haven, shook itself vigorously to life. It was an extraordinary school year. A lot of veterans were mixed in with the regular young students. Combat boots and khakis stood out in stark contrast to the tweed jackets and rep ties of the big eastern prep schools. This, it seemed to me, was a dynamite expression of the times, and I reveled in it. One day early in the semester, a white fellow with red hair, carrying a bassoon case, bolted through the door of the music building. Almost busting into me, he introduced himself as Bill Skelton. As we got into conversation, it came out that we were both there on the GI Bill. Soon he was introducing me to other veterans who'd come there, like me, for the express purpose of studying with the great Hindemith. Everybody ended up exchanging war stories. I was one of the few there with a discharge but no adventures to lay on them. One fellow asked me where I'd served and with what outfit. I was cool and said I'd just left a special base in Ohio, Lockbourne, where the Ninety-ninth Fighter Pursuit Squadron was stationed. Bill Skelton's mouth flew open. He grabbed me around the shoulders.

"Oh my God," he said. "Those are the guys who saved my ass more than a dozen times! I flew bombers in the Eighth Air Force from England over Germany, and those pilots were always in the air to meet us and escort us to our targets in Germany and take us back home to England again after we'd dropped the bombs. They shot the German fighter planes out of the air before they ever got close to us. And I want to tell you—we never lost a single plane while under their escort."

It was the same old story I'd heard so often, but I never expected to hear it from the mouth of a white music student who'd actually flown the bombers.

"Those pilots were stationed somewhere in Italy," Skelton said. "We never saw them on the ground, but they were some flying sons of bitches! I even heard they sank a destroyer, and *no* fighter plane pilots ever did that before, or since. I'd sure as hell love to meet some of those men someday. Jesus! Is it ever a small world."

Bill Skelton was a very likable fellow and became a special friend of mine at Yale. He also had my respect as a musician; he could blow the varnish off that bassoon.

Even before I had attended all my classes, I got the good news from Professor Wilson that I had been hired to play horn in the New Haven Symphony Orchestra. I'd been hoping for the practical experience of playing with a real symphony orchestra and not just a student group. Professor Wilson would also be my horn teacher, and I considered myself lucky to have him helping me along. He began working with me on the symphony music even in my first lesson. I knew I was going to love studying with him, because he was such a fine musician and the best clarinetist I'd ever heard. He could even transpose the horn parts of the symphonic literature on his clarinet and play right along with me while correcting my phrasing and intonation. He was also a big help to me with interpretation. Working with him was an altogether new experience in learning. As the conductor of the Yale concert band and various ensemble groups I played in daily, he, more than anyone, could properly check my progress.

One day at a lesson he told me something that—mundane as it was—gave me a jolt: "You're going to need a tuxedo to wear for the symphony concerts." I'd never worn a tux before, and having already spent a wad on the beginnings of a civilian wardrobe, I would have to make this purchase cautiously.

One October afternoon, I was walking home from school, stopping to listen to the World Series broadcast coming from radios in business establishments along the way. In the window of a small used-clothing store I had noticed on my walk to school each day, I spotted a well-cut tux.

"Come on in!" said a pleasant-faced man, wearing a hat and a conservative business suit. "What can I do for you?" I told him I was interested in the tux in the window.

"Oh, are you going to a dance, or prom, or something?" Just then a roar came from the radio, a wild Yankee Stadium roar. The announcer screamed, "There it goes . . . it's gone, gone, gone! A home run for Joe DiMaggio!"

The storekeeper, who I presumed was a Yankee fan, gleefully parroted what the radio man had said. After a moment, he recovered and got back to business. "You going to a dance?"

"No, sir, I'm going to play in the New Haven Symphony."

"Holy Joe!" he exploded. "*Moses* hit *this* home run! A *schwarze* in the New Haven Symphony!" Stretching out his open hand to shake mine, he said, "Put it there, pal. The millennium must be here. Congratulations!"

It was all too much, and too fast. I hadn't caught on right away to the Moses bit or the mention of the millennium in connection with the symphony. But there was something about the strange double-talker that got to me.

"Where do you live, son?"

"Three blocks up Grand Avenue."

"Do you go to Hillhouse High?" I bristled at even the suspicion that I was a mere high school student.

"No, sir. I'm a Yale Music School student."

He whacked his forehead. In a surprisingly testy tone, he said, "Paul Hindemith . . . modern music, schmodern music! What the hell's wrong with C major? A little melody never hurt anybody!"

I thought: What would a secondhand clothier know about Hindemith, the New Haven Symphony, and modern music's faults? I tried to sort it all out as he wrestled the tux from the window rack, still talking a mile a minute.

"Feel this material, hard as a rock, custom made in London. A real sharp job." Helping me out of my own jacket and into the tux, he said, "Fits like a million bucks. Try on the pants." Then he said, "You got a good eye for clothes, son." (It was the only tux in the window.) "I just took in this baby from an Englishman a few days ago. Paid him twelve dollars. For you, a young symphony man breaking in, take it for twelve bucks. Cost, for Pete's sake!"

Perhaps it was the change in the smile on his face, or the conviction in his voice, or the shine in his warm eyes. "Sold," I said, and we shook hands on the deal.

We exchanged names. His was Morris. Morris Widder. Then I bolted toward the door. I was late for dinner, and Sister didn't like to be kept waiting.

"Wait," he said. "I've got some sterling advice for a young guy in your shoes in a place like Yale."

"Which is?" I asked. Morris's face became half serious through a yet softer smile.

"Always remember," he said, "in this town, and on that campus, and especially when you grow up a little more: Dress British, think Yiddish!"

On the night of the first concert of the symphony season, my clothier showed up backstage, took one look at me, and shook my hand. "You're the best-dressed man in the house tonight, Raggs." I would learn that Raggs was Morris's tag for his closest friends.

I began stopping in his store every day on my way to and from school. The routine was, he'd always send me out to get coffee—two cups; his treat. With the World Series behind us, he kept his radio tuned to New York's classical music station, WQXR. He knew all the music and often hummed or whistled it expertly and in tune. All except the modern composers. With a grunt, he would turn them off and complain, "What the hell is wrong with C major?"

Morris finally confided in me that he had been a musician. With real sadness in his voice, he said that the violin had been his love since early childhood and that he'd even played in the New Haven Symphony until family responsibilities made it necessary for him to go to work with his father and brothers in the used-clothing business. Morris became a good and steady friend to me; one of my best.

Another friend at Yale was Bob Cecil, a white South Carolina ex–tail gunner, who already had a master's degree from Juilliard. Bob, too, was studying the horn at the School of Music. He introduced himself to me on the first day of school in a musical down-home drawl as thick as mine, and we struck up a friendship that has lasted to this day. In addition to our southernness, we share a love of jazz, good jokes, and, of course, the horn. We played a lot of concerts together at school and with the New Haven Symphony, and we car-pooled wherever horn players were needed in orchestras all around the state.

After a week or so on campus, I was beginning to breathe a little easier about the choice I had made. Every now and then I thought about Mr. Ruffin's offer to help get me into West Point. Some of the sages of Lockbourne had caused me to wonder if the silent treatment, or some other form of the social isolation our Colonel Davis had experienced in his cadet days at West Point, would be my lot as a Yalie; there were only about a dozen black students on campus then.

But campus life gave me no trouble. With the comforts that went with living with my family after such a long separation, dining on my two big sisters' fabulous home cooking, plus the friendship of Morris, Bob Cecil, Mr. Greenlee, Professor Wilson, and the musicians at school, I figured I had the richest social life of any man I knew at Yale, and then some. School was going just fine so far, and I knew that whatever academic challenges lay ahead could be managed.

Playing classical music in the symphony orchestra meant joining the union. All the other nonunion players from Yale were told to pay up. I went to the bank and withdrew some of my GI savings and tagged along with a small group of musicians to the union office. Right away, I ran into trouble. The union official at the desk took one look at me and said, "You have to join the colored local."

I told him that if my application was unacceptable, I wanted it in writing. Of course, he refused. The white students paid their money and left. My money and I went back to the bank. For months, I was the busiest, best-paid scab in town. I went on playing the symphony concerts, did my usual jazz playing, and was in no hurry to pay good money to get into a segregated union I didn't need anyway. But the more I thought about a segregated union, the angrier I got. I finally wrote a letter to James Petrillo, the reigning czar of the international musicians' union. I listed my veteran's status and asserted that the racial segregation of artists in the American Federation of Musicians was intolerable. Petrillo had bigger things on his mind and never acknowledged my letter. Then I really got mad.

I had met a lawyer I admired at a black church in town. George Crawford, the only black corporation lawyer in New Haven, had come from Alabama (no, he didn't have a banjo on his knee either). And when I learned that he was a graduate of both Talladega College and the Yale Law School, I liked him even more. I made an appointment to see him at his office. He listened to the story. I asked him if he could help me take on the Jim Crow union. He rubbed his hands and said that not only would he represent me, he would do it without fee.

"Results will take time," he said. "Meanwhile, go on with your education. Don't be distracted by this problem. You've known worse injustices in Alabama, and your military experience before coming here should have taught you something. Keep your eye on the ball and keep on stepping. We'll make em cry uncle."

About midway through the first semester, Bob Cecil called early one morning to tell me about a new part-time job he'd taken. "Man, you've got to meet this guy I'm working for! He's marketing a new toy that has caught on like a house afire, and he's hiring Yale students. He is a class act, our kind of folks. I know how busy you are with your jazz work and all, but you gotta meet him even if you don't want to work."

It was true that I probably didn't need the work, for I was playing for pay almost every night in the week, but Bob knew I was a sucker for interesting characters.

I found Bob one afternoon in an old house at the edge of the campus (Yale rented several of its properties to tenants not associated with the university). There, on the first floor, I saw Cecil and a busy group of undergraduates, looking like kids in nursery school. They all seemed to be wrestling large blobs of soft but very stubborn plastic material from fifty-gallon drums. What was this all about? I watched, more than bemused. They were flattening the stuff out on a table, forming it into long rolls like cookie dough. Still others were cutting the rolls into chunks and weighing them on postal scales—they had to form a one-ounce blob, precisely. The ounce then went to the next man in the crude assembly line, who put it into a plastic package that looked like two halves of an egg.

"What the hell is it?" I asked Bob.

"Silly Putty."

"Come again?"

Bob put down his egg and took me into another room, where he poured me a cup of coffee and handed me a copy of *The New Yorker*. The "Talk of the Town" section was all about Silly Putty. Brendan Gill was captivated by the adult plaything that children loved. And *New Yorker* readers began flooding the Silly Putty mailbox with orders faster than the staff could fill them.

When I finished reading the *New Yorker* article, I saw that there was a piece of Silly Putty lying near the coffeepot, along with a hammer and a newspaper comic-strip page. I had picked up a piece of the stuff to test some of the properties Mr. Gill attributed to it. I rolled the blob into a ball and slammed it against the floor; it rebounded and whacked the ceiling. I put the ball on the floor and bashed it smartly with the hammer; it shattered like glass and flew everywhere. I gathered up the shattered pieces from all over the room and reconstituted them into one piece, then, picking up the funny paper, I laid my putty flat onto Alley Oop's face and transferred Alley, in full color, onto the wad. Alley's face stretched comically in whatever direction I pulled Silly Putty's edges.

Watching Bob Cecil and Silly Putty's college crew wrestling and packing the stubborn stuff was more fun than playing with it. There seemed to be no systematic process that would speed the job along. The meanest task of all was coaxing the substance out of the large barrels in which it arrived from General Electric. The workers tried training a heat lamp on the barrel to soften the material inside, figuring to make the extraction easier. Even when it was heated, only modest handfuls would break free. Since shattering was one of the things *The New Yorker* said it did well, somebody decided to try a sledgehammer, then take out the pieces for packing. Bad thinking. The sides of the barrel dissipated the hammer's shock, leaving the Silly Putty lying there in a hellishly obstinate state somewhere between a liquid and a solid. Even the strongest Yalie in the house, a football player, gave up in rage and disgust after wearing himself down with the sledgehammer.

I had to leave without meeting the boss on my visit that day. Later on, I did meet Peter Hodgson, a large, relaxed, and elegantly dressed Virginian. Bob had been right; Pete had class, and we became fast friends. Pete often drove me into New York in his new elegant maroon Hudson convertible to listen to Duke Ellington, Louis Armstrong, and other jazz greats. We went to expensive dining spots on the Silly Putty expense account, places I'd never have been able to afford. Although I wasn't on the Silly Putty payroll, Pete made me the firm's unofficial music director and put me in charge of purchasing new jazz and classical recordings I felt he and his kids should be listening to. Silly Putty was a boon to my already hot and broad exposure to good music, and thanks to Pete and that expense account, I learned my way around New York's music emporiums while at Yale.

I became friendly that first year with yet another musical army vet studying composition at Yale; a well-known jazz prodigy in my entering class. He was Mel Powell, the pianist, who as a teenager had been one of the most brilliant stars in Benny Goodman's musical galaxy. After his army stint, Mel wrote movie music in Hollywood. The pull of Hindemith's reputation drew him from Hollywood to Yale with the rest of us that year.

Now he was turning out new "academic" music that was as modern as tomorrow. My horn and I played a lot of Mel's music that first year although he and I never got around to playing any jazz together. However, I discovered another of his surprising gifts: he was one hell of a talker about music—one of the best I ever knew. The scintillating experiences he'd enjoyed years earlier as a kid rubbing musical elbows with some of the icons of the jazz world was magical stuff to me. Hearing him describe those experiences, I felt like I was right back there with him in the thick of it all. He'd been the bus and airplane seat mate, and main confidant of Benny Goodman's first black drummer, the great Sid Cattlet. The delicious tidbits Mel dropped on me about those times made conversations with him even more rewarding for me than his handily crafted music. Never before had I met anyone with such boundless enthusiasm for American jazz and the descriptive gift of the gab it takes to make a story about an impromptu Louis Armstrong trumpet solo come alive. Once or twice during the year, whenever we'd get into conversations about jazz, I'd nudge Mel towards a nearby piano and make him briefly sit down and illustrate some ingenious facet of the intriguing Armstrong mystique for me. His reverence for old Pops was right up there with his feelings for Hindemith. But even if we never had a jam session together at school, we became good buddies, laughed a lot together, and ended up always calling each other "uglier than me."

At the end of classes that year, Mel surprised me. It happened when his old boss, Benny Goodman, came to town to play classical music with the New Haven Symphony. In the middle of the program Benny brought Mel Powell and the drummer, Mousy Alexander, onstage to play some jazz with him. Just before the downbeat, Mel spotted me sitting in the Orchestra, got up from the piano, and whispered in Goodman's ear that a hot "bass man" was sitting in the French horn section. Goodman walked over and invited me to lay the horn aside and borrow a bass and play my first public performance with real jazz all-stars. I was eighteen, and the local papers made a big deal of it. The notoriety brought me a lot of extra paid work around town. Sister beamed and swelled up with pride about what the papers said about the "kid from Sheffield playing with the greats and sounding like a pro." I got a heavenly reward: Sister cooked me the biggest and best pot of turnip greens and cornmeal dumplings I ever sat down to. And all through the feast and even as I worked on the dessert—sweet potato pie, bless her heart—she was still wishing Mama could have heard that big bull fiddle and her boy rhythmically driving ol' Benny Goodman on.

No—there was definitely no grass growing under my feet, socially or musically, that first year of my switch from Lockbourne to Yale; I thought my stuff was hot and still heating.

CHAPTER TWENTY-FOUR

Hindemith, at Last

IN THE EARLY PART of my first year at Yale, Bob Cecil and his wife, Dottie, invited me to drive with them into New York to visit Denny De Intinis, a New York Philharmonic horn player who'd been Bob's classmate at Juilliard. We stayed overnight at Denny's apartment and went with him the next day to hear the orchestra. It was my first trip to Carnegie Hall, as well as my very first time listening to a live performance of the great Philharmonic. Dimitri Mitropoulos conducted. I couldn't believe my good luck.

The concert was the ear feast I had expected. The next-best thing was Denny's invitation for the Cecils and me to come to the musicians' locker room after the concert. The backstage room buzzed with the exhilaration that comes over musicians hot off the stage following a rousing performance. Everyone talked at once. Mr. Gomberg, the oboist, congratulated Mr. Vacchiano, the trumpeter. The manic patter and the hurried motions of a hundred musicians anxiously coming out of their black tailcoats reminded me of a noisy flock of penguins.

Over near the corner, the man snatching off his white tie was Saul Goodman, the flashy timpanist I'd just seen playing his drums with the elegant body English of a ballet dancer. He was great. And the man packing away his silver French horn was James Chambers, who'd just

204

taken our breath away with his solo in the overture to *Oberon*. I'd heard so much about his sound and incredible musicianship from Abe Kniaz back in Columbus, and Bob and Denny had been Chambers's students at Juilliard. Denny gave me the thrill of an introduction, and I learned just how small the professional musicians' world is. I had lost touch with Abe Kniaz. He seemed to have disappeared from Columbus without a trace. My letters to him had come back unclaimed. I mentioned this to Mr. Chambers, who'd taught Kniaz at the Curtis Institute years earlier. Chambers called out to Mark Fischer, the orchestra's third hornist. "Say, Mark, didn't you say you'd seen Abe Kniaz playing somewhere here in New York recently?" Fischer said he had, and suggested I contact Kniaz through the musicians' union.

As soon as I got back to Sister's apartment, I wrote a letter to Abe care of the New York union. About a week later, he called me with an invitation to New York. I asked if I could bring my horn for a lesson. "Why?" he said, laughing. "What could I teach a Yale man?"

He, Judy, and I had a reunion that wouldn't quit. We caught up with each other that day. "A few months after you left Lockbourne for Yale," Abe said, "the Columbus Orchestra suddenly collapsed because they fired our conductor, Izler Solomon. We were all left without jobs, so I came to New York to see what it's like."

Judy and Abe asked me about my life at Yale. I told them that I'd made the dean's list so far, was holding my own with the prep school crowd and even leading them in the French class I was taking every morning in Yale College. Thanks to Mr. Brice's ear-training and theory classes back at his Lockbourne Khaki Conservatory, I found some of the first-level musicianship classes at Yale profitable and pleasurable, though not always a breeze. I had stopped worrying about keeping up and was giving myself over so completely to playing and learning exciting things that sometimes I wouldn't even remember to stop to eat until I got to the door back at my sister's apartment and smelled dinner working on the stove.

Kniaz was wrapped up in the high adventure of free-lance music-making in New York: Broadway musicals, chamber music, and the recording studios. I resumed my lessons, and they turned out better than ever, because now I knew more.

Once while I was there for a lesson, I tagged along with Abe to hear him play a Frank Sinatra show at the Roxy Theater. Sinatra's lushly orchestrated arrangements featured several exposed horn solos, which Abe played fabulously, putting in all the little musical seasonings he'd begun teaching me back in Columbus. Sinatra acknowledged the horn solos by graciously signaling the spotlight operator to swing his beacon downstage to Abe.

After a season of New York commercial work, Kniaz accepted the principal-horn chair of the National Symphony Orchestra in Washington, D.C. The big time for him, a drag for me; Washington was too far away for me to keep up my lessons.

During this time I began thinking a lot about the world of classical music, which I was getting deep into at Yale. I grew increasingly aware of European traditions that still dominated classical music performance in America. The principal players and conductors of our symphony orchestras either were European or were students of European masters who'd made their way here from the Continent earlier in the century. Even Kniaz, my own teacher, a product of European training at the Curtis Institute, fit that mold. At Yale I couldn't escape the haughty pant of Mother Europe's hot breath down my collar.

But after all, I had come to Yale because of Paul Hindemith. Unfortunately, he was on leave from Yale, giving the Norton Lectures at Harvard. While waiting for Hindemith, I studied his past. And studying his past, I became more and more intrigued. In his native Germany, his music had been declared decadent, and all performances of it were banned by order of Adolf Hitler. Prominent German musicians were fired for ignoring the ban, among them the brilliant conductor Furtwängler. Hindemith was also severely criticized for "being at home in the company of Jews." In 1940 he arrived in the United States from Switzerland, having fled Germany a year earlier. It didn't take long for me to learn that this exotic musical hero of Charlie Parker's was a thundering paradox. For one thing—and this floored me—he'd spent no more time in school than I had. The precocious young Hindemith didn't bother to show up much for school—he was too busy teaching himself. And he taught himself so effectively, and played the violin so brilliantly, that much to the envy of other boys his age, his truancy went unnoted or, worse, unpunished by the authorities. To support himself, he played the drums in jazz bands, or at least what the Germans called jazz then; he also wrote music for films, mechanical instruments, stage plays, and school minidramas. The most glaring paradox in the whole complicated life of Paul Hindemith—a learned professor of greatest distinction who taught medieval Latin and mathematics at the Hochschule in Berlin, who revamped the entire music education system in Turkey, who shuttled between the lecture halls of Yale and those of Harvard—was that he had all his life passionately avoided schoolhouse book learning for himself.

Hindemith returned to Yale, and I was finally in his History of the Theory of Music class. At the first lecture, I had to elbow my way through the packed hall to find a seat. I didn't know what to expect. I hoped Hindemith might want to talk about modern chords, elaborate on weird dissonances, or at least address some subject close to the new ideas in twentieth-century music—a theme that would have interested the progressive Charlie Parker.

Hindemith was a small, tightly packed man who exuded self-assurance; his intense, piercing eyes reflected firmness and strength rather than arrogance.

His first lecture confused me. It put me off; I kept asking myself: Why is the man so hung up on the past? He talked at length about Boethius, Pythagoras, and the music of the spheres. We heard about the ancient Greek notion that all things are number or explainable by number.

"The quadrivium," Hindemith said, "those four subjects whose concerns are measure—geometry, astronomy, mathematics, and music—formed the core of an educated person's learning in olden times."

He then filled the blackboard with a long string of numbers representing the ratios of vibrating frequencies that made up musical tones and the resulting harmony of musical tones sounding together. Directing his steady gaze at us and rubbing his hands, Hindemith said:

"The list of great scientists and philosophers through the ages who have also written on music theory is long and impressive. They include Ptolemy, Euclid, Descartes, and, of course, Johannes Kepler. Johannes Kepler, a seventeenth-century mathematician and astronomer, was driven in his work by a musical idea. In the process of exploring and laboring to prove those same musical ideas, he was to lead to some of the most intriguing discoveries in the whole history of science."

I didn't know then that Hindemith had a peculiar obsession with Kepler's lifework; that for nearly a decade he'd been laboring at an opera, "The Harmony of the World," based on the bizarre details of Kepler's dogged life.

Again, in that large lecture hall, he harked back to the ancient Greeks and their notion of the music of the spheres. Still rubbing his hands, he said, "The Pythagoreans imagined that each planet, in what they thought to be a circular orbit, would sweep out a note and that all their notes taken together produced a chord. There was, in their view, a constant cosmic chord sounding in the universe."

A faint glimmer of hope broke over me, and I wondered if those old Greeks could have been right about a truly celestial model of the music we humans hear down on earth. But still, how did Hindemith intend to connect up his preoccupation with the history of science to the concerns of our class? Back again to Kepler and his discoveries:

In a 1619 treatise, Hindemith explained, Kepler published the first reliable data showing that there are musical principles involved in the march of the planets around the sun. However, they are not as the ancient Greeks imagined them.

"Kepler's first law of planetary motion states that planets move in elliptical orbits at constantly changing rates of speed, and not in perfect circles at a constant velocity, as the Greeks had thought. Further, the constantly changing relationships of the planets to each other cannot produce the single cosmic chord the Greeks had imagined."

Hindemith then read to us from a large book, *Harmonice Mundi*, the 1619 treatise he'd referred to, translating the Latin to English as he read. "The heavenly motions are nothing but a continuous song for several voices, to be perceived by the intellect, not by the ear; a music that, through discordant tensions, through syncopations and cadenzas, as it were, progresses toward certain predesigned six-voiced cadences and thereby sets landmarks in the immeasurable flow of time." What would Charlie Parker think of *this?* I wondered. Hindemith went on to say that Kepler had thrown out a challenge to his musical contemporaries to set the musical march of the heavens to a sacred text; he himself would demonstrate the celestial harmonies in numbers.

The clock on the wall said that it was time to bring the lecture to a close, and Hindemith summed up what he wanted to leave with us: "The science of music deals with the proportions objects assume in their quantitative and spatial, but also in their biological and spiritual, relations. Kepler's three basic laws of planetary motion . . . could perhaps not have been discovered had he not had a serious backing in music theory. It may well be that the last word concerning the interdependence of music and the exact sciences has not been spoken."

This was a puzzling beginning to my long-awaited encounter with the man "Yardbird" Parker had said he wanted to study with. I could see that what Bird had supposed were Hindemith's musical passions would not be what I'd be learning in that class. "What *will* I learn?" I asked myself, and, "Will the man ever get beyond those ancient Greeks and get modern?" That cosmic music box he'd talked about, the music of the spheres, the idea of planets that sing, kept me in my seat long after the other students and Hindemith had left the room. Had I come to the right place to study music?

I finally made up my mind to take my professor as I found him and to wait and see where his concerns would lead me. "After all," I told myself, "just a short three years ago you were in a Wyoming barracks boiler room with an instrument that confounded you as you fumbled through a book that you struggled to read with your lips moving!"

A few weeks into the semester, when Hindemith started passing out sheets of music in his own neat script, I got the feeling my patience was about to pay off. As he distributed the manuscript he said, "Now we will make some music together."

I was ready! But to my horror, the sheets of music were not his own compositions; the music wasn't even of the twentieth-century at all. Rather, he'd given us transcriptions he'd made of some of that medieval music he'd already talked about, which I had hoped was behind us.

Hindemith tested our voices individually, and he carefully divided the class into singing sections of tenors, sopranos, altos, and basses. Then he stood in front of us and began conducting our singing. A sudden miraculous transformation took place: Paul Hindemith, the real musician, broke free of the tight little lecturer-teacher who'd been confounding me for so many weeks. The surprising sounds of music written in twelfth- and thirteenth-century Europe were making sense to me. Day by day, as we sang those long-forgotten relics from Europe's Middle Ages, a far clearer understanding of the importance of what had happened in the musical past began to come into focus. We worked our way on chronologically, and with Hindemith's expert choral direction, our performances came alive. Then he grew more adventurous: we took up music of a later period, with instrumental accompaniment. He insisted on our hearing the authentic instruments of the period and fetched them, when available, from dank museum basements for us to play. Miracles began to happen. From our shaky beginnings on the creaky and out-of-tune instruments, here and there in our rehearsals a stunning combination of sounds would leap out, which would have turned even Charlie Parker's head. For me, connections gradually became clearer. Then, a little later in the semester, I really got an earful as we worked our way forward in time all the way up to sixteenth-century Venice.

Hindemith began putting on public concerts in Yale's acoustically sumptuous Sprague Hall, with us playing and singing the work of a miraculous body of music that had been written for performances in St. Mark's basilica in the 1500s. We even took our show on the road to New York's Metropolitan Museum of Art, where our large group stood on the grand staircase in the foyer and raised the roof with the majesty of our sound. So here I was at the Met playing my horn and singing in that huge, high-ceilinged space, getting my kicks from the living energy in Gabrieli's invigorating chunks of harmony, the stunning echo effects, the exhilarating rhythms, and Gesualdo's grinding dissonances. Hindemith was so pleased with our sound he arranged for us to make recordings.

All this lavish Venetian church music that Hindemith was insisting we know set up reverberations in my memory of W. C. Handy's message to the children at my Alabama schoolhouse way back in 1937. I was not absolutely sure of it, but I had the distinct feeling that the religious music of my world—those spirituals Mr. Handy had admonished Sheffield's children to sing with pride in their voices—and this rich body of Old World religious music were connected. Years later, I was to find the connection.

I never had much private contact with Hindemith, but he did listen to me play his horn sonata and a sonata for four horns that he'd written while at Yale. There was a handful of Yale students Hindemith took on as composition students, but I was not nearly ready for that. I always suspected his heart was less in teaching composition than in advancing the larger notion of music as metaphor and in making the connections he loved to make between our craft and the dynamics of life itself.

CHAPTER TWENTY-FIVE

"They Got Flies in That Buttermilk Yet?"

OPPORTUNITIES TO LEARN NEW THINGS seemed endless in my musical comings and goings around New Haven. I was soaking it up and loving every minute of all the different kinds of music I was learning. Though music, European history, English, and foreign languages were claiming my attention at school, I couldn't shake the feeling that I was leaving something undone.

I can thank Mr. Greenlee for gently pulling my coat. He used to check up on me when I came to the Monterey with my bass on Saturday nights.

"Hey, Red, what's shaking, baby? . . . What the white folk learning you downtown?"

I'd recite the menu for him. Each semester, when the fare changed, I'd have to make a report: "German, French, English, History, the Theory of Music . . . ."

The mention of European languages was enough to set Mr. Greenlee off hoofing and singing in his show business German, French, and Russian, all fluent and full of spice. Grinning and landing lightly from a neat leap off the floor, he'd say, "I used to kill em with that number in Berlin in 1927." I was often treated to his Paris routine. Then one night during an intermission, he got serious with me,

"Whatcha gonna *do* with all that book learning, man?"

"*Do* with it? Well, Mr. G., I want to learn how to teach, but mostly I'm gonna try to play the horn in a *major* symphony orchestra."

"That a fact?" he said. "*Major* symphony, eh? They got flies in *that* buttermilk yet?"

"Fly in the buttermilk," popular since slavery times as a metaphor for black people moving into all-white situations, was often on Mr. G.'s lips. Jackie Robinson had recently become the fly in the buttermilk of major league baseball. Ralph Bunche had flown into the major diplomatic milk bowl of the United Nations. As we talked on about the musician-entertainer's world, my future in it, and his past, Mr. Greenlee allowed that Jackie Robinson's example might cause some barriers to fall in other areas of professional possibilities. "*But*," he added as he snatched his cigar from his teeth and pressed his strong forefinger hard into my chest, "if your paint job stands in the way of your playing *major* symphony music for society, then sell that jive-assed society something it can't do without. Somebody got to keep society *outta* jail or put their sick asses *in* the hospital. You git what I'm telling you, Red?"

And there it was again, law and medicine occupying the top spot on Mr. Greenlee's list of "hustles" a smart music man ought to be thinking about. I had, by then, begun to look on him as another of my sophisticated father substitutes. His advice that I stay ready to shift hustles if my preferred one fizzled endeared him to me even more. And I thought back to what the Lockbourne chaplain told me the day he got me discharged:

"Remember, take advantage of as much as you can outside of music at Yale. It would be a sin to learn just one thing in so rich an intellectual environment. Music is fickle, you know, and Jim Crow ain't going to lay down and die because Mr. Brice taught you a thing or two and you bought an instrument and got yourself into an Ivy League school."

It certainly was not lost on me that the majority of few black undergraduates on campus were either premed or prelaw students. So I began to diversify with courses I might need for admission to medical or law school, should it come to that. It was university policy to allow its students to study outside their major anywhere on campus, with no additional fees. When the next semester rolled around, I began adding classes; my little appointment book looked a fright. Music classes and rehearsals were interspersed with biology, physics, economics, cost accounting, and chemistry. Through it all, Mr. Greenlee was the model of support and encouragement. When I showed up for work at the Monterey on weekends, I often brought books along to study during intermissions. Every time I hit the front door with a load of books along with my bass, Mr. Greenlee would holler, "Kill em, Red!" then go off to prepare me a little table in the back storeroom, where I could read away from the noise of the club. Always, when it was time for the second intermission of the night, I'd lay down my bass, dry off the sweat, and head for the storeroom, where I'd find on my study table—a stack of Rheingold beer cases—a chicken sandwich, a glass of milk, and a cloth napkin, compliments of the house.

In spite of the absurdly cheap rent Sister accepted from me for my room in her apartment and despite her great home cooking, I decided I now needed more privacy, and room to study and practice. It was time to move on. I answered ads for apartments in the vicinity of Yale until I grew tired of slammed doors and direct refusals to rent to blacks. Then I thought of buying a multiple-dwelling house, which I would share with my sister Mary, who was raising Nathaniel, now eight years old. Mary had recently been divorced and was struggling to raise her own two tots and our little brother. Her small flat over the beauty shop Sister now owned was cramped. I needed to be sure I would be on solid ground making such a purchase, and again I telephoned Lawyer Crawford for an appointment.

He shook my hand warmly, asked what news there was from our Alabama. "I'd be surprised if you came here to tell me that there's trouble with the musicians' union again, because Mrs. Crawford and I see you playing your horn at all the symphony concerts."

I told him no, this time I was having housing problems. He nodded understandingly as I recited my frustrations at the doors being slammed in my face. "Yes, I've been there too," he said. But when I told him what I proposed to do about it, his smile grew into a face-stretching grin.

"I've been *there* too." He thought my plan to buy a two- or three-family house was right on the money. He himself had purchased a house on Orchard Street. He proceeded to give me a short lesson on accumulating equity, current and future cash-flow projections, income-producing properties, taxes, owner's insurance, and contingency reserves. He scribbled some numbers on a sheet of paper.

"These are some hypothetical prices of homes, along with what you can expect in the way of down payments and reserves. If you think you're 'long enough of pocket' to handle that kind of responsibility, take it on!"

Once again I blessed Mr. Ruffin for starting me out on a savings program back when I was a fifteen-year-old corporal in Wyoming, for there was nothing on Lawyer Crawford's paper beyond my reach now that I was an eighteen-year-old civilian. With my regular earnings playing music and my little bankbook balance, I could swing it. I thanked him and got up to leave, but he stopped me. "Ruff, hold on a minute. You should know that in the state of Connecticut, a contract is legal and binding only if *all* the parties involved are above age twenty-one. You want to tell me how old you are?"

I hesitated, muttered, and stammered, until he said, "Never mind. I get the picture. We'll cross that bridge when we come to it. You know your way back here by now."

Even after Mr. Crawford's reassurance, something made me want to discuss the idea further with Mr. Greenlee, another savvy property owner. When I'd finished telling Mr. G. essentially what I'd told Mr. Crawford, he snatched the cigar from his mouth, grabbed the lapel of my jacket. "Man," he said, "you already done your homework. Now, if you don't cop you a pad, and *quick*, I'll kick your little rump so hard you'll taste shoe polish!"

That did it. My sister Mary with her children, little Nat, and I all settled into the two-family house I bought just down the street from Lawyer Crawford.

CHAPTER TWENTY-SIX

Falling in Love

ENOCH WOODHOUSE had been an officer at Lockbourne, having arrived there from Godman Field, Kentucky, after the famous court-martial. He'd also been stationed on the Yale campus during the war, when a lot of servicemen—including Glenn Miller—were billeted at the college. Now he was a civilian and back at Yale as an undergraduate. The two of us, the only ex-Lockbourners in town, got together frequently.

Woody was the son of a Boston bishop and was a "heads-up operator" in his own right. He had an inner sense of the practical, was smart as a whip, and planned to go to law school after he graduated. A French major, he spoke the language like a native, and was president of the Yale French Club.

"Hell, anybody can learn the law," he told me. "I want to go another step and practice internationally. That's why I'm getting my French together—the international language, dig? Then you can watch my smoke when I begin my practice in international law."

His plan was to sign up for the Junior Year Abroad program, for which Yale would give him credit while he lived lavishly in Paris on his monthly GI Bill stipend. One day, he said to me, "Listen, man, you ought to consider studying for a year at the Conservatoire in Paris.

A lot of jazz cats are living there. You could work all you want to, and with your GI Bill, you can live like a king. Take a break from New Haven, see the world." He was sounding like Emil, who still came to all my Yale performances and applauded louder than anybody in the hall. But as good as Woody made it sound, I was having too much fun where I was.

A t that time, Woody spoke often and admiringly of a young lady, Emma Mitchell, a native of New Haven who'd been studying French at Fisk University in Nashville.

"Man, this lady is rare. Got beauty *and* brains," he told me.

Woody had been in Paris a few months when I learned that Emma Mitchell was by then a graduate student at Middlebury College in Vermont, getting another degree in French.

Later that summer of 1951, I called her at her parents' home in New Haven and introduced myself. We met. Woody hadn't exaggerated. I was charmed. We liked the same music and could talk together endlessly and late into the night. As I learned more about her tastes and her passion for teaching, bells began ringing.

The Crawfords were friends of Emma's parents, and Mrs. Crawford especially had been one of her chief rooters during Emma's triumphant march through the city's Hillhouse High School, where she excelled in all she touched. Hillhouse, in those days, ranked among the top public schools in the nation, just after Boston Latin. Our common interest in college teaching was strong, and our ideas of the differences good teachers could make seemed to mesh.

The "buttermilk" of the major state and private universities and colleges in America was painfully free of flies then, and we both fully expected to go to black institutions to work. In fact, Emma had already accepted a teaching job at a black college in Texas. I hoped I could find a school somewhere near a symphony orchestra that could use me and my horn.

By the time Emma went off to Texas, I had discovered how much I liked her mother. So I continued going to the Mitchell house to visit even while Emma was in Texas. Perhaps I was seeing in her mother some of what my own mama might have become with a less brutal life, a chance at schooling, and a few up-north advantages.

Our long-distance relationship was too long and our meetings too few, but by the time Woody came back from France the following year, Emma and I had become engaged.

Meanwhile, Lawyer Crawford was getting deeply involved with the union desegregation matter. He showed me a sheaf of correspondence between Governor Chester Bowles's office, the new Office of Human Relations that Bowles had recently created for the State of Connecticut, and the musicians' union. "We are ready to challenge the American Federation of Musicians," Mr. Crawford said. "Either they admit you to their local or we sue them, with the backing of the state, the Governor's Office, and the Office of Human Relations. If I have your permission, I will write a letter advising the white union to accept your application, or else. How about it?" That's how I became a union man early in 1952, shortly before Emma and I set the date for our marriage that June.

Our wedding took place at the Dixwell Avenue Congregational Church, just down the street from Mr. Greenlee's. Bob Cecil was my best man, and Abe Kniaz, Enoch Woodhouse, and my favorite Yale jazz trumpeter, Johnny Glasel, were in the wedding party. Even though the wedding was on Saturday, the Sabbath for Orthodox Jews, my main man, Morris Widder, sat beaming in the congregation, wearing his yarmulke and looking like a saint brightening my day. I was wearing the pants to the classy twelve-dollar tux he'd sold me three years earlier, and a white formal jacket for which he'd refused to take my money.

Abe and Judy Kniaz kept in touch from Washington after the wedding, and Emma and I went down to visit several times. Hearing Abe play in the National Symphony Orchestra in Constitution Hall was always thrilling. And as Emma and I sat in the hall, we couldn't help thinking of Marian Anderson's 1936 cause célèbre and Eleanor Roosevelt's involvement.

In my senior year at Yale, 1953, the Kniazes invited us down for another visit. But this phone call was different. I could hear that something more than visiting was on Abe's mind. "The orchestra will have a vacancy for an assistant principal hornist next year," he finally said during the phone conversation. "Don't get your hopes up—and I will try not to hope for too much too—but I want to approach the conductor, Howard Mitchell, to ask that you be considered for the job." Certainly, I knew better than to allow myself to hope for anything. Abe had been preparing me to expect nothing since I was sixteen years old back in Columbus. But he added, again with cautious optimism, "I might be able to get the conductor to at least give you an audition, although this orchestra has never even auditioned a Negro before. It's just possible that if you're asked for from inside the orchestra, by me, it might make a difference. If I asked for any white horn player I wanted as my assistant, there'd be no question. But Washington *is* the nation's capital, after all, and it just might be the right time for them to accept a Negro in the orchestra. Who knows, Willie?"

With the horn vacancy a full season away, it wasn't hard for me to put the whole notion on the back burner. Besides, I was planning to stay on at Yale for a master's degree.

One day about two months later, Abe called. This time the casual cheerfulness was missing from his voice. He said he had talked to Howard Mitchell about me. Mitchell said he certainly would like to have a Negro in the orchestra. But he was concerned about bookings in the southern states. The orchestra played a lot of concerts in the South, where the laws did not allow Negroes in hotels and restaurants.

Emma was the only one besides the Kniazes who knew about my hopes for a position in the National Symphony. While she hadn't really expected I'd be auditioned, she'd worried that a refusal might cause me to lose heart and give up my aspirations as a professional musician. But what hurt me more than my rejection was the effect it had on Abe. Even after his years of trying to protect and prepare me for what I would surely face in trying to break down the barriers in American orchestras, he'd stuck his neck out and got hurt himself. I'd been instructed and prepared by Mama, and by many other benign influences all my life, on handling racial rejection. But nothing along the way had prepared me to cope with so hurtful a disappointment to a champion of my cause. The more I thought about Abe's feelings, the angrier I got. My anger took the form of silence; I didn't open my mouth to speak for three or four days. It was the only way I knew to contain myself, for I was afraid that if I did open up, I would explode. It was a silence that worried Emma, but when I finally started talking again, it was to say to her that it would take more than one rejection from Washington, D.C., to get me out of music. But I knew I would always remember Abe's frustration, and I would find a way, one way or another, to make a career in music that would justify his faith in me.

PART FOUR

Performing

CHAPTER TWENTY-SEVEN

Tel Aviv or
Lionel Hampton?

SHORTLY AFTER I GOT MY MASTER'S from Yale, in 1954, I went to New York with Pete Hodgson, to hear Erich Leinsdorf conduct the Boston Symphony in an extremely moving all-Beethoven program at Carnegie Hall. A few days later, in a musicians' union newsletter, I saw an announcement that the Tel Aviv Philharmonic Orchestra, the pride of the new state of Israel, was auditioning horn players. Leinsdorf would listen to several Americans and would recommend the one he liked best. He was a regular on the podiums of Israel, and he knew the American musical scene and its players as well as any conductor alive. The newsletter gave his phone number.

The more I thought of the Leinsdorf concert I'd heard at Carnegie Hall, the stronger was the pull of the audition. I called the Westchester County, New York, number in the newsletter. Leinsdorf himself answered the phone. I introduced myself and said I was calling from New Haven about the Israel horn position. Leinsdorf said the position hadn't been filled, though he'd heard a lot of fine players. He asked about my background, and when I reported the Yale years, he wanted to know if any of them had been spent making music with Hindemith. I told him I had been taught by Abe Kniaz, and he said he knew Abe's work. After a cordial and warm few minutes, he made a date with me.

I prepared myself for the audition, which would be held at Leinsdorf's home, in every way, including sartorially. I dressed up in a good-quality medium-weight suit Morris Widder had sold me (at cost), shined my best pair of conservative shoes, and stopped by the clothing store to kill a few minutes before the drive down to Larchmont. Morris, I knew, would want to wish me good luck: give me his "mazel."

It was a hot summer day, shirtsleeve weather. As I approached the store, horn under my arm, Morris spotted me and left his customer, who stood in new pants with pins down the seat and in the cuffs.

"Wrong suit!" he yelled to me. "It's summertime. Too heavy. Besides, you're not going to a funeral. Brighten up, man! A well-dressed man *looks* comfortable. Look at you: you're sweating, for crying out loud! Maestro Leinsdorf will take one look at you in that schmatta and say, 'Uhh uhh, another schlemiel schlepping to the Holy Land.' "

"This is the best you ever sold me," I said.

"How much time we got?" he asked as he marked the cuffs and seat for the man in the new pants and sent him on his way with a "Next Tuesday. So long." To me he said, "Gimme ten minutes, and I'll make you a new man. Do you think I'd let you go to Israel looking like *that?*"

"Morris," I said, "I'm not going to Israel today, just to Westchester County."

"Same difference. Don't argue; we don't have much time. You'll borrow a new suit, something right for the season." Manipulating a long broomstick with a hook affixed to its end, he jiggled loose from a high rack a new light-tan linen suit, threw the jacket at me, and plugged in the iron.

By the time he'd pinned and sewn the pants cuffs, the iron was hot, and he sponged and pressed the whole suit. I was ready. I admired my image in his full-length mirror, while he checked and tugged at the jacket from behind. He turned me around to inspect the jacket front and recoiled. "My Gawd," he said. "I *hate* that shirt! You'll never get to Israel wearing that." He was off to the back room, returning with a bundle, the laundry ticket still stuck to it, of his own shirts. Ripping the paper off, he took from the stack a button-down oxford shirt with a quiet stripe, held it under my chin. No good.

"We need something more muted," he said. When I tried a muted one, Morris complained, "Cheez, that tie is a dog!" He ran his hand into his pants pocket and yanked out a bill.

"Here, take this ten bucks and run around the corner to J. Press and buy a four-in-hand rep stripe tie with a little red, green, maybe a hint of yellow. But no blue! Tell em it's for Morris, they'll give you a discount. Understand?"

I pushed the hand with the bill away. "Thanks anyway, Morris," I said, "but I can at least afford a tie." J. Press had the tie, but no discount. When I came back, Morris said, "That's better. You're going to be the hottest shofar man in Jerusalem!"

"Tel Aviv," I said. He followed me to the door, and as I sprinted in the heat for my Ford, he hollered after me, "Slow down. Don't sweat in my suit! Play well, Raggs!"

D riving down the Merritt Parkway, I tried to remember all the pointers Kniaz had offered along the way about playing for conductors. "Don't be flashy. Don't play horn concertos unless you're asked, but show that you know more than just orchestral music. Remember that the audition starts with the first warm-up notes you play. Be relaxed."

I arrived in Larchmont nearly a half hour early. Once I'd spotted the house, I drove on down the block, found a parking spot in the shade, took out the horn, sat in the car, and warmed up with soft slow scales. I played through the melody of Rossini's *Semiramide*, one of my favorites for the instrument. Everything felt fine. My clothes were comfortable. No more sweating.

Going up the long walkway to Leinsdorf's large house, I could hear a piece of very modern music coming from a piano inside. I guessed it was Leinsdorf though I didn't know he was a pianist. It was one o'clock, time for my appointment, but I waited for the final cadence before pushing the doorbell. A woman answered, I introduced myself, and she asked me in. "My husband just left the piano and went upstairs. He'll be with you shortly," she said. "He said you may warm up there in the music room." Kniaz had been right; of course Leinsdorf would be listening from upstairs. I continued with the easy blowing I'd started in the car, playing a quiet phrase or two of *Semiramide;* it was on my mind.

After a few moments, Leinsdorf came into the music room, carrying a few sheets of an old *New York Times,* extended his right hand to me, and in a resonant, warm, and friendly voice said, "Good afternoon, Mr. Ruff. I'm glad to see you." So far so good. He then spread the *Times* on the floor next to my chair to protect the carpet from the water that horn players must constantly empty from their horns. "He's done a lot of this," I told myself.

Taking a seat on the nearby piano stool, Maestro said, "Tell me some more about yourself." I recited all I thought he would care to know about my military experience and Yale. Then he said, "What have you prepared that you would like to play for me?" Well, of course, *Semiramide.* I played it through to the end this time. "A very nice approach, and an interesting tone," was his comment.

Then I put a book of orchestra excerpts on the music stand and asked if he would like to choose something for me to play. He fingered through the book and asked for samplings of orchestral horn writing from the eighteenth century to modern composers. I had practiced everything in the book; there were no mishaps in the dozen or so excerpts he chose. The last thing he asked me to play from the book was a bit from a Haydn symphony. The part, written before the horn had valves, required transposing. The symphony was in the key of D, not one of the more difficult transpositions a horn player must learn and keep in his professional baggage. I played through the passage, and near the end there was a slip of a finger, or the lip, or of my concentration. Anyway, a note of the melody was not right. Not a *missed* note but a wrong one.

When I was finished, Leinsdorf asked me if transposing was troublesome for me. I said it was not ordinarily. But I didn't want to make excuses for the slip and offered to play other transpositions from the book. He said, "No, I'll take your word. However, you might want to pay more attention to your transposing for future auditions." He then asked if I wanted to play anything else. I thought it was a good time to do as Kniaz had advised: play something that was not from the orchestral literature. Abe had shown me a piece from Schumann's *Carnival* piano suite, in which one movement, a musical portrait of Chopin, elegantly shows off the best of the horn's lyrical qualities. Nobody ever plays the piece on the horn. "Wonderfully effective for encore pieces or auditions. Use it," Kniaz had said. I played the movement once through, not too loud, not too soft, then made the repeat at a hushed whisper. It worked. I hoped that I had made up for the earlier slip. Maestro smiled at me.

The audition was over, and Leinsdorf said some very complimentary things. Then he pulled the piano stool closer to my chair and said, "Would you care to tell me why you, an American, are interested in the position in Israel?" I told him that all my working life in music, from my fifteenth year till then, had been devoted to preparing myself as a horn player. I wanted to play in a symphony orchestra, perhaps not for the rest of my life but for now.

"I am certainly aware that positions in the professional orchestras in this country are not available to Negro artists," he told me. "I know these orchestras and the communities that support them." Then he mentioned an alternative to the job in Israel.

"I'm the music director and conductor of the Buffalo Symphony Orchestra. I can definitely offer you a position in the horn section. It might be a more direct route to your later entry into another, larger American orchestra. The Tel Aviv position would also be good for you, and you would certainly be appreciated there regardless of race. There are no laws that would separate you from anybody else. I suggest you consider both these options, but don't short-change Buffalo."

I thanked him and he saw me to the door, where his wife met us to shake my hand. We would talk by phone in a week.

No matter what would happen as a result of the encounter, I was glad to have had the frank talk with an artist I admired as much as Leinsdorf.

Shortly after my audition, Emma and I sat home one night watching television, the Ed Sullivan show. Lionel Hampton and his orchestra were announced. When Lionel and the band started his theme song, "Flying Home," the camera panned across the full band and stopped on the piano player. He was Ivory Mitchell, from Lockbourne! I raced for the telephone. Manhattan information gave me the CBS number. I dialed. The CBS switchboard rang through to the theater's backstage. I asked the person on the other end to give my number to Hampton's piano player.

"The band just came off. Hold a second, I'll call him. What's his name?"

"Mitchell," I said.

The next voice I heard said, "Hello, who's this?" It was the same old fall-in-the-ditch Ivory Mitchell's voice. Instead of answering, I sang the deep bass-notes to "All the Things You Are," the way he'd taught it to me for our first radio program back at Lockbourne: "Thum thuuuum thum thum thum thum thum thuuum thuum." At about the third bar, he screamed, "Ruff! Aww man . . . Ruff!"

All of a sudden, he was going, "Kyah . . . Kyah . . . heekh, heekh, wheeeew, huuu—awwwww, Jeeeesuuuus!" I picked up his giggle fit, until Emma, showing serious concern, asked, "Do you two ever talk? Or is it all bass fiddles and guffaws?"

"Your timing was perfect," Mitchell said. "You got me just as I came off the bandstand. But the band is working at Basin Street, here in town, and we're due on now. Everybody is leaving."

"Well, at least I got you, at last," I said. "I will probably be leaving soon to play in the Israel Philharmonic Orchestra."

"Naw, man, don't do it. We got to get together. Israel is a very hip place; we go there often with Lionel. But you ought to join this band, and we can work out that duo we always talked about back in Mr. Brice's band. I think about him all the time, man, God rest his soul.

"Listen, Ruff, we're playing in Bridgeport, Connecticut, tomorrow night, at the Ritz Ballroom. Bring your horn; I'm sure Lionel will hire you. We gotta get our shit together now. I can't wait to see you. Gotta go. Don't forget tomorrow. Later!"

When I arrived at the Ritz Ballroom, Hamp's musicians were about to go on the stage. Mitchell spotted me and tapped Hamp on the shoulder. They came right over. "Hey, Gates"—Lionel's name for everyone, and the one he likes to be called—"Mitchell told me all about you. Just take a seat anywhere and move around in the band. Blow with the different sections. Hell, make yourself at home wherever you think it sounds good." Mitchell and I saved our reunion until later, but I wondered if he knew what he was getting me into. We had spoken again on the phone earlier that day. Would it be possible, or practical, for us to organize our duo and work up a repertoire while traveling on the road? The one thing I was certain of was that I wanted to sound good that night and not embarrass us both.

The opening number with Lionel is always a fast and active piece of pyrotechnics called "Big Slide." Sitting between the two trombonists, I discovered that playing in that band was not so much a musical challenge as one of showmanship, that dominant feature of any Hampton performance. After the intermission, I played a few numbers with the trumpets, then I moved my chair forward to play with the saxophones and finally found music to suit the special character of the French horn. The horn's tone, when mixed with a saxophone section, enlarges and adds color to the ensemble. The lead alto saxophonist, Bobby Platter, sitting in the chair to my left, guided me through the best of the band's library. Platter was a large but quiet and gentle man, who had been the band's assistant leader for many years. He had also composed the great dance-band classic "The Jersey Bounce." As we read through "Midnight Sun," we reached a point where Platter nudged me and said, "Big reed section solo coming up. Double the lead part with me." We began the phrase together, and from the sound of our first note, I could imagine that a midnight sun did break through the smoky haze of the ballroom. Matching Bobby's lyrical tone was even more effective when we played softly, accompanying Lionel's vibes solos. Lionel got inspired at one point, stopped midphrase in his solo, turned from his vibes with a grin, his mallets high over his head, and yelled at me, "Yeah, Gates, blow, blow, blow!"

Platter signaled the other saxes to tune up and to pay more attention to the expressive shadings in the music. "Shhh, way down, man. Don't drown out the French horn!" Almost immediately our blend and balance improved. Platter looked at the saxophonists and said testily, "That's a whole lot better! Yeah. Damn. Why don't you cats play like that *all* the time?" Lionel's chief musician was tuning his section to a level he'd apparently had difficulty sustaining otherwise.

Before we started again, Bobby searched through the music on his stand, trying to find ballads that would show off our new saxophone–French horn mix. We experimented like that for the rest of the night, turning up beautiful ballads to play, which, according to Bobby and Mitchell, the band hadn't touched in years.

During the next intermission, trumpeter Wallace Davenport came to shake my hand. Others followed. Some of the men were interested in arranging, and had questions about the horn: its range, pitch, and mixing characteristics. Lionel asked me to play solos on a few ballads with his vibes during the last set of the evening. I was in horn heaven.

When the night was finished, Bobby, Lionel's main musical adviser, said, "Sign him up, Gates. You heard that sound!"

"Yeah, ain't no other bands got no French horns, except Claude Thornhill and them cats. It's something new. I'll call Gladys and ask her." He went for the telephone booth to consult long-distance with the real boss of the band, his wife.

Gladys Hampton was the force that kept the Lionel Hampton organization afloat. A glamorous and adroit businesswoman, she did all the hiring and firing in the band, made all the business decisions, and supervised the tours. Mrs. Hampton, as she was addressed by band members, controlled one of the all-time-big-grossing packages in the music industry. Arrogantly secure in what she'd had to teach herself about show business, Gladys flaunted her power. The industry was not yet ready for a black woman representative, so Gladys left the hard contract negotiations to the white agent Joe Glaser. Lionel was but one star on the roster of jazz greats the Glaser office booked. Others commanding big money through Glaser's Associated Booking Agency were Louis Armstrong, Duke Ellington, Woody Herman, Sarah Vaughan, Stan Kenton, Billy Eckstine, Billy Daniels, and on down. But from the moment a Hampton contract was nailed down by Glaser, Gladys took over.

Lionel, speaking to his wife on the pay phone, was saying, "Gladys, I just heard this musician up here in Bridgeport. He sat in with the band tonight. It sounded great. We're still short a trombone player, you know, so we can put him in there to bring the band up to full strength." Gladys said something, to which Lionel replied, "Naw, he ain't no trombone player, he plays the French horn." There was a long pause, presumably Gladys giving her husband fits. Lionel broke in.

"I *know* I ain't never had no French horn in the band before, but you oughta hear it. The whole band sounds bigger. It's something *new*, Gladys. It's classy, and the people will dig it! Bobby Platter and Mitchell can tell you. This guy was in the Air Force with Mitchell. . . . Come on, Gladys, can we hire him?" Finally, Gladys gave a tentative OK, but she was going to have to check it out for herself when the band came to Harlem in two days for its annual month-long stint at the Apollo Theater.

The next day, I called Erich Leinsdorf's house to say that I was no longer "in the running" for the job in Israel. I wanted especially to thank him again for his thoughtful offer of a job in the Buffalo Philharmonic. It was a kindness I would never forget.

The news that I would probably be going with Lionel Hampton was a relief to my New Haven family. Israel seemed such a long way from home. My sister Mary had wanted to know, "How the devil are you going to even talk to those people way over there, boy? You can't speak Hebrew!" To them, Hamp's band, no matter how far it traveled abroad, was still familiar territory. And what better place than the Apollo to start one's band career?

CHAPTER TWENTY-EIGHT

At the Apollo

M ITCHELL HAD a thirty-dollar-a-month cold-water loft on the top floor of a building with several studios, situated over a bustling ground-floor bar. It was right on the Bowery, near First Street. I moved in with him for the month we'd be at the Apollo, bringing along not only my horn but my bass and bow, so that we could begin work on our duo material. For our rehearsals, we rented an upright piano, five bucks a month.

Following my first night in New York as a member of the band, Mitchell and I headed for the subway and took the A train to Harlem, in the early-morning press of rush hour. We had to be onstage at the Apollo at 9:00 A.M. sharp for a run-through. Besides our own show, we had to rehearse another act on the bill. The stage manager told us our schedule, and I now knew why Hamp's band was known as the "work-horse" of the industry. We would open the theater each day with "Big Slide" at 11:30 A.M. The last show ended with "Flying Home" at 1:00 A.M. the next morning! We alternated with a seventy-minute movie. Meals and rest (two luxuries I never caught up on at the Apollo) had to be snatched while the movie played.

Lionel's yearly stints at the Apollo were celebrations for his New York fans. There was no audience in the world like his Apollo loyals.

Count Basie, Duke Ellington, and Billy Eckstine had their Apollo followers too: the sophisticated elite of the jazz fans, who came like worshipers at a holy shrine. But it was Hamp's "funky butts" who flocked back year after year to rock the Harlem edifice to its foundation.

In an effort to learn as much as I could about the music I was sight-reading, I spent a lot of time leafing through the folder I shared on Bobby Platter's music stand. I took a few sheets from the trombone folder I'd played in Bridgeport, electing to add my horn's voice to their section where needed.

As I sat next to Bobby before the first show, my eyes fell on a folder of music that the band had recorded years earlier. I fingered sheets written by bassist and composer Charlie Mingus. There was "Mingus Fingus," a virtuoso composition for the band and the solo bass fiddle as only big Charlie Mingus could have written and played. A record of "Mingus Fingus" had stunned our whole band back at Lockbourne, and the sight of the handwritten music in the folder before me, all that remained of the original composition (unplayed since Mingus quit the band years earlier), was a special thrill. There were sheets on which Clifford Brown's name appeared; Quincy Jones's arrangements were well represented; Dexter Gordon, Fats Navarro, Art Farmer, Illinois Jacquet, and Arnett Cobb's old showpieces were scattered through the folder like loose pages in a history of jazz.

Finally, my eye fell on a piece called "Second Balcony Leap," but it meant nothing to me and I kept leafing. Bobby Platter chuckled slightly, pointed to the sheet, and said, "Now, that's a *mean* one." Apparently, "Second Balcony Leap" took its name from an Apollo performance by the band some years back. The piece, a scorching house-rocker, written by a player in the band, had been untitled until its first Apollo performance, one Saturday night. "Man," Platter said, "we played that piece and a cat in the second balcony got carried away and started dancing in the aisle up there." His finger was pointing toward the ceiling at the back of the theater, way off in the dark void. "When Gates put down his mallets and started playing the drums, this guy up in the second balcony started walking the seats." All the seat-walkers I'd ever known were Holy Rollers and Sanctified.

"That night," Bobby Platter went on, "Gates and the band was wailing! This cat was on the seat backs all over the balcony, till Gates came to his big drum finish with a cymbal crash. That cymbal was too much for my man in the balcony, and he leapt off the seat back, over the rail, landed in the aisle on the first floor, and kept on boogying right on up here on the stage with us!"

"Cheez!" I said. "That's a fifty-foot leap. I'm sure sorry I missed *that*." I wanted to know if it was likely to happen again.

"Don't worry bout it," Bobby said. "Schiffman made Lionel cut that number out of the program. Said the theater can't afford that kind of insurance!"

Mr. Schiffman, an Apollo presenter of some great longevity, had a keen eye for presentation at his theater, and he was smart enough to balance the heavy heat of a Lionel Hampton appearance with an act that moved at a different pace. He scored heavily that summer by booking opposite our band a child act of two little brothers who tap danced. Part of the enormous appeal these children had for the Apollo audience was that the smallest of them, a five-year-old named Gregory, had lost his front teeth to the tooth fairy. South of his nose, he was all gums. He and his brother, Maurice, a year or two older, had mastered the show-biz-sibling stage-rivalry routine. Gregory reveled in his professional role of "stage pest," feigning his puckish unwillingness to follow the sage direction and learned advice of the straight man, his elder brother. Gregory played his onstage role, royal pain in the big-brotherly neck, to perfection: a natural mimic, an exceptionally controlled hoofer, and a ham par excellence, he always ended his virtuoso skits of dance and deviltry with his big bright eyes blazing, as he flashed out across the Apollo footlights the most splendid set of gums in show business. The audience was his. And Lionel was smart enough to have Bobby Platter conduct the band for the Hines Kids. Even the mighty Hamp dared not stay on the stage with that kind of competition.

The final curtain came down on the first show of the first day with the audience roaring and Hamp and the rest of us sweating buckets. Mitchell and I rushed, half starved, out into Harlem's streets. Seventy minutes for breakfast and a fast tour of the Apollo neighborhood. In all the rush to get into the band, I hadn't caught up with Mitchell and his news.

In the five years since he had left Lockbourne, three had been spent with Hamp, playing all over Europe and the world. An old Harlem hand by now, Mitchell knew the Apollo neighborhood as only a Lionel Hampton sideman of long standing could know it.

Mitchell took off at a trot. "Come on, boy. I'm going to take you to the best place in Harlem for a good southern breakfast at the right price." Seated at a booth in a café run by Florida people, we ate the southern food like we were GIs again, and then the talk turned to our boss, Gladys. She still had to approve of my performance with the band, or I'd have to see if I could still shuffle off to Buffalo with Maestro Leinsdorf.

I pressed Mitchell for information. "What's Gladys really like, Mitchell?"

"Well, Ruff, I'll tell you. When I first joined the band, she would travel on tour with us more than she does now. Lionel and the rest of us usually travel in the band's bus, but Gladys drives her Jag XK120. We see more of her when we play in Europe than here in the States. She and I used to talk a lot out on the road. Her story was really very interesting. She comes from Oklahoma, where she was raised by an aunt. Once, when the band played in Oklahoma, Gladys and I drove out to visit the old lady. And, man, I'll never forget it. The place was in the sticks. I mean, there was *nothing* else anywhere *near* that place. Gladys told me that when she was a child, she had worked like a dog to learn a trade so she could get the hell away from there. She took up sewing and tailoring, and she got good at it and ended up working in California. She worked in Hollywood, sewing for movie people; wardrobe mistress or something. She was working for Joan Crawford when she and Lionel first got together."

Mitchell talked on of Gladys's earlier years, while we waded through the Harlem bustle back to the Apollo. It made me smile to see him— "man of the world" and old Harlem hand—his nose, eyes, and ears dazzled right along with mine by the familiar food smells from the South, the musically built slang, and Harlem's own "eye music," that high evidence of a social originality expressed in the swagger, in the color and style, of the clothing all around us.

"When did Gladys take over the business end of the band?" I asked.

"She told me that Lionel started his own band after Benny Goodman's mixed group with Lionel and Teddy Wilson broke up. After he left Goodman, Lionel had a pretty big name in the business, and his band did far better than anybody else, from a money standpoint. Gladys said all she ever saw of the money was a new Cadillac and a new mink coat every year. But no real *green*. She said she didn't know *what* the hell was happening to the money. She asked Lionel. He didn't know. She asked Joe Glaser, and he didn't know. So she said, 'Shit! I'm going to find out and manage it myself, then I'll *always* know.' So I guess that's when she started handling the money, and that's when she started investing and buying property, like the house they live in right up here on Sugar Hill.

"Lionel doesn't even *touch* the money now. You'll see for yourself when we go out on the road. When Gladys pays the band at the end of the week, Lionel stands in that line right along with me and you and the rest of the band to get his little allowance. She's definitely in control, and nothing gets by her. But I gotta tell you, man, if it wasn't for Gladys, Lionel wouldn't have a damn quarter today. Now, *anybody* will tell you *that!*"

As our Apollo shows alternated with the movie that first day, I was surprised that no two of them were the same. All it took for Hamp to switch gears and tear into something not in the plan was a call from a fan in the audience. "Hey, Hamp, blow 'Hamp's Boogie,' " and he would run to the piano to join Mitchell for a showy boogie-woogie duet, Lionel playing with two fingers on the high keys and Mitchell walking the bass and giving him chords underneath.

These deviations from the way we rehearsed the show were always exciting and often challenging; everyone but me knew all the music by heart. When Hamp pulled a fast switch, I alone had to grab frantically for the music. I was getting no closer to a routine that would impress Mrs. Hampton. I finally decided to treat Lionel's big changes less urgently. Instead of the mad rush through the folder to locate a piece when he threw me a curve, I told myself, To hell with the folder, and began blowing improvised obbligatos. It seemed to work. At least my lines were fresh every time, and very often it worked better than something I'd tried to sight-read and transpose. Bobby Platter encouraged me, and as I became more comfortable with it, I began choosing spots to add an occasional line along with Lionel's vibes solos.

Using my ear to accompany Hamp had its own rewards. Listening to his vibes playing more closely made me understand why he was such a durable attraction in our business.

Lionel, while still a child, began his musical life as a drummer and was taught the trade by a nun. Although he never became a great drummer, his mastery of timing, his formidable ear for melody and harmony, and the uncanny drummerly instincts that he brought to the vibraphone quickly made him one of the world's greatest jazz soloists. No show during our month at the Apollo came and went without my hearing some fresh and original example of Lionel's synthesis of all his gifts.

The New York newspapers always wrote up the band's annual Apollo stay. Several writers came during that first week, one after the other. The stage manager, a foul-mouthed old Southerner whom everybody called Puerto Rico, handed me a copy of the *Daily News* one day. Walter Winchell mentioned Lionel's new sound, which included a French horn played by "so-and-so."

Puerto Rico ripped into me. "Shows you what Walter-fucking-Winchell know bout jazz. Shit, you sound like a goddamn billy goat blowing that racket on my fucking stage. If you don't quiet down, I'm gonna have to git my hook for your ass." I finished reading what the paper said, handed it back to him, and left.

Bobby Platter had witnessed it all. He caught up to me and whispered, "It ain't like it sounds, man. Don't get mad. He doesn't say *anything* to anybody he doesn't like."

"Well, why is he talking about cutting me with his hook knife?"

"No, no, no." Bobby laughed. "He means his long neck-hook. He's the cat that runs the Apollo's Wednesday night amateur show. When the amateurs' acts stink, Puerto Rico always reaches from behind the curtain with that long hook and yanks them off the stage. He's been doing that stuff for years, since Ella Fitzgerald sang on the amateur show here back in the thirties! He really is trying to encourage you. He's just trying to see if you can take some ribbing."

Still, I decided to stay out of Puerto Rico's way. But the next day, as Mitchell and I came in for the first show, there stood Puerto Rico, his hook in one hand, and again he thrust folded paper at me. Another columnist had mentioned the show, Hamp's new sound, and, this time, my name. As I read, P.R. waved the hook back and forth in front of me, threateningly.

When I finished reading, I said to him, "You can save that hook for your mammy, Puerto Rico." He shoved his hand out for a shake. As soon as I took it, I saw it all. I'd passed the test by playing the old "swap insults" game. Putting him in the dozens as we call it in the South. His eyes lit up, and he made a quick little fake pass in the direction of my neck with his hook and laughed like hell. I had a new friend.

Finally, Saturday arrived and Gladys Hampton came to the show. Life backstage shifted into a new mode. Puerto Rico cooled his mouth and Hamp put on a new face to fit the sedate presence of the "boss lady." There wasn't time for me to take in the full effect of Gladys's entry, for I was preoccupied greeting my own pretty wife and my sisters, who'd driven down from New Haven. We all took pictures with Hamp and Mitchell and the Hines Kids. Mitchell took my little family group backstage to meet Mrs. Hampton.

Shaking Gladys's hand, Sister said, "I've read and heard so much about you and your work, and what a wonderful manager and businesswoman you are. I'm a businesswoman too. Our people *need* smart women in business and management." Gladys then said some complimentary things to me about the horn playing and welcomed me to the "band family."

Later, when she was out of earshot, Sister said, "Well, I bet she won't let Lionel end up with the white folks taking all his money and him going broke, like poor Joe Louis. Too bad Marva Louis didn't have her qualities, so she could have helped Joe that way."

I felt fabulously lucky to have got "tenure" in the band through Gladys's nod. Now, between shows, I took in the sights of Harlem, soaking it up with renewed pride in my step. At our dinner break next day, Mitchell said to me, "Ruff, let's hang out with the other guys for supper. You haven't seen all the right places yet." Wallace Davenport, our lead trumpeter, was from New Orleans, and so was the bassist, Chuck Bade. "Homeboys" tended to stick together on the road. Mitchell's Florida homeboy was Nat Adderley, our Tallahassee hot trumpet soloist. Most of Hamp's musicians were from the South and congregated in the abundant Harlem eating joints run by fellow Southerners.

That day, a large group of us went to a soul food joint for dinner. The owner, a lady who loved Hamp's band, knew we had less than an hour to eat and get back to the Apollo. She didn't bother with menus for us. Her verbal shorthand for the fare she served was only partially familiar to me. But it had an engaging logic. She called the musicians not by name but by their hometowns. Seeing Davenport and Bade caused her to holler out, "Hey, N'Awluns!" Then to the cook she yelled, "Two pianos on a plate, and two sides of wrinkles." Turning back to Chuck and Davenport, she asked, "Y'all want treaders or waggers, baby?"

Presently, the plates arrived with a fine order of ribs, the piano on a plate; there were chitterlings on the side, the wrinkles. Chuck Bade had declined the pig ears, or waggers; and Davenport waved off the treaders, saying, "Naw, never did like no pig feet."

I hadn't realized how much I had missed living in the language of the professional jazz musician.

CHAPTER TWENTY-NINE

On the Road

I T WAS TIME TO BOARD THE BAND BUS and crisscross the Midwest on my first road tour of one-night stands. Life on a band bus would be something new for me. In a band like Hamp's, it involves strict attention to long-established rituals, and the matter of seating is far from casual. Seniority and rank dictate choices. The third row back, to the right of the aisle, was Lionel's. He spread himself over two seats, his gear handily stacked in the overhead racks: home for a day or two, sometimes more. George Hart, Gladys's lieutenant, was a man with the body and mind of a dance hall bouncer. He was our road manager and paymaster, and his seat was just to the rear of Lionel's. Bobby Platter, Mitchell, and the other long-lived members of the band owned seats away from the bus wheels; seats over wheels are noisy, and the bumps in the road disturb sleep. And Lord help the man who stashed a suitcase containing shoes in the rack above George Hart's head.

"Every-damn-body knows shoes up over somebody's haid is bad luck, man! You wanna hava damn wreck widdis bus, fool?" he'd holler as he chucked the offender's Florsheims and Stacies out the window.

I enjoyed the talk and the lies that rang through the coach those first few minutes after boarding. Everyone seemed to go at it like a chorus—all jawing together about the highlights of the last engagement.

Lionel sounded off right along with everybody else, raising his voice above the raunchy din of jazzmen sharing close quarters. But Lionel seemed to have an inner clock buried somewhere deep in himself, which reminded him of some dark duty or a somber promise somewhere in his distant past. Suddenly he'd break off his woofing, settle into silence, stare off into the space before him as if looking hard at his own thoughts. It was the same look that took over his face when he played, *not* clowned but *really* played the vibraharp. There on the bus, that look always came just after boarding, and when it did, he settled himself silently in his seat to pray. After an interval, past his prayerful silence, he'd switch on his seat light, take down from above his head a little leather satchel in which he kept his reading glasses and Bible, and as his pointing finger followed the words on the page, he'd move his lips—on, and on, into the lonesome late night down the diesel-perfumed road.

There was one nagging matter I needed to get straight with Mitchell. All during our stay at the Apollo, I'd heard Lionel introduce Mitchell to the audience as " 'Dwike' Ike Eisenhower Mitchell." Up till then, I'd forgotten to ask Mitchell why the boss didn't just use Ivory, like everybody else, or even Gates, which he called me and the rest of us. Now, with quiet time on the bus, I finally asked.

"Well," he said, "you knew back at Lockbourne that I didn't want Ivory as my professional name. When I got out of the Air Force, I talked it over with my mother, up in Jacksonville. She spelled out the letters D-w-i-k-e. I don't know how she came up with it, but she said, 'You should call yourself that,' and that's how I took the name.

"Lionel likes Eisenhower; he calls himself a Republican, you see. And in his onstage clowning, he put Ike and Dwike together for those stupid-assed introductions." I'd never known a name change that became so quickly politicized.

Even with the rented piano we had in Mitchell's New York apartment while we played the Apollo, we did very little duo rehearsing. We were too beat when Gates let us off the Apollo stage. Now, on the road, we doubled our determination to make up for lost time. Whenever the band bus pulled up in front of a hotel in a new town on our schedule, the two of us would dash into the lobby, book a double room, stash our gear, and head for the nearest music store to rent a bass and a studio with a piano. Since Mitchell and I are both lusty snorers, single hotel rooms would have been a welcome luxury. But the cost of studios and instruments for our rehearsals demanded cutbacks in personal comforts. The few dollars we saved booking double hotel rooms were applied to rent for rehearsal studios. The more we economized, the more rehearsals we could afford. Unfortunately, not all music stores had basses or studios with pianos. If we found a store with a bass and no studio, it was often possible to persuade the owner (for the price of the bass rental) to call around town for another store, with a room for rent with piano. It was tricky, but generally we found space. When there was a piano and a room but no bass, we'd work on our new repertoire for horn and piano.

One afternoon in an Ohio town, we paid a music shop owner seven dollars for the use of a Baldwin in his display window and threw ourselves—French horn and Baldwin—into the lush sonorities of Ravel and Debussy. At a single session we arranged both "Reverie" and the lovely "Pavanne for a Dead Princess."

My first road payday brought me a shocking revelation. The pay envelope George Hart shoved at me was short—very short. I could only blame myself, for I had neglected, in my excitement over working with Hamp, to discuss pay with Gladys. At the Apollo, the pay was union scale; the six-day week (thirty-six shows) brought me $124, which I assumed would be the rate on the road as well. But in Cleveland, when I looked at my week's check, which had been prepared by Gladys, there was pay for only those days when we'd worked, and by Gladys's own reckoning, the days were calculated at twenty dollars a night. I'd made only eighty dollars that week, for dances in Cincinnati, Columbus, Dayton, and Cleveland; out of it, hotels, meals, and rehearsal studios were to be paid. There wasn't enough left from a week's pay to trouble a postal clerk for a money order to send home to Emma. Mitchell said that what I saw there was what I'd get.

"Why do you think Nat Adderley left after the Apollo?" he said. "Gladys is like that. She looks out for Lionel and for herself, but you'll see that it is usually at the young musicians' expense."

I was hopping mad at myself for not asking before I left New York. "We can make twice this much in New Haven," I said, "and have all the time in the world to rehearse." Mitchell patiently heard me out and then suggested that some of the places on our tour schedule would be worth experiencing: Los Angeles, and the Bay Area again. There'd be money from the recordings we were scheduled to make in L.A., *and* we were booked for a month in Las Vegas, at the brand-new Moulin Rouge, the only first-class hotel with casinos in that town where non-white people were allowed as guests. One of the hotel's chief attractions was Joe Louis, who was their "official greeter." I'd seen a picture of Joe standing at the front door, shaking the hand of every guest who entered. The promise of a handshake with Joe Louis was enough to take my mind off the pay for a little while.

Mitchell said, "The union scale for musicians in Las Vegas more than doubles what we got at the Apollo. That should give us time to write and rehearse a lot of new music. Maybe enough so we can come back to New York and get *real* work."

But the Moulin Rouge engagement sat way down at the bottom of my typed schedule, months away. Before getting there, we'd cross the continent, our bus dipping through and circling the Canadian provinces, followed by a week in Chicago's Blue Note nightclub. I splurged and sent for Emma to come to Chicago for a week. When we left Chicago for the ride to Salt Lake City, the band boarded the bus with the tight-jawed resolve of soldiers going to battle. It was a trip we'd have to make nonstop, because all the hotels in between were white-only. Mitchell and I curled up in our seats to sleep those nights away, telling ourselves that the money we saved on hotel rooms could go toward rehearsal studio rentals.

After the long days and nights of riding, and dining on sardines, cheese and crackers, cold cuts, Twinkies, and milk from grocery store sacks, Salt Lake City loomed in our thoughts like the Promised Land. The band had eyes only for the Saint Louis Hotel, a small black-owned establishment of a dozen rooms, known to the seasoned American motorists of color as an oasis in the desert of Jim Crow hotels. The Saint Louis wasn't much, but it offered the only showers and beds we'd see on the overland route from Chicago to the West Coast.

Our bus eased into Salt Lake City around midnight, in the chilling night-desert air. Lionel and the whole band came awake as we snaked our way through the streets and circled the imposing Mormon Tabernacle, in the shadow of which sat the Saint Louis Hotel. Bleary-eyed jazzmen up and down the bus pulled themselves awake and looked reverently out the window at the tabernacle, its outline lit with soft pastel electric light: a musical shrine, famous, like Carnegie Hall, as a site of landmark recordings and broadcasts. We all thought of the great choir; of Stokowski and the Philadelphia Orchestra; of the great organ—

The hiss of the bus's air brakes broke the spell. We were at the Saint Louis. Mitchell and I made our run ahead of the crowd into the lobby, where a sleepy nightman met us, shook his head, and said he was full. He had received mail reservations for only three of our group; Hampton, Hart, and Platter.

"I'm sorry," he said, "but it gets crowded here in the summer. Look at all those eastern license plates out front."

The mood of the fifteen bone-tired, sweaty black men was heavy but familiar. We all knew where we were. I knew I would be able to sleep better yet another night in that bus seat if I took a good walk. One turn around the tabernacle in the cool, fresh air would be enough exercise to bring on deep sleep.

On my way back to the bus, I passed a sign, HOTEL, under which there was an arrow pointing up a set of stairs. It was less than a hundred yards from the Saint Louis Hotel and on the same street. Mitchell and a small group of musicians were talking and smoking outside the bus door; their mood had improved. Getting Mitchell's attention from where I stood near the sign, I signaled that I was going to try the place upstairs. I figured that even if it was a white-only joint—there were no signs in Salt Lake City that I saw—then perhaps somebody there could tell me where we could rent a room, maybe even in a private home. It was worth a try. As I mounted the stairs, I could see that Mitchell was following. At the top of the steps was a door to a small, dingy lobby. Inside was a closed door with a night bell and a sign: RING FOR NIGHT

CLERK. I rang. The door opened, and a haggard white man in his dirty undershirt stuck his head out, and without a word slammed the door in my face.

Entering the lobby, Mitchell asked, "Anything happening?"

"Maybe the guy knows another place. Anything would be better than the bus." The door cracked open again just enough to accommodate a long double-barrel shotgun, shoved by its owner directly into my face. Out of the darkness within, I heard two clicks, followed by a voice saying, "Just ring the goddamn bell one more time, you nigger son of a bitch!"

"Ohhh shit!" Mitchell gasped.

That a person about to die sees his life flash before his eyes was only partly true for me as I stood peering down the double barrels. Alabama did flash through my thoughts, but it was all Fort McClellan, basic training, and Sergeant Display. The gun was too close to my face for me to try to wrestle it away from the man. If I just turned around and walked away, would I be shot in the back?

Mitchell had already made it to the stairs and out of the line of fire, and his voice was urgent. "Ruff, come on here! Just walk, man. Come on, Ruff—this is no place to die." I began walking slowly toward his voice, putting one foot in front of the other—the longest journey of my life—half expecting each step I took to be my last.

When I reached the bus, Mitchell was already there, telling everyone what had happened.

"No shit?" said Billy Brooks, our high-note trumpet man. There were murmurings of revenge. More than a little shaken, I got to my seat, needing quiet: time to think. Gradually, the other men without beds came aboard, and after a while we all settled down for another night.

It was Billy Brooks, still seething, who broke the silence. "Man, the world would never believe that in the very shadow of the mighty Mormon Tabernacle, a man can get his head blown off for asking for a hotel room." More murmurings, about "Molotov cocktails" being too good for the chicken-shit night clerk–gunman upstairs.

I thought hard about it and for a long time. Perhaps sending Ambassador Molotov up those stairs as my diplomatic emissary would have brought me some satisfaction. But my last thought before dropping off to sleep in my seat was: Joe Louis is waiting at the Moulin Rouge. Shaking his hand would be a greater satisfaction than any revenge I could get upstairs, and it would last longer. Maybe even a lifetime.

After we finished the dance that night in a Salt Lake City amusement park, the bus continued west across the desert, headed for a string of California towns. Late in the night—*Blammmm!*—a heavy thud came from the front of the bus. The wheels wavered, bags and horns spilled down from the overhead racks, gravel and sand pounded the bus's undercarriage and slowed us to a bogged-down halt on the roadside. The driver went, "Whew! Sorry, fellas, we just hit a horse. Musta been one of them wild mustangs. He came out of the dark, panicked at our lights, and ran right into us. The bus knocked him down, but he got up and took off again."

George Hart came out of his seat, screaming, "Whut sommich put his damn shoes upovva mah fuggin haaid?"

Billy Brooks said, "Aw, man, go on back to sleep. Ain't no shoes over your head, but you damn near had a face fulla horse's ass."

We limped on into the Los Angeles skid row district, where hotel rooms were cheap, so cheap that Mitchell and I decided to treat ourselves to one each. Since most of our southern California engagements were easy bus hops away from Los Angeles, we got even better rates on the rooms by paying weekly. Our days were free, and we found a music store just a few blocks from the hotel, where for a few dollars a day we could rehearse.

On our first day at the music store, Mitchell found his way into the little practice room, and with the door still open, sat down and began playing his heart out. His bombastic chords and the dazzling runs that covered the whole length of the keyboard seemed only to whet his appetite for playing on an instrument whose eighty-eight keys all worked. The piano was the best instrument he'd played on since Chicago, weeks before, and he celebrated his good fortune by indulging us both in a Baptist-flavored blues that sounded like a lament for Salt Lake City and other seats of sorrow. Mitchell seemed to be shaking off the bad times and mean manners of the desert. The music store owner perked up when we put the two additional instruments together with the piano. He sent out for coffee and exchanged the bass he'd rented me for a better one and a new bow. That doubled our sound and inspired Mitchell to start working out a bass line to "Yesterdays" modeled on the towering harmonies of Bach's Chaconne. The bowed bass, along with his full-voiced piano chords, sounded at times like a full orchestra, and I knew we were on our way to our real musical identity as a duo.

While still in Los Angeles, the band did a record for the energetic impresario Norman Granz. Nat King Cole came to the session. Nat had a deep love and admiration for Lionel's powerful gift. One of the great pleasures of that summer was witnessing the adulation Hamp enjoyed from the greats of jazz music. All the way from the Apollo to the West Coast, wherever we went, any jazz personality within earshot came.

We weren't at the studio long before word got around. Buddy Rich dropped by to play with us just for fun—off the record. Drummers Shelly Manne and Chico Hamilton, bassist Red Callender, trumpeter Harry "Sweets" Edison, and a crowd of other old friends all came. Benny Carter, the dean of the Los Angeles jazz cadre, was conspicuously absent, but Nat Cole said we'd see him when we got to Las Vegas. Carter had been retained by the Moulin Rouge as its music director that summer; another indication, along with Joe Louis at their door, that a class act awaited us there.

The bus pulled into Las Vegas on the afternoon of our opening night, and we rode slowly down the "strip," where the marquees of the major hotels advertised the names of their headliners. Louis Armstrong, Lena Horne, Billy Daniels, Billy Eckstine, Red Skelton, Spike Jones, Frank Sinatra . . . they were all working in town. Our driver followed the written directions on his map to the Moulin Rouge. We drove on and on, leaving the strip far in the distance. But there was nothing to see but barren desert. Our driver said, "Where the hell is it? These directions must be right." He stopped at an intersection and asked directions.

"You're going the right way," a man told him. "It's straight ahead of you and to the right." As we came to the right turn, the parched scrub brush turned into an oasis that might have been in French North Africa. There was the Moulin Rouge, looking lush and fabulous. In the parking lots and all over the grounds were men wearing the full-dress uniforms of French gendarmes. Everything was new and tastefully planned, with nothing of the gaudy bad taste of the neon palaces we'd passed on the strip.

I asked the uniformed doorman a most important question. "Where's Joe Louis?"

A little bemused by the urgency in my voice, he said, "He won't be on duty until the dinner hour, sir." Inside, the band assembled into a huddle in the lobby and the manager welcomed us, explaining the rules of our stay, our room rates, meal discounts, etc. "Your shows don't begin until eleven each night. We planned it that way so patrons and entertainers from the strip can come here after their last show, about midnight."

I took a cab to a music store, which rented me a bass for the month. We'd begin our duo rehearsals at three-thirty each morning, after the last show.

When I returned with the bass, the dinner hour had started and Joe Louis was shaking hands just inside the air-conditioned lobby by the main door. Joe stood there listening and talking to all his admirers. I took a side entrance to the pool area, near my room, reserving the thrill of my first handshake with Joe until I had time to savor it at my leisure.

When Mitchell and I, wearing our best street clothes, finished our discounted dinner, I left him and took a side exit, for a place in the Joe Louis line. Standing there, I rehearsed all the things I wanted to tell him. Just ahead of me were white couples, snapping pictures, shaking Joe's hand, saying: "You're a great American." "To us, you'll always be the champion." "It was a great day for America when you whipped Max Schmeling."

At last it was my turn. I stepped forward and looked up into Joe's kindly face. He stretched out his enormous mitt, which swallowed mine, and my vocal cords froze. While I tried to clear my throat and make my lips work, he squeezed my hand and said, "Welcum to the Moulin Rouge. Glad ta seeyer."

All my thoughts collided and locked in my jaws. Nothing seemed to work from the neck up. I nodded, and struggled to say something— anything. Finally, I gave up, bowed nervously to Joe Louis, and skitted away. I'd blown it.

Lionel called a rehearsal to go over the show an hour before show-time. It was lucky I'd memorized all the music by then, for my mind was busy composing letters to Emma, my dad, and my sisters, which I would sign: "From the hand that shook the Brown Bomber's, even if I was too nervous to talk to him."

Our first show had the usual enthusiastic opening-night crowd, consisting of Moulin Rouge hotel guests, well-wishers from L.A., and "strip regulars," who'd come to see Hamp from their digs across town. After our first show, while most of the band milled around the front lobby, watching Joe Louis, Louis Armstrong came through the door, giggling. He stopped to cut up with Joe Louis and spotted Lionel on the opposite side of the lobby. Lionel hollered, "Hey, Pops!"

"Gates!" Armstrong growled back. "I knew you was gonna stay here at this fine palace with me and the rest of the cats. Boy, you don't get no older. Gladys treating you awright?" After Pops and Gates caught up with their visiting, and our two New Orleans sidemen, Davenport and Bade, shook hands with their homeboy and got autographs, Armstrong went back to Gates, to announce: "Looka here, man. Lena Horne and her cats are on their way, and Billy Daniels too. We all got reservations for your next show, man. We gonna let you know if you're any good—heh heh heh!"

Armstrong had given us only a hint of the number of headliners there would be in our audience that night. Spike Jones came with a huge party of friends that included some of his musicians and Red Skelton. Our last show was twice as long as the first one had been. Once Hamp got hot, he couldn't be stopped. After it was over, Mitchell and I changed clothes, had breakfast, and brought the rented bass down to the bandstand for a long work session.

Until then, we had spent most of our rehearsals arranging and composing new material. None of what we'd learned was written down. We worked on new material by playing it over and over through countless repetitions until it was fixed in our minds and muscles. Little time had been spent polishing the music's performance. Now Mitchell said, "Ruff, let's spend some time getting our things tight before we begin adding any more music. Let's just work on performance and play what we already have the best we can." Even as we did just that, we couldn't resist making some changes, for we found that certain pieces worked better in different instrumental settings. For instance, if the true bass line, the bottom notes of chords, was taken from the bass and played by the piano, while the bass took different notes of the chord, new colors emerged. We found that we could add and sustain musical interest with devices such as switching the traditional or expected roles of our instruments and using the French horn alternately as an accompanying voice and a solo voice. Another kind of interest was added when we stressed the color tones of chords while exploiting the French horn's wide tonal range.

One morning after the show, we were rehearsing Mitchell's arrangement of "Yesterdays." We played through sections of it several times, polishing as we went. When we came to the big ending of the song, two musicians came out of the dark, applauding. They introduced themselves as the Dozier brothers. I recognized them. They were part of a band of five musicians who played every night in the gambling lounge off the lobby. They wore beautifully cut formal wear, and their manners matched their dress. They were not a jazz band but a middle-of-the-road group that sang familiar lounge favorites and played music calculated to serve as a congenial, nonintrusive background for the gambling casino. The senior Mr. Dozier, the group's leader, was very excited about our music. He led his brother up to the stage and extended his hand, asking us, "What are you guys doing here? You should be in New York, playing on the East Side!"

These were the first musicians to hear our duo. The senior Dozier said to us, "You guys don't know how glad I am to see somebody who wants to perform first-class music. My brother and I heard you rehearsing from outside, and came in and got the surprise of our lives. We recognized you both from Hamp's band, because we get to see a little of the show on our breaks every night." Mitchell told them something of our hopes. "Ruff and I used to play together in the Air Force, and now we're working on material while we're with Hamp. We aren't ready yet to take off on our own with our duo, but it's coming."

Over the next several days, the Doziers came back often to listen. Whenever we met around the hotel, where they, too, had rooms, they were full of advice for us about our music's presentation, how much of a classical music sound we should project and how much we should "swing," and the way we should dress onstage. "You guys should only work in clubs where you can play in white tie and tails," they insisted. "There's the Blue Angel, in New York, a classy East Side supper club. Lou Jacoby and Max Gordon own it. Max owns the Vanguard too; maybe that would be a good spot for you to get started. And don't forget about arranging. With your training, you guys could do a hell of a job and could earn a *lot* of money writing for other acts and singers. Look at Benny Carter."

Benny Carter's career as an arranger was not news to us. We knew that he had lived in Europe during the thirties because the doors of Hollywood and the radio networks were closed to all but white writers. Mitchell and I still had not met Carter. Though he had written a lot of music for shows that had preceded us at the Moulin Rouge and was still retained by the hotel, he did his work at home in Los Angeles, where he lived and wrote music for a weekly television drama.

It was near the end of our month's stay in Las Vegas when Carter came to the Moulin Rouge. A large revue called Larry Steele and His Brown Skin Beauties would take the stage in the main showroom after Hamp's show moved on. Carter, who had written music for the show, came to begin long collaborative sessions with Steele and company at the hotel. There were fast-moving, high-kicking dance numbers featuring the "beauties," musical numbers for singers, and tons of music from Benny Carter's pen. One night as Louis Armstrong was leaving the lobby with his band for their job on the strip, Benny came into the lobby from the coffee shop. Seeing each other, they rushed together, hugged heartily. Armstrong said, "King Carter! Man, you just keep on arranging and writing that music, cause I don't want you blowing no more of that mellow trumpet round here; you might put old Pops outta woik!"

I had known that Benny was a formidable "triple threat" in our business—a master of arranging, saxophone, and trumpet. But did anyone but Louis call him King? Maybe it was a private joke.

The next day at the swimming pool, I saw Armstrong watching his singer, Velma Middleton, a three-hundred-pounder, making beautiful swan dives from the pool's high diving board. Louis and a crowd of swimmers stood poolside, rapt with admiration for Miss Middleton's wondrous form. She went to the high board several times, leapt, arched her ample torso gracefully, and broke the water, making barely a ripple. It made Louis cry gleefully: "Lord have mercy, what little water that gal knocked out of that pool wouldn't even fill up a teacup!"

When he finished applauding the diver, I went to him and asked, "Mr. Armstrong, I heard you call Benny Carter *King* Carter last night. Is that be—"

He interrupted me: "That's cause he *is* a king, man! You got Duke Ellington, Count Basie, and my man, the Earl of Hines, right? Well, Benny's right up there with all them cats. Everybody that knows who he is call him King. He *is* a king!" We were interrupted by Mrs. Armstrong, who had business with Louis. He excused himself, saying, "Catch me later, man. I can tell you a whole *lot* about that cat!"

Mitchell and I had wanted to ask Carter to listen to us; perhaps he could give us some pointers and maybe he had some compositions we could play. But there never seemed to be time. And Louis Armstrong checked out before I caught him again.

I still had unfinished business with Joe Louis, and I got my chance at it one night during a lull at the main door before our first show. Joe was taking a short break and sat in the lobby, enjoying a tall fruit drink. I didn't want to spoil his rest, and waited until he took his place again by the door. Then I approached him, extending my hand, which he took, saying: "Looka here, champ, haven't I seen you before? You're one of Hamp's men, right?" I confessed that he had seen me before in the greeting line, and happy to find that speech was still in me, I said, "Champ, I'm from Alabama just like you are, so I wanted to shake hands with you, but I kept getting nervous and coming back."

"You know," Joe said, "people don't know how tough it is to shake hands all night. Look at this!" He held up his right hand and showed me that it was swollen and irritated. "Man, my hand didn't get this sore boxing Max Schmeling! I soak it and put talcum powder and stuff on it, but it still gets sore every night."

We talked a little about Alabama. "A whole lot of people from Alabama come here to see me, both colored and white people, and all of em very nice. They must be proud of coming from there, cause they all tell me about it." Seeing how sore his hand looked, I didn't have the heart to ask him to use it to sign yet another autograph just for me, so I let him go.

Gladys checked in at the Moulin Rouge about midway through our stay. Learning that Mitchell and I were working all night every night after the show, she sent George Hart to talk to us and find out our plans. While we rehearsed one night in the auditorium, Hart strode from the back, where he'd apparently been listening for a while. Slouching up to the bandstand, he asked, "Whut chal doing?"

Mitchell said, "Jamming."

"Jamming, my ass! I ain't no muzishin, but I can *damn* sho tell jammin fum prakzin. You sommiches prakzin an gittin ready to go off on yo own, aincha?" Mitchell's piano sounded the opening chords of "Moonlight in Vermont": all the answer Hart would get. We both knew our days with Hamp were finally ending, even though we weren't ready to go. Hart left, obviously more than a little annoyed at being ignored.

We packed up the bass and went back to our room, and each of us wrote out the customary two-week notice: we would be leaving the band at the end of the Moulin Rouge engagement. The two-week notice is a courtesy the musicians' union demands of sidemen and bosses about to part ways. Mitchell shoved his notice under Hart's door later that night. I gave him mine the next morning in the coffee shop.

Gladys phoned Mitchell in the hotel room the night after Hart's visit; she wanted a meeting. He returned from the meeting shaken.

"Man, I just can't believe the things that woman said to me."

"Like what?" I asked.

"Like how ungrateful I am, after all she's done for me to make me a star! Me, a fucking *star!* Hell, I make union minimum—scale when I'm lucky—and twenty-five dollars a night on one-nighters. I'm supposed to be *grateful* for all she's done for *me.* Oh, incidentally, she says that you are a disruptive influence in the band. She doesn't want you to work out your two-week notice. You're fired. She's ordering your ticket back to New York now." I said, trying to be cool, "OK, but tell me what else she said."

"Well," he went on, "I told you that when I first joined the band, she and I were pretty close. She liked to hear me play the piano, she said, and we'd go to parties after the show sometimes—especially when we played in Europe and in Israel, because the newspapers and reviewers over there wrote complimentary things about my playing. I often got asked to play alone on television and radio over there. Gladys got upset when I played without the band or Lionel, and said I shouldn't negotiate my own terms; she would do it. She wanted me to sign a management contract with her and promised to get me record contracts and engagements apart from the band. Of course, I would still be the band pianist. Figuring that Gladys Hampton could really promote my career if she wanted to, I signed the damn contract with her for three years. It's probably expired by now."

I asked him, "How much work and how many record contracts did she negotiate for you?"

His eyes blazed. "The same damn number she negotiated for *you!*" Then he added, "Now you can bet that she's going to do *anything* in her power to hurt us. Lionel sure as hell doesn't need us in this band, and Gladys really ought to be trying to help us in the business rather than hold us back."

George Hart paid me off the next day, giving me my plane ticket and a final remark: "Listen, Ruff, don't you know Joe Glaser ain't gonna book y'all?"

"Who asked him?" I said, knowing how he hated short, smart-assed answers.

Even though I was excused from playing with the band, I stayed on at the hotel, and Mitchell and I continued rehearsing, only harder. We had learned twenty or so pieces; twice that number was our goal before we'd launch ourselves as a working duo.

Bobby Platter, our staunchest rooter and closest friend in the band, had heard about the row and came to say how sorry he was. Mitchell really respected Bobby, so he asked him to come listen to us and give us his suggestions and an honest critique. He came often and was the model of encouragement always. To each of us, he privately offered any help he could give, even money if it came to that. "You cats *got* to make it, as long as you play the kind of music you're working at now," he said.

Lena Horne's bassist, George Duvivier, was staying there at the hotel. A master of the bass fiddle, he had played and recorded with the best bands and musicians in our business. His bass work and professional carriage made him one of the most valued and highest-paid classy sidemen in all show business.

One morning he bounced into the rehearsal room with his bass, and Mitchell said, "G.D., take the cover off that thing and let's play something. Let me hear you bow it." G.D. obliged. The sound was unbelievably balanced and pure. Mitchell said, "So that's the way a *good* instrument is supposed to sound!" George shoved the bass at me. "Here you go, ol' buddy—have at it." Then he sat quietly and sipped vintage Scotch from a paper cup, as Mitchell and I played through "Yesterdays" and "Stella by Starlight." When we were through, we asked him for suggestions for improvements.

"Improve on *that?* I love it. Just do more of it. Well, maybe a thing or two you could do." He took back his bass and demonstrated how I could more easily negotiate certain phrases, reduce unneeded hand movement by simply playing in a different position on the fingerboard, use a different bow stroke; he suggested how Mitchell might heighten an effect by revoicing certain piano chords. What Lena Horne was paying long money for was ours for the fun of it. At last we had some experienced musical advice, our own "resident coach."

By the time we met Duvivier, we'd stopped using the bandstand in the main auditorium. I slipped one of the night janitors five bucks to leave unlocked a door to a smaller banquet room that had a piano. At about 5:00 A.M. every day, George, Mitchell, and I made that room our hangout, safe from intrusions by hotel staff and Gladys's lieutenants.

Having arrived at his musical maturity and good station after years of grueling study and application to his craft, road experience with bands, the usual color bars in public accommodations and employment, Duvivier still exuded a refreshing cheerfulness. We were in the coffee shop one morning after rehearsing when I noticed that Mitchell was slyly urging George to talk about himself. He was probing for secrets to George's cheerfulness. "G.D., you got to be the jolliest sommich I ever met in my life, man. Didn't you ever have bosses like Gladys?"

"Well, ol buddy," George said with a sympathetic shake of his head, "I've been at it longer, much longer than you, and I've had my share of the slickest in the business, but Gladys never gave me the pleasure!" He exploded with laughter that shook him into a quick little up-and-down bounce in his seat.

Mitchell pressed on. "Well, I know you live in New York, but you're on the road with Lena a lot. I want to know how you all deal with that segregated-hotel shit. Do you all fly to all your engagements?"

George said, "Lena does. Not me, at least when I can help it."

Mitchell asked, "Well, how do you and your bass get from New York to Las Vegas?"

"Easiest thing in the world, ol buddy," said George. "I drive."

"You mean you drive to Chicago and stop to sleep, then to Salt Lake City to the Saint Louis Hotel, then drive on here by yourself?"

"Oh, no," said George. "That's Stone Age segregation-dodging. I drive from New York to Las Vegas—period. Nonstop!"

"But that's impossible," said Mitchell.

"Finish your coffee and come go with me."

In the parking lot sat George's new Cadillac.

"Get in. Let's go for a ride in the desert." The front seat on the passenger side was specially made to slide back and down to accommodate his bass fiddle for a cushioned, cradlelike ride. We headed for the open road, as George explained a new feature for Cadillacs that year—alcohol fuel injection, with which a mixture of high-octane fuel and alcohol injected into his four-barrel carburetor turned his vehicle into a rocket.

"I love sophisticated machinery that delivers what it promises," George said. "It's like music to my ears." The Cadillac purred, and George's grin spread.

"I only use the fuel injection on straight roads when the cops aren't out. You see, I don't need a lot of sleep. Driving coast to coast nonstop is my *thing*."

We cruised past the strip and out into the desert, picking up speed at an awesome rate. I cried, "*Wheee!* George, that fuel injection sure is powerful!"

"Not yet, ol buddy. I didn't kick it in yet."

Mitchell and I looked sideways at each other, but mostly kept our eyes glued to the speedometer. When the needle on the dial touched 110 mph and we felt ourselves still accelerating, Mitchell and I hollered in unison: "That's OK, George, that's OK. We'll take your word for it."

George eased back the fuel injector, to our great relief, and broke into his bouncing chuckle. Mitchell took a moment to relax. "Whew!" he said. "Man, that ain't fast driving, that's low flying!"

"Well," said George, "you cats asked how I deal with segregated living on the road, didn't you?"

Mitchell replied, "Yes, George, but at speeds like that, I'll stick out the segregation for a while!"

The day came when Benny Carter's music and Larry Steele's Brown Skin Beauties replaced Hamp's show on the Moulin Rouge stage. Mitchell, having worked out his two-week notice, was a free man, and the Mitchell-Ruff Duo was launched. All we needed to complete the launch was a job.

Instead of flying east with the tickets Gladys provided, we cashed them in and took the train to save money. In Chicago, Mitchell made a train connection to Jacksonville, Florida, for a visit with his mother and stepfather. I boarded a train for New Haven.

One evening, fully recovered from the long summer season on the road, and stuffed full of delectable Virginia fare from my mother-in-law's table and the turnip greens my sisters cooked, I went over to the

Monterey to visit Mr. Greenlee. He jumped up from his chair when he saw me. "Hey, Red!" he said. "Man, I thought you might be dead or something!"

"What do you mean?" I asked, puzzled.

Mr. G., looking really serious, answered, "Didn't you hear the news about Hamp's band in that bad bus wreck out west?"

I told him that I'd left the band a few days earlier to form a duo with my old army buddy.

"Well, your timing was right on the money. They say somebody got killed and nearly everybody was hurt."

Mitchell called me that night with the details. Bobby Platter and Lionel had no serious injuries. George Hart and Wallace Davenport had both their legs broken, and Wallace's pelvis had been crushed. The new driver, not the guy we knew, was killed instantly. "I talked to Bobby's wife," Mitchell said. "It sounded like a nightmare. But he's on his way home. Naturally, the band won't be working for quite a while. Man, I knew that bus had to crash someday. You and I sure were lucky to leave when we did. You keep praying for Wallace and George, Ruff. I know I will."

A couple of weeks later, Mitchell called and said he was playing piano in a little joint in Jacksonville. He'd play a couple of hours in the late afternoon for cocktails, break for dinner, and play again from nine till midnight. The owner wanted to hire the duo, he said, and the job would be a good chance to perfect our material while making a paycheck. I started packing.

We played our first music as a duo for pay in the Biltmore Bar in Jacksonville. We made twice what Gladys had paid us on the road, and the customers were civilized. Musicians started coming in regularly to hear us, and a local paper ran an article that drummed up more interest. Suddenly the Biltmore was the hottest joint in downtown Jacksonville.

With a piano we rented for daytime rehearsals at Mitchell's mother's house, we arranged repertoire that we could try out on the bandstand at night. In a few weeks, we were able to perform an entire evening of music from memory without repeating: not jamming or endless improvising, but "worked" material. After a couple of months of hard rehearsing, we knew we were ready for New York.

CHAPTER THIRTY

The Summer of
Our Baptism

NEW YORK, in the fall of 1955, was a beehive of jazz activity. There were a couple of dozen clubs midtown with a strictly jazz policy. Only the established "name" groups—Miles Davis, Dizzy Gillespie, Max Roach, Clifford Brown—had agents. Club owners preferred to hire players without big reputations at union minimum wage, without adding the agent's commission.

We visited all the clubs the Dozier brothers back in Las Vegas had told us about, Mitchell as the music director, I as business manager. The Blue Angel did a showcase one night a week. One way of advertising a new act was to arrange a showcase and invite club owners, agents, managers, and concert promoters. Lou Jacoby, the Blue Angel's owner, gave us a showcase spot, and I got busy phoning every jazz club owner, manager, and promoter I could identify in New York. Mitchell and I showed up, as instructed by the Doziers, in white tie and tails (rented) and played our most sophisticated "East Side" material: mostly songs from Mabel Mercer's elegant portfolio, but also lots of Cole Porter and Noel Coward. The audience buzzed. At the intermission we heard things like:

"What elegant music!"

"Great East Side material!"

"Those tails look mahhvelous."

At last I put away the bass and made ready to talk with the club owners, bookers, and promoters I'd invited.

It was a long wait. Nobody from the jazz world had come.

After that fiasco, I just went around asking for auditions in the clubs; I was astonished at how easy they were to come by. Nightclub owners regarded auditions as part of doing business. The Embers, an East Side restaurant famous for its good food and strong pianists, was run by Ralph Watkins, a gentleman and a piano enthusiast. Ralph listened and encouraged us to keep on the path we'd chosen; he hired us for a Monday night while his regular headliner rested.

All entertainers and musicians working in New York were required to pay a fee to the police department for a cabaret permit. Fingerprints were a must, along with a mug shot that went on a card the applicant had to carry at all times on the job. The card, according to the police, ensured that New Yorkers would not be entertained by felons. Among the legends sitting out that season was Billie Holiday.

We got into a routine. Our first couple of months in town consisted of long morning rehearsals at Mitchell's loft. Afternoons were for auditions. Avoiding expensive taxis, we worked out a system to hustle my horn and the bass around the city on foot, on buses and the subway. With one man carrying the neck of the bass and the other gripping the tailpin and the horn, we could scoot onto a crosstown bus, up and down subway staircases, and through rush-hour jams with the agility of moles in moss.

The sight of two fast men hefting a bass fiddle and a French horn overhead while streaking through turnstiles and traffic was enough to shock and immobilize even New Yorkers just long enough for us to ease in and out of situations of astounding tightness. Even rush hour never slowed us down—a good thing, because restaurant auditions always ended just before the "happy hour," at five. That threw us into the evening press of downtown traffic toward Mitchell's loft for supper.

On a very good day on the circuit, if the Muses were with us and we made a well-executed run for the bus while a Samaritan held the door, it was not unusual for little old white ladies to spring to their feet and offer their seats, even to dig deep into cavernous purses and shopping bags for a tissue to sop our dripping brows. And more than once, a cookie or a salty pretzel accompanied the tissue, along with a good wish. Once, a virtuoso bus-boarding with both instruments on the Fifth Avenue line prompted a small baby to clap and squeal with glee, and plead for an encore; "Do again. Again. Make them *again*, Mommy!"

Club owners, wherever we auditioned that season, wanted records. "You guys ain't got no records? How the hell good can you *be?*"

Jimmy Garafola, the boss at the Café Bohemia down in the Village, was not a man of Ralph Watkins's sophistication. He listened to our audition one day and gave us a job as "intermission band," to start the following month. He didn't say who the main attraction was. We heard him explain to his brother, Spunny, who helped run the place, why he had hired us.

"It's simple rithmatic, Spunny. Just two fucking guys! They make as much noise as three fucking guys. Why keep paying three? Who needs trios!"

Mitchell and I were already out the door after the audition when Garafola hollered to us, "Every group wot woiks heah got records. Even *bums* got records, like that fucking wild man Mingus ya woiking opposite. He got lotsa records."

Outside, Mitchell shook his head. "Damn, Ruff, imagine getting hired because you are the world's smallest and cheapest group, by somebody who calls *Mingus* a bum with records!"

As we hiked back to the loft, with records on our minds, it occurred to me that I had nothing to lose by telephoning the only record executive I'd ever met. Marvin Holtzmann at Epic had produced a record I'd played on with Art Harris, a Yale student composer, Jo Jones, Milt Hinton, and Billy Taylor while I was still a student in New Haven.

I called, and Holtzmann remembered me. He said, "A duo, huh? Well, that's sure not expensive." I asked if he wanted us to audition.

"No, I believe you're good. Besides, how much can we lose paying union scale to two guys?" We went to the studio the next week and finished our first album in two sessions.

We were not about to rest on our laurels just because we had a job at the Bohemia the next month opposite Charlie Mingus and a record in the can. I kept telephoning club owners for auditions, and it paid off a few days later with something on the East Side, a supper club called the Composer. The room was lovely, and it regularly booked piano soloists and trios. We showed up there early one afternoon to audition for the owner, Sy Baron, a sly-looking ex-tailor. The room was dark, and all tables were empty, except for the one where Baron and a big, flashy blonde dined. From their conversation, we gathered they hadn't known each other long. But even in the darkness we could see Baron, his hands underneath the table, urgently exploring everything the blonde had. Mitchell pouted for a minute, then whispered to me, "That man's mind isn't on this audition."

We began playing "Stardust," and before we'd played two measures, the blonde took a firm hold on the boss's hands and placed them solidly on top of the table, saying, "Oh, I just love 'Stardust'; it's my favorite song." Baron, showing disappointment at his loss, nodded at us and said, "Yeah, good number, good number." He came over while we were still in the tune, and said, "Nice sound for just two guys. Can you start next week?"

We both nodded, and Baron said, "I've heard enough. You can go."

But it was the Café Bohemia job that was our baptism in the working world of thoroughly modern jazz. The Charlie Mingus Jazz Workshop was newer than next week. Mingus showed his blinding bass virtuosity only on occasion; it was his compositions, and the performances of them his musicians rendered, that brought audiences to the club. His music set him apart from all his peers at that time. He had taken up serious protest music. "Fables of Faubus," a portrait in music of the Arkansas governor who refused to allow the racial integration of schools or any-thing else public in that state, was a raging, poignant statement in which the band made wide use of dissonance, and Mingus admonished his drummer, Danny Richmond, to sound lots of sirens, rasps, pistol shots, and gongs. So learned were the harmonic, contrapuntal, and rhythmical elements of his music that all but the most "socially aware" jazz critics stayed away from him in droves. One night, on Mingus's birthday, a well-meaning young white writer and jazz critic came to hear the band. A true fan, the young man approached Charles confidently. "Happy birthday, Charlie," he said. Without a pause, Mingus replied: "Ain't no more happy birthdays for Emmett Till."

Garafola, who'd heard the exchange, yelled to his brother: "Ya see, Spunny, I told ya he was a fucking wild man!" Then to Mingus: "Jesus, Charlie! This guy didn't lynch that little colored kid in Mississippi. I bet he never been near the fucking place. Ya oughta 'pologize, Charlie, fer Chrissake!"

But there was another side to the Mingus personality, which showed itself in some of his music. This was especially so in an arrangement he'd made of the poetic ballad "Laura." When he chose to let his lyrical side shine through, Mingus's music could challenge the tender elegance of Schubert. During one of our Café Bohemia intermissions, I persuaded him to teach me his special "Laura" bass line, and I later made it the basis of a composition.

Mingus was also one of the first of his crowd to declare himself a Dwike Mitchell fan. He often sat and listened to our sets. One night he said to Mitchell, "Dwike, I heard a lotta cats play piano, but nobody has your 'attack,' loud or soft." He invited us to his house to hear some of his music, which he taught us by rote, refusing to write it down. I'm sorry we didn't write it out for ourselves, for it was interesting, lovely, and unique. There seemed never to be enough time to continue the rote sessions with him or to arrange and rehearse all our own music. Fortunately for me, I found enough time to take a few bass lessons from him, for which he always refused to let me pay.

The Café Bohemia was one of the busiest clubs in New York that summer. Jimmy Garafola had come to know the importance of records because one made by another great bassist, Oscar Pettiford, put the joint on the map. Oscar wrote and recorded a piece called "Bohemia After Dark," featuring Cannonball Adderley. Jazz radio stations played it a lot, and soon the place was packed every night with New York's hippest modern-jazz fanatics.

When the Charlie Mingus Jazz Workshop moved on, our Epic record was just coming out. Garafola, not a man to fight success, kept us on at the same ninety bucks a week each, and we became the intermission band for the Miles Davis Quintet.

"Ya see, Spunny," Garafola boasted, "we got one of the most expensive acts in jazz right along with the cheapest, all together on the same stage. This jazz business is simple fucking rithmatic, I keep telling ya."

Coming out of an afternoon movie on Broadway one day, I spotted two very familiar-looking men walking toward me. As my eyes adjusted to the sunlight, I recognized Bill Doll, a celebrated and highpowered press agent Pete Hodgson had introduced me to while I was at Yale. Doll was Silly Putty's press agent, and Pete and I had visited him often to pub crawl around New York.

I stopped Bill and we shook hands. He was walking with the English actor David Niven.

I caught Bill up on my career: told him about having left Lionel Hampton to form the duo, our new record, and that we were working in a jazz joint in Greenwich Village opposite Miles Davis. Doll got excited. "Oh, good. I'll come to see you and bring some people."

Niven perked up too: "Jolly good, Bill! Count me in, will you? We all need a bit of diversion. We're working too hard."

A few nights later, the duo was on the Café Bohemia bandstand when a waiter put two drinks on the floor by the piano, said they came from the party along the wall with David Niven in it. He handed me a note from Doll, saying he'd arrived with a large group of his staff that was publicizing Mike Todd's new movie, *Around the World in 80 Days*.

When we took our intermission and sat with the Doll-Niven party, Bill took out a little notebook, asked me a bunch of questions as he wrote, and said he'd call some press people next day and get our names in the papers. In an aside to Niven, he said, "Don't tell Mike Todd I'm moonlighting."

Mitchell and I didn't expect anything to come of what Doll said, but he kept his word, and newspaper columnists began mentioning our names. Some of them actually came to hear us, and before long Garafola had *our* notices plastered on the walls and put pictures of us on the marquee under those of Miles Davis. We stayed on at the Bohemia for months, working as the intermission band and learning from people like Max Roach, J.J. Johnson, Jimmy Smith, Horace Silver, and Stan Getz. It was definitely the summer of our baptism.

The hottest and most expensive name in jazz that year was the team of Count Basie and Joe Williams. Their recording of the lusty blues number "Every Day" kept them at the top of the record charts and sold out all their club engagements.

Birdland, the famed basement jazz club on Broadway, was Basie's New York home base at the time. The owners took a cue from Jimmy Garafola and booked jazz's smallest and cheapest group—us—as Basie's intermission act. That was great, but also not so great. I mean, no band of *any* size could hope to come onto a bandstand left hot and rocking by Count Basie and Joe Williams and expect anything of a Birdland audience except certain death.

The subway ride uptown to Birdland for that first night opposite Basie seemed like a ride into the darkest doom of hell.

I said to Mitchell, "It would be better for us to just get off this subway and sit on the third rail. We're gonna die anyway opposite all that sound." Mitchell just sat there looking grave.

Our first set started at nine o'clock; Basie's show would begin at ten. All tables had reservation signs on them, and by nine forty-five the place was packed. We could feel the audience's anticipation mount as Basie's showtime approached. We finished our set to nothing but tepid applause from the audience and sneaked offstage as the lights went down. Basie's men filed onto the stage one by one and sat in the dark. And then a bright light flooded the whole bandstand, showing the band primed and confident. Birdland's master of ceremonies, Pee Wee Marquette, a brash midget with a hard face, bellowed over the microphone:

"Ladies and gentlemen, Birdland proudly presents *Count Basie* and his band, featuring *Joe Williams!*" The crowd came roaring to life, and for one and a half hours, Basie led his men through the musical romp his audience had come to hear. Master showman that he was, he paced his presentation to steadily excite his listeners out there until they were primed for Joe Williams and "Every Day." One time through "Every Day" would never be enough; the crowd screamed for more. As the band held on to the song's final chord, Basie smiled his inimitable little smile into the spotlight and cooed into the microphone: "One more time!" "Every Day" and every living thing in Birdland rocked on. After several more encores, it was time for Basie's intermission. The audience couldn't stop buzzing. Even the waiters danced around the joint, hustling drinks with hot excitement.

Just before we went onstage, I said to Mitchell, "I don't want to do this. I just wish I had died when I was a baby."

Such talk always unnerved him. Wringing his hands, he said to me, "Hush, Ruff! Just remember the plan, and keep praying."

The plan could be described with just one word: contrast. We took the bandstand knowing it was our only chance of surviving the experience. The louder Count Basie played, we had resolved, the softer we would play. The hotter the pulse of his rhythm section, the more of our florid piano–French horn repertoire we'd do.

About midway through our first soft and florid French-horn-and-piano song ("Stella by Starlight"), I saw Count Basie ease from the table he shared with his wife's party and slip around the bandstand to a spot that gave him an unobstructed view of the piano and Mitchell's hands. He motioned to his guitarist, Freddie Green, to join him, and in a little while, other men of the band were hushing conversation around the room. Suddenly, as if commanded by the angel of silence, Birdland was quiet.

The room's stillness hovered as a soundless echo. The audience's attention followed our sound down to the faintest whisper. Our fears and nervousness faded away. We were free.

As we ended "Stella by Starlight," it was Count Basie who led the applause from where he stood. The audience, following his example, applauded with an enthusiasm to match his, and Freddie Green's, and Joe Williams's, and Joe Newman's, and Frank Wess's, and Snooky Young's, and Frank Foster's, and Thad Jones's.

One of my best memories comes out of that moment. Basie, by leading his audience's attention to a couple of defenseless young musical neophytes, proved his noble heart. When I later said as much to Mitchell, he replied, "You can call it his noble heart, Ruff. I call it his religion."

That night, Count Basie and his musicians became our musical godfathers. In the weeks that followed, they brought friends to hear us, and they talked to us in the dressing room about what they liked or the things in our presentation that needed work: solid, reliable, and free show business counseling. Birdland became our New York home whenever the owners booked a high-price group that needed an intermission band; and for years, we continued to come back to Birdland to reaffirm our commitment to "contrast" opposite Dizzy Gillespie and his big band, Miles Davis, Dinah Washington, Sarah Vaughan, Lester Young, Carmen McRae, Oscar Pettiford, and Stan Kenton.

CHAPTER THIRTY-ONE

The Legacy That
Is Yours

AFTER ABOUT A YEAR of club work and recording, Emma and I were able to begin saving to buy our own first house. She was working as a substitute teacher in New Haven's high schools while the duo was playing the club circuit in a string of cities across the country. Things slowed down in New York from time to time, and Mitchell and I, when not traveling, happily brought the duo to various New Haven clubs. I knew all the club owners, and old friends always came to hear us. One of the best things about being at home was that Mitchell and I had time to get a lot of rehearsing done and learn new material.

All my family, and especially Emma, adored Mitchell, and from the moment we formed the duo, he immediately became a member of the clan. Emma was happy to see us work out our plans and fix our musical directions. All my musical priorities now were bound up in the duo; my earlier aspirations to play in a symphony orchestra were transferred to the more personal challenge of building the duo into a world-class enterprise.

The major frustration for Mitchell and me in those days was the difficulty of expanding our work beyond nightclubs. We had our eyes on the concert circuit, where we could reach the audiences we wanted most to hear us. Nightclubs, with their long hours, low pay, and often unwholesome atmosphere, were, at best, limited. So we started to look elsewhere.

One day in 1956 we got lucky. My good friend the trumpet player Jonny Glasel, whom I'd loved playing with at Mr. Greenlee's and in other clubs when we were students in New Haven, was now living and playing in New York. It happened that his girlfriend, Gilly—Ruth Mary Gilfillen—worked for an antique wholesaler on Fifty-seventh Street, next door to a small booking office. Through them she heard that a midwest agency specializing in college concerts was coming to New York, looking for new acts. She and Johnny gave me a call at Mitchell's New York apartment.

"Show up with Mitchell at Fifty-seventh Street, ready to play 'college-type' jazz," Gilly said.

"When should we be there?" I asked.

"In an hour."

We made it on time. Pryor-Menz was the name of the booking agency. Its seat of operations was, of all places, Council Bluffs, Iowa. We learned that the agency had been booking concerts and lecture tours for over a hundred years, had presented attractions as far apart in their appeal as Mark Twain and Huddie Ledbetter. Dave Brubeck's concerts were sweeping college campuses, and Pryor-Menz wanted in on Brubeck's domain.

Our audition went well enough for the Iowa bookers to sign us up for a three-week tour of midwestern colleges the following summer, 1957. They promised that if we did well, they would arrange for another agency, in the South, to take us on and combine two tours into one. We signed contracts on the spot.

Even as we played in New York jazz clubs, our minds worked over the challenge of the upcoming college tour. We asked ourselves: What kind of programs should we be preparing for college audiences? Much sooner than we expected, and in the most surprising way, we got our chance to find out.

It all began when a group of New York white socialites came to Birdland to hear the duo play. These women had pioneered an organization called Young Audiences Inc., which presented music in an enriching educational setting to schoolchildren in New York. Now they were covering the country. Among the organization's founders was Mrs. Edgar Leventritt, sponsor of the Leventritt Competition, one of America's earliest world-renowned contests for young musicians. Another spark plug in the group's engine was Mrs. Lionello Perera, of the international banking family. Mrs. Perera, an intimate of the Toscaninis, was also a major contributor to the Giuseppe Verdi Home for retired musicians in Milan. She regularly sponsored young musicians and gave them rehearsal space in her comfortable Madison Avenue home. Mrs. Perera's daughter, Nina Collier, of Baltimore, was similarly committed to the service of music and avidly followed in the footsteps of her indefatigable mother.

These were the three board members who descended the steep stairs to smoky Birdland one evening to observe the Mitchell-Ruff Duo in action while Dizzy Gillespie and his big band took their break. The women were hunched up tight around their tiny table, jammed close and looking uncomfortably out of place in the midst of New York's hippest Dizzy fans. A waiter passed me a note and pointed to their table. Would Mr. Mitchell and Mr. Ruff join them at intermission? We would.

We'd never in our lives come across anybody like these women, but it didn't take long for us to find out that they were not New York's "artsy-idle." From the moment we sat down and were introduced, the matrons were all business. As they talked about their work, the smile on Mitchell's face told me that he, too, was impressed. They weren't there to offer us a job, they said. Rather, they wanted to find out if we had the potential for their kind of work; a member of their board who'd heard us thought we might. Mrs. Perera kept cursing her cane, which wouldn't stop slipping off the edge of the little table onto the floor. Finally, exasperated, she left it there, put her foot on it, drew herself up straight, and said testily:

"Gentlemen, we won't beat around the bush. None of us in our organization knows anything at all about jazz, and I'm not sure any of us even like it. But that is beside the point. Young Audiences thinks it is time for responsible music education in America to include jazz music. It's as simple as that. No music is more American than jazz, and we are looking for the right ensemble"—nobody had ever called us an ensemble before—"to get behind and include in our organization. We want a good and solid program on jazz that American children can understand and learn from."

I saw Mitchell's smile broaden.

Mrs. Leventritt added: "We have a good roster of young classical performers; piano trios, string quartets, brass ensembles, and woodwind quintets. We even introduce the children to opera scenes and minidramas. Of course, the young artists we hire, like you gentlemen, haven't yet made large reputations. By working with rising artists who are *good*, we can keep our costs within reason."

Mitchell and I said we thought their plan was admirable and that we would like to visit some of the performances, if they didn't mind.

"Mind?" said Mrs. Perera. "That is why we came to talk to you. We want to invite you to observe what we do, and see if you are interested in joining us as pioneers to put jazz where it belongs. Birdland," she said with haughty disdain, "can spare you for an even more important audience: the audience of the future!"

Mitchell said, "Amen!"

We agreed to come, a few days later, to a public school where a young string quartet would be playing a children's concert. With that, the ladies rose en masse and stomped out of Birdland.

As we watched them climb the wickedly steep stairs, Mitchell said, "The one with the cane reminds me of Miss Whitehead back in Dunedin." For years I'd heard of his troubles with Miss Whitehead, his first-grade teacher, but I feigned amnesia. "Which of your teachers was Miss Whitehead?" I asked.

"She was the one that used to wait by the door with that strap to whip my ass *every* morning, because I lived right across the street from the schoolhouse and was late for school *every day*."

The quartet we'd been invited to hear played enthusiastically and well, and the children liked their presentation of Mozart's music and the little word images they gave them of the composer's harried life. Their demonstrations of their instruments were humorous and informative, and they asked for questions from the children, drawing them into the transaction.

At the end of the concert, the committee cornered the quartet.

Mitchell and I watched the exchange and listened as the women offered suggestions for the musicians to improve their presentation. Mrs. Leventritt was reminding them that they must not lapse into old habits. "Don't mumble!" she said. "We keep telling all of you that you must speak more clearly when you explain the music."

"And stand up straight when you demonstrate your instrument," said Mrs. Collier to the first violinist, as she pulled his drooping shoulders back and straightened his tie. Mitchell and I had to admire the quartet; they were heroic to put up with the grueling instructions they were getting. We could see that working for these women could be tough going, maybe like army basic training, but it seemed like work our duo could learn. Before we went home, Mitchell and I told Mrs. Perera we'd like to be considered.

As we left the school, the quartet's cellist came over to us and said, "Good luck. These are some tough old babes, but if you can put up with them and get a solid program down pat, the work is really rewarding."

Nothing could have prepared us for the rigors of fashioning and presenting an introduction to jazz music to young children under the fierce collective eye of those overseers. They didn't pretend to know anything at all about jazz and accepted the fact that we were the experts. That was the only notable advantage that separated us from the young classical groups they sponsored. It was up to us to fashion a credible account of the story of jazz and demonstrate its main features on our instruments. Actually, that fact made the challenge even richer for us. Inventing a format on our own, we felt, would make us think harder and do better work.

We agreed to prepare a trial program and to have it ready for auditioning before the committee in a week. Mrs. Collier admonished Mitchell, "We'll be your audience. Just pretend you're playing for a small group of fourth graders, and in your spoken explanations, tell us what jazz is, and where it came from, and how it got to be what it is today. Remember not to talk down to your audience. Keep the language simple. Tell us as much as you can, but keep in mind that we are fourth graders, with attention spans to match."

When the day of our first session with the committee rolled around, Mitchell was just as nervous as he'd been the night we opened Birdland opposite Count Basie.

"How," he asked as we opened Mrs. Perera's door, "am I going to imagine that I'm playing and talking to fourth-grade children when I'm looking into the faces of grown white women with blue-tint hair, wearing pearls round their necks?"

Mrs. Perera's large and comfortable Madison Avenue living room buzzed with about ten other formidable-looking women. They were having afternoon tea. After we'd been given tea, we took our places.

I addressed them: "Good morning, boys and girls!" No response. But I heard a half-stifled snicker from the direction of the piano: Mitchell's clue to the committee that a response was expected.

Again I tried: "Good morning, boys and girls!"

This time the ladies loosened up, smiled out loud, and said, "Good morning, Mr. Ruff."

Mitchell wore an expression of triumph and looked them in the face with a gaze that said: That's better.

I was ready to continue. "We are here today to share with you a celebration of a legacy that is *yours*. It should make you very proud. We are going to play some jazz music for you. But before we play, there are a few things about the music you should be aware of. Of all the music you've heard through the generous and learned efforts of Young Audiences, none is as American as jazz." Several ladies moved forward in their seats, and a few took notes.

"Mr. Mitchell and I want you to know that Americans, and nobody else, invented jazz. Nobody else invented the blues. Nobody else invented Negro spirituals. Nobody else invented tap dancing. Before I continue with all the important things about this music, which nobody else but us invented here in America, let me introduce you to the sound of jazz in the hands of one of America's virtuoso pianists."

I began then to play a walking blues vamp on my bass. It had the rolling lilt of a line I copied from the great bassist Walter Page, who'd played it on a 1930s Count Basie recording. Mitchell joined me for the first number of the afternoon. We had agreed beforehand that our initial rendition for the committee should do nothing more than show our musicianship and that we had a reliable technical competence. The blues number ended, and I went back to the story of the origins of jazz.

I explained that jazz music, like classical music, is made up of three structural elements, rhythm, melody, and harmony. I told them a story about rhythm and the importance of an instrument that was conspicuous by its absence from our duo—the drum.

"Girls and boys, as you go on listening to jazz music throughout your lives, you will hear a lot about the music being made up of both African and European influences. I want to tell you something of that musical element—rhythm—I just mentioned and its place and function in West African society. In that society, the drum has no rival as the instrument of greatest importance. The drum has several functions. One of them is ceremonial. You are all familiar with ceremony, whether it is the ceremony of a religious sort, or a ceremonial behavior required of you by your parents when you sit at the dinner table. Still another of the drum's functions is obvious already to you. That is the function of entertainment—it can make you boogie! The last but not the least important of the drum's functions is communication. Let me hear you say 'com-mun-i-ca-tion.' "

The ladies said it. Mitchell, who had for some inexplicable reason become emboldened, said: "I don't hear you, girls and boys. Say it again!" When the word had been enunciated to please Mitchell, I went on to tell them about drumming in the speech mode, in which precise messages can be sent over great distances.

"Drum language sounds very much like spoken language and is useful, in addition to message sending, for the recitation of proverbs and tribal history. You should know that drumming in the speech mode is so complete and precise that tribal history, and the stories of epic deeds, can be played and understood without recourse to speech at all. Imagine, please, a tool of communication so vital and efficient that a document such as the Gettysburg Address could be recited *without* words! Naturally, only those persons with a knowledge of the tribe's spoken language could understand its drum language.

"Remember, now, that when African slaves were brought to America, they had a language that only they, and not their slavemasters, could understand. A secret language spoken on the drum was soon perceived to be dangerous to the slaves' owners. Can you tell me why? Raise your hand if you know." At first, there were no hands. I got concerned. Perhaps I was giving them too much too soon. Or they might not agree that the mention of slavery and its cultural consequences was important to this story. Just then a hand went up: Mrs. Collier's.

"Perhaps," she said, "a secret language was feared because it could be used to organize revolts or insurrections."

"Not bad, my dear, for a fourth grader," I said, to the laughter of our elite auditors. "Now, girls and boys, let me tell you one of the consequences of the slavemaster's fear of the talking drum. Because it was feared, the talking drum was outlawed. Even the language that the drum and the African slaves spoke was similarly outlawed. Since that time, 'drum substitutes' have sprung up in our society: substitutes for the drum that are unique to America. They have taken several forms. Mr. Mitchell has insisted that I show you one of them. He thinks I am very good at it. It is called the hambone. The hambone is a rhythmical contrivance, and it requires no drum: just your own hands, thighs, and chest. I learned it as a small boy in my native Alabama." After I demonstrated the hambone, our presentation went on for another few minutes, along with musical examples.

We had worked our way up past spirituals to ragtime, when Mrs. Leventritt interrupted. "I think it is more effective for you to play more," she said. "You're spending a lot of time on information and, I think, not enough on playing the music itself."

Mrs. Collier said that there could be a better balance of talk and music. The points they raised were good ones. After gallons more of Mrs. Perera's tea, we all agreed to meet again in a few days and try to script out a balanced presentation for several different grade levels.

As we rode the subway back downtown, I was surprised at how cheerfully Mitchell had taken it all. He agreed that the committee's comments were in the right direction. "If we can come up with a program that works for children, this could be a worthwhile thing for us to do. I bet Mr. Brice would really get a kick out of what those women are trying to accomplish. I can't get over their commitment to including jazz in their work, though. Ruff, I'm telling you, man, this is important!"

Over a two-week period, we spent a lot of afternoons in Mrs. Perera's living room, taking tea and advice, before we were allowed to visit a schoolhouse. But in that time, we did develop a program that worked in classrooms all over New York. After we'd played a dozen or so school performances, the ladies gave us their stamp of approval and Mrs. Collier took us on the road to Baltimore, where she had established a residence and a Young Audiences chapter. She was a natural teacher, eager to present challenging ideas to the very young, and to us. By the time we got to Baltimore, Mitchell had convinced me that in order to illustrate an example of how jazz improvisation works, he could pull off what I still think is an amazing feat of spontaneous performance. It seems all the more amazing to me because he does it so effortlessly.

At the Park School in Baltimore one morning, after we'd worked our way up to the subject of improvising in that morning's program, I asked for a volunteer to come to the piano and give us a melody that we could improvise on and make into a jazz piece. A little boy about nine years old came to the piano, said his name was Terry, and, to the delight of his fellow pupils, began to play a simple Schubert piece. After a few measures his fingers stumbled, and without breaking the rhythm, he repeated the passage that had tripped him and went on to the end. Terry finished the piece but was devastated that he'd goofed in front of his friends. He went slinking off the stage in a funk, but Mitchell stopped him, shook his hand, and thanked him; actually, Terry's recovery was remarkable. Then Mitchell sat down and began playing the piece just as the boy had. When he came to the measure where Terry had tripped, he approximated the lad's moment of hesitation and made it sound like a controlled hiccup. Each time he brought the theme back during the several variations, he accommodated the little hesitation differently. After a few more variations, he signaled me to add my bass, and together we washed over the Schubert composition and turned its character to American jazz. By then I had got Mitchell's message: we were to demonstrate for the boy and his friends that hesitations, hiccups of memory or finger muscles, or just about any impromptu occurrence during a performance can become material for the improviser's art.

As we worked on into the Schubert variations, I looked out in the audience and saw Terry's face; he was beaming. All traces of the exasperation he'd carried off the stage had vanished. As our improvisation came to a close, Mitchell insisted that Terry stand up with us and take his share of the applause.

We were almost certain we'd brought a better understanding of a unique American performance tradition to our Park School audience. We needed only to listen to the applause to know for sure that Park School was celebrating a new musical hero: Terry.

While we were still concerned about fashioning the right kind of presentation for the crowds we'd be facing in the colleges out on tour a few weeks thence, the Young Audiences experience had sharpened our understanding of the performer-audience transaction; we felt better in our musical skins; we'd become used to talking to our listeners, to communicating.

Back on the Birdland bandstand one night, we made a surprising and fortuitous discovery.

It was the club's policy to encourage minors and college-age youngsters to listen to jazz music, without serving them liquor. Birdland had a special section of cheap bench seats at the side of the room, where young people could sit and listen without waiters pressing them to spend money. The modest student ticket prices they paid at the door covered their obligation to the establishment. The bench seats were always full when we came to play the first set every night—the students' assurance of a view of the headliners who would be following us. Birdland's big spenders seldom came early enough to hear the opening act; we had the students in the cheap seats to ourselves.

That particular night when we got to work, Mitchell and I saw that quite a few of the young people were wearing sweaters with college letters sewn on front. That gave us an idea. Why not start right there with that captive crowd and preview our routines for the upcoming college tours? The students already knew something about jazz and what they liked. Several college radio stations close to New York played jazz records regularly, and more and more students were finding their way to the music and coming to places like Birdland.

I began talking to the young people in the cheap seats about the repertoire we would play for them and found out right away that they enjoyed being told about its origins, its form, the circumstances under which it came into being, who had recorded it: all the things the Young Audiences ladies had been drilling into us. If there was something funny or socially significant to say about the music, so much the better: we'd share it with them. Audiences, young and old, we were learning, loved stories.

In time, Birdland's manager, Oscar Goodstein, and one of the main young owners, Morris Levy, saw that we were doing well with the student crowd. They encouraged us to keep talking. Levy also owned Roulette Records and thought the college market had promise. So he had us record an album for the label, *Campus Concerts*. Day by day, we were sharpening up our presentations for Pryor-Menz and getting ready for the college crowds across America.

At the same time, we were learning from the great artists playing all over New York that season. At the Café Bohemia, we listened to Miles Davis's repertoire and paid attention to the kinds of music that attracted him and the way he made his choices of material to play and record. He would offer us repertoire suggestions. Enthusiastic about Mitchell's playing and the arrangements he made for our three instruments, Miles especially liked the Mitchell versions of such standards as "You're a Sweetheart," "My Heart Stood Still," and "Yesterdays," which feature quirky and totally unexpected key modulations. One evening at the Bohemia, before the room filled up, Miles stood next to the piano, watching Mitchell's hands as we played. Suddenly I was distracted by a question he asked Mitchell in his gravelly voice:

"Why did you go to that key, Dwike? Damn! I like that."

"From D major to A-flat minor," Mitchell said, "is a very natural shift for *this* piece."

After our set, Mitchell and I went to the bar. Miles came over and led Mitchell back to the piano. He wanted to see Mitchell modulate again. The Bohemia's Davis fans, much to Jimmy Garafola's annoyance, were kept waiting while Miles and Mitchell explored key shifts.

Another night at the same club, Miles, Mitchell, and I had a conversation about Miles's preference and acknowledged genius for playing songs with words even though he never had a singer in his band.

"I'm the singer in my band!" he told us. "I always learn the words to a song before I play it. It gives me a feeling of what to do on my trumpet when I'm trying to phrase an idea. I go all over New York just listening to great singers. I even buy a lot of singers' records." Then he looked directly at me. "Now, take your French horn, for example: its sound is very distinctive and voicelike; nobody says that you have to make it sound like a trumpet or a saxophone. Shit, you'd sound silly trying to sound like Dizzy, or Coltrane. It's just not that kind of an instrument. If I were in your place—I mean, starting out in jazz on an instrument like that—I'd listen to all the great singers, like Mabel Mercer, Sarah Vaughan, Carmen McRae, and Billie Holiday: those people with that perfect and classy diction. Listen to the words and use that as your guide for shaping lines."

Not long after that, home in New Haven, I got a call from Gil Evans, whom I admired tremendously for his arranging for Claude Thornhill and for the writing he did for the early Miles Davis recording *Birth of the Cool*.

Gil didn't know me or my playing, he said, "but Miles Davis asked me to call you about an album we're working on. He wants you to play the French horn on it. I just want to check a few lines I've written for you to see if they are comfortable and present no problems." Gil began singing the melody of Kurt Weill's lyrical song "My Ship." I said that what he sang was fine, and it turned out to be the solo I later played on the collaborative album of Gil and Miles and a nineteen-piece band for Columbia Records. That record, *Miles Ahead*, immediately became the world's best-selling jazz record, and it remains a classic. Having my name on *Miles Ahead* and a later album with Gil and Miles, *Porgy and Bess*, brought me and my horn more recording work and recognition in New York than I ever expected.

Weeks before the college tour began, a thick letter arrived from the Pryor-Menz office. There were road maps, a credit card for gas and a rental car, and a detailed itinerary. In addition to a list of the many schools we'd been booked into, there was a roster of rooming houses, hotels, and private homes where traveling musicians of color could find rooms and food. The letter also named the few white hotels that would rent rooms to Negroes—provided they were booked in advance by a white firm. A Sedalia, Missouri, hotel had that arrangement with Pryor-Menz, and on our typed itinerary we found a dining recommendation: "You can order meals from the dining room for delivery to your rooms. Good Kansas City steaks here! Try the T Bone. Booker Reed is a great chef. Tell him hi for us."

For what other artists besides Leadbelly had this outfit needed to work around Jim Crow in the Midwest? With Pryor-Menz, we learned, these details were an old story. Even before Leadbelly had sung his way across their circuit, the agency had booked black classical musicians and singers into the territory.

Our tour started in Council Bluffs, Iowa. When we arrived by air at the Omaha airport, just across the river, Phil Pryor, a great-grandson of the agency's founder, and Cliff Menz, with a similar ancestral connection, met us at the plane. They took us to a Council Bluffs hotel and left us to freshen up until dinnertime.

Dinner at Cliff's home that night and the activities of the following day were congenially contrived to allow us all to get to know one another. We covered the vital points of touring on their circuit. Over Sunday cocktails, we learned about the histories of all the schools on our list, who the campus sponsors were, along with their backgrounds, and the condition of the on-campus guest facilities. Phil and Cliff dazzled us with what they knew about the black families we would "room" with. All these details were in the heads of Cliff and Phil and their secretary, Twyla. All three had obviously kept their contacts alive and could guarantee that every bed we'd sleep in and every kitchen from which our food came had the Pryor-Menz stamp of approval.

We came away from that weekend with a better idea of how to conduct our end of a professional musical tour.

As we packed our gear into the rented car we'd take with us on most of the tour, Phil Pryor gave us some last words of advice. "Gentlemen, remember this: the job isn't over when you play the last note. The sponsors give receptions after the concerts. There isn't a lot to do out here on the prairie, so people like to mix when artists come to town. For our sakes, you gotta go to the receptions even if you don't want the cookies and punch. We want to build audiences we can send you back to. So keep in mind that what you do and how you do it at the receptions is often more important than what you do onstage. The performance ends when you're out of town."

Then Cliff Menz shook hands with us and offered his wisdom. "Good luck, and drive carefully, fellers. Some of the distances between towns are long—three, four hundred miles. Watch your gas tank, and no matter how good and how rested you feel, always drive fresh. In this heat, you can get sleepy before you know it. Switch drivers *every* hour, no matter how good you feel. It might save your lives."

Our Pryor-Menz tour that summer took us to the teachers colleges in Bemidji and St. Cloud, Minnesota, Hays State College in Hays, Kansas, Clovis State in Clovis, New Mexico . . . places we never knew existed before.

Bemidji was hot and dry, a small, barren-looking place whose main action that summer was the college. Instead of the undergraduate crowd we'd played to in Birdland, the auditorium was packed with late-middle-aged schoolteachers from around the state, returning to summer school to upgrade their teaching credentials. Jazz was new to them. After our first number, which was received with civility but not much enthusiasm, Mitchell gave me an undereyed look that said, "This might be tough."

I decided to talk more and tell our audience as much about the music as I could think of. I recalled for them the story of a famous Minnesota musical family of mixed American Indian and Negro blood. Dr. Pettiford, a veterinarian, trained his children in music, formed a family orchestra, and toured extensively. One of the Pettiford children was the great bassist Oscar Pettiford. We played Oscar's "Bohemia After

Dark" and some of the music associated with his bass playing in Duke Ellington's orchestra.

Instead of sticking to what we'd prepared for a younger crowd, Mitchell and I fell back on more of the great standards these teachers knew, and soon we were all having fun.

After the concert, just as Pryor and Menz had told us, we had to hang around a long time, talking and nursing the cookies and punch. The sponsor waited until after the long reception to tell us: "You fellers went over right well. We're going to tell Cliff and Phil we want you back again."

When we'd worked our way through the first half of the fifteen concerts on our list, we fell into Sedalia, Missouri, for our first free day. No driving. No receptions. Sedalia was the town on our list that had the hotel with the great T-bone steaks and the room service that was mandatory for its black guests. Mitchell and I both relished good room service, but we laughed like hell at the thought of it being forced on us there in Sedalia.

Sedalia was Scott Joplin's home. After the good room service and several long, restful naps, I went out in search of remnants of the bygone Joplin days, but nobody I talked to even knew who Joplin was. His rags hadn't hit the charts yet.

In the middle of one of my afternoon naps in the hotel, my phone rang. Phil Pryor was on the other end, excited.

"Willie, I've been getting enthusiastic reports from your concerts. We've already got requests to bring you back to about half the places you've played. I think we got onto something with this jazz thing out here. I've telephoned the people in Atlanta that booked the southern leg of your tour and told them how well it's been going." This was the Alkahest Famous Artists Agency. Like Pryor-Menz, Alkahest was a venerable office with a long history of southern college and community bookings, and we were glad to have the guarantee of two weeks of concerts in their territory.

When we crossed over the line onto the Alkahest turf, Mitchell and I were in familiar territory—at home in the Deep South. The Atlanta office had sent us a special travel packet, similar to the one we lived with from Pryor-Menz. But in the South, we had no need for the "social" road maps we'd used in the Midwest. Most of our dates were in Negro colleges we'd known about and admired all our lives—Fisk University in Nashville, and Bethune-Cookman in Daytona Beach, Florida, and Morehouse College in Atlanta, and Talladega College in Alabama. We did play a few white colleges: Duke University, Catawba College, Clemson, and Georgia Tech.

But for us, the trip to the Tuskegee Institute in Alabama was our own personal pilgrimage. Without Tuskegee, we would never have known the people at Lockbourne, Mr. Brice, or each other.

While Tuskegee was the school that held a special significance, every one of the black college audiences we encountered had one basic association with our music that we had missed in the Midwest: they all were intimately connected to the music of the southern church. And from the first audience we played for, at Fort Valley State in Fort Valley, Georgia, to the end of the tour, in my discussions of how African-American music developed in the New World, I always cited W. C. Handy and elaborated on what he'd told the children at our school in Sheffield years earlier. Now I told the students, "Hold up the spiritual, guard and be proud of it, for from that has come all of the later forms of our music."

No pianist I know has a more authoritative command of church music of this genre than Mitchell. And there in the South, when he played examples that showed the progression of secular music out of the music of the church, there always came a spontaneous "Amen!" or two from the audience; and we knew that the concert and the reception later that night would be interesting and nourishing.

We learned that audiences at college campuses across America were all different; but though they came from varied social backgrounds and religious persuasions, they had this in common: with careful attention to the music we chose to play for them, we could reach them all on some emotional level. We were picking up more skills, and learning to develop more of the tools of our trade, with each concert. College concerts, to this day, are still a big part of the Mitchell-Ruff Duo's annual itinerary.

PART FIVE

International
Relations

CHAPTER THIRTY-TWO

A New Language
and a Large Loss

I N 1958, while resting in New Haven from the rigors of concertizing
for Young Audiences, playing colleges and clubs, and recording, I
happened to run into a Yale Music School classmate, Denis Mickeivich.
Denis, a young Latvian with a crackling personality, had immigrated
to America with his parents at the end of World War II. He was a good
pianist and accordionist, and the first immigrant "hipster" I'd ever
known, whose command of the jazzman's jargon was total and electric.
We'd played a few jazz dates together as students and had become good
friends.

Intensely intelligent and full of good ideas, Mickeivich always had
something working. One of his most inspired ideas as a student had
been to form a singing group of Yale undergraduates studying Russian.
He convinced some of the Yalies he tutored in Russian Studies that
singing Russian songs was the perfect way to develop their pronunciation
and speaking skills, and his Yale Russian Chorus soon became one of
the most impressive musical organizations at the college.

That day on the street in New Haven, Denis yelled to me out of a
crowd in his unmistakable voice, which had the lingering charm of a
faint Eastern European accent.

"Willie! Man! What's happening? Speak of the fucking devil! You're just the cat I want to see." He told me that he and his Yale Russian Chorus had just returned from a singing trip in the Soviet Union.

"Man," he said, "you can't imagine how much interest in jazz there is in Russia now. Wherever I took my singers to sing, we got bombarded constantly with questions about jazz music. They asked us to sing jazz, which would be fucking ridiculous for us to try. They wanted lectures on jazz, which would be a drag without hearing the music itself. We sang a couple of Negro spirituals. That was pretty good, but how much could they expect from a group of white Yalies? Shit, Willie, you've got to come back with us next summer, with Dwike. The Russians will go nuts hearing the real thing!"

The interest in jazz in Russia had been heightened by the Soviet prohibition of it; jazz was considered decadent. Russian youths were told that such music begot riots and bad habits, and represented the worst elements of a capitalist society. To prove what jazz riots looked like, *Pravda* published photos of English rock-and-roll bands raising hell!

By then, Louis Armstrong and Dizzy Gillespie were veterans of goodwill tours overseas. But Russian officials said *Nyet* to both great artists. Even Sol Hurok, the king of American impresarios, with all his Soviet connections, couldn't break down the resistance. When he offered pianist Errol Garner, the Kremlin held firm. I asked my friend Denis how he expected to get Mitchell and Ruff on a stage in Russia if the powerful Hurok couldn't swing a booking for Louis Armstrong and Garner there.

"Simple, man," Denis said. "Those dumb-assed booking agents are going through official channels. Who needs official? We're just a student group that sings on street corners, at parties, in dormitories—anywhere at all. I guarantee you that we can find a way for you cats to play, once we get you there!"

Several months later, Denis came to hear the duo at the Hickory House in New York. He brought a group of Yale students who'd been on the Russian trip the previous summer. Denis and his committee sat in the club all through our performance and outapplauded the other patrons. At intermission, he charged backstage and grabbed Mitchell in a bear hug. "Holy shit, man! The Russians are going to go wild over that blinding technique. I can't wait for them to hear you cats." Then he pulled me into the discussion.

"Willie, the details of the trip are already worked out. Our grant came through. We've raised enough money to easily pay expenses for everybody, including you two, but, unfortunately, no fee for you cats." Mitchell's face fell and mine with it. Neither of us could afford to give up work for a month and a half. I could afford such an extravagance least of all, since Emma and I had bought a house with a big mortgage and we had a new baby girl, Michele, born in the summer of 1957. I was a truly happy new papa, playing with the baby of my dreams and glad to be home. But Denis was undaunted. He pressed on.

"The only other thing we have to do is to teach you cats to sing all our songs in Russian. You will have to look like one of us."

"That won't be easy, Denis," Mitchell said with his characteristic patience.

But Denis came back: "You have a big advantage, Dwike! Did anybody ever tell you how much you look like Paul Robeson? Shit, man, Robeson is the biggest star in Russia. What other foreign musician has ever been given the fucking Stalin Peace Prize?" I looked hard at Mitchell for a moment. Denis was right: there was a striking resemblance to the young Robeson. Mitchell remained skeptical. Denis and his committee went back to New Haven with the understanding that we'd need to sleep on the idea some more.

I couldn't rid myself of the thought of actually going to Russia. Then, a few days later, Birdland's manager, Oscar Goodstein, phoned me in New Haven. Goodstein was a tough, energetic, thick-bodied man of middle age, who, together with his wife, made Birdland click. Oscar said he was calling on behalf of Teddy Goldstein, a club owner in Miami.

"Willie, this guy Teddy is a hell of a nice guy you'll love when you get to know him. He wants an 'affordable New York–type jazz group' down there." Oscar's advice to Teddy was to hire the two "clean-cut" guys he always hired to work opposite Basie and the big names in Birdland. Mitchell and I agreed to work for the last month of that 1959 winter season for Teddy, then come right back to Birdland to open the summer season opposite Count Basie again. With that much steady work already on the books, we thought we could afford to take a chance with Denis and the Russians. We decided that our trusty Young Audiences program would be what the Russians would hear if we got to play there.

I didn't know a word of Russian, but I felt sure that in the three months remaining before the tour, I could learn enough of the language to present a respectable public lecture. Our Silly Putty friend's son, Pete Hodgson, was a senior at Yale, majoring in Russian; he had been to the Soviet Union himself, and I knew he spoke the language with style. Perhaps I could hire him as my Russian-language tutor.

I typed out my speech—essentially our Young Audiences program—in English and called the Silly Putty office, still in the house Hodgson senior rented from Yale, to arrange a meeting with the two Petes. I explained how the invitation to go to Russia had come about and handed the pages to young Pete.

"This is all I need to learn how to say," I told Pete junior, naively.

Squinting at the paper in astonishment, Pete said, "This is *all* you want to say? Jesus, man! This is a hell of a lot of Russian, my friend. If you can say this, you can say damn near anything."

Big Pete's eyes danced as he opened beers for us. Over his shoulder, he quipped to his son, "Take the damn job, and charge Ruff plenty. Your old man needs the dough. Besides, Silly Putty deserves some return on the inflated tuition we're paying our goddamn uppity landlord to educate you!"

Young Pete read on in my written speech. "Well, Willie," he said finally, "I think I can cram Yale's regular one-year course into you in a couple of months. Then we can get to translating this goddamn dissertation. This isn't a speech, it's a tome, pal!"

We went to work. The fee for lessons was affordable, and Pete was eager to show his dad that if I could take it, he could teach me Russian in that short time. We went at the lessons daily, three or four hours at a clip, in the Silly Putty office and the campus libraries, in parks and in Pete junior's dormitory room. I even tried sleep learning, playing prerecorded word lists and grammar drills while I slept. I don't think I learned much of anything useful while asleep, but in time, my tutor had me confident enough to believe that I could stand up in Moscow and tell the story of jazz music in decent Russian.

One night, I arrived early at Birdland to work on my Russian in the dressing room. I was playing my vocabulary and grammar drills loudly on a wire recorder, when Count Basie entered. He smiled and took a seat to listen.

"Go on with your gobbledygook, Ruff. I want to hear some of that stuff." The trained voice on the machine said a few Russian words, and I imitated it. Basie laughed at each sentence, asking, "What the hell does that mean?" I told him how to ask for the post office, how to inquire about trains and hotels and to drink a toast. After a while, he put on his reading specs and picked up a word list I'd been studying. He would drill me from the list, speaking the English word, with me giving him back the Russian equivalent. What more symbolic way of learning to communicate with Russian jazz fans than with the great Count Basie's help?

While Mitchell and I continued to play dates everywhere and prepared music for the Russian trip, troubling word arrived from Evansville. My father had severe lung problems. He had smoked cigars heavily all his life and worked around deadly coal dust. Suspecting either TB or lung cancer, I went to Evansville to see him. It was cancer. Uncle Grover had moved back to Evansville from Detroit and had taken his brother in to live with him and Seculia. But after a while my father had to be hospitalized, and I went back. I brought him a present he'd asked for: a picture of Emma, Michele, and me.

I left Evansville for a duo concert somewhere, expecting never to see my father alive again. I think I began my mourning even as I watched him lying there in the hospital. I thought a lot about our good times and bad. Though the bad times mostly outweighed the good, I loved my father and knew how much he'd always loved me, even if he didn't or couldn't always show it when I was young. I saw how much he suffered over his failure to oversee my upbringing after Mama died. In my travels since I'd left him to join the army, I had seen enough black men in his circumstances to begin to soften my judgment of the chinks in his armor and to understand the iron independence of will that had been his curse.

I remembered the time in New Haven when he gave me the surprise of my life. It was just after Emma and I were married. He breezed into town as casually as he'd done when I was a child back in Alabama, when he always showed up without notice. This time, he'd come on the bus, not hopped off a midnight freight train; but he'd forgotten, or not even bothered, to bring my address. Somebody in downtown New Haven showed him how to hike from the bus station to the heart of the action in the black business and entertainment district. Then my phone rang. It was a waitress at Mr. Greenlee's Monterey.

"Ruff, a tall red feller just came in here, looking just like you, baby! He says he's your dad. I'm looking at him right now, and, honey, I swear I don't figger this cat is lying!"

I had to smile at the old hobo holding to his habits. I picked him up, and we had a whole week of good times, driving around the countryside, talking about the teaching and playing I wanted to do after I finished my education. His new daughter-in-law and my half-sisters and -brothers made a big fuss over him, and once in a while, as we sat among them, or off somewhere by ourselves, I'd catch him gazing at me with the love I never much got from him directly but always knew was there.

Even more surprising than his popping into town unannounced was a question he threw at me one day on that New Haven visit. "Looka here, buddy. You know, this Ruff family ain't getting no younger or no bigger. When you and Emma gonna make me a granddaddy, man?" He didn't let it go at that but kept it up until it was time to get back on the bus for Evansville. Grandfatherly sentiments rumbling around in a man like my father: it was hard to figure.

One day, the call I was dreading finally came from Uncle Grover: my father had died in his sleep. When I reached the modest Evansville funeral home, I found myself taking part in the smallest burial service I've ever witnessed. Besides me, there was only the officiating preacher, a little man who boasted of having baptized my father the day he died;

Uncle Grover, Seculia, and a woman I remembered visiting with my dad while I was on furlough once from Lockbourne.

I thought I'd made peace with my father's death and finished most of my mourning before I got to Evansville this time. But as Uncle Grover sat beside me, shaking with grief, I knew I was still in for a rough time. The majestic, beatific look that ennobled my father's face in death made me think of loss. If only he could have come to know his granddaughter, even this late in his dogged life. And music, our strongest common bond: if only my dad could have heard me play just once as a professional. It was the thought of his missing the music that undid me. Uncle Grover saw it and put his arm around my shoulder, and the two of us sat there side by side, shoulder-hugging and consoling each other as we remembered.

CHAPTER THIRTY-THREE

To Russia, Truly with Love

IN JUNE 1959, the Yale Russian Chorus, the duo tucked in with them, left New York for Europe. The accommodations for our flight were strictly steerage class. The whole Yale chorus, thirty strong with Mitchell and me, crammed into an old chartered DC-3, which flew from New York to Bermuda, then refueled again in the Azores before limping in to Berlin twenty-nine hours after we left New York. In Berlin, after the numbing roundabout route, we needed a few days' rest. Mitchell and I had shopping to do. We had to rehearse more with the singers and learn all the songs in Russian. I also did the rounds of East Berlin music shops to buy a bass fiddle to take into Russia. The choir was to buy me a bass for the trip; I would not drag my second, brand-new DiLeone bass, this one made by the old master's son Luigi, across Russia. I figured a bass would be cheaper in the east than in West Berlin. For $150, I found a good enough instrument.

We took a long, two-day train ride through Poland, then a day later reached Moscow. I had by then hit my stride in conversational Russian, helped tremendously by the pronunciation drills Pete Hodgson had insisted on. Denis had sharpened my ear through regular dialogues beyond my level. By then I had begun to have dreams in Russian, the best sign for a student of a new language. There was a bonus I hadn't counted on: the Russian vocabulary I'd had to master in order to tell jazz's story enabled me to engage in ordinary conversation.

Settling baggage and the East German bass fiddle into the Central Hotel, a comfortable and surprisingly aristocratic-looking Old World building just down the street from the Kremlin, I went out walking on my own. When I came back to the hotel, the singers headed into the streets for the first night's work. Work meant singing to attract a crowd. One of the choir's favorite crowd-drawing ploys was to assemble outside a movie house, concert hall, or theater just before the audience exited. As soon as the crowd surged into the street, the booming sound of a herd of energetic Americans singing Russian songs at the top of their lungs would stop the Muscovites cold. Mitchell and I blended, at least vocally, into the otherwise all-white choir, he with the basses and I with the second tenors. It was an inspiring sound, and the Russians applauded their heads off.

After the singing, members of the choir broke off and talked to Russians. But most of the Russians flocked around Mitchell and me. And just as Denis had said back at the Hickory House, people asked Mitchell time and time again if he was Paul Robeson. There was always a Yalie around to translate for him. Denis had also been right about the Russians' interest in jazz. They constantly asked us about the "exotic" music.

These singing and talking sessions often lasted late into the night and sometimes ended up in parks, or on long walks, or in our hotel rooms.

Although Soviet Intourist guides were assigned to the choir to keep us busy, we could go anywhere alone without police problems. But we noticed that whenever we went off on our own, a "tail" usually followed, at a civil distance. A torrential rainstorm caught me late one night out in the suburbs, at the home of a French horn player. As I came out of the house, I lucked out, snatching the only taxi in sight. But then I spotted the familiar and soaked tail, who been watching me from under a tree, and offered him a ride back to town. He accepted.

Mitchell, a man who needs the solace of the piano when far from home, was getting antsy. One morning, over our hotel breakfast of common caviar, black bread, tomatoes, and tea, which we ate with music on our minds, he said to me, "Come on, Ruff, let's make something happen."

"OK, I'll try." Not quite sure what I intended, I found myself going off alone in a taxi to find the Tchaikovsky Conservatory. When the taxi stopped at the front door, I burst into the building and asked a serious-looking uniformed attendant to show me the director's office. Without even blinking at my Russian, she took me to a secretary, who immediately showed me into the office of the director. Startled, to say the least, he couldn't figure out my nationality. But when I started talking in Russian, a large smile broke over his face.

"Good day," I said. "My name is Vasily Vasilyevich Ruff. I am an American musician of African descent, traveling in your great country with students. I would like to know if your students and faculty would be interested in a performance of the music of my people, along with a lecture concerning our music's development and growth in America." I had purposely not used the word "jazz," and I had emphasized "people," a word of great weight in the USSR. But I was not prepared for the director's response. He leapt up from his desk, seized my hand, and shook it vigorously.

"Welcome to our conservatory," he said, a big smile lighting up his face. "My faculty and students will certainly attend a performance of the music of so courageous a race as yours. It will be an honor for the Soviet people to sponsor the artistic expression of our oppressed Negro brothers in America!"

He called the secretary back and gave instructions to send word all over the conservatory that a convocation was to take place that same afternoon at 3:00 P.M. in the small concert hall. All students and faculty would be privileged to witness a performance of the music of the American Negro people.

I rushed back to tell Mitchell of our good luck. Once again there was a call to assembly for us, but this one was different from any that had gone before. We trembled into our clothes—you might say we were nervous—and headed back to the conservatory.

At exactly three o'clock that afternoon, the conservatory director came onstage and welcomed the audience of about three hundred colleagues and students to "the first instrumental presentation of American Negro music in modern Soviet history."

We were greeted by uninhibited applause as we took the stage. Having rehearsed over and over for this moment, we began our program with a strong blues. But it was a blues we made up on the spot. Unveiling a new blues inspired by the feeling of the moment is our way of establishing our musical bearings. The audience applauded warmly. Then it was time to talk to them in my best Russian.

"I speak Russian very badly, and for that I apologize. But I want you to know that what you've just heard is the blues. The blues has come to be one of the most serviceable musical forms of people's music in all of Western civilization. Even though its roots are to be found in the spirituals and other early musical outcries of our people in slavery, it is now appreciated by free people all over the world. The blues was one of the many musics of a transplanted people taking on a new identity in a new nation. It could only have happened in America. But why is the power of the blues so obvious? And why is it admired by so many societies of the world today? Paul Robeson has preceded us here to relate to Soviet audiences some of the surprising and charming ways in which various of the world's people express themselves in music.

"On his many visits here, Robeson demonstrated with his extraordinary singing that there are similarities between the music of Russian serfs and the religious music that sprang from American slavery. We will not repeat that demonstration here, because I can neither sing nor speak Russian like Paul Robeson. But my partner and I will play for you some of the instrumental high spots in the story of Afro-American music."

We began by playing much of our Young Audiences program but with the luxurious stimulation of having real musicians in the audience, for whom we could use material that would have been beyond children. We started with spirituals, wondering how music with religion at its center would set with the Russians. As Mitchell and I sang, "My Lord, What a Morning," I looked out at the faces and saw several students with their eyes closed, swaying. No problem with ideology. Their response to the blues and to Mitchell's virtuosity brought spontaneous applause several times during the afternoon.

When we'd played our final encore of the concert, the conservatory director led a crowd of well-wishers backstage. He spoke for them: "Extraordinary! More Soviet musicians should hear what you did here today. Can you come back tomorrow and play the same program in Bolshoi Hall, our large hall here at the conservatory?" I thought I understood him correctly.

"Really tomorrow?" I said.

"*Nu, kaneshna!*" he assured me.

The next afternoon, back at the conservatory, a student led Mitchell and me to a comfortable dressing room near the stage, where we settled down for strong Russian tea and a quiet five-minute rest. Through the closed dressing room doors we could hear the audience buzzing. Mitchell, with mounting anxiety, sneaked out of the dressing room and tiptoed to the side of the stage for a peek out at the crowd. What he saw made him jump back and scurry through the door, wringing his hands.

"Ruff! Ruff! Man, come here and look. You won't believe it. There's not an empty seat in the whole house. People are standing in the aisles, and that place looks as big as Carnegie Hall! How the hell can they draw a crowd like that in just one day?" I wouldn't look.

A congenial young man, an instructor at the conservatory, came backstage to greet us and introduce himself in easy and accentless English. He was Lev Vlasenko, a pianist who'd been runner-up to Van Cliburn at the International Tchaikovsky Piano Competition there at the conservatory two years earlier. Vlasenko told Mitchell, "The piano we have for you onstage is excellent. Van Cliburn loved playing it, and it is the favorite of our own great Richter, here at the conservatory." Then he led us out the door to wait at the side of the stage, saying he would speak to the audience first, welcome them, then bring us on. Mitchell looked out at the giant gleaming black piano, its keyboard facing away from us, making it impossible to tell what make it was. All the while Vlasenko was telling the crowd what they would be hearing, Mitchell had eyes only for the imposing grand piano glistening on the sunlit stage.

He whispered sideways to me, "That's the biggest damn piano I ever saw in my life. I wonder if it's one of those old prewar Hamburg Steinways."

Vlasenko finished, to applause, then Mitchell and I went out. Rounding the keyboard side of the piano, Mitchell stopped in his tracks and gasped, "Well, I'll be damned. Thank you, sweet Jesus—a Bechstein at last!" He sat down and reverently ran the palms of his large hands over the smooth surfaces of his first Bechstein concert grand, his face bright with expectation. He gave me my tuning note, playing the piano's G. It was a gorgeous G, round, resonant, and full of promise. I adjusted my bass string to match that magnificent G. Bass players need only one note from the piano in order to tune all four strings, but in his impatience for his first feel of the fabulous piano, Mitchell let a curious finger fall in turn on the other three notes, sounding them out along with me as I tuned the D, A, and E strings. Coming to the low E, I watched him lean gently into the note with upper-body English, and the big piano moaned its mezzoforte. There was a hush from the audience, then silence.

The main features of the program were to be identical to those of the day before. But since many in the audience would be hearing us for the second time, we played different music to illustrate the origins of jazz in America, with its secular and religious antecedents. Mitchell and I sang two spirituals we'd not sung at the first concert, as examples of harmonic devices in common use in the twentieth century that had their origins in the music of slavery. While we sang, my eyes fell on a Russian woman, her head tied in the traditional babushka. She was rocking back and forth in her seat, clasping both hands before her, tears rolling down her age-lined face. Mitchell and I proceeded up the chronological ladder of the story of jazz and played "Do Re Mi Blues," our excursion through the C-major scale and the twelve-bar form of the blues. Whenever we play it, we stop to take questions. This time I wanted to be sure that our Russian audience was getting the point. In Russian I asked, "Are there any questions?"

The old woman who'd been crying during the spirituals came alive and with surprising energy threw up her hand: "*Tavarish, pazhalta, igriet grusnia, grusnia Negratanski pesnyi.*" She wanted more of the mournful, sad, sad Negro music of slavery. I asked her if a sad, sad blues written in this century would do just as well, and please, could we just play it and not sing? She raised her shoulders in a shrug of compromise and said in her poignant Russian, "All right, comrade, play! But make it sad; good and sad!"

Mitchell attacked the Bechstein with a long solo blues introduction of his own invention, and in it I could hear the pathos of his Baptist church roots, sad and mournful. I could tell that the lady was happy again; we could see it through her tears.

The afternoon sun left the auditorium as we played. It was time to close the concert, and Mitchell said, "Let's go off with the new Russian popular song we learned." So we played "Moscow Nights," in the key of E minor. The very last note of the concert was the same big E Mitchell had leaned into earlier in the afternoon for me to tune the bass. Basking in the applause, Mitchell looked out at the clusters of Russians rushing down the aisle, their arms loaded with colorful bouquets.

"Well," he said, "looks like they dug us—the music *and* the talk."

Lev Vlasenko came forward, along with the flower bearers, and stood in a group at the edge of the stage to translate questions the piano students had for Mitchell. Some wanted to learn to play what they had heard; they asked where they could buy the sheet music. Even when Vlasenko reminded them that I had said in my talk that improvisation was the lifeblood of the jazz performance, they nearly all insisted that what Mitchell did was more than that. My Russian was not good enough to catch all the points of the debate. But it was clear that "improvisation," as we use it in jazz, meant something entirely different in the Russian musical experience.

"You have a fantastic memory to play such a long program without sheet music," said one of the young pianists to Mitchell.

"Memory had little to do with it," said Mitchell in English, Lev translating. "Most of what you heard was spontaneous—made up and performed at the moment of conception. Yes, the harmonic form is constant; that is our only guide. For instance, the twelve-bar form Ruff explained to you was all we have to remember whenever we play the blues. We could never repeat that exact same performance again, no matter how hard we tried." Vlasenko was hard-pressed to translate Mitchell's intended meanings.

"But what a pity it is not written down," said a professor of composition. "I would like to see how the sad, sad Negro blues is notated on paper."

Several minutes after the concert ended, I was called away from the group near the stage. A young man, loaded with flowers, had just come rushing into the hall, and he thrust at me the biggest and most elaborate bouquet of the day. He smiled and said in Russian, "From Konstantin Polex, my father. He is at a dress rehearsal at the Bolshoi theater and very much regrets he could not come to greet you."

I was thrilled by what this youngster told me. I own records made by the great Polex, the principal hornist of the Bolshoi Theater Orchestra, and was overwhelmed that he had sent me flowers. Young Polex asked, on behalf of his father, the name of my hotel. His father would call next day to invite me to their home for dinner. Now I wondered even more about the speed and efficiency of the Moscow musical grapevine. I went back to Mitchell and his admirers, wondering what Polex's connections were with the conservatory.

Some of the hard-core jazz lovers (youngsters schooled on the Voice of America radio jazz programs) and a crowd of conservatory students helped us carry our flowers back to the hotel. It was a sensationally colorful parade.

Mitchell and I were wakened early the next morning by a messenger with an official-looking envelope containing two tickets and a note. I opened the envelope, looked at the tickets and the accompanying note, written in Russian longhand (which I decipher badly), and realized I needed an interpreter. We knocked hard on Denis's door.

"Sorry to wake you, Denis, but I need help reading this." Denis, wiping sleep from his eyes, took the envelope and mumbled something about "pain in the ass." Then he complained about the difficulty of reading such "bureaucratic scrawl practically in the middle of the fucking night." Suddenly he jerked himself out of his drowsiness.

"Holy fucking shit, man!" he said. "I know you cats blew your asses off at the conservatory, but this is tremendous!"

Mitchell looked worried. "What is tremendous, Denis? Are they deporting us?"

"Deport, my ass! You two are invited to attend a historic event tonight at the Bolshoi Theater: Ulanova's final performance. I don't have to tell you what an important figure she is in Russia. This is an invitation to sit in a box reserved for guests of the state. You two lucky bastards will see Ulanova dance *Swan Lake* for the last time in her life. Jesus, what an honor!" I wondered if the horn player Polex and the conservatory director had finagled our tickets, for as the day wore on, we learned that the performance was Moscow's theatrical "do" of the season. Tickets were as precious as gold.

When Mitchell and I arrived at the theater, a short walk from our hotel, the orchestra was tuning up. A uniformed usher took us to our box, situated just left of center of the mezzanine, and we settled down in the most sumptuous theater we'd ever seen. Every inch of its lavish red and gilt decor was meant to herald the strength of the Soviet state as well as that state's reverence for its arts and artists. An adoring Soviet public was turning out to salute a woman, past sixty, who, since early childhood, had danced her way into their history. As premier teacher and artistic example for a new generation of dancers, Ulanova was onstage that night to give back some of herself and to receive from her people a hero's farewell.

The houselights dimmed slowly, the orchestra hushed, and I became aware of movement in the box only a few feet to our right. A group, speaking softly in Russian, filed into the box, making way for a stocky man and a woman of about the same build. Mitchell and I recognized Nikita Khrushchev and his wife. All the members of the Russian party, still standing, made way for a second group: brown men, who themselves opened ranks for a diminutive but regal figure who floated like a royal sepia ghost dressed in white-braided military attire, complete with an elaborate white visor hat. The Russian staff, Premier and Mme Khrushchev, and the dark men remained standing. The majestic small personage then lowered himself into the red velvet chair with kingly grace. Then, raising a most elegantly shaped small hand, he removed the visor hat. Mitchell leaned in my direction and, in a side-mouth whisper, said, "Now just a damn minute . . . is that *really* who I think it is?" Yes, it was the Lion of Judah, Haile Selassie, king of Ethiopia.

At that moment, the conductor gave the downbeat, Tchaikovsky's music washed over us, and Ulanova glided onto the stage, bringing the entire house to its feet, including the Lion of Judah. The applause reached a thundering peak and held. From several parts of the theater came disruptive but adoring cries, making it impossible for Ulanova to continue her dance. The audience wouldn't stop applauding. The ballet came to a halt: a reverent pause for adulation. The music went on, but the conductor and orchestra tapered their volume down to a mezzo piano and vamped smartly while Ulanova, looking not a day older than eighteen, faced her audience, looked toward heaven, extended both arms wide, and slowly leaned her elegant torso forward, touching her forehead to the floor and holding it there. The house went crazy. When, at last, the standing audience sighed and reseated itself, *Swan Lake* proceeded.

As I sat listening to Tchaikovsky's music played as no other ensemble in the world can play it, my thoughts were of Mr. Brice, under whose baton Mitchell and I as teenagers had first learned and played Tchaikovsky's concertos and symphonies. How the old soldier would have smiled at the way Mitchell played the hell out of that great old Bechstein at Tchaikovsky's own conservatory the day before. How it would have awed and pleased him to know that his Lockbourne boys were now seated practically side by side with one of the most powerful world figures, watching a sixty-year-old dancing woman in a tutu bring the Lion of Judah to his feet!

When at last Ulanova made her final curtain call, with the theater roaring and everyone standing, Mitchell and I sat back down and kept stone-still and silent. The houselights brightened, and the musicians put away their instruments. Khrushchev led King Haile Selassie and their entourage out into the Moscow night, and we were among the last souls to leave the theater. For the first time in all the years we'd known each other, Mitchell and I remained completely silent, as we walked back to the hotel. Neither of us uttered another word that night.

The next day, a small group of young Russian musicians showed up at our hotel. One fellow had a snare drum and a cymbal, tarnished green, with a long split running across it; others carried battered horn cases. Denis had them all in tow. "Willie, these guys are amateur jazz players," he said. "They have organized a little party and jam session for us all." Denis, our duo, a few Yale singers, and the Russian jazzers all squeezed into a small flat out near the university to jam. But the jam session got off to a slow start. The Russians were bashful and too modest to play for us. Mitchell tried to put them at ease.

"Let us hear something. Play anything you like." The drummer begged off, saying that Tollye, their tenor sax man, would come along shortly, then they would all play together. Meanwhile, they asked us about the jazz scene in the States. "Dizzy is great hero for Soviet jazz players," offered the drummer. "Miles Davis great stylist too," said the trombonist. "Miles student of Dizzy, no?" Then to Mitchell, he said, "I think you know Miles, yes?" When Mitchell assured him he did, the whole room gasped, "He *know* Miles!" Mitchell told a Miles Davis anecdote or two and allowed that Miles was a great composer and stylist.

Then it occurred to our hosts to take advantage of this rare chance to replenish their store of hip expressions from real American jazzmen. Mitchell rubbed his hands. "I'll bet cosmopolitan jazz fans such as yourselves know lots of American slang jazz talk."

"Hep cat!" offered the clarinet man.

Mitchell threw up his hands. "Naw, man, not 'hep.' That's old-fashioned. Say 'hip.' No e in the word. Say i, like in 'lip.'" He then hipped the Muscovites to "bad," which meant "good," and "Blow, blow, blow," which they read as "Get hot." But it was Denis who shed the brightest light on the American jazzman's vernacular for our hosts. Not only was he a master of the idiom; he could also offer the corresponding Russian word to just about any thought a Soviet hipster might want to express. Every Russian in the room fell in love with, and rehearsed to perfection, two of Denis's chief contributions that evening—"split the scene," for leave, or go, and "make the scene," for come, or arrive. Another usage that broke them up was "most bitch." Dizzy was a most bitch of a musician. Of course, words like "cool" were already firmly rooted in their repertoire: Miles was cool. Our hosts all agreed that, as a group, the American jazzman was, linguistically, a most bitching and formidable inventor.

The language lesson subsided, and Mitchell got up and sauntered over to the upright piano that stood in the corner. It was out of tune, and several of its aged brown keys had been stuck for years in the down

Hamp—the exuberant Lionel Hampton—with trumpeters Billy Brooks and Eddie Preston. Mitchell and I formed our duo while in Hamp's band in 1955.

: The duo in Yale's Sprague Hall, the site of a lot of musical highlights for me.

My daughter, Michele, (ABOVE), age 14, en-route to the Central African Republic's rain forest with me. We had stopped off in Paris for her to meet and hear master drummer Kenny Clarke (RIGHT), whose virtuosity swept us away.

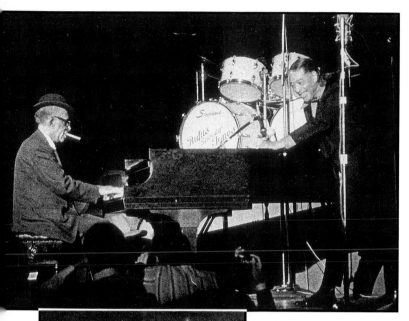

In 1972 I persuaded Yale's president, Kingman Brewster, to honor forty great names in music and inaugurate the Duke Ellington Fellowship Program at Yale. We had an astounding group of musical luminaries, among them Willie "The Lion" Smith, (ABOVE), shown here playing for Ellington, pianist-composer Mary Lou Williams, (LEFT), and singer Joe Williams (BELOW).

Charlie Mingus.

ABOVE: Eubie Blake, piano, Noble Sissle singing.

TOP CENTER: Dwike Mitchell at piano, Max Roach, drums, Clarke Terry, trumpet, me playing bass, Sonny Stitt, tenor sax.

LEFT: Odetta, with Kingman Brewster and the "impresario." Right behind us (top): Harry Carney, William Warfield, Dizzy Gillespie, George Duvivier, Charlie Mingus, Noble Sissle, Ray Brown, Jo Jones, Lucky Thompson, Max Roach.

William Warfield.

ABOVE: Cootie Williams.

LEFT: Benny Carter.

BELOW: President Brewster presents his medal to the man who made it all possible—Duke Ellington.

ABOVE: Dizzy Gillespie teaching and playing with the duo at Troup Junior High School in New Haven in 1973.

LEFT: Jo Jones, a longtime favorite of mine. He came to my house in Alabama and talked into the tape recorder for a solid week, "just to set the record straight about this jazz music!"

ABOVE: The Mitchell-Ruff Duo singing the spiritual "My Lord, What a Morning" for a class of music students in China, 1981.

ABOVE: Major General Joseph Wheeler, an ex-Confederate general from my Alabama, who, from the grave, helped me make sense of my journey.

RIGHT: Uncle Grover Ruff, my father's only brother. He was good to me when I was young. Shown here at 90, he is, believe it or not, still going strong at 95, as Evansville's oldest World War I veteran.

The duo, resplendent in modern times.

mode. Mitchell noodled for a while, memorizing the out-of-tune and the stuck notes he'd want to avoid. Soon his fingers found enough working keys to play the blues, and when he'd played a chorus or two, the little cherub-faced trombone player got carried away, took out his horn, and joined in. It made the strangest, most interesting mismatch imaginable. The Russian's harmonic and melodic thinking was modern and logical, and came close to matching Mitchell's, as long as he left off imitating "jazz." His approach was avant-garde in the sense of that time, but his phrasing and rhythmic focus was stuck in 1929. I thought: Here's a thoroughly modern Soviet, shackled stylistically in New Orleans. It was the kind of outrageous and beautiful paradox that Mitchell loves more than anything. He grunted encouragement to the Russian: "Yeah! Blow, blow!" The other Russians crowded close, and their man picked up steam, pumping his slide furiously. Mitchell's accompaniment took on a new dissonance, which excited and encouraged his soloist even more. The pace quickened. Mitchell fed his partner more daring, short, choppy chords. Then I heard him using the expression the American jazz avant-garde had invented to characterize an excursion "outside" the established tonality, or key center. "Outside. Yeah, outside."

Mitchell and the Russian took a break just long enough to refresh themselves with orange soda and discuss the "outside" crowd back home, which included Ornette Coleman, Mingus, Sun Ra, and others the Russians had wind of. Everybody around the room tried "outside" on for size. The two then struck up Thelonious Monk's lovely ballad " 'Round Midnight," and everybody sighed. *"Kak prikrashnya!* Thelonious most bitch!" The soloist stuck to Monk's melody's own rhythm but masterfully substituted certain melodic keynotes for the ones Monk wrote, going "outside" more daringly and giving the song an engagingly balanced yet bittersweet verve. All the Russians were tapping their feet and swinging their shoulders along with mine, as orange soda and some newly arrived pepper vodka made the rounds. Every few seconds, somebody in the crowd hollered out the "outside" word.

I noticed a few among our hosts looking and acting anxious. When I asked the drummer what was the matter, he said his pals were worried because Tollye, the tenor man, shouldn't be taking so long. The trombonist said, "Perhaps emergency at hospital where he works. Perhaps work late." Every few seconds, someone hung out the window to see if Tollye and his sax were on the way. Through the door, at last, came the robust Tollye, bubbling and out of breath, his horn in a pillowcase. Under one arm he clutched a curious large, flat envelope, about which he was very excited.

The crowd, much relieved that he'd finally made the scene, encouraged Tollye to take his horn out of the pillowcase and get "outside." Tollye's eyes widened. Was he being asked to leave? It was the trombonist who explained in Russian the true meaning of "outside." Quick-witted Tollye brightened at the explanation and came right back with, "OK, goddamn! I give you fucking *outside*, man."

He laid down his pillowcase, snatched from under his arm the large envelope he'd brought from the hospital, and yanked out a big sheet of X-ray film showing a very sharp picture of someone's chest and rib cage. He went to a small record player near the piano, turned it on, and placed the X-ray film flat on the turntable. I hadn't noticed before that the square film had a hole at its center to accommodate the turntable spindle. Nor had I noticed that there were small grooves cut into the film, like those on a long-playing record.

"What's that, Tollye?" asked Mitchell.

"Just a minute you see, man." Everybody in the room gathered around as Tollye placed the needle in the groove of the spinning rib cage. Miles Davis's blistering trumpet filled our ears.

Mitchell howled, "Aw, shit, now I've seen everything. Come on, man, is this real?" The song was "Springsville," the album was *Miles Ahead*, Gil Evans's arrangements for Miles Davis and a nineteen-piece band. It was one of the Miles Davis recordings on which I'd played the French horn several months before.

Tollye then turned to me, pointing an index finger proudly to his head. "You see, man, Soviet jazz fan use goddamn head! One Russian jazz fan is airline pilot, my friend. Go to Helsinki, bring back Miles Davis record. I borrow lathe, some wire, and make copy on X-ray film. Outside, no?"

Tollye knew the names of all the New York players on the recording. He listened for sections of the album where certain players were prominent, and he called out names as they played. He said loudly, pointing at the X-ray, "Cannonball," whenever the alto sax played the lead part. At the masterful drumming all through the album, more than once he asserted, "Philly Joe Jones. Beautiful fucking drummer, man!" And during "Blues for Pablo" he told us we were listening to Paul Chambers, Miles's young bass-playing genius. When the ballad "My Ship" rolled around and the French horn melody leading up to Miles's entry sounded out, Tollye called out my name without connecting me up with the horn player he was listening to. In his mind, it was a cat back in New York, working with Miles, and not in a crowd of Soviet jazz fans listening to an X-ray. Then suddenly I saw his brow furrow. He snatched the cigarette from his mouth, narrowed his eyes, and walked tentatively in my direction.

"No," he insisted, "is not you! *Is* you? *No!* Is you, really?"

"Is me, Tollye." The trombonist, crouched near the record player, shook his head and mumbled, "Fucking outside."

The jam session we'd gathered for flew out the window. Everybody wanted Miles Davis stories. What was it like making the album with Gil and Miles and Philly Joe and Paul Chambers and Cannonball and the great trombonist Jimmy Cleveland?

The French hornist Polex, true to his word, called and invited me to his home for dinner. As an artist much valued by his government, he lived with his family in an apartment that was comfortable and generous by Russian standards. His wife prepared an excellent meal, with plenty of hard-to-get meats, desserts, imported brandy, and good Russian vodka. After dinner, Polex and his children wanted to hear some Negro blues played on Polex's horn. I played W. C. Handy's "St. Louis Blues" until Polex's wife reminded us that it was time for their early-rising neighbors to begin their night's sleep.

After a week in Moscow, the Yale group took the overnight train to Leningrad. A large crowd of conservatory students, Lev Vlasenko, the jazz players, and dozens of fans came to say goodbye. The conductor said, "All aboard," and Mitchell and I tore ourselves from the bear hugs and kisses just in time to scurry onto the already rolling train.

We did a performance in Leningrad, which was full of jazz enthusiasts like those we had met in Moscow. Then we went on to sing and play in Lvov, Riga, and Kiev. Finally, it was time to end the Russian tour, in Yalta and Sochi, on the Black Sea. Sochi, the last stop before our return home, was a large resort where outstanding Soviet workers were given a vacation with their families as a reward for high productivity. The place had the air of a sanatorium, with no young people around, no good pianos anywhere, and no jazz action.

One afternoon, a Yalie came running toward us out on the beach, waving a *New York Times* he'd miraculously found somewhere in Yalta. On the front page was an article about our Moscow performance. Once we got back to the States, we discovered that the *Times* story had brought more interest in us than we could believe. Suddenly every TV producer, club owner, and concert agency wanted us.

Seymour Krawitz, a young press agent Bill Doll had trained, called Dave Garroway and got us on the *Today* show, the *Tonight* show and an appearance on *What's My Line*. We were hot.

But that wasn't why we had gone to the Soviet Union. We had gone, I suppose, mostly because it was *there*. We wanted the experience of visiting a foreign country that had been sealed tight to American modernism. And it had all worked out beyond our wildest dream. We had given some Russians an "opening" to a part of our culture they had known nothing about—to the music that had been invented in America and had evolved in amazing ways over the years. That we were the first jazz ambassadors to the Soviet Union since the 1920s—well, that was our gift to them. In return, they had given us memories that would never leave us and a new perspective on a world that, just maybe, was beginning to come closer together.

As for our new notoriety, which we knew would be transient, it was those Russians who had welcomed us and our music whom we had to thank. And I must say, it did set our minds to thinking about other worlds to conquer.

CHAPTER THIRTY-FOUR

"Sitting in the Catbird Seat, Baby!"

IN 1962, three years after that fabulous Russian excursion, we had a new opportunity to go international. It would be our first as a trio.

The year before this came about, two momentous events happened in my life: (1) we decided to add a drummer to our act; and (2) I became a nightclub owner. Here's how it all happened.

Mitchell and I had been feeling we'd like to hear another instrument added to our sound, an expanded expressiveness to the music. This growing feeling that something was missing might have come from our hearing so much of, and often playing with, some of the best drummers in jazz—Elvin Jones, our old Lockbourne colleague, and the phenomenal Philly Joe Jones. Philly Joe, who was Miles's drummer at the time, used to sit in with us as we played opposite Miles's band, laughing like a wild man while laying down with his brushes a simple little pulse that totally changed our sound.

Billy Taylor's piano trio had been a mainstay on the New York nightclub scene for a long time by then, and my favorite of all the drummers I heard with Billy was Charlie Smith. Charlie was a small group's dream. Having started his professional career at seventeen years old, playing for Ella Fitzgerald, he'd worked with most of the greats of jazz while still a youngster: from Ellington and Errol Garner to Charlie

Parker and Dizzy Gillespie. No longer with Billy Taylor, Charlie told me one day that he was tired of New York and wanted a change. After a few days of talking it over with Mitchell, we invited Charlie to join us as a trio. And that started the other thing in motion.

We needed a home base where we could play regularly, work daily in detailed rehearsals, and make a trio record album. We wanted to be away from New York.

New Haven came to mind as the place to organize. I was home one day, driving down the street with my four-year-old Michele, when I spotted a bar for sale. With work, it could be turned into a very good jazz joint, I thought. I drove on, telling myself I didn't want to own a club, I just wanted a steady job in a club for our new trio. Time dragged on. Mitchell and I started to get itchy, afraid that Charlie Smith might get another offer. I went back and looked at the bar and decided to go into hock to buy it. I hired a crew of unemployed waiters I knew in town—jazz fans from way back—and we completely tore the old building apart, rebuilt it, and opened a club I named the Playback. Charlie moved to town, and Mitchell and I worked on a new repertoire that suited the addition of the drums.

It wasn't easy. Right off, we found it troublesome to integrate the drums into the duo sound. The slow, lush ballad music from before worked well, and Charlie added interest and excitement with his percussion shadings, but the kind of hard-driving drumming he was known for somehow didn't take hold. When we all wanted to turn on the steam and bear down, the rhythm wouldn't flow. We weren't meshing as a group.

One Sunday afternoon, a ski lodge operator nearby hired us to play for a party. As we got into the music, our already shaky rhythmic focus degenerated into an unbearable blur. I didn't know what to do to bring us back in sync, nor did Mitchell or Charlie. It felt like heart disease. Finally, in my frustration, I said to the other two, "Let's take a break."

We went out in the snow to talk. "I don't know what our problem is, but this just can't go on. Why don't we just call it quits with this trio while we're still friends." Mitchell and Smith looked at me askance. They both protested. When I suggested we forget about the rest of the job and pack up the instruments and leave right then, Charlie, who was never at a loss for words, said, "Who's *that* rich, baby?"

We gathered about the fireplace and drank hot toddies in silence. We felt whipped. But when we went back on the bandstand and started playing the blues, the very first note seemed to be coming from a new trio. Every rhythmic idea was nailed squarely and solidly, as if the three of us had suddenly got wired to one brain. Perhaps there was some special mojo in the blues we played. Whatever it was, it felt fabulous.

No more heart disease.

Tight and elegant musical details we'd never discussed before sounded through the music: we made stunning crescendos and decrescendos together, built colors and emotional counterpoint that groups learn to do only after playing together for years. After that session we rehearsed every day, holding on for dear life to the newfound feeling and learning new material. We couldn't wait to get onto the Playback bandstand. Charlie's mood and appetite for music-making soared and became infectious. On any night when we were really cooking, Charlie would yell out one of Red Barber's trademark sports expressions:

"We're sitting in the catbird seat, baby!" We were.

One of our regular patrons, Dr. Walter Cory, a local physician and a talented recording engineer, began bringing in professional equipment and taping our sets in the club. Over a period of several months, he captured our sound on tape, and Atlantic Records released it as our first trio record album, *The Catbird Seat*. Charlie was laying another layer of rhythmic awareness on Mitchell and me, and we never got over it.

Owning the Playback brought me into another arena of the business of music: I learned the role of impresario and discovered I had a knack for it. Whenever the trio went on tour, I hired jazz artists from New York. Since the room could seat only a hundred patrons, it was impossible to pay the fees well-known artists were used to. But we were close enough to New York for artists who had a week off, or were recording there, to want to come up to play. Stan Getz, Marian McPartland, Roy Eldridge, Chico Hamilton, Slam Stewart, Teddy Wilson, Bobby Hackett, Henry "Red" Allen, Horace Silver, all played at the Playback. Even Langston Hughes, sponsored by The Artisans, a group of black women in which Emma was active, came several times to read his poetry on the Playback stage.

Soon our New Haven audience got a reputation among New York musicians for its musical taste, and everybody in the jazz world was suddenly eager to come to play. New York agents began calling me whenever artists they represented were idle in New York.

One night at the club, I got a telephone call from John Hammond, the Columbia Records producer in New York. John had hired me for New York studio work with several jazz artists he'd recorded, and he liked coming up to the Playback from New York to hear his old friend the pianist Teddy Wilson and others. A descendant of the rich and famous Commodore Vanderbilt, John was cultured, and his speech still bore the traces of his upper-class upbringing, even if his sentiments didn't. Not one to put on airs, he was at home with the folk in the jazz world.

"Willie," he said on the phone that night, "I would like to ask a favor of you. I am recording a young girl from Detroit on Columbia Records. It's her first album, and she's just sensational. Her experience is the gospel tradition. She is only eighteen years old and is away from home for the first time and alone in New York, with nothing to do over the weekend. Her father, a Baptist preacher of the old school, has insisted on my promise of personal responsibility for her. If you can find a spot for her at the club with Charlie Smith and you, it would be terrific."

I said, "I don't think gospel music would go over well in the club, John."

He hurried to correct me. "Oh, no, that's not what I'm suggesting. I'm recording her on an album of show tunes and Broadway standards. She has a hell of a repertoire of those things, and she plays piano for herself, and rather well. That's why I think the experience of her playing and singing with you would be good for her. I don't want to twist your arm, but if you can present her there, you need only pay her expenses; Columbia Records will take care of everything else."

John's expert judgment was good enough for me, and I agreed that the girl could alternate with our trio for the weekend, with Charlie and me doing double duty playing for her.

"I'll put her on the train here in New York," he said, "and you can pick her up at the New Haven station and take it from there. I'll come up for tomorrow's show."

"Now, John, tell me: who am I picking up at the train station?"

"Her name," he said, "is Aretha, Aretha Franklin, and I guarantee you, this is the last time you'll need to ask who she is."

A year later, we were on our way to Italy for a series of children's concerts. We'd also play the San Remo Jazz Festival on the Italian Riviera, a big event that would be televised nationally.

The sponsor of our trip had never presented jazz to Italian children before, but she had heard from some of Mrs. Perera's Milan connections that we were pretty good at it. Could we present the children's show in Italian? I knew that learning to present a program in Italian had to be easier than one in Russian. Besides, I already had some Spanish and French, and I could read Italian newspapers, so abundant around New Haven. I went to a record shop one day and bought a set of Teach Yourself Italian records off the shelf. Then, after a couple of weeks, I put myself in the hands of neighborhood Italian friends, who helped me translate what we wanted the children of Italy to know about jazz and its origins.

A month or so later, I called the French steamship line and bartered part of the trio's passage to France in exchange for a performance or two aboard the new S.S. *France*. That was a ploy to get us to Paris for a few days of listening to some of our favorite American jazz artists living there, all heroes to us. Kenny Clarke was one of them; a former star of Dizzy Gillespie's big band and the original drummer of the Modern Jazz Quartet, he had left the MJQ to work in Paris. Kenny was a role model for Charlie Smith, and I had been a special fan since hearing him on record the first time, back in the army band in Wyoming. Charlie promised Mitchell and me an introduction.

As soon as we landed in Paris, we took off for the Blue Note, a jazz club not far from the Champs Élysées. A sign outside the club read: AMERICAN JAZZ—BUD POWELL—KENNY CLARKE. We paid the admission charge (steep) at the door and stood at the bar to listen to two of the original pioneers of the modern jazz that all three of us worshiped.

The great pianist Bud Powell was on the bandstand with a French drummer and bassist. They sounded OK, but the drummer was not Kenny Clarke.

When Powell finished his set and came off the bandstand, Charlie rushed him: "Bud, baby! whatcha know?" Bud knew nothing. There was no response; no sign of recognition. He was in a daze. "Meet my two partners, Mitchell and Ruff." Bud extended a lifeless hand to Mitchell. Mitchell glowed. Of all the geniuses in the progressive jazz movement, Powell has always been his favorite. With more than a little emotion in his voice, Mitchell said, "Oh, Mr. Powell, I'm so happy to meet you!"

"Buy me a drink," interrupted Bud. Mitchell complied, but Bud had nothing more to say. He just stared vacantly. Charlie attempted to fill the void. "Remember that night in the joint on Fifty-second Street, Bud?" The emptiness in Bud's eyes signaled "nobody home."

In a little while, Kenny Clarke came in. Charlie again took the lead, grabbed Kenny in a bear hug, and introduced Mitchell and me. Then Kenny went to work. Mitchell, noticing that the man sitting at the piano in Kenny's band was not Bud, said, "What the hell is *this*? Where's Bud?" Kenny's pianist was a very able young Parisian, but he was not Bud. The same bass player who'd played with Bud was doing double duty with Kenny. And then we got the point. The Blue Note owner had hired these two American giants separately and paid them a few francs more than he had to pay the local sidemen. That way the club made a lot of money, while Kenny Clarke and Bud Powell made little more than a living wage. The shameless exploitation of the jazz artist stretching all the way across the Atlantic was an old story.

The whole Blue Note scene was so depressing I left Mitchell and Charlie and went to the Left Bank to find Don Byas, the tenor saxophone master whose records had been favorites with the Lockbourne crowd. Byas, after playing with Count Basie and Coleman Hawkins, then working with Dizzy Gillespie and the new breed of modern jazz players on Fifty-second Street, left the States and had been living in Europe for years. I found him in a little cellar club, on the bandstand with a young trio of French musicians not half as good as those back at the Blue

Note. But even with substandard sidemen, his playing had all the fire and authority I remembered from his recordings.

When he came off the stage for his break he was staggering, and I guessed that he drank to make it easier to tolerate the amateurs he played with. I tried to imagine what a trio of Byas, Kenny Clarke, and Bud Powell would sound like. Combining such an array of American jazz talent would be a record producer's dream. I also suspected that if the three men pooled their musical resources and insisted on working strictly as one unified American aggregation, their earnings would increase ten times over. I waited until Byas came to the bar, then I introduced myself. He could not have known my name, because he'd left the States years before Mitchell and I formed the duo in 1955.

"Mr. Byas," I said, "I am a great admirer of your playing, and I treasure every recording of yours I've ever heard. May I buy you a drink?" We toasted each other, he asked what I was doing in Europe, and I told him of the trio, and that our drummer was Charlie Smith.

"Oh, yeah," he said, "the little left-handed cat that's so great with the brushes. Where you working?" He was surprised to hear that we had come to Europe to play for children.

"Jesus! That's a hell of an idea. That sounds like something I would really enjoy doing. I'm crazy about kids." Perhaps it was the subject of children that made our exchange easy. I gathered up my courage and asked him if he would consider asking his band to sit out the next set, so I could play the bass with him—just the two of us.

His hesitation spoke volumes.

It was an absurd request, and I realized it immediately. I hadn't then heard the masterful duet of "I've Got Rhythm" that he'd recorded with Slam Stewart, or I wouldn't have asked to play at all.

Trying to make amends, I said, "Well, how about the two of us just playing one tune, 'All the Things You Are'?" More hesitation, but after a moment he said, "OK, come on. I'll tell the cats and ask the bass player if it's OK for you to use his bass." I had noticed that when he'd played with his band during their previous set, he'd talked to his audience in quite good French, easily managing the usual show business patter in his adopted tongue. But when the two of us went on the stage to play, he didn't say a word to his audience. I knew then just how apprehensive he was about playing with me. I tuned up the bass and began playing the bass introduction the way Slam Stewart did on the classic Charlie Parker–Dizzy Gillespie recording of "All the Things You Are"; it was also the way Mitchell and I had done it back at Lockbourne. The borrowed bass had a robust tone, with quick and easy response, and its bottom register was rich and deep. At the end of my eight-measure introduction, Byas entered, his big pure round tenor tone singing out the song's elegant melody in a delivery reminiscent of the great lyrical singers—Eckstine, Sarah Vaughan, and Ella Fitzgerald. He was that rarity, an instrumentalist-balladeer, an artist who plays a song's words with lyrical detail as clear and as transparent as speech.

I knew, even during the four beats of the first bar of the melody, which is exactly how long the first note and the first word, "You," lasts, that I had embarked on the jazz ride of my life. When we'd worked our way through the first chorus, Don anchored himself in a spread-legged, bent-kneed stance, grunted his preparedness, took a big breath, then soared. What followed was a harmony lesson via an unimaginable excursion through the intricate chord progressions of "All the Things." We both finished in a lathering sweat. Don's French audience stomped and cheered him. I extended my hand to congratulate and thank him. He took me by the hand, grinning. "You said you wanted play a whole set, man. Where you going? Let's play 'Body and Soul.' "

At the children's concerts in Italy, the kids listened attentively to my Italian spiel, but they went wild for Charlie's drumming. Charlie, a natural teacher and an experienced showman, laid it on them, and it took no time for Mitchell and me to see that the children's favorite instrument on our stage was the drum set. In our routine, Charlie would demonstrate each part of his set as I described it in Italian, a demonstration that he made slick, graceful, puckish, and such a delight to the children that they danced in their seats and hollered, "Bravo, Signor Charlie!" In Sicily, where we always played the children's concerts in churches, the little ones sat with riveted attention to the piano playing and our musical explanations, but they, too, couldn't get enough of Charlie's drums.

In Brescia, we got the children to sing an Italian folk song for us, so we could use it to show them how improvising in the jazz fashion can completely alter the nature of a song even if we, the musicians, played back the exact notes they sang. The rhythm, we wanted them to understand, made the difference. After they'd sung, we gave the opening of the folk song over to Charlie and his drums. He played a hot rhythmic introduction using lots of tom-toms and mallets, then signaled for Mitchell and me to enter and the children to sing the ancient song along with our trio in the new style Charlie had just laid out. It was a new moment for us and the herd of singing, bouncing Italian children: we rocked the staid old hall to its foundations. The bravos sounded up and down the boot of Italy, and though our triumph with the Italian children was all too brief, we knew we would be coming back again and again. And come back we did.

CHAPTER THIRTY-FIVE

Breakup

TRAVELING WITH THE TRIO was never as easy as being on the road with just Mitchell and playing as a duo. Charlie had met his new wife in New Haven, and they now had a lovely baby girl, Wendy.

Traveling began to wear thin for Charlie, and again he wanted a change. Actually, a kind of musical restlessness seemed to be settling on all three of us. And the Playback, once a workshop for building the trio, was suddenly a burden. Financial responsibility for the operation was mine alone, and while it had served a musical purpose, it had never turned a profit. I'd had to plow back my share of the earnings from concert tours into the business just to pay salaries, taxes, and utilities. It was only with the loans of a few hundred dollars here and there—from my generous mother-in-law, from Pete Hodgson at Silly Putty, from Morris Widder, and from a couple of jazz-loving patrons—that I was able to keep open.

For a time, we ran a successful series of Playback children's concerts. Sunday-afternoon chamber music programs also did well and gave me a chance to play the horn with some of the fine local musicians I'd known for years. But that didn't save the day for us.

It was in the winter of 1963 that I felt myself stuck in a quagmire, with never enough money or energy to pull myself clear. I don't know where the fatigue came from, but it was there, and the worrisome day-to-day drudgery of running an unprofitable restaurant began to take its toll with me, both at work and at home with Emma. My marriage was falling apart. And when I came down with a series of mysterious health problems—puzzling and excruciating boils and fevers—my doctor could only attribute them to depression. I seemed to feel better only when work took me away from New Haven; but away, I missed my little girl, and got further depressed over the sinking marriage.

Some men take their broken marriages to their preacher, to their psychiatrist, to bartenders or other confidants. I tried to suppress mine in music and learned that music expresses; never suppresses. My main talking buddy, Morris, who had a marriage that was literally killing him, could only tell me how lucky I was in mine.

One day I got a message that Mrs. Tribett, a neighbor and longtime friend of Emma's family, wanted to see me. Would I drop by the house soon? Though I knew Mrs. Tribett fairly well and liked her, I thought the call to visit a little unusual.

But I went to see her, and she sat me down, gave me a cup of coffee, and got right to the point.

"Willie," she began without preamble, "I gather that you and Emma aren't happy. I hope you won't mind my not telling you how I learned this. And I especially hope you won't mind what I would like to tell you. No marriage, even the ones that look most perfect, is easy. You must know that, of course. But I'm telling you what I *know* about marriages—not what I *heard*—because I've been in the same fix as you.

"Mr. Tribett and I have a considerable age difference between us." (I very much admired Mr. Tribett, New Haven's only black licensed electrician and a Tuskegee graduate. A call from *him* to visit would have been easier for me to understand.) "But," Mrs. Tribett went on, "that wasn't the biggest of our problems. I don't even know if I could tell you what the problems were if I tried, but they seemed big enough at the time to split us up. Somehow, later on, we did manage to go back together, but we had to work at it, brother, and so far, it's a good thing. A marriage sometimes needs working at.

"I just wanted you to hear this from me because I think you know how much I think of Emma and you and that baby. And I wanted you to know that even if you two decide to go through with a divorce, even then it won't be too late to try again. . . . But maybe you can try harder before that happens."

No preacher's inner office or bartender's sympathetic ear could have done better, and I never got to properly thank Mrs. Tribett, for she died of cancer before I got around to it. But the marriage wasn't saved.

On the day Emma and I agreed on the divorce, neither of us had very much to say beyond wondering what effect my leaving would have on Michele, who was then five. There had never been any temperamental eruptions or abuse; we both had probably seen it coming for such a long time that we were too worn down and depressed about it to explode. Emma said, "Whatever happens, I'm sure we both want what's best for Michele. Whatever we do, we have to keep that in mind." It was quiet and straightforward enough, but still there were tears. She must not have had any misgivings about my commitment to our daughter's welfare, for she agreed to my choice of a lawyer, a quiet blind man whose Seeing Eye dog often led him to the Playback, where the two sat quietly, listening to the music.

When Emma and I showed up at his office, this lovely man said, "Mrs. Ruff, I want you to know that my main concern in the matter is the welfare of the child. You can be certain that she and you will have all of whatever assets there are."

Emma and I were divorced in 1963. When we sold the house we'd lived in, we used the money to settle her and Michele in a house near the best elementary school we knew of in town. I closed the Playback and, with my DiLeone bass, my horn, and fifty bucks, moved to New York and stayed in Mitchell's apartment until I earned enough money for a month's advance rent in a midtown hotel.

Living in New York hotels as a "permanent" took getting used to. At least New Haven was close enough for regular visits with Michele. And being in New York put me in touch with elements of the broadcast and recording industry I'd not known before. I worked hard. John Hammond found me and put me to work playing bass on a variety of jobs; among them was the first album of the Canadian singer Leonard Cohen. Then I became involved in an interesting new situation that would mean some more foreign travel, quite unlike any I'd ever done.

CHAPTER THIRTY-SIX

Seeking Out the Samba

ONE NIGHT shortly after I'd moved to New York, Mitchell and I were playing at the Hickory House when Jeff Goldstein, a twenty-four-year-old associate producer from WCBS, came in. Goldstein introduced himself to me and said he was from New Haven. His visit that night had nothing at all to do with his work, but as we talked he showed some interest when I mentioned that I'd met some Brazilian musicians in town who'd got me thinking about a documentary film I wanted to see made. I told him about how the idea had me dreaming about working on the film myself. I wanted to try and find out how the samba had taken root in Brazil and flourished. How was it that the samba's African origins, its direct rhythmic bloodline from an Angolan past, still coursed so forcefully through Brazil's musical veins?

I wanted especially to see the Brazilian equivalent—Candomblé—of the American black Sanctified Church. Candomblé still used pure African drums and dancing in its ritual, and I wanted to learn how the drumming contrasted with what my Mrs. Nance back in Alabama had played on her single bass drum. Brazilian religious dance and spirit possession had counterparts in North America; all shared an African past. Tracing that past would be the musical odyssey I wanted to film.

A few days later, Jeff called me at my hotel. "Say, Willie, is your passport up to date?" My passport is always up to date, I told him. "Well, get ready for this: that Brazil idea you were talking about? It can fly, if you're really serious about it. I was just at a meeting with my boss and the staff of the local WCBS program *Eye on New York,* and get this: the end of our fiscal year is nearly here, and there's dough left over from this year's budget. They'll have to return the goddamn money to the network if it's not used, so they are now looking for a 'class' project. I told them about your Brazil idea. Of course, you'll have to take me along, goddamn it, if I sell them this idea, right?"

What sold the idea to his boss at CBS, Jeff told me later, was the popularity at the time of the quasi-jazz "new beat" (bossa nova), which had brought such a formidable horde of Rio musicians to America. Bossa nova was everywhere. My film idea was timely and appealing because *Black Orpheus,* a film from Brazil, was sweeping the world and winning international film awards, including a Cannes Film Festival prize. A large part of *Black Orpheus's* appeal was its musical score. Luis Bonfa, one of that film's composers, was in New York and in the inner circle of the dozen or so Brazilians I'd come to know.

Jeff arranged a meeting for me with the WCBS brass. I reviewed my idea for them, and we made a deal on the spot. I prepared to leave for Brazil immediately for a two- or three-week scouting tour, beginning in Rio, then going on to Bahia, where the strongest concentration of Africanisms survived. I had a list of subjects of musical interest I felt were vital to my plan: I would film an interview with the widow of the celebrated composer Villa-Lobos and visit the samba schools in Rio, where neighborhood clubs practiced all year for the annual carnival spectacular. The clubs played the authentic hot, two-beat, African-rooted samba, not the diluted Carmen Miranda kind.

A few nights before I left for Rio, John Hammond took me up to Minton's Playhouse in Harlem, to hear the new jazz guitar sensation, George Benson. George was barely out of his teens, and he played the instrument like nobody's business. When we left Minton's, I told John about the Brazil trip, and he said, "Oh, you must talk to Goddard Lieberson before you leave. He knew Villa-Lobos very well and would be very interested in what you are going to do." John called Lieberson, Columbia Records' president, and made an appointment for me.

The next day, I met Lieberson at his office. He was very suave, elegantly dressed, and thoroughly charming to me. And he seemed genuinely interested in my project.

"What an exciting idea you have! I would love to go with you. Of all my musical memories, my visit to Brazil at the invitation of Villa-Lobos stands out and stays with me." I could feel him bursting to share the details: "Villa-Lobos was an extraordinary man; really, a delightful and charming mystic. He loved his country and its cultural mix. African music, and especially the music of Bahia, fascinated him. It must have been twenty years ago that I got word that he was hard at work making the rounds of all the schoolhouses in Rio de Janeiro for the sole purpose of teaching small children to sing. When he was satisfied with their performance, he assembled a hundred thousand of them in Rio's municipal soccer stadium, where they all sang together. You see, Villa-Lobos had the idea that the vocal cords of young children are nature's own living, dynamic, biological 'strings,' and that they produce the most pure and natural of all musical sounds—a rather engaging notion, I thought. The sound of a hundred thousand children singing together had been one of his lifetime musical dreams, and he invited people from all over the world to come to Brazil to hear it. Well, I was one of the invited, and I promise you, it was unforgettable. I get chills just remembering it."

I knew then that talking to Villa-Lobos's widow was the first thing I wanted to do when I arrived in Rio. Lieberson found her address and phone number for me and said he would call her on my behalf. Then, just as I was leaving his office, he stopped me and smiled.

"Tell me this—how the hell did you wangle your way into a giant corporation like this one and engineer a trip to Brazil on *our* expense account, when I, the president of the record company, am stuck in New York? Wanna be my agent?"

I went to my Brazilian musician friends in New York and got the names of the best musicians and sources for my project. Since the film would have, wherever possible, some interactive performances by our duo, Mitchell stood by to fly to Rio with the CBS crew. Luis Bonfa had agreed to take part in the filming and was returning to Rio for a vacation just ahead of me.

Mme Villa-Lobos was the first person I called in Rio. She had heard from Goddard Lieberson and was expecting me. In quite good English, she invited me to her home. And for yet another reason I had to admire the departed Maestro. Madame was a much younger and more energetic woman than I had imagined. Her elegance and Brazilian beauty brightened when she talked of her husband, and her world turned around his memory. She showed me the guitar he used for composing, as well as stacks of unfinished or unpublished manuscripts in his neat handwriting. We talked about his interests that bisected those I was in Brazil to document, especially the African music connection and Bahia.

It didn't take long for word to spread through Rio's musical grapevine that a "CBS man" was in town, making a music documentary. Musicians, dance troupes, and voodoo artists rushed out of the woodwork to find me. I was put upon to listen to all sorts of performers, proposals, and acts not even remotely related to what had brought me there. It was astonishing how many doors flew open at the mention of those three magical letters: CBS. Politicians and functionaries of every stripe were anxious to assist me.

After a week in Rio, I traveled to Bahia, met drummers and dancers, and arranged permission to film churches and old Candomblé religious ceremonies and capaera, the lethal African combat dance-game. The governor of the state, eager for CBS coverage, offered a car, a guide, and a driver, and within a week all my locations and subjects were in place.

A Rio-based German cameraman, Jürgen Neumann, and a Dutch soundman made up our crew. When we began shooting in Rio, we had no way of knowing how well or how badly we'd covered our subject each day. Without the luxury of a fast lab in Brazil to process the daily footage, we were working in the dark. Were we getting everything? Were all the subjects properly focused and lit; was the accompanying sound well balanced? The WCBS office insisted we send each day's footage back to New York by jet, for them to process and then give to their chief film editor, John Carter. Carter's daily phone calls to us were mostly raves and praise for the camera work and the music. Neumann and his camera seemed to be everywhere at once. He was at work before and after we shot each location, filming cutaway details to bridge the various sections of action. Mitchell said of him, "I don't know what the stuff is going to look like when it's projected, but that cameraman even *looks* like a virtuoso."

When we'd finished shooting in Brazil, Mitchell and I stayed on in Rio to record an album with several Brazilian musicians. By the time we arrived back in New York, John Carter—today an internationally famous film editor—had assembled a rough edit of the footage. In the screening room one afternoon, he pridefully switched on the projector, and within minutes we knew we had a winner. No film, I learned, is altogether without disappointments. My one regret was that the executive producer felt Mme Villa-Lobos's English was too strongly accented in the interview: American audiences, he insisted, wouldn't understand her. I thought he was wrong, but he was the boss, the real CBS man, and to my horror, the interview footage ended up on the cutting room floor, never to be seen again.

Even before it aired on the network, our film, *The Distant Sounds*, won several awards, including the Peabody Award for excellence in a documentary film. It took longer than usual for the network to give us an air date. They kept saying they were holding out for a prime-time slot. So we waited.

Even before John Carter had finished his editing, I had made up my mind, with his encouragement, to invest a great deal of concentrated time and energy in learning the basic technical details of film-making. I knew for sure that film would be an important tool for exploring other of my musical interests, and I wanted a "from the ground up" indoctrination. So I moved to Los Angeles and enrolled as a full-time film student at the University of Southern California. USC had other musical attractions for me as well: one was the Swedish music professor and composer Ingolf Dahl, whose music I had played under Professor Wilson back in New Haven. I arranged to study composition with Dahl. I knew, too, that David Raksin, the composer of the wonderful film score and the ballad, *Laura*, taught a class in composition for film at the school. Classes with Dahl and Raksin would round out the musical focus of my film study; the rest of the time was for classes in editing, cinematography, screenwriting, sound editing, and the history of film. I was into a new life, at a time when I felt I really needed one.

CHAPTER THIRTY-SEVEN

The Search for Our
Musical Roots

B Y THE SUMMER OF 1967, several of my New York colleagues, jazz arrangers and composers, were relocating in Hollywood. Jazz-flavored musical scores were in demand in the TV studios, and Quincy Jones had come west a year or two before me. Oliver Nelson, Benny Golson, and J.J. Johnson followed. When I got there, Quincy had just given his *Ironside* series to Oliver Nelson before he moved on to *The Mod Squad*, feature films, and other things. All these musicians made me and my horn welcome, just as they had done back in New York, and before the USC film classes even began, I was recording sound tracks for *Ironside*, *The Dean Martin Show*, and a wide variety of other shows. Several times a month, Mitchell, still traveling from his New York apartment, would meet me on some college campus for duo concerts.

Benny Carter came to visit Oliver Nelson at Universal Studios one day while we recorded an *Ironside* episode. I had narrowly missed meeting him in Las Vegas twelve years earlier. This was my chance. Oliver introduced us and mentioned a connection with Yale. "Oh, we know another musician here from there," said Benny. "He's the dean of the composers and arrangers here at Universal. In fact, he is one of the great ones in town." Pause. "No, I take that back: in the *business!* He must be in his office or around here somewhere. I'll find him and bring him in during the next break."

Benny was talking about Sidney Fine, the musician Universal Studios retained on staff to score pictures and "put out fires," as Fine sometimes described his job of "fixing" musical problems others found insoluble. A compact man whose eyes sparkled, Sidney was of Benny's vintage, and like Benny, he was easy to know, well-spoken, and laughed easily. After he'd graduated from Yale, he had studied composition with Arnold Schoenberg in New York, written for network radio as a regular at NBC, and, in addition to his work for music publishers, composed for the New York musical theater.

I admit to complete shamelessness when it comes to enlisting experts among my elders to teach me. I told Sidney that I was in California to learn something about the craft of film-making and that I was also interested in composing for film and related media. Then I asked if he would consider teaching me something about writing dramatic music.

"Oh, no," he said. "I have no experience or qualification for that sort of thing. That's best left in the hands of others. No; my career, such as it is, has been concerned with just putting on paper what's required. I have nothing of importance to pass on." Later in our friendship, I learned that he'd been "required" to put music on paper for a host of legends of the film world, including Charlie Chaplin, Walt Disney, and Mike Todd; that the work of his hand carried the names of an impressive list of composers, who, when pressed by demanding deadlines, thought nothing of calling him in the middle of the night for help. This "putting out fires" was a common Hollywood practice, and when Fine found himself in a similar pinch, other composers, some with large names, had in turn doused a flame or two for him.

Though he'd waved off my plea that he take me on as a student, Sidney did invite me to visit him at home. "We'll talk about New Haven," he said. We made a date for Sunday morning, and when I arrived at his house, he and his wife, Rose, a teacher of theatrical children in Hollywood, led me to a lavish breakfast table. After the meal, Sidney got up from the table and called me to the piano, where there was a tall stack of well-used volumes of music, including that of

Bach and Beethoven; but most in evidence were songs by Schubert. Fine sat at the piano and motioned me to look over his shoulder.

"The other day at Universal," he said, "you mentioned an interest in scoring dramatic music. Well, let me show you some surprising examples of dramatic music in a different dress." He began playing the "Erl-king." I knew the music, but Sidney called my attention to the song's piano accompaniment, so descriptive of the mood and meaning of the Erl-king legend of Germanic folklore: the evil spirit, malicious toward children. Everything in the story, the sinister and the urgent, was there in the few notes Schubert had written. Sidney's point—that simple musical ideas often have dramatic elements built into them— opened me to ways of thinking about drama and musical emotion.

"Imagine this orchestrated," he said, and for three hours or so we explored the music stacked on the piano. I was learning new ways of listening. I thanked Sidney and Rose for the morning and prepared to leave. Sidney said, "We're home Sundays. Come again."

The next Sunday morning, I called, and Sidney said, "Come at ten." After breakfast, we again went to the piano, and we worked through a stack of music he'd prepared for me. And again the time flew. I didn't go the following week; I thought he should have a rest. Besides, my mama always warned, "Learn not to wear out your welcome, boy." But at half-past ten, my phone rang.

"It's ten-thirty. You're late!" Sidney had become my teacher without saying so. For the next four years, 10:00 A.M. on Sundays was my time for learning at the Fine house.

No part of my studies at USC served me better than the weekly private composition lessons with Ingolf Dahl. His teaching and musicianship were so inspiring that I crawled out of bed every morning at four to spend four to five hours writing music for his criticism: it was the most concentrated musical learning of my life. On the few occasions when concerts and work in the recording studios kept me from composing, I took my horn to the lessons. Dahl loved playing Paul Hindemith's horn sonatas as much as I did, and he astounded me by sight-reading the full orchestral score of Hindemith's concerto for horn just as easily and effectively as he'd managed the sonatas. Our little chamber music jam sessions were like cool refreshment in a parched desert. We played every piece of music I owned for the horn and piano, in addition to what I wrote.

Meanwhile, my courses at USC's film school were so stimulating that my interest in college classroom teaching surfaced again.

One day, I made an appointment with Professor Walter Rubsammen, the chairman of the music department at UCLA. I had an idea for a new course: an introduction to Afro-American music. UCLA had a jazz history course but no such offering as I proposed.

Rubsammen was very interested. However, I had practically walked in off the street; references had to be checked. Having done his homework on me and my background, he called several days later and said that if I could develop enough teaching materials to support my idea, he would hire me as a part-time instructor.

There were no models for the class I had in mind. After reading all the books on the subject I'd not read before, I knew I would have to start from scratch, writing my own syllabus. Then began the long process of listening to every recording I could find of African, European, and American music that related to my subject. I bought records by the dozens. There were films on African music made in the field, but hardly anything had been organized in a digestible format for teaching. Mantle Hood, chairman of UCLA's ethnomusicology department, put me in touch with West African master drummers around town. In a few months, I was ready to begin sketching ideas for a series of lectures using film, recordings, and live performance.

In my search for new teaching materials to use for my lecture class, I learned from a local dentist, who was an amateur drummer, that one of the world's richest deposits of recorded American music was right there on the UCLA campus—not in the music department but in the collection of folklorist D. K. Wilgus.

Wilgus had long ago recognized the importance of song, music, and dance as guides to facets of American culture and had brought together the earliest recorded spirituals, Sanctified sermons, and every genre of American popular music. Thomas Edison's experimental footage of black dancers performing the cakewalk, the buzzard's lope, and other dances, all filmed in the 1890s, was part of his treasure. And from Wilgus I learned the whereabouts of other African and African-American musical films, for sale or for rent for classroom use. Then I used what I'd learned about editing at USC's film school and threw myself into my lesson plans.

Nearly four hundred UCLA students were in their seats in Arnold Schoenberg Auditorium the first day my class met. It was the largest audience I'd ever faced alone, without Mitchell or an instrument to play. After thirteen years of evangelizing for jazz music on four continents, there I was, feeling the heavy weight of my solitary challenge as a classroom teacher. Stage fright crept into my knees, and I asked myself why I had not brought along my bass or my horn to help me break the ice. But I remembered that I was there to teach, not to entertain.

The visual reinforcement I'd prepared—the slides, maps, film clips, and taped musical examples—began to do their work, and my terror receded. Sidney Fine had graciously listened to several of my trial lectures and he helped me organize my ideas. He'd been right when he'd advised, "Choose your musical examples well, Willie—then trust them to do their work."

It was not long after the start of the first semester in 1968 that CBS aired the duo's Brazil film as a Network Special. It was a big success but best of all, the program had meaning for my students and was very much to the point of what we were studying in class. Then, about midsemester, Mitchell came to town to spend several sessions at UCLA, helping me illustrate musical examples I wanted to present to the class. He was anxious to go before an audience that had already had an introduction to the historical materials. In all our years of playing before audiences new to jazz, this was our first opportunity to spread our presentation out over several sessions. It was at our first class that a simple question by one of the students led to a colloquium that stunned us to our marrow.

One young woman asked how we'd started playing together. Mitchell took the answer. It was simple, he said. "We met in the army at an all-black air base in Ohio, where we learned our craft under a musician and teacher, Chief Warrant Officer John Brice. Mr. Brice taught us that this music is one of our culture's strongest and most honorable legacies and that we should do all we can to serve it well."

Instantly, other hands went up. I believe they all had the same question. "Why was there an air base just for blacks?" UCLA was crackling with revolutionary zeal that year, as were most California campuses. But my students, about half of them white, couldn't even imagine that black men had ever been refused training in military aviation in America; or that black officers had organized themselves to challenge racial segregation in the army. The very idea that America ever had had a Lockbourne snatched their breath away. It was hard for Mitchell and me to believe just how much the subject took hold of them. In the end, I had to insist that we lay aside twentieth-century "military history" in favor of the musical subject we were there for. Even so, more students asked for appointments to talk about Lockbourne during my office hours. Suddenly there was a swell of renewed interest in the Tuskegee episode.

After our next class, two days later, a young woman brought a picture to my office showing several black airmen gathered around a group of fighter planes. The picture was obviously of men of the Ninety-ninth, and it had been taken in Italy during the war. The student said, "Mr. Ruff, I was telling my parents what you and Mr. Mitchell had said about the Tuskegee pilots and your own experiences on the Ohio air base. My dad said, 'Oh, yeah, my brother, your Uncle Wiley, was one of those pilots.' Then my dad showed me this picture of Uncle Wiley and his friends here. I mean, I raised hell with both my parents, because I shouldn't have to go to college to be learning this kind of thing about my own people in a *music* class!"

It made me proud that a music class had illustrated to the young lady how quickly our story, a significant story in the American experience, erodes if not reinforced from generation to generation. That realization kept nagging at me like an itch needing a scratch. I couldn't get it out of my mind.

Several days later, Carmen McRae, a longtime friend, whose musicianship and heart I've always admired, called me. She wanted me to meet Richard Quine, a film director and a fan of our duo. Quine had used some of our recorded music in one of his films. He had directed *The World of Suzie Wong, The Solid Gold Cadillac,* and *Hotel.* He'd also been a force in bringing Count Basie's band to Hollywood to work on an early Blake Edwards picture, and he was on the scene when Fred Astaire, who lived just up the lane from Richard, made a dancing record with Count Basie playing piano.

We soon did get together and became friends. Richard's home was just down the hill from the UCLA campus, and some afternoons after my lectures I'd stop by to unwind and listen to his rich record collection. He had everything. I even borrowed a few historical sides from his collection to play for my class.

One day when I came to his house, I found Richard in his living room, talking with a couple I didn't know. One of them was Hesper Anderson, a writer and the daughter of Maxwell Anderson, the playwright-lyricist. Introducing me as "a music teacher from up the road," Richard went to the record player to put on a new duo record I'd given him. After a couple of minutes of intense listening, Hesper's hand went up. "Where on earth did you find that fantastic piano player?" I talked about meeting Mitchell in the Lockbourne band, described Mr. Brice, the Tuskegee officers, what the all-black air base was about, and how it came into being—the court-martial and its resolution.

Immediately, both of them thought: why not a movie?

Why not indeed. In my enthusiasm, I told them about B. O. Davis, Sr., the only black general in the army; his son, Davis, Jr., at West Point, then at Tuskegee in the first group of cadets; the unit's fighting record in Germany and the mutiny charge in Indiana that brought on the court-martial. Hesper flew into a flurry of notetaking. Richard scrambled to the gadget box to switch on a tape recorder. Did I know how and where to find any of the Tuskegee men who'd flown with the squadron overseas?

I had heard that Colonel John Whitehead, Lockbourne's most celebrated daredevil, called "Mr. Death," had become a member of the Chuck Yeager crowd of test pilots at Edwards Air Force Base, not many miles north of where we sat. I said I would call him when I got home.

"Call from here," Richard said. "I'll throw a party for everybody. Maybe the colonel knows where we can find some of the others from the group." I dialed Edwards Air Base information, got Whitehead's home number. He was flying. I left my home number.

Mr. Death called me back that same night. He remembered Mr. Brice, Ivory Mitchell, and a lot of characters in the band, but he couldn't place me. No matter. Would he come to a party in Beverly Hills to talk about the Tuskegee story and tell us how to contact other "Spookwaffe" pilots and officers? Hell yes; and he would also make some calls and get back to me with phone numbers and addresses. "But you can start right now and call Marsden Thompson and Ed Gleed for yourself. Gleed works for the City of Los Angeles, and he can tell you how to contact Marsden." I asked if the Gleed he meant was the same major who was the executive officer back at Lockbourne in the old days. "Same one. Brilliant guy, you'll recall. He retired early a few years ago and went to law school. Call him. But don't shortchange Marsden Thompson, man, because he was one of the ringleaders in busting through that goddamn door of that Freeman Field white officers' club. He and another Los Angeles guy were among the three who were court-martialed when the army saw they couldn't get away with that crap any longer. They ended up dropping the charges against the hundred and six of us, to focus on and court-martial those three. Hell, Marsden and those guys started something. You call Marsden. See you later!"

Within a week, Mr. Death, Hesper, and I had made contact with about a dozen Tuskegee men and planned a big party at Richard's. To add to the occasion, Richard and I invited Sarah Vaughan and Carmen McRae. I called Carmen to make sure that they would come, and she confirmed, "Sarah and I *will* be there!"

CHAPTER THIRTY-EIGHT

The Reunion

O N THE SUNDAY AFTERNOON of the party, I stood in Richard's driveway to greet the airmen and their wives. Men and women piled excitedly out of their automobiles, clutching photo albums, scrapbooks, snapshots, newspaper clippings, pamphlets, memorabilia, and official documents relating to the war and their part in it. One car pulled up with a single occupant, and even from a distance I recognized Major Gleed, the classy master administrator back at Lockbourne, now, according to Mr. Death, a lawyer helping run the City of Los Angeles.

Another man pulled up and introduced himself and asked for a projector; he had a film made at Tuskegee. Marsden Thompson was in the car with him and had a copy of the transcript of the court-martial. When Mr. Death's car drove up, with his wife at the wheel, no introduction was needed: he looked exactly as he'd looked at Lockbourne, with the addition of glasses and perhaps three extra pounds, pushing his weight up to, maybe, 126. I had expected to see more Lockbourne men among the vets. Of all the men there, only Gleed and Mr. Death had stayed in the Air Force after the court-martial and served at Lockbourne.

When the last car was parked, I went in to join the party and bask in the warmth of reunited war buddies reminiscing and hugging and introducing their wives. We were buzzing away when, all of a sudden, a new person entered the room. Everyone seemed to hush at once. It was Sarah Vaughan. The center of attention shifted, and it took Carmen McRae's entrance to quiet the room. Then the crowd brought out their records and autograph books for the two stars to sign. But in no time, the imposing presence of Mr. Death quietly reminded us all of why we were there. I looked at his compact frame and those familiar ultra-streamlined steel-chiseled features, and I remembered what a star he'd been back at Lockbourne. But even in Beverly Hills, in civilian clothes twenty years later, he was every inch the dashing ace, our Tuskegee man turned test pilot, an Edwards Air Base heavy, the daredevil aviator I'd envied as a boy.

When the moment was right, Richard tapped several quick clinks on his highball glass, welcomed the airmen and their wives, Carmen and Sarah. He reiterated our interest in filming the story and asked, "How can we help Hesper write the kind of script this valiant and untold story deserves?"

Somebody suggested that we begin by looking at the film made at Tuskegee, an official War Department documentary meant for black audiences. We watched it mostly in silence. The film avoided the racism implicit in the fact that the "Tuskegee experiment" was needed at all, and its wartime message was upbeat and inspirational. We saw young black men in classrooms, studying the complex elements of navigational math and physics. They were pictured in flight, in physical training, and on parade. Every few seconds, some man at the party would point energetically to the screen and shout out of the dark, "There I am! And look at old Thompson!" There was precision marching to the music of the band I'd heard as a boy in Sheffield. A segment near the end of the film showed men marching and singing their fight song. As great music, the fight songs of the world generally fall short. But Sarah Vaughan was so stirred by the spirited young voices on the film that she came up out of her chair.

"My God!" she said. "Listen to that sound! You don't ever hear anybody singing with that kind of conviction and spirit anywhere except in *church!*"

The film wound down in the dark with the young men of Tuskegee marching to their own singing. As Richard flicked on the lights, the men in the room spontaneously took up the song again, invigorated by the sight of themselves and their fellows in the full blossom of youth, twenty-eight years earlier. Their singing stirred us all and rang out into the Beverly Hills afternoon.

Mr. Death's wife, whom he'd married years after leaving Lockbourne, repaired her tear-stained makeup and said, "I never heard that song before, and John never talked much of what Tuskegee, in this context, was really all about. I'm so impressed."

Carmen McRae interrupted. "Why are we only now learning that all this really took place? Something has definitely been left out of our history."

Ed Gleed said, "When this occurred, none of us thought it was anything special or historic. Certainly we felt challenged in a very special way, but hell, *all* of life for black people was a special challenge then, as it still is now."

Richard asked to interrupt. "Folks," he said, "that's exactly why this is such a great story. Hesper wants to hear as much of it as you can all remember, starting at the beginning at Tuskegee. Later she and I will get back with you all individually for greater details. Today we'll be doing fine to get the broader picture of what took place, how, and why. That's why we asked you to bring the snapshots, clippings from the black press, and your scrapbooks."

Bob O'Neil transfixed us all as he told how his plane, while escorting an American Eighth Air Force squadron on a bomber raid over Germany, was shot down. By the time he was captured, the Ninety-ninth had done so much damage to the Luftwaffe that German intelligence officers had assembled thick files on the black aces, knew their names and the number of German pilots they'd shot down, where they'd gone to school and details of their lives back in America.

Gleed, who had been a young flight leader in combat, said that before taking his plane up into those daily sorties he'd led, he would routinely stretch himself out flat on his stomach on the wing of his airplane and vomit himself empty.

"It was just that nerve-racking, and anybody who was not scared was either a goddamn fool or a liar."

"The irony in all this," O'Neil said, "is that I got more humane treatment as a prisoner in the hands of German officers than I ever got as an officer at home. I was often asked during my interrogations why we blacks fought so valiantly for a nation that treated us like 'swine'— a favorite German word. In a very real way, my captors changed my life."

Marsden Thompson talked about the events leading to the court-martial. "When we'd made up our minds to challenge the authority of the Freeman Field base commander and force the bastard to arrest us, we had to take several factors into consideration. Never before had any confrontation like this come about. This was a full decade before black American civilians organized their protests. We pioneered civil rights by insisting on human rights in the military. Martin Luther King was still in school when we took our stand! So we were ahead of our time in several ways.

"You also have to take into account that many of our men were career officers—for instance, Chappy James and Whitehead here—and we wanted to see them succeed. Some of us knew we were not staying in service, so we decided to shield the career men from the stigma of arrest and a general court-martial. Regardless of the results, win or lose, any involvement in a general court-martial would be an indelible mark on any career officer's record; and even worse for a black officer. We all knew that. I had nothing to lose: I knew damn well I was getting the hell out of the Jim Crow army, and that's why I volunteered to be the first one in the damn door when they ordered us to stay out of that white officers' club in Indiana. And you know something? Chappy James was here in Los Angeles last year, and he came to see me. He pointed to his shoulder and said, 'Marsden, you help put these four stars on my shoulder.' Damn right I'm proud to have been a part of it all, and I think this story would make one hell of a movie. It's time!"

Gleed broke in. "You're right, Marsden. Whose idea was it, anyway, to get us all together like this?"

Richard, pointing straight at me, said, "We got the idea from one of your own, Mr. Willie Ruff, right there."

Gleed looked at me for a long moment and said, "I beg your pardon, mister, but I don't remember you."

"That doesn't surprise me at all, sir. I was just a kid, sixteen years old and lucky enough to be in Mr. Brice's band—one of the proud teenagers who were watching and admiring what you all were doing. I can tell you that no part of my education before or since Lockbourne can match what I came away from there with."

Mr. Death said, "Hell, Gleed, you were too busy running the damn base to see everything and everybody. I don't remember the man either, but I sure as hell remember marching to Brice's music, and dancing to the jazz band too! Who could forget old Warrant Officer Brice and that band?"

I wanted them to know about the broad interest in their story, so I explained: "Whenever I talk to young people about this story, their mouths drop in disbelief that it could have happened the way it did."

After a pensive moment, Gleed said, "So the band at Lockbourne was your only connection to us?" I said it was, but that Mr. Brice's teachings, and the powerful example of them, the officers, and the tutoring and encouragement I got there, had set both me and my partner on our paths to becoming professional musicians.

Gleed's brow crinkled. Looking at me, he shook his head. "I swear to you, never once during that whole time did I suspect that anybody at all really saw us that way. I doubt that any of us realized that some youngster coming along might be paying any special attention."

Richard floated from group to group, listening to episodes he hoped would flesh out the story on film. He came to our little cluster, where Gleed, the two singers, and a few of the airmen's wives stood. "This is the classiest party I've seen in Beverly Hills in thirty years." And to me he added, "You mentioned writing the music to this picture; maybe we'd better sign up these two divas for singing parts right now."

Before the party broke up, Richard suggested a song by Carmen and Sarah. I asked for "September Song," to which Hesper's father had written the words. I was sorry I didn't have my bass or the horn. Though Sarah and Carmen were both fine pianists, it was Carmen who sat at the keyboard. Her fingers began searching for Sarah's key, then Sarah sang the first chorus—divinely. Carmen's elegant piano style, acquired through long years of accompanying herself in public, showed to fabulous advantage. During the second refrain, she added her voice to

Sarah's, and spontaneously, as had happened during the Tuskegee film, voice after voice in the crowded room took up "September Song." When it was over, there was Hesper, sobbing. "I've always loved that song," she said, "but I never expected to hear a performance of it like this one."

Nor did I. "September Song" on that unforgettable July afternoon underscored my own reverie. Never in my whole life would I have expected that two of American music's great women would join me in Beverly Hills to celebrate the military heroes of my boyhood.

Although nothing came of the script Hesper, Richard, and I worked on, now, twenty years later, I receive word that *Star Wars*'s director, George Lucas, is producing a film on the Tuskegee pilots, and that he might start shooting it this year.

Now, maybe, the pilots' story will receive the audience it deserves.

CHAPTER THIRTY-NINE

Back to Yale

MEANWHILE, UP THE HILL AT UCLA, I was struggling with the excessive and unwieldy crowd of nearly four hundred undergraduates in my class. Even with two teaching assistants, I saw no way of ever clearing enough time to read and evaluate each student's exams and term papers to my satisfaction. After worrying the question a long time, I went to class one day and suggested an alternative. Students could form themselves into teaching teams of up to five persons and, equipped with the same audiovisual materials I'd used, go into the Los Angeles public schools and teach young children what they'd learned in my class. The idea was an enormous hit. Students signed up in droves.

Once again, my timing was lucky. In those days, campuses all over America were moiling; students were rising up to demonstrate and speak out on a wide variety of issues. The war in Vietnam, racial inequities, affirmative action, truth in government, and women's liberation were but a few of the issues. California campuses led the nation in student protests, and UCLA was a seething caldron of confrontation. Outreach programs, such as the one I proposed, were an unexpected town-gown social boon, and the city's schools were thrown open to my students.

But it didn't take long for me to see that what I had contrived as a time-saving idea suddenly took on a life of its own: my part-time teaching job demanded a full-time commitment. Before the student teams could begin teaching, I had to approve their course outlines and audiovisual materials, verify their suitability, and match the teams with public school classroom teachers. I also promised to visit at least one of the four sessions they were required to teach. Many of my students were graduates of Los Angeles schools and wanted to return as college students to do their work where they were known. I have to attribute a large part of the success of the plan to just this factor.

When I'd proposed the team teaching, I had not expected that four college students presenting a single story could so thoroughly involve and charm a classroom of schoolchildren. Word of the effectiveness of the teams spread around town, and we had more schools interested in us than we could possibly accommodate. The students went far beyond what was required of them for grades from me, and more than one team did its work so well that school principals asked them to take on other grades.

What we were doing leaked beyond Los Angeles, and in 1970, Mitchell and I accepted an offer from Dartmouth College to be artists in residence for a semester. Dartmouth's President Kemeny, the inventor of the computer language BASIC, was pushing computer "literacy" for his faculty at a time when I very much wanted to learn how computers might serve my work. Written into the Dartmouth deal was a budget to bring a special guest artist to campus for a concert with the duo. Whom did we want? Dizzy Gillespie leapt to mind. Mitchell and I both remembered that at Ellington's Strayhorn concert in Lincoln Center, Dizzy Gillespie had said he wanted to play with us. Dartmouth was the perfect opportunity. Dizzy came, and the concert was memorable, and we even recorded it for Mainstream Records, one of our happiest and better recordings, I always thought.

Even during the semester of the Duo's Dartmouth College teaching residency, many weekends found me flying between New Hampshire and Hollywood to record film-scoring assignments. I had lucked up on my first film a few short months after moving to California when artists' manager, John Levy, invited me to dinner along with the actor John

Astin. Astin heard I was at USC's film school, and described a lyrical no-dialogue short film with the musical title, *Prelude*. He was writing it as a vehicle for himself even as his television comedy series, *The Addams Family*, was on the air. It caught my fancy; we kept in touch and ultimately made the low-budget but very high quality work, and booked it into a Beverly Hills theater just in time to be considered for a nomination in the "short drama" category for an Oscar that year. We got a nomination! But the Oscar went to a documentary on the life and recent death of Bobby Kennedy. My biggest ace in the hole during all this, my security blanket you might say, was having Sidney Fine looking over my shoulder, ready to offer advice and even "put out fires" if I ever lit one that got out of control. He was there when the owner of a small industrial film production company, who also taught the screen-writing class I was in at USC, gave me a chance to score a promotional film for Andersen Windows.

Another kind of film came my way shortly after the CBS Brasil Special hit the network. I was out on the road with the Duo when a phone call caught up with me. Maynard Orme, a young producer with the Los Angeles public TV station, called me in Lewiston, Idaho. He'd seen and loved the Brasil film, knew the Duo's records, and wanted to talk. The Duo ended up taping three jazz shows for his station. Then over the next several months Maynard threw some small nature film scoring projects my way along with a documentary on the innovative artist-furniture building genius, Sam Maloof. Then came the real plum: a short Bill Cosby film called "Cosby on Prejudice." Cosby strolled into the studio one afternoon and completed the whole show in one take; a half hour of steady rolling perfection. No stops. My guitarist friend, John Pisano, and I recorded the music to it in the same amount of time. We scurried about the studio alternately playing a whole roomful of string instruments as Cos's puckish and poignant work flashed on the screen. One take also. That little film's considerable profits went entirely to the United Negro College Fund, and, to Cosby's credit, it still produces revenue today.

It was about this time that another desperate call came from John Hammond back in New York. John was still having problems with famous singers.

"Willie, Mahalia Jackson is doing a gospel album for CBS records there in L.A. I knew Dwike has been there working with you for some time now," John said early that Sunday morning. "Mahalia's pianist had an accident on her way to the studio and nobody comes to mind as a replacement who can even come close to Dwike Mitchell." John sure did have that part right; nobody could. "The producer there, my friend Irving Townsend, is waiting in the studio with Mahalia," John said. "Would Dwike consider helping us out? We're desperate." I was a little worried, for I knew Mitchell was locked in a morning-after-a-big-Saturday-night-party sleep.

"Any interest in a gospel gig in twenty minutes?" I asked gently from his bedroom door. "Don't be ridiculous!" he croaked.

But I went closer and said in his ear, "With Mahalia Jackson, fool!" He came up off the pillow and groaned that he couldn't possibly appear in the presence of "Her Holiness, the queen of Gospel" in so unpurified a condition. John Hammond and I negotiated a short delay to the start of the session, and in a little while Brother Mitchell left my house clutching a cup of my strongest java. I said a silent prayer or two. Perhaps I overdid it. A few hours later, Mitchell came back sparkling with the news that the great Sanctified diva had offered him long, long pockets to forsake the "sin music" he'd been playing with me and get on board the gospel train.

I was scoring a short film, a nature project Richard Quine and the Delaware Nature Conservancy had hired me to do, when a call came from Dean Philip Nelson of the Yale School of Music, inviting me to join the Yale faculty. I was extremely flattered, but I knew it was a decision I would have to sleep on and take up with my adviser on all musical matters, Sidney Fine. I had been in California nearly four years, learning and profiting from every kind of musical experience I'd come there for; it had never been my plan to blend into the Hollywood musical landscape. So there was nothing holding me there. I went to Sidney to ask if he could think of reasons why I should accept the Yale offer.

"Yes," he said immediately. "Playing chamber music regularly again with that great clarinetist you speak of so often, your teacher Keith Wilson. That alone is reason enough. Be a participant in more than just one kind of music, Willie. I don't have to tell you that in spite of all your activities here, there is no substitute for making great music."

That advice, coupled with the bonus of living close to my daughter again, settled it. I called Dean Nelson and accepted the Yale offer.

Sidney Fine had been right. Working at Yale as Keith Wilson's colleague was all I had known it would be, even if we never seemed to have enough time to play as much chamber music together as I would have liked. It thrilled me that a new crop of clarinetists from around the world was flocking to Keith's studio for lessons. Young Richard Stolzman, one of today's leading soloists, was one. The next-best thing to playing with Keith was using what he'd taught me about ensemble performance in my own teaching, for now one of my duties was coaching chamber music. My biggest class, however, was for nonperforming undergraduates, the same introduction to Afro-American music I'd initiated at UCLA and later taught at Dartmouth. More than two hundred students showed up for the first class, and as I'd done in Los Angeles, I contacted the New Haven public school system with the idea of my students team teaching throughout the city. The schools had a pressing need for teaching materials on the subject and welcomed the collaboration.

Since I'd last lived in the city, the excellent music and arts programs that had flourished for generations in the public schools had been cut to the bone; student orchestra and band participants had dwindled. Still, a dedicated group of music teachers around town fought hard to build a new curriculum and hold on to what remained.

I duplicated my collection of teaching materials from California, making extra copies of the films, tapes, and rare recordings to share with my Yale students. Then several music teachers and principals set up a team-teaching network for schools all over town. Sometimes New York professionals came to town to join the undergraduates for performances in the children's classrooms.

Once, Dizzy Gillespie teamed up with Mitchell and me for five straight days, during which we played twenty-eight school performances. Dizzy surprised both teachers and children with his numerical wizardry, which comes to him as easily as his trumpet playing. Mitchell and I had always heard that Dizzy was something of an arithmetic genius and chess whiz. But seeing him at the huge blackboard at Troup Junior High School, instructing while entertaining his pupils with his number magic, was nearly as much fun as playing bebop with him.

Our "schoolhouse road show" grew that year to include, besides Dizzy, the two great tap dancers Honi Coles and Charles "Cookie" Cook; the comedian Pigmeat Markham; bass-baritone William Warfield; and Bessie Jones, a specialist in the music of the Georgia Sea Islands. Mrs. Jones came back to town later to spend a week in workshops, where she taught music teachers to pass on the musical ring games, riddles, and folk stories that have survived since slavery. Dizzy, Mitchell, and I were so impressed with her work that we went with her to the Sea Islands to make a film, in which she acted as hostess and guide and traced African musical elements in Sea Island music.

The juices of the impresario would surge in me in New Haven every time I saw my undergraduates teaching and interacting with school-children, each group learning from the other. The lessons I had derived from the Young Audiences days continued to nourish even this work, and along the way we also discovered how to address some of the specific needs of children with physical handicaps, language and learning de-ficiencies, or no experience at all in listening to live music. Our town had them all. And as the duo continued to make new recordings and play college concerts across the country and around the world, the New Haven classroom work, on and off campus, was like a magnet that kept pulling us back.

CHAPTER FORTY

Living with the
Ba Benzele Pygmies

ALL DURING MY FIRST YEAR of teaching in New Haven, I had felt a distant pull on my ears coming from French Equatorial Africa. It had begun back in my Los Angeles apartment, while I packed the books, films, records, and teaching materials I would need at Yale. It was only then that I rediscovered a record I had bought and misplaced without ever having heard it. It was a UNESCO album, made in the rain forest, of Ba Benzele Pygmies singing and drumming their spellbinding music. I was particularly struck by their yodeling, a totally new effect for me. I knew that John Coltrane had an interest in the music of another group of Pygmies, the Mbuti, living in the forests of the Belgian Congo, a people whom anthropologist Colin Turnbull had visited and recorded. But what I was hearing was a musical tradition that was worlds away from the Congo Mbuti.

The more I listened to the Ba Benzele drumming, the more it sounded like twentieth-century jazz drumming in America—the subtleties of Big Sid Catlett, Kenny Clarke, Jo Jones, and Max Roach. But the singing made me think of the elegance of the sixteenth-century Italian liturgical music masters Palestrina, Gabrieli, and Merulo. How had Stone Age people arrived at such music? I couldn't stop listening, and after a couple of days I began playing the record over the phone for Mitchell, back in New York. I told him to ask Coltrane's drummer, Elvin Jones, now Mitchell's next-door neighbor, if he knew the tribe and their music. I made tapes of the album to send to my daughter, Michele. And the longer I listened, the clearer it became that I had to go to Equatorial Africa to find these people and perhaps make a film about their music: my first independent ethnomusicological excursion and my first chance to use the filmic skills I'd gone to USC to learn. Now the first year at Yale was behind me, and I wanted to do something special for my ears in the Central African rain forest, and I knew I wanted to take my daughter with me.

In the summer of 1972, Michele and I flew off on the first leg of our trek. The capital city of the Central African Republic, Bangui, was as close as airplanes fly to the Pygmies. But one cannot fly from New York to Bangui without first going to Paris. However, that mandatory stopover had a hidden advantage.

Michele was fourteen, a time of life when many of the world's people mark their children's coming of age with ritual ceremonies. Somewhere in my private self, I had come to think of this journey as a symbolic rite of passage for Michele. I liked having the drum so central to our pilgrimage. But a visit to Africa's oldest drummers shouldn't be approached without a prelude; we needed a strong preamble, properly rooted in what drumming in America has become since its African beginnings. I knew that Kenny Clarke, who still lived in Paris, was just the man to send us on our way.

We found him and his band of French musicians playing in a small club on the Left Bank of Paris. I introduced him to Michele and described our musical odyssey.

"You, better than anyone I know," I said to Kenny, "can connect her to her roots."

He looked down at the floor, shook his head for a moment, and grinned. "Wheh! That's a tall order for any drummer, my friend. You flatter me. But—I will do my best."

After the band's intermission, Clarke left his musicians standing on the sidelines and, striding with immense dignity and stately ease to the stage, sat down at his drum set. As he folded his arms across his chest, the lights shining on the drums, tom-toms, and cymbals cooled down to a warm glow that radiated the colors of daybreak. From the floor, we sensed—not in our ears, but deep down in the solar plexus—a rumble resembling a faint but steady heartbeat. Though Kenny sat motionless, his arms still folded, the pumping heartbeats throbbed through the floor. And gradually, as the gut-rumble moved up through a steady crescendo, with his fingertips he stroked soft rhythmical resonances from two large tom-toms. Then he punctuated the mix with tight, crisp sock-cymbal statements that made the bronze disks flash like Fort Knox gold in the reddish light.

As I listened, I thought of Clarke's long career at the forefront of jazz. I knew he'd been there to propel the music's march into the conscience of America and the world. And I remembered that his drumming days stretched all the way back to Louis Armstrong's orchestra and on into those seminal days of Bebop experiments in Harlem's after-hours joints. I thought of Minton's Playhouse, where Kenny was so integral a part in the shaping of modern jazz—Kenny, and Charlie Parker, and Dizzy Gillespie, and Thelonious Monk, and the other young black musical intellectuals of the 1940s. And it came back to me, too, that he, Ray Brown, Milt Jackson, and John Lewis were the original Modern Jazz Quartet, the old rhythm section of Dizzy Gillespie's Things to Come big band. How incredible that this distinguished man, who personified so large a slice of the continuity of jazz and its story, was offering this musical baptism for a fourteen-year-old black American girl he'd never met before!

With his attention fixed on our table, he was working straight at the initiate, stroking drum magic solidly into Michele's adolescent metabolism. Then came a subtle acceleration of the bass drum's throbbing heartbeat, which compressed time and became a new tempo. Kenny's complex rhythmic inventions lifted us up and swept us along with him through his musical autobiography.

Michele glowed, smacked the table hard, and said, "Jeez, that's so fine!"

Kenny brought his seven- or eight-minute discourse to an end with a reference to the opening bass-drum heartbeat, and his audience, led by Michele, stood up and gave him a thundering ovation. His gift had done its work. We were ready for Africa's first drummers. As we were about to step out of the club into the Parisian night, Michele approached Kenny.

"So that's the stuff of my roots," she said. "What an introduction! Thank you, Mr. Clarke."

We were bumping over dusty potholes, lurching through a four-day ride in an ancient bus from Bangui to Carnot, in the Central African Republic. Michele and I had been impatient to get into the forest with the Pygmies after having spent our first days on African soil in the nation of Chad, holed up in the old city of Fort-Lamy. The French presence (we saw only French people in the vital businesses) was so strong there, it didn't feel like Africa at all. When we arrived in the Central African Republic, President Bokassa's administration in Bangui kept us in an expensive government-owned hotel longer than we wanted or needed to stay: their treasury could use the American hard currency. Minister So-and-so would have to return from somewhere to stamp our travel visas, and until then, "be comfortable in our wonderful hotel." Then I was called to the American consulate and advised to visit the Central African Republic's minister of the interior and get a letter to help ease our passage through the bush; all this in addition to the travel visas that kept eluding us as we shelled out our dollars in the high-rent hotel. The natty minister of the interior disapproved of my interest in the Ba Benzele and suggested, with some pompousness, that the CAR had far worthier attractions than the "uncivilized" Stone Age people of the forest. He listed the discomforts we faced—four days on the bus, sharing the space with chickens and other livestock and all their accompanying smells. But in the end, he grudgingly gave me an official letter on his letterhead, requesting hospitality from a village chief who ruled near our destination.

Victor, an African boy of fifteen, boarded the bus about two days down the line, at Beberati. His Christian missionary boarding school was out for summer vacation, and like us, he was headed to the end of the line.

Though Michele and I were traveling light, I had brought along my French horn, because I wanted to hear how its notes would sound backed up by the exotic equatorial birds and beasts in the forest. I knew I wanted to play something of my musical world for the Pygmies, who'd probably never even heard of Duke Ellington or "Mood Indigo" or "Sophisticated Lady."

Victor spent a lot of time looking over my electronic and musical paraphernalia and at Michele. His missionary school French was clear and correct. Mine, he said, was understandable; I should use it to tell him all about America, about James Brown and television and rock music. He said he had assumed that Michele was my wife—alliances between young girls her age and middle-aged men were not uncommon in his world. Were we Christians? Why had we come to the CAR? My answer, "To hear Pygmy music," jerked his head around.

"Why in the world would anybody leave James Brown country to listen to Pygmy music? We never see Americans," he said, "and the first black Americans I meet here came just to listen to Pygmy music. *Sacré bleu!*"

I liked the way Victor took my mind off the discomforts of the old bus, the butt-busting bumps, the bugs, the stifling heat, as well as the money-draining delays we'd suffered back in Bangui.

I showed Victor my letter, written in very correct French. He examined it closely and said he knew the chief to whom it was addressed; he added that he himself was no stranger to Pygmies and their ways. He'd grown up enjoying the splendid elephant meat his tribe acquired from the fierce Ba Benzele Pygmy hunters. After his year of boarding school food, the mere thought of elephant steaks made him smack his lips: "*Zznyauuum!*"

The nomadic Pygmies, he explained, often appeared at clearings at the edge of the forest, where they traded their freshly killed game for salt, knives, and scrap metal from which they expertly fashioned spears and arrow tips. Victor seemed to enjoy instructing us: "With their spears and arrows dipped in deadly poison, the Pygmies charge the elephants head-on and deftly drive their poisoned spears through the great beasts' underbelly, straight into the heart. *Phumpfh!* They fall!"

Full of wide-eyed admiration for the Pygmies' athletic prowess and agility, Victor whirled his two fists in tight rapid forward-traveling circles and said, "They can run up tall trees as if they were climbing steps all the way to the top. They climb to gather wild honey and birds' nests and to catch monkeys—all for food. Non-Pygmy children living near the forest even learn to speak the Ba Benzele language." Pygmy children commonly find playmates among the people they trade with, and he himself had learned to speak their language that way. But that is as far as they go with the forest people.

"Nobody but Pygmies dare venture deep into the forest," he warned us. "Even tax collectors, census takers, and missionaries stay out of the Pygmy terrain if they know what's good for them."

At the end of the road we piled off the bus seats that had been our beds for three nights and four days and put down in a settlement of about a dozen houses near the forest. Victor pointed out the village chief, whose neighbor had a place Michele and I could sleep in that night. They all assured us that finding a guide who could translate from French into the Ba Benzele tongue would be no problem. As Victor and I shook hands in our leavetaking, I mentioned that I was prepared to pay for a translator-guide, and I thought I saw an idea flash across his large, intelligent eyes.

Our host, Pappa Cadre, a thick-bodied and gentle widower, could have been the twin of old Corporal Talley from my army basic training back at Fort McClellan. The chief had suggested we sleep at Pappa Cadre's modest mud-thatch house because it was just next to the forest and had a new room recently added on. The addition had no furniture and the floor was smooth, clean, hard-packed dirt, on which Michele and I gratefully unfolded our blankets. Having come prepared to rough it in the forest along with the Pygmies, we'd brought heavy-duty mosquito nets, a well-stocked first-aid kit, some medicines, and emergency food—sardines and rind cheeses. Though Michele was the consummate camper, a few items of Pygmy diet she'd read and heard about before leaving New Haven moved her to declare, "No monkey meat or roasted termites for this explorer, Daddy!"

Very early the next morning, while still in our blankets, we were awakened by a jarring knock on the door. It was Victor. He wanted the guide-translator's job. Furthermore, just since last night, he'd scouted out three different Pygmy encampments, and he urgently informed me: "They're not too far into the forest. You can meet at least one of the groups this morning, if we move fast."

Pappa Cadre agreed that Victor would do just fine as a guide, but he pointed to his own gray hair and wagged his finger at me, saying, "The Pygmy elders will know that your intentions are honorable if you take this gray hair along." I liked being so close to a world where somebody else's gray hair vouched for me.

To be absolutely certain that Michele and I would be offering the appropriate gift in exchange for the Ba Benzeles' hospitality and their music, I asked Pappa Cadre and Victor if, indeed, salt was really the thing.

"Oh, *certainement*," they said, nearly in unison. I had read that nothing from outside the forest has as much value to the Pygmies as salt—"white gold"—nature's simple sodium chloride, a scarce commodity there on the equator, where it is naturally leached from the soil.

"The Pygmies love *du sal*," Victor said, "so much that they will eat it like candy. You will see for yourself." He and Pappa Cadre led the way to a little traders' shack, where, for a few dollars, I filled two large shopping bags with coarse rock salt.

As Michele and I lugged our loot down the narrow footpath, trekking behind our guides, I felt swept backward into biblical times, when salt was a highly prized medium of exchange and currency—"salary." Our shopping bags were so loaded with mythical symbolism, I had to remind myself that we were just two twentieth-century pilgrims, following our ears.

Stepping into the forest was a baptism, a total immersion into a subtle, color-drenched world whose muteness dazzled us. The intoxicating colors and flashy fabrics so prized by Africans living outside the forest were nowhere in sight. The biggest color show beneath the verdant overdome took place in the faces of the Ba Benzele people.

Pygmies are not black. Nor are they simply brown, or yellow. Wherever the sun rays struck their compact bodies, there lay all the colors of the rainbow, imprinted in the texture of their skin, vibrantly mixing themselves into a subdued miracle. Want a color? Take your pick.

And every face in the crowd looked familiar; could actually have come from my Alabama childhood. It was Baptist Bottom set down in Central Africa, enveloping us in its welcoming circle. Over there, among the girls, the pretty face of Hazel Nell; and there, Maverne and Mary Gladys; and damned if the man with the mustache and beard wasn't the spit of Bitsy Pillar, who never in his long life grew any taller than a Pygmy.

Suddenly, out of the crowd, strode an old woman about four feet tall, with gray hair and great long sagging breasts that flopped against her bare chest as she jogged purposefully toward me.

"The tribal elder, no doubt," I said to Michele. She marched herself right up to me and began talking and laughing all at the same time. From time to time, she interrupted her monologue to cover her laughter with both hands. Whatever it was she was saying made the other Pygmies around us double up and add their laughter to hers. And just like in Baptist Bottom, the Ba Benzele, when tickled, lustily slapped their thighs, grabbed their sides, sagged to their knees, and rolled themselves in the dust, kicking and hollering. Musical laughter rang through the trees. Even Victor and Pappa Cadre covered their mouths. I asked Victor, "What's so funny?"

He shook his head and said, "Pardon, Monsieur Willie, I'm just a schoolboy, and a Christian. I'm too young to translate *that*. Please, ask Pappa Cadre to tell you."

Finally, Pappa Cadre recovered and translated for the grandmother. "Before anybody says a word," the old woman was saying, "I want to take this tall creature of strange color to my hut. I'll put him in my bed and work him down to half my size!"

Pappa Cadre, still giggling, pointed once more to his gray hair— proof that his mojo was working—and insisted that the sexual reference was a good sign. Then the grandmother's already gentle face softened further and she flashed me a snaggled-toothed grin that needed no translation. "Just funning, son," her laughter and her eyes told me. The ice was broken: the reigning matriarch had acknowledged nature's bodacious regenerative engine with a joke. Humankind's chief social taboo had been defanged, blown away with a tribal belly laugh. Michele looked amused: "Hadn't expected I'd find a stepmother in the forest anyway!"

We had decided to leave the movie cameras back at Pappa Cadre's on this, our first trip. We brought only the rock salt and a cassette player with a tape of selections from the UNESCO recording of Pygmy music I'd bought in Los Angeles. We passed the rock salt around, and just as Victor had promised, the Pygmies popped amazing quantities of it straight into their mouths to eat voraciously, as if driven by a chemical need. When they saw I had more salt in the shopping bags, they scurried through the foliage, tearing large green leaves off trees to wrap up the reserves for future use. Michele said, "Ecologically neat, man—chlorophyll doggie bags!"

While the salt feast went on, Pappa Cadre and Victor sat with me and the group's chief, Pumba, to translate some of the many questions I had about their world. I was struck by the design of their huts, whose superstructures looked much like Buckminster Fuller's geodesic domes and, I was told, required less than an hour to build.

Pumba, who'd been elevated to the high status of chief of his group because of his outstanding hunting skills, seemed set on showing us the tools of his trade. When he passed around arrows dripping their lethal poison for us to inspect, Victor cautioned, "One slip, Monsieur Willie, and *pooof*, you're finished!" Pumba softened the caution and explained that a clumsy stab would be no problem at all to fix: "Where there is a poison, there is an antidote nearby." Pumba's people live by hunting and will remain in any one location for only as long as food—game and vegetation—is plentiful. The group of a dozen families he ruled was the optimum size for successful travel and mobility through the forest. They serve no flag, recognize no national boundaries, and pride themselves on the freedom of their movement among the Central African Republic, Zaire, and the Cameroon.

I was enjoying being instructed on life in the forest, when I noticed that Michele and I were conducting a one-way inquiry; Pumba, quite unlike Victor and Pappa Cadre, showed no curiosity at all about Michele and me. We'd dropped like strange tall aliens into their world with salt and what looked like friendly intentions; who we were and where we came from was our own affair.

Something told me it was time for some music. Besides, I wanted Pumba's people to hear the UNESCO selections. I was still not certain that we'd found the people to match the music I'd brought. I counted on their reaction to the tape as an indication. I hit the red start key on the cassette player, and as the first note sounded, children jumped up off the ground and came running toward the machine. "Huudi huudi!" they shouted. Women pounding manioc flour dropped their mortars and pestles and crowded around; men with arrows laid them down and pressed into the circle. "Huudi huudi!" they sang, along with the cassette.

The *huudi huudi* song is, for me, a marvel among the Ba Benzeles' musical inventions: a duet for one. A singer alternately blows a single sweet note on a reed whistle and sings a note that is different each time it enters the exchange. The result is an ingeniously varied blown-hummed melody. Pumba told Victor and me that he'd never heard Pygmy music on a machine before. How had the *huudi huudi* musician got in the little black box? Victor went into action, translating for me.

"A white man, years ago, visited another Ba Benzele camp, and they gave him the music on the machine." Victor's translation of my explanation seemed only to half-satisfy Pumba. I let the tape roll on, and in a little while, Michele and I were finally satisfied that all the music on the tape was traditional: everybody in the camp knew each song and joined in to sing along with the machine. Every once in a while, someone would stop singing and listen to hear if the machine would keep up, then the singer would take off into the song again. During one piece, a little boy found it impossible to keep still and not dance. From his movements, a graceful pantomime of spear strokes and arrow shots, I gathered we were listening to a hunting song.

The cassette was the life of the party, and Michele and I glimpsed a hint of a small success; at least we'd matched up the sound we'd lugged from the other side of the world with the right Pygmies.

As I gathered up our salt sacks and the cassette player at the end of our visit, the little grandmother who'd made me the bogus sexual proposition piled fruits and berries into our shopping bags. Children handed Michele mangoes, wild bananas, and avocados. We had to decline a freshly roasted monkey haunch for lack of room.

I asked Pappa Cadre to find out if we could come back the next day with more salt and our movie cameras. It was agreed that one of the young men would come to fetch us the first thing in the morning. But on our walk back to the outside sunshine, I wondered about the reliability of an appointment with people who keep neither clocks nor calendars. Pappa Cadre, looking stern, said, "You can trust a Pygmy's word."

Next morning, Victor and Pappa Cadre called us out of our blankets just after daybreak; Pumba and another man were waiting at the edge of the forest. All our cameras and recording equipment were packed and ready. We'd bought a hundred-pound sack of salt the previous day, out of which we'd filled two shopping bags. We'd also packed in enough fresh batteries, tapes, and film for a full day of work.

Now that Pappa Cadre's gray hair had done its work, he said he would entrust us to Victor's able care and expect us back at the end of the day.

Then Michele and I learned one of the cardinal principles of life with the Pygmies. As we approached Pumba and the young man waiting at the edge of the forest, we smiled our good morning and I extended one of my flight bags of camera gear, hoping for a helping hand from Pumba—the salt alone was heavy. I should have known better. Pumba chilled me with the most sophisticated snub of my life. He said nothing. He simply looked through me, eyes fixed on some distant scene, miles beyond my back.

"Oh, well," I said to Michele. "I guess Pygmy chiefs don't carry baggage." I tried giving the bag to the young man. He stood stone-still and gave me a look that seemed to say: You brought it; you carry it.

I hadn't remembered that we were with the original light travelers: people whose survival is defined by the size and weight of things they need. Everything—tools, babies, food, hunting regalia—must be portable, small, and light enough for them, the world's most diminutive race of humans, to heft and carry long distances on their backs. No frills. No nonessentials and certainly no baggage services for big folk from New Haven.

As we strained under our load of salt and electronics, Victor described for us the Ba Benzeles' view toward work. "*Non*, Monsieur Willie, Pygmies have no capacity for work as we know it. They shun money and prefer to trade or barter for salt and metal objects. Local coffee plantation owners have tried to hire them to pick coffee. It never works. They try it, grow tired of the work and the hot sun, and vanish into the forest without a trace—*PHOOF!* No Pygmy has ever drawn a payday around here."

When we got to the camp, life there was at full flower: women who had been gathering firewood were lugging huge loads of it in slings on their backs and heads; men who the day before had been occupied with arrows, bows, and poison were tending babies. I asked Victor if Ba Benzele hunters minded baby-sitting. "Oh, no—look there." He directed our attention to a hunter carrying a baby on each hip and one perched on his shoulders. "I think only one of the babies is his. Pygmy men play with the children because they enjoy them."

We began passing out the salt. Small boys gave us freshly cut *huudi huudi* whistles and a sample performance. The salt seemed to bring out the party mood in our hosts.

"Pygmies are the world's greatest party people," Victor said. He pointed to a small circle of women sitting on the ground, singing softly, nibbling salt, and clapping their hands. "*Regardez!*" Their song was familiar from the UNESCO recording. And I recognized the metallic timbre that has become the trademark of the modern jazz drummer: the rich sound of rare and expensive Persian spun-bronze cymbals such as those Kenny Clarke had played in his Paris performance. I heard Michele giggle behind me.

"Daddy, check out what's behind you." A woman sitting on the ground was holding a short stick and tapping a complex rhythmic pattern on a rusty and severely battered lard can. Michele said, "Wait until Kenny Clarke hears what a fortune he's been wasting all these years on Persian cymbals!"

A man emerged from among the little huts, carrying three small drums, which he placed close to an open campfire. Every few seconds he thumped a drumhead to test its timbre, as the fire parched the forest moisture out of the drumskin and tuned it. He then struck the head of a long, slender drum, and its deep and resonant *boom* sounded like a large bass drum: a roaring gut-shaker; a marching-band rumble. I asked Victor to ask the man how they had made such a deep, booming drum with so little wood and weight. The Pygmy laughed at the question; he then said a word that Victor translated as "experience."

I asked if they took the drums with them whenever they moved. Again the man laughed. "We take our drums *and* our fire with us always. This fire that tunes our drums, cooks our food, and lights our night is older than any person alive." With that, he got up and snatched from a nearby tree one of the versatile green leaves we'd seen so much of, cupped it in his hand, and flicked a smoldering coal from the fire into the leaf. He blew gently on the coal until it was ruby red, then wrapped it up. "This fire," he said, "will stay alive for days as we travel with it through the forest."

I thought about how arrogantly the minister of the interior back in Bangui had referred to the Pygmies and their Stone Age ways. But watching them interact with the forces in their world swelled my admiration for them and their independence from the language and customs of the French colonialists who for four hundred years had ruled the world just outside their forest.

I had expected that settling on a serviceable language would be more of a problem than it turned out to be. Michele, for her part, seemed to manage among the women using made-up sign language and gestures. But we would soon learn that nothing carried as much tacit meaning as the wide variety of Ba Benzele laughter. And we would learn, too, that each laugh carried its own distinct and precise meaning, which almost never needed translating.

By the end of our first day of casual work, we'd collected all the music we'd heard on the UNESCO record and more. I'd also let the tape roll to preserve a group of legends and hunting stories.

Going back to Pumba's camp the next day, we arrived with the cassette machine playing the music of the day before. Even before we'd passed out the salt, the Pygmies pressed into a tight little circle around the machine and stood riveted by the unexpected sound of their voices. A spontaneous game erupted: Identify the voice. Whenever a conversational voice on the tape came on, the whole crowd howled and named the person speaking. But each identified speaker vigorously denied that the voice belonged to him! Then everyone went into a wild laughing fit until his own voice came up for him to deny.

I remembered that people I knew outside the forest never thought their recorded voice sounded real. But the Pygmies' confused and emphatic denial of their own voices worried Michele. "This is really spooky, Daddy, and I don't think I like it."

We were seeing frowns on Pygmies' faces for the first time, and I felt a trace of fear. Were they convinced that a part of themselves— their voices or their spirits—had been imprisoned in my little machine?

I stopped the tape and urged Victor to ask Pumba if his people were comfortable with the machine. But as soon as the sound stopped, the crowd began to grumble. Victor went into conference with Pumba, then said, "Monsieur Willie, at first they were frightened of the machine, but now they will be very uncomfortable if you don't let the tape play to the end."

I hit the fast-forward button to run the tape ahead to a conversation between Pumba and another man, but the speeded-up chatter was funnier to them than anything. They and the whole settlement collapsed in giggle cramps.

We let the tape play itself out, and the laughter finally subsided. Then we passed the salt around, relaxed, and had a feast.

For me, the high level of energy and obvious good health of the Ba Benzele were a constant marvel; the children were as robust and energetic as their parents. I wondered what went into the education of Pygmy children. For them to learn all they needed to know to master their environment and live successfully in their world obviously required a lot of teaching. Pumba said that in the long and strenuous process of

Pygmy children's training, they learn first to have no fear of even the fiercest of animals in the forest, for they believe that all creatures are set down in their world to serve human needs. He wanted us to notice an elderly woman together with a young man gathering medicinal plants, berries, and roots to make into medicines, tonics, and purgatives.

The woman assured us, "The plants in the forest are not only here to feed us; they also keep us well." She showed us their age-old methods of ingesting—chewing, smoking, sniffing, rubbing, soaking, etc.—the rich and potent substances into their systems. And we saw and savored dried plants and roots of indescribable pungency and strength and heard amazing accounts of the ills they healed. Then she had something to show Michele, a fine, soft, and superabsorbent moss—the Ba Benzele equivalent of Tampax. I had the feeling we were in the world's largest and most complete green pharmacy.

I wondered if the leisure we saw all around us was typical. When I asked Victor to tell Pumba I wanted to know more about their leisure, he hesitated.

"Oh, Monsieur Willie," he finally said, "I don't know the Pygmy word for *loisir*." I said, "Ask him, then, if work—hunting, gathering, and making shelter—takes as much as a third of their waking lives." At first, Pumba's face registered disbelief at the question. But after a moment, he broke out in laughter, and it was a laugh that only slightly veiled a sharp and edgy ridicule. I tried another tack.

"Where I come from, an eight-hour day—a third of the twenty-four-hour cycle—is what is required of most people for their living." Now Pumba's laugh no longer veiled his ridicule, and it hovered in the air like sewer gas. Michele picked it up and suggested we put the question yet another way.

"Instead of leisure or work," she said, "ask him about pleasure or entertainment."

That was different. When Victor said the "pleasure" word, Pumba sprang to his feet with a spear in his hand and, on his face, the look of a man in joyous celebration. He floated through his hunting stances, which were at once a dance and a demonstration of his awesome power to bring down beasts the size of elephants. I knew I was watching something more than entertainment.

Pumba finished his hunter's dance and sat back on the ground, laughing wistfully to himself. "Hunting serves two functions here," he said. "It gives our people sustenance for our bodies, but it also nourishes the spirit." Suddenly the Stone Age looked different. If "affordable leisure" is the standard by which the "quality of life" outside the forest is measured, then we were observing a man who enjoyed the highest living standards of anyone I knew; and he was laughing at us and ours.

Our living arrangement with Pappa Cadre worked so well that we decided to keep sleeping at his house as we made daily excursions into other nearby Pygmy groups to hear their music. It was a convenience for us, and he enjoyed the rent. The other Pygmies had essentially the same music we'd heard from Pumba's people and the UNESCO recording. We did hear, in a nearby camp, a colorful harp virtuoso with an instrument made of vine strips stretched over a carved wooden body. The only stringed instrument we found anywhere in the forest, it was used mostly as an effective accompaniment to the player's singing. Every Pygmy group we heard had and loved their *huudi huudi*.

When we'd recorded and filmed all the music we could from the other camps, I asked to be taken back to Pumba's camp, on the outside chance that he and his group were still around. Everyone was there and acted very glad to see us again.

I had come back and brought my horn because there was something special about the acoustics around Pumba's camp. I wanted to play in nature's own architecture, where the vaulted shapes of the trees gave me the feeling of being in a vast, green, breathing cathedral. I took the instrument out of the case and softly blew the opening notes of Duke Ellington's "Sophisticated Lady." From the very first note, I could tell that the Pygmies' acoustical environment was more perfect than I had imagined. Unlike any music I've played inside the stone walls of cathedrals and concert halls around the world, the horn tones didn't ricochet or bounce back in echoes. There in the misty green quiet, the notes flew out through the foliage and rang with a vibrant clarity and resonance I could hardly believe. "Sophisticated Lady" floated out into the distance and, at moments, overshadowed the monkey chatter and bird song. Two or three times, birds and creatures from their high perches spoke back as if in imitation, and for the briefest moment we were an orchestra.

I blew on and closed my eyes to better enjoy the melodic twists and turns of the melody as it went softly caressing the trees and teasing all twelve notes of the chromatic scale. I thought: What a sound Ellington's orchestra would make out here beneath the big trees. Then I felt a sharp tugging at my sleeve. It was Michele.

"Daddy," she whispered, "you're being ignored. I think you're bombing!" I looked around and saw children, after short glances in my direction, go back to their noisy games up in trees. Pumba's crowd resumed their smoking. And only then did it strike me that the elaborate twelve-note scale of "Sophisticated Lady," nine of its notes already there in the song's first phrase, was outside the whole musical language and experience of the Ba Benzele. Nothing like its complex melodic construction exists in their five-note, pentatonic musical scale. Not only was my gift of music no gift at all; Pygmies all around me were covering their mouths in gaping yawns of darkest boredom. If, earlier, I'd misjudged their attitudes towards visitors with excess baggage, now I'd gone beyond absurdity and fallen into the old "Music is a universal language" trap. I should have known better.

Hoping for a chance to redeem myself and "Sophisticated Lady," I played a couple of themes from pentatonic-flavored spirituals I knew whose scales sounded similar to what we'd heard in the Pygmies' songs. But when "Nobody Knows the Trouble I've Seen" brought as many yawns as "Sophisticated Lady," I knew I was bombing with the Ba Benzele for reasons other than the differences in our respective scales. Perhaps it was the solo performance, I thought, or maybe the instrument was wrong for them. I hadn't seen a single solo instrumental performance of anything in the forest; singing is solidly at the center of all their music; even *huudi huudi* playing is half singing.

I must have looked dumb and impotent standing in the great forest with my gorgeous French horn and nothing to play. Keenly aware of my discomfort, Michele, bless her, had an inspiration.

"Daddy, why don't you play the hambone?"

It wasn't easy for me to switch my musical focus away from "Sophisticated Lady," "Take the A Train," and " 'Round Midnight," examples of the American jazz music I so wanted the Pygmies to hear. But it was clear I hadn't a prayer of leaving them with anything really representative of jazz. So what could I lose by narrowing my focus to pure, raw, and unadulterated rhythm? I handed Michele my horn and sat down on a fallen tree, and with my open right hand, I began slapping out the hambone rhythm on my thigh and chest. Pygmies stopped midstride. A hush fell over the camp. The manioc pounding ceased, Pumba and his friends quit yawning, and boys skittering overhead in trees turned their gazes downward. There was suddenly nothing but the sound of the birds, the monkeys, and the hambone. Michele looked satisfied and cried, "Hot damn! We got em now!"

When I saw Pumba's mouth stretched in a wide grin that matched the enthusiasm in his flashing eyes, I was encouraged. I then added the left hand in unison with the right and made double hambone. Shoulders and heads all around the camp began dipping and bobbing to my beat. The little grandmother pressed in close, and her feet made small, tentative steps that got bolder as she swayed in bigger movement and loosened up. Suddenly she was dancing. Little boys tightened the circle and slapped at their thighs and chests, trying to catch and reproduce my sound.

Victor laughed and said the French equivalent of "Monkey see, monkey do." Then he, too, tried his hand at it. Out of the corner of my eye I caught sight of Michele, motioning with great agitation. She was silently slapping her puckered lips, a signal for me to add the resonant puckered-mouth pops to the hambone's rhythmic arsenal. I did, and the sound "*Puuk*-a-tah *puuk*-a-tah *puuk*-a-tah *puuk*" rang out with the clarity of a log drum. It was more than Pumba could stand. He lost control and hollered out his first raucous laugh of approval of me, or of anything I'd brought to his forest. I'd played all the hambone variations I could think of on my body before it occurred to me to recite some of the ditty rhymes I'd learned in Alabama as a boy. I began reciting along with the hambone accompaniment:

Hambone, hambone, where you bin?
Been around the world and I'm back agin.
Hambone, hambone, hambone shoulder,
Bring up a pretty gal, I'll show you how to hold her.
Way down yonder in Jay Bird town
Jay Bird slapped his Pappy down.

I eased up on the meatskin,
And creeped round on the bone,
I gave that hamhock one mo chance,
Then made them molasses moan.

Certainly the Alabama words went flying right over the Ba Benzeles' heads, but not the rhythm or the rhyme. Pumba laughed wild and excited encouragement straight at me. Victor's voice rang out: "Pumba says don't stop now, Monsieur Willie!"

When I finally had to pause to get my breath, Pumba grabbed the man who'd tuned the drums by the fire—their best drummer—and brought him to me for a hambone lesson. I began by playing the thigh-chest strokes slowly at first, so that my Ba Benzele pupil could catch the movement better. But it was tedious work. I've had quicker results teaching the hambone to children in Switzerland, Italy, and Russia. After several tries with the pucker, the Pygmy drummer lost heart and asked for a rest. The grandmother asked me, "What do you call it?"

"Hambone," I said, and several people in the circle repeated that word:

"Hamoone."

I was ready to let it go at that, but Pumba and the grandmother wanted to hear about who made it, and how. The crowd pressed in closer for my answer, and I began by saying that the hambone was invented where I came from, far from the forest; that it was a spontaneous expression of an African people whose drum had been taken away centuries before, in slavery. "Hambone playing, along with tap dancing, the blues, spirituals, and jazz, all of them uniquely American music which I'm sorry I can't demonstrate alone, could be considered drum substitutes."

All that information was certainly a mouthful for Victor to translate but something about the story of a displaced African people who'd lost their drum seemed to go straight to the hearts of the Pygmies. Suddenly their relationship to us was changed; Michele and I weren't aliens anymore. Now we had a past, and we had a story, and it related to their Africa, which, in a small way, was our Africa too. Individuals who had earlier made a point of keeping their distance from us now reached out their hands and touched us. Even little children pressed food on us as never before. I could hardly believe that the hambone's lowly story could make such a powerful impression so far from its origins way back home in America's Deep South.

By then our real work with the Pygmies was done; we'd collected on film and tape all the music and dance they had to give us. Now we could relax and enjoy our last day in the forest with them and start thinking about going home. But small boys wanting hambone lessons refused to let me rest. Before long, several kids were gaining the knack, and I even heard the beginnings of good strong popping sounds on their puckered lips.

Just as we were gathering up our machines, salt sacks, and other belongings to say goodbye, the drummer I'd been teaching the hambone to stepped out of the crowd, carrying two drums under his arms. He marched up to me and handed me the larger of the two, then handed the other to Michele.

Pumba laughed approvingly and said, "Now you have a drum again!"

As Michele and I stepped out of the forest, back into the stark sunshine, we could still hear the sound of Pygmies slapping their thighs and bare chests. The *puuk*-a-tah, *puuk*-a-tah from their lips mixed naturally with the monkey chatter and the sound of the birds. For me, the circle was complete; I had the film and the tape of their music, and the bonus gifts of Pygmy drums; they had the hambone.

But then I was startled by the sudden and loud eruption of laughter. It was coming from Michele. "What's the matter with you, gal?"

"I just thought of something," she said, still grinning. "What a mess it's going to be someday when some musical anthropologist hears these people doing the hambone. They're gonna write screwed-up dissertations on how the hambone came all the way from the Ba Benzele Pygmies to America instead of the other way around. Hell, I just love it!"

CHAPTER FORTY-ONE

The Conservatory
Without Walls

NOT LONG AFTER OUR RETURN from the Central African Republic, I
called Duke Ellington. I had an idea for him. I asked if he would
bring his orchestra to Yale. I wanted him to play a concert for schoolchildren and then give an evening public program at Yale similar in
scope to his 1968 "dream concert" for the Billy Strayhorn Juilliard
scholarship.

"Why, we would love to come back to the campus. Anytime. You
know," Ellington added, "that yours truly is now among the exalted:
Mother Yale awarded us the degree of Doctor of Humane Letters in
1967. We're a Yale man now!"

Well, of course I knew that, but when he reminded me of it I
thought of another idea, a lot bigger than the one we had just talked
about. "Maestro," I urged, "give me a few phone numbers where I can
reach you out on the road for the next week. I have some homework
to do before I get back to you."

I went to Dean Phil Nelson and Yale president Kingman Brewster
and persuaded them to follow up Ellington's honorary degree with a
permanent visiting fellows program at the university bearing Ellington's
name. My dream was for world-class artists to come regularly to the
campus and give performances and workshops for Yale students as well

as children in the public schools. President Brewster was enthusiastic, and everything began to fall in place.

Within a week, forty artists were selected as the first Ellington fellows, and President Brewster agreed to welcome them to the university and present them with a special medal in a gala ceremony. No other university had ever honored so many great names in music at one time.

When I tracked Ellington down, somewhere out on the road, I had the details, the finances, and the convocation worked out. A local foundation headed by Ernie Osborne, a jazz fan I knew from the Playback days, funded the event. I had two concert halls booked at Yale for three days of concerts, workshops, and jam sessions. Ellington's orchestra would be the centerpiece of the convocation, along with the forty artists from across the United States and Europe. Our lineup included Benny Carter, Dizzy Gillespie, Eubie Blake, Joe Williams, William Warfield, Roland Hayes, Marian Anderson, Charlie Mingus, Max Roach, Kenny Clarke, Ray Brown, Clarke Terry, Slam Stewart, Milt Hinton, George Duvivier, Odetta, Mary Lou Williams, Lucky Thompson, and Harry Edison. The remaining names we wanted among the forty would confirm after schedule adjustments.

When I called Kenny Clarke in Paris, he said, "Man! This is going to be the biggest reunion in music." I hoped it would be that. To me it was shaping up as the world's most lavish and prestigious jam session.

A couple of days after my conversation with Clarke in Paris, I called Charlie Mingus in New York. "Yeah, definitely count me in," he said. "Dizzy already told me about Kenny Clarke coming all the way from France, and Ray Brown and Benny Carter and Harry Edison all flying in from California. That's Christmas in October! I'll be there with my bass. Maybe I'll even get to play something with Duke; wouldn't *that* be a gas!"

The classical artists—Marian Anderson, William Warfield, Roland Hayes, and Dorothy Maynor—were equally enthusiastic. Of the entire venture, nothing could have meant more to me than having Miss Anderson graciously agree to come out of her retirement and near seclusion to help me host a press conference at Yale two months before the convocation. Her appearance in New Haven gave me my first chance to meet her. When the day came, I found her powerful aura and quiet dignity so stunning, I couldn't take my eyes off her. At one point I asked her, "Miss Anderson, why did you so readily agree to come out of your retirement to help me publicize this convocation?"

In her rich and serene contralto, she said, "When you called me and said you wanted this university to honor so many pioneering artists of our tradition, it struck me as a very positive idea, and one that is important for the music. I also heard an urgency in your voice that I couldn't ignore. I had to respond, Mr. Ruff, and do what I could."

Paul Robeson, though hospitalized and sinking, assured us that had he been well, nothing could have made him miss the gathering and the music of "my good friend Dizzy Gillespie and all those other lifelong musical favorites of mine." I had almost forgotten what tremendous fans our musical giants are of one another's work.

When Ellington and I began the "dream list" of those he wanted Yale to honor, I knew that scheduling around the availability of so many busy stars and President Brewster's calendar could be a nightmare. I was right. But as the date approached, Ellington went to work on the "impossible to reach" musicians. Miles Davis, for instance, was incognito that year and beyond even Ellington's long telephoning arm; Ella Fitzgerald was out of the country; and Lena Horne, Roy Eldridge, Sarah Vaughan, and Teddy Wilson all had bookings. Sadly, the invitation we sent Don Byas in Europe reached his house the day after his untimely death. Ben Webster, also living in Europe by then, was not well enough to come.

But we were lining up some good ones, and as the confirmed roster of performers grew, so did the considerations for programming: what to have whom play, and when, and with whom. Not since the Strayhorn Juilliard scholarship concert four years earlier had Duke involved himself in so large and varied an enterprise. And even that hadn't approached the scale of the New Haven celebration. But there he was, right on track again, full of new ideas. I had to fly cross-country to some of his concert and festival sites just to squeeze in hurried meetings with him backstage and in taxis, in elevators, airports, and hotel rooms.

"One never knows about time, baby," he said to me one day as room service in his Madison, Wisconsin, hotel spread his dinner before him in bed. "Eubie Blake, Noble Sissle, and Roland Hayes are crowding ninety, and Willie the Lion isn't far behind. They're the ones we want center stage. Tomorrow is, too often, too late. We should honor the greats among us while they can still smell the flowers." I loved learning the ropes from the "master of situations."

Finally, with all our artists' confirmations in hand, I set about ordering forty handsome medals bearing Duke's likeness. Studying the list of medalists at that moment, I realized that this assemblage of musical immortals represented a virtual living conservatory: an informal and uncredited school through which the lifeblood of jazz music had quietly perpetuated itself. Furthermore, I recognized those same elderly musicians Ellington wanted center stage as direct musical descendants of the generations that preceded them—the music's originators. Taken all together, our honorees came very close to spanning the history of jazz music. And the classical musicians—Hayes, Miss Anderson, Robeson, and Dorothy Maynor—had been role models for those of us who followed them on the American concert stage back when that possibility was systematically denied African-Americans.

For days I could think of nothing but this invisible conservatory. I reviewed again and again the teaching materials I'd developed for my classes at UCLA, Dartmouth, and Yale; the recordings and films I'd collected over the years, featuring these same artists. I discussed the "conservatory" and its cultural weight with Sidney Fine and Benny Carter in California; with Dizzy, Max Roach, Kenny Clarke, Joe Williams, and Jo Jones. Then I phoned Ellington.

"Maestro," I said, "have you come up with a name for our celebration yet?" He hadn't. Had I?

"Well, what we are really preparing to celebrate here is a real conservatory, a conservatory without walls. Why not just call it that?"

Duke paused a minute. "Conservatory. Hmmn. 'Conservatory without walls'? I think I like it. We do have all those specialties of the conservatory—the instrumentalists, singers, and composers—don't we? The bassists, for instance, with Slam Stewart, Charles Mingus, Milt Hinton, Ray Brown, and George Duvivier. And the pianists: Eubie, a great composer too; and of course Willie 'the Lion' Smith, who was Fats Waller's piano professor and mine, breaking us in way back in our 'kid' days in Harlem. And while we are on the pianists, don't forget the fabulous Mary Lou Williams, also a great composer and arranger. And we have the drummers: Sonny Greer, Jo Jones, Max Roach, Kenny Clarke. The saxophonists, trumpets, singers . . . I'm out of breath. But I can't beat that title, man. Print it!"

I wasn't through with the Maestro. I said, "And when President Brewster presents the medals, why don't we have all forty of those legends sit there on the stage together; and for each of their instrumental and vocal specialties, let's have a young world-class artist perform something special in their honor. We'll get a young trumpeter to play for Dizzy, Harry Edison, Cootie Williams, and Clarke Terry while they're sitting there onstage. We'll have a saxophonist play for Harry Carney, Benny Carter, Sonny Stitt, Russell Procope, Lucky Thompson, and Paul Gonsalves. A pianist for you, Eubie, the Lion and Mary Lou. A singer for Joe Williams, Bessie Jones, Marion Williams, Bill Warfield, Odetta, Roland Hayes, Dorothy Maynor, and Marian Anderson."

There was a pause. Then from Duke:

"Like I said before: Print it, Willie!"

We printed it. Printed and distributed it in press releases and in thousands of posters and brochures, until the three-day jubilee was upon us.

All day long on Thursday, October 12, 1972, the musicians began to gather. Little cells of old friends and mentors had cropped up all over the campus, in hallways, in classrooms, and on street corners. Musicians who'd been out of touch for decades were hugging one another and reminiscing.

Ellington's drummer Rufus Jones, my seatmate on Lionel Hampton's band bus when he, Mitchell, and I played with Lionel, spent that afternoon in Sonny Greer's hotel room. Greer was Ellington's original drummer, fifty years earlier. Jo Jones and Kenny Clarke also stopped by.

Rufus, a confident man who is seldom flustered, said to me later, just before going onstage to play, "I never saw so many from the generations that came before us! Just having Sonny Greer—who helped invent this band—out there in the audience tonight listening to me gives me goose bumps."

That night, students at Yale and Ellington devotees from around the world were treated to a full concert featuring the Duke Ellington Orchestra. The orchestra strode to the stage without its leader but with its collective chest thrown forward and gave "Take the A Train" a rare fire and celebratory lift. I knew they were playing on the inspiration that surfaces whenever professionals perform for an audience of their peers.

Just as "A Train" was ending, Ellington made his entrance, and his audience stood in a roaring welcome. He went to the side of the stage and brought out Willie "The Lion" Smith and introduced him as his "artistic overseer and custodian of good taste."

I joined several other musicians in the audience, then began to move all around the hall to hear from different vantage points. Mingus, Dizzy, and Sonny Stitt were lined up along a side wall, listening. "Imagine Harry Carney," Mingus said, "after all these years, still playing with that great big sound, making the whole band sparkle!"

Just then, onstage, Cootie Williams eased up out of his chair and, with his plumber's plunger, bent his deep-throated trumpet growls all around the melody of "Concerto for Cootie."

Dizzy Gillespie grabbed his face. "I don't know if I can stand three days of this much excitement!"

The next afternoon was given over entirely to that jam session I had thought so much about. I directed traffic, putting the various dream bands onstage. Joe Williams had given me some preliminary guidelines beforehand: he wanted to sing with Duke at the piano, Benny Carter at the alto sax, and Jo Jones, and Ray Brown filling out the rhythm section. Dizzy said he wanted to play with his old friends Kenny Clarke, at the drums, Mary Lou Williams, at the piano, Sonny Stitt and Lucky Thompson, playing saxophones, and Slam Stewart, playing bass. Even with such explicit directions, there were latecomers to accommodate, and other surprises, such as Jo Jones moving Max Roach over and himself playing a number with Harry "Sweets" Edison, his old friend and soulmate from their days as stars of Count Basie's band.

The oldest team performing on the bill was Eubie Blake, eighty-nine, and Noble Sissle, eighty-three, giving what was to be their last public performance together; Sissle died shortly afterward. Their young audience, mostly students, gave their songs, from *Shuffle Along*, one of the most heartfelt standing ovations I've ever witnessed. Dizzy, Kenny Clarke, Mary Lou Williams, and Sonny Stitt were backstage, getting ready to play and recalling the spirit of the 1940s Harlem jam sessions they'd had at Minton's Playhouse with Charlie Parker and Thelonious Monk. Kenny said, "Charlie Parker would have loved this whole thing. He used be around Minton's and other places, talking about the new music he liked. Hindemith was one of his favorites. Bird would really be in his element here today."

At one point the stage filled up spontaneously with musicians wanting to play "How High the Moon," one of the all-time-favorite jam session numbers. From somewhere came the idea to feature solos by all the bass players in the house: Mingus, Ray Brown, Milt Hinton, George Duvivier, Duke's bassist, Joe Benjamin, and Slam Stewart. Duke even asked me to play, but I wisely declined in that company. All I wanted was to be out front to hear it all, and it was something to hear. Had an earthquake at that moment swallowed up Woolsey Hall, jazz would have been very wanting in the bass clef. But I knew I shouldn't even be *thinking* like that.

In fact, in the midst of all that jumping with those bassists, plus Benny Carter, Lucky Thompson, Sonny Stitt, and the nineteen-year-old Dizzy protégé, Jon Faddis, a police captain rushed backstage. "Clear the hall!" he yelled. "We're on bomb alert! Somebody called in that a bomb has been planted in this building."

My levelheaded assistant, Brent Henry, immediately went to the microphone. "Ladies and gentlemen," he said calmly, "we've just been informed that a bomb alert is in effect in the hall. The fire marshal and the police are searching the building now. Please go calmly to the nearest exit and leave the building. In twenty minutes we expect the building will be safe to reenter, and the concert will go on."

The audience moved easily out the exits, and with Michele and my bass in tow, I watched the huge concert hall emptying itself. Musicians, clutching their instruments, took safe ground across the street. The music was silenced. But not for long. One who hadn't deserted the hall was Charlie Mingus. There he was onstage with his bass, talking on the microphone as the police captain tried to get him out of the hall.

From the door I heard him say to the cops, "You all just get Duke, Eubie, Noble Sissle, Harry Carney, and all of my musical forebears out of here. I'm staying. I'm not moving, do you understand? I'm staying right here! I've got to die sometime, and it ain't ever gonna get better than right now. Racism planted that bomb, but racism ain't strong enough to kill this music; if I'm going to die, I'm ready. But I'm going out playing 'Sophisticated Lady.' "

The bass version Mingus played of the song was so great I hated to have to miss it. My daughter and I walked slowly toward the exit, and we could hear the tune going on, with Mingus's verbal counterpoint hotly expressing his righteous indignation while he played. Ellington, standing among the waiting crowd out on the street, smiled as he listened through the open doors. Mingus was getting hotter, and the police captain's pleas for him to leave the stage couldn't have fallen on deafer ears.

Kenny Clarke, standing near Duke, shook his head. "I wouldn't have believed it if I hadn't seen it and heard it for myself," Kenny said. "Listen to all that music coming out of Charles even while he's raising hell! Charles sure *is* a bitch, bless his heart."

Mingus's indomitable spirit rained on the old devil's hellfire and completely defused the ugly trick.

"False alarm," declared the police captain after about twenty minutes, and the musicians returned to the stage, hell-bent on raising the roof—with music.

We got tremendous press for the whole event—Radio France, the BBC, and German radio and television covered it. At least two major American magazines listed the preconvocation activities and the programs at Yale. But I was disappointed that American network television felt that Duke Ellington and forty of America's greatest musical artists at Yale lacked "audience appeal"; they all passed. Our publicists were shocked, but not Ellington. His stoic serenity was never more biting:

"We learn from our experiences, don't we, Willie?" he said. "We're honoring all those beautiful musicians *because* they have become great *even* in their invisibility. Maybe Fate is trying to tell us something about invisible. Why spoil a good thing, man?"

Sonny Stitt didn't spoil a good thing. As soon as the crowd was seated again after the bomb scare, he marched onto the stage, playing his saxophone with a fire that made Kenny Clarke shout, "It never got *this* hot even up at Minton's!"

Harry Edison responded, "Nothing *ever* got this hot."

I fell back in the spirit of it all and saw my chance to practice what I'd watched Duke carry off so masterfully back at the Lincoln Center Strayhorn concert. Looking over the waiting sea of legends standing backstage, ready primed, I called out to Duke: "Maestro, will you play with Kenny Clarke, Mingus, Dizzy, and Benny Carter now? And oh, yes—Slam, do you want some of this? Mary Lou, how about you and Milt Hinton, Max Roach, and Joe Williams teaming up Lucky Thompson, Cootie Williams, Sweets Edison, and Sonny Stitt." I was hitting my stride as a new master of situations. Mingus had been right: I knew it would never get better than that day.

But that night, at eight o'clock sharp, it came close. The stage of Woolsey Hall was filled with forty chairs, and in them sat the artists who were to receive the Ellington Medal. Sidney Fine had come East to help keep me straight. Watching that stage fill up with legends, he, from his perils backstage, passed me a note saying, "Go to the mic. *now* and say, 'I declare this house sanctified.' " When I did, a strange hush enveloped the stage and spread over the waiting crowd.

Kingman Brewster came onstage and presented the medals to the artists individually according to their musical specialties. The trumpeters came first: Dizzy Gillespie, Clarke Terry, Cootie Williams, and Harry Edison. Then young Jimmy Owens, a New York trumpeter of great stature, came forward and played his heart out before the elder masters of his instrument. The effect of such a spirited musical offering was all I could have hoped for. How can I ever forget the prideful look on the great musicians' faces as Jimmy played his musical synopsis of what the trumpet meant to him and his feeling about honoring its place in the history of jazz? Owens's improvised essay covered it all with wit, humor, and style.

Then Odetta, herself an honoree that night, sang a song called

"Black Woman," performing without accompaniment. Her singing hushed the hall, and she began building the drama and pulling her audience right along with her, right up to her grand emotional climax. It brought the house down. Ellington led the musicians on the stage in applause, and the audience came to its feet.

I thought it fitting for Odetta's lone rendition to be followed by a solo from the young drummer Tony Williams. About ten years earlier, Tony had, at age sixteen, joined Miles Davis's band. Weeks before the convocation, Max Roach had told me why Tony was the young drummer to play for his elders at the convocation. "Tony," Max said, "of course, is a young master himself. But more important than that, he never stops giving credit to Jo Jones, Sonny Greer, Kenny Clarke, and all of us who came before him. His last album is dedicated to Papa Jo." I hadn't expected that a drum solo could have so much music in it. Max had chosen correctly. Tony showed us all that he was the man for playing drum honors that night.

Mitchell hadn't wanted to play for the pianists. He was nervous. "What am I going to play for all those people on that stage, Ruff?" he pleaded. But several of the honorees helped me talk him into it, and he followed Tony Williams and played the pants off "I Got It Bad and That Ain't Good." Willie the Lion, who had only heard Mitchell the night of the Strayhorn concert, leaned over and whispered to Duke, "That boy has promise." And then it was time for Lucky Thompson's soprano saxophone. As Lucky played "In a Sentimental Mood" as nobody on the stage had ever heard it, I watched Benny Carter's face shine with pure admiration. The same admiring smile played on Harry Carney's face, and on Russell Procope's. And when Lucky was finished, he spoke eloquently of his debt to the late saxophone masters: to Johnny Hodges, Lester Young, and Coleman Hawkins.

Then Richard Davis brought to the stage the very same bass that the late, great Jimmy Blanton had played in Duke's band in the 1940s. Richard also spoke some admiring words for Ray Brown, Slam Stewart, Milt Hinton, George Duvivier, and Joe Benjamin, and went on to make us all proud with his original improvised solo, which he dedicated to Blanton. I thought I saw a tear rise to Ellington's eye.

Now all the departments of our conservatory were honored. But there was still the unfinished business of the medals for those absent heroes who'd been kept away because of illness. I had asked Dizzy Gillespie, who enjoyed a close friendship with Paul Robeson, to accept Robeson's medal and deliver it to him. Dizzy said a few words about what the great Robeson meant to him, then he quoted Mary Bethune's famous statement: " 'Paul Robeson is the tallest tree in our forest.' "

Joe Williams accepted Marian Anderson's award, and as he looked hard at the medal in his hand, he, too, had a quote to pass on, from Miss Anderson's past. He said he'd once heard her relate a piece of sage advice her grandmother gave her as she was about to launch her career: "Always remember, darling, wherever you go, and whatever you do, try always to do your best, for someone will be paying attention to what you do and the way you carry yourself, in order that they may pattern themselves after you."

William Warfield stood in for Roland Hayes. Holding Mr. Hayes's medal in one hand and his own in the other, Warfield said to the audience, "I am here tonight because a legend came to Buffalo, New York, my hometown, when I was a boy. I heard the great tenor Roland Hayes sing, and from that magical moment on, I knew that I had to be a singer too."

We still had a screening, the next afternoon, of my film made with Bessie Jones and Dizzy Gillespie in the Georgia Sea Islands, to be followed by yet another jam session.

But now we prepared to cap the concert's magnificence with a party, which President Brewster would host.

As we were leaving, the hall buzzed with high excitement. People like Ray Brown, Benny Carter, Harry Carney, Cootie Williams, and Harry Edison all came over to me with warm words of praise for the event and the role I'd played. But the impact of what had taken place didn't come into sharp focus until Charlie Mingus, with the full force of his nearly three-hundred-pound frame, surrounded me and gripped my hand in both of his with a surprising warmth. "You gave me the greatest gift of my life just by making it possible for me to see Duke and all these great artists get the honor they deserve," he said. I got misty and felt a huge tear begin to blur my vision. Mingus saw it and with a forcefulness that was startling at such a moment, said, "Oh, no.

Naw, man. Hold that tear! Call it back. Don't let that one fall. Call that one back. I mean it. Call it *back!*"

It scared and stirred me. I was lost inside Mingus's new tone of voice for a whole symphony of reasons: primarily because I'd always admired him so much, yet I knew his reputation for physical chastisement. But there was no hint of violence in his tone now. Rather, there was that old teacherly manner Mama had used so often to preach at me: "Read between the lines, boy!" Now, a grown man of forty-one then, I was locked in Mingus's terrifying clutches, with him bearing down on me: "Keep that tear. Save it for another time on down the road. You need to keep that one—it's special. Hold it in reserve!"

My vision cleared, and though I would have sworn it was physiologically impossible, I managed to call back the tear.

CHAPTER FORTY-TWO

Toward the Harmony
of the World

IN 1974, we would celebrate the one hundredth anniversary of W. C. Handy's birth, and that was a birthday I wanted to observe in a special way. Over the years, two books of spirituals arranged by Mr. Handy and published by his own firm have become favorites with me. According to his foreword to the first book, Mr. Handy was worried that we as a people were in danger of forgetting what our original sacred music had sounded like. By setting down the old spirituals the way he recalled hearing them as a boy in the church his father preached in, he felt he could help preserve something of their character.

After I'd begun teaching at Yale, I would go back home to Alabama to visit. I liked to see my old neighborhood and visit some of my Sheffield teachers. One day I was sitting in Miss Frances Pollard's living room in Florence, and her aged mother just up and talked about Mr. Handy. She said that long after he'd become rich and famous, he would come to spend quiet time away from New York, visiting and resting in the homes of his friends. "We all thought at first that William was trying to write another 'St. Louis Blues' when we saw him spread out on the floor with his music paper scattered everywhere, writing down these spirituals the way he remembered hearing them around here." Mrs. Pollard went on: "He went to a lot of expense to get those spirituals printed up, too, and he ended up giving most of the books to musicians and schools if they wanted them. But that's what he wanted to do. He didn't need the money it cost him. So he was satisfied."

Nothing could be a more fitting or a more useful celebration of that hundredth birthday than a full Handy concert at Yale that included several of those spirituals as he'd arranged them. With the help of Wyer Handy, Mr. Handy's son, who ran Handy Publishing in New York, we found choral and orchestral versions of a wide range of music his father had written. Sidney Fine, who was by then retired from Universal Pictures, contributed two excellent arrangements of Handy works for orchestra and chorus. On November 7, 1974, the actual birthday, I called an assembly and went onstage in Yale's Sprague Hall to conduct a full orchestra and a large community choir. Marion Williams, the great gospel singer, and Dwike Mitchell were our soloists, and we lifted our voices and instruments in a glorious noise to celebrate with the music Mr. Handy wanted us never to forget.

In 1972, I had finally got my chance to begin exploring some of music's relationships and connections with other arts and sciences. It had happened when Dr. Gilbert Glaser, chairman of the medical school's neurology department, mentioned at a cocktail party one night that he would like to see a program staged on campus that would serve as a memorial for a mutual friend of ours, the neurologist Warren S. McCulloch, who'd been at Yale early in his career. I had been introduced to Dr. McCulloch by his daughter, Jean, and her husband, who had met me at Birdland several years earlier. Warren was the best talker I ever knew—about anything. I fell under his spell on my first visit to his farm in Old Lyme, Connecticut. He later mailed me several of the papers he'd written on his brain research; most of them, but not all, were beyond me.

Dr. Glaser put aside his drink, led me to a quiet corner at the party, and said, "Actually, in the six or seven years since Warren's death, I've wanted to do something here at Yale to celebrate his life. But how do you honor such a gifted character—a doctor, engineer, neurophysiologist, mathematician, poet, cybernetician, and neuropsychiatrist? Certainly not the usual stiff stuff memorials are famous for; Warren would hate that." I left the party having agreed to try and think up some kind of fitting celebration for Warren McCulloch.

A few days later, I found a recently published book of papers by McCulloch, *Embodiments of Mind*, in my mailbox, with this friendly inscription: "To W.R. in mutual memory of a kindred soul, from Gil Glaser." I smiled when I saw printed there some works that had showed up in my mailbox years earlier. "Where Is Fancy Bred?" and "Why the Mind Is in the Head" had been heavy going, but "How We Know Universals" rang my bells: it dealt with the perception of musical tones and chords. For that paper, Warren had collaborated with young Walter Pitts, and the work was a seminal study of visual and auditory perception.

Then I read the famous old story Warren loved to tell of his student encounter with Rufus Jones, the Quaker philosopher and the president of Haverford College. Having watched Warren's many undergraduate successes at Haverford, Jones called him into his office at graduation time to ask: "Warren, what is thee going to be?"

"I don't know."

"And what is thee going to do?"

"I have no idea; but there is one question I would like to answer: What is a number, that a man may know it, and a man, that he may know a number?"

Jones rubbed his face and said, "Friend, thee will be busy as long as thee lives."

Warren claimed, indeed, that he had been. And far too modestly, he also claimed that whatever his scientific contributions were, they'd simply been "promises kept to Rufus Jones." But then, he was never above playing to the crowd.

As I laughed again and imagined that even the ghost of McCulloch must still be preoccupied with number and knowing, I suddenly saw a theme for Dr. Glaser's celebration: Rhythm, in all its interdisciplinary numberness! Why not organize a colloquium on rhythm here at Yale, at which scientists, scholars, and the world's best performing rhythmicians could come together to discuss and demonstrate it as it applies to their fields? Such a program, lasting several days, could be interspersed with a stunning series of world-class performances. Now the impresario in me really got involved. Dr. Glaser encouraged the idea, and we took it to Rook McCulloch, Warren's widow, in Old Lyme.

"I know one scientist you will certainly want to have there," Rook said. "Try to find Cyril Smith, the metallurgist from MIT. He is a very likable person, and he and Warren loved talking together. They would talk for days about the most fascinating things. They liked each other enormously."

I found Smith. Stimulated by rhythm's challenge and the chance to celebrate Warren's career, he agreed to prepare a special talk.

Some months later, our three-day colloquium opened at the Yale Medical School, with Dr. Glaser talking brilliantly on "The Role of Brain in the Control of Rhythmic Movement." The hall was full; brain seemed to be on everybody's mind. And the same audience sat fast for John Hollander's talk on "Rhythm in Poetry" and for Gary Schwartz on "The Psychophysiology of Rhythm." T. J. Fraser, a founder of the International Society for the Study of Time, spoke on "Time and the Ecstasy of the Dance." Then, as a finale to the morning, Geoffrey Holder danced his seven-foot-tall Jamaican presence onto the stage and intoned in his deep bass voice James Weldon Johnson's "The Creation" while performing a breathtaking speak-dance to its rhythm.

In the afternoon, Jo Jones played his drums onstage at the School of Music—the consummate expression of timed arithmetic. His drum solo set the tone for a talk and slide presentation on rhythm in painting by Malcolm Cormack, curator of painting at the British Art Center. "Translation of Rhythm into Dress and Dress into Rhythm in the Black Atlantic World," by Robert Thompson, a Yale art historian, was an electrifying examination of the visual rhythmic principles in the colorful quilts and clothing of West Africa, the Caribbean, and the American South.

We were in a mounting crescendo. Cyril Smith, tall, slim, and elegantly dressed, took his place casually just in front of Jo Jones's drums and began speaking about how objects, and especially molecules, fill space. "Space," he said, "is the rhythmic domain that concerns the metallurgist, just as time is music's dimension." Then, switching on a projector and flashing onto the screen slides made from old and faded drawings of cannonballs stacked in various arrangements, he pointed out for us the principles of "close packing," arrangements that, by their symmetry or dyssymmetry, permit the greatest number of balls in the stacking. With a smooth transition from cannonballs to crystals, he projected drawings of large, beautifully shaped snowflakes onto the screen and showed that while no two snowflakes are alike, all are hexagonal in their crystalline arrangements. Smith's guided tour through the alluring sixness of snowflakes led him to the end of his short talk. He summed up by saying that the materials he'd used—the pictures of faded old cannonballs and snowflakes—were the work of the seventeenth-century German mathematician-astronomer Johannes Kepler. And the memory flooded in of how, twenty-five years earlier in that same Sprague Hall, I had listened to Paul Hindemith discuss this same Kepler.

"The science of music," Hindemith had said, "deals with the proportions objects assume in their qualitative and spatial, but also in their biological and spiritual, relations. Kepler's three basic laws of planetary motion . . . could perhaps not have been discovered had he not had a serious backing in music theory. It may well be that the last word concerning the interdependence of music and the exact sciences has not been spoken."

Cyril Smith had called up those voices from the distant past that shook awake resonances in me. I knew I would have to try to keep the interdisciplinary momentum alive in my own teaching.

A year later, I introduced an interdisciplinary seminar on rhythm, which happily continues to this day; it is based on the spirit of Warren's colloquium. Dr. Glaser, John Hollander, Malcolm Cormack, and Robert Thompson continue with us, and we make regular visits to the labs and offices of biologist G. Evelyn Hutchinson, geologist John Rodgers, and professor of philosophy Robert Brumbaugh. Our musical guests have included the harpsichordist Ralph Kirkpatrick; the singer Phyllis Curtin; the composer Elliott Carter; the tap dancers Honi Coles and Chuck Green; and the fabulous Juilliard eurythmics professor, Robert Abramson.

Kepler's notion of the "music of the spheres" now was gnawing at me harder than ever. I wanted to hear that aural planetarium both Cyril Smith and Hindemith had spoken of. I went back to read Hindemith's long, musically challenging opera based on Kepler's bizarre life, *The Harmony of the World*, and I realized that Kepler's three-and-a-half-century-old dream of hearing his data translated into sound was possible at last. In 1619, Kepler had written: "The heavenly motions are nothing but a continuous song for several voices; a music which, through discordant tensions, through syncopations and cadenzas, as it were, progresses toward certain predesigned six-voiced cadences and thereby sets landmarks in the immeasurable flow of time." If he was right about planetary motion following musical principles, then I would be able, with the help of the new computers and tone generators, to finally hear these relationships for myself.

This new technology, which Kepler never knew and Hindemith had known only in its primitive infancy, was fully capable of doing the skull-twisting calculating, synchronizing, tracking, and sound synthesis that should give me the audible sounds representing the planets in their march around the sun.

I knew I would need a collaborator, so I enlisted my neighbor and old friend John Rodgers, professor of geology at Yale, who is also an accomplished musician. Mark Rosenburg, a Princeton graduate student, wrote a computer program using the astronomical data John Rodgers and I developed that ultimately gave us an audiotape of Kepler's *Harmony of the World*.

When Rodgers and I heard with our earthly ears the music Kepler and Hindemith had heard only with their intellects, we knew it was time to release the tape as a phonograph record. No commercial record company carried such things, of course; we would have to create our own. We did, and in tribute to Kepler's great and indomitable spirit, we named the little enterprise The Kepler Label.

From the day the story of the new "planetarium for the ear" appeared on the front page of the *New York Times*'s Science section, floodgates opened. Scientific publications, radio stations, astronomy magazines, newspapers, and science buffs from around the world began crowding Yale's telephone switchboard. Kepler's musical astronomy was launched on tape, and it continues in its lively orbit even now.

CHAPTER FORTY-THREE

Improvising in Shanghai

O N THE AFTERNOON of June 2, 1981, Mitchell and I were in Shanghai, facing the most challenging audience of our musical career. Several hundred students and professors at China's oldest conservatory waited to hear their first American jazz concert. Mitchell sat at the piano. I was out front, holding a few sheets of paper on which I'd written crib notes for this, my first lecture in Chinese. I noticed no sign of the nervous "dry mouth" that often comes when I have to talk publicly in an unaccustomed language. But then, for two solid years I'd been strenuously instructed, drilled, tutored, and encouraged by a team of Yale teachers who could teach a stick to speak like a Mandarin.

The story of jazz in China first seduced me in the 1950s, when I learned that trumpeter Buck Clayton and trombonist Dickie Wells had played in a Shanghai British men's club in 1937. Wells told me a sign in the club's window read: "No Dogs or Chinese Allowed." Later, in the 1970s, I saw jazz elude the Chinese once again when China reopened her doors to foreigners and our government rushed them symphony orchestras, chamber ensembles, and great soloists: the best performers in America—of European music. But when Beijing and Shanghai natives began arriving in my classroom believing that the

Stephen Foster they'd heard back home was jazz, I knew it was time to knock on the door of Yale's Chinese department.

After several months of grueling classwork, I had enough Mandarin to add private work with Professor Vivian Lu, who gave me the vocabulary, special expressions, and confidence I would need to talk about my people's music before native Chinese.

Isaac Stern's *From Mao to Mozart* had just won an Academy Award, and music teachers from all over China flocked to America to observe how we teach and learn music. Several came to my door, and word spread in China that a strange black music man in New Haven wouldn't shut up in Chinese. More of the curious came, and from them I learned more Chinese. Then one day a call came from Columbia University. A Professor Tan, deputy director of the Shanghai Conservatory and a central figure in *From Mao to Mozart*, wanted to see Yale. Would I be his host? I jumped at the chance.

Western music of all kinds had been silenced in China from 1966 to 1976, that trying decade of the Cultural Revolution, in which schools were closed all over China. Professor Tan Shu-chen, like teachers everywhere in the People's Republic, was publicly humiliated, locked away, kicked and beaten by his own former students, as an accused "tool of decadent cultural influences from the West." Yet the cheerful eyes of the seventy-three-year-old musician crossing my New Haven threshold were not the eyes of an abused political prisoner. His face, I thought, looked like a composite of all the good teachers I'd ever known. There was no trace of a foreigner's accent in his easy and perfect English. In fact, his conversation had the resonant and pleasantly cadenced music I remembered from Lockbourne Air Base.

In spite of these similarities, Professor Tan was of another tradition. Born in Shanghai in 1907, he learned the languages of Europeans along with his music studies as a boy. His violin teachers were Italian and Dutch. Musicians from England, Russia, France, and Germany were playing in Shanghai then. By 1930, he was teaching in six Shanghai colleges.

I asked him about those times. "Were there really public signs such as the one warning off Chinese and dogs when the jazzmen played at the Shanghai British Club?"

He smiled. "Oh, we saw such signs everywhere, even in our public parks. The Europeans were so strong and they controlled so much of Shanghai that it was the only city in Asia with a Chinatown. When I joined the symphony orchestra there in 1927, I was its first and only Chinese member. That was Shanghai!"

On his third and last day at Yale, our talk turned to jazz, and I suggested that Professor Tan visit a classroom where Mitchell and I were going to play for undergraduates. He sat among the students and listened intently, working to take it all in. At one point I saw that his eyes were closed, and I thought: Uhh uhh, jet lag's got him. He's out like a light! But then I recognized the closed lids of a musician in deep concentration—not those of an old man napping. From time to time he stirred and rapidly wrote Chinese characters on the back of an envelope.

After the class, he had several questions about technical aspects of jazz and its origins. But his central interest was improvisation. He was puzzled by it. "Is that kind of improvising," he asked, "similar in some ways to what the Europeans did in the time of Bach, Mozart, and Beethoven?" Mitchell went to the piano to illustrate certain clear similarities between the two musics. Then Professor Tan nodded and broke into a chuckle. "If only our conservatory students back in Shanghai could hear you! They have no idea that relationships exist between this music and the classics they are studying. I have to keep reminding myself that only in the last three years have our students been able to practice even Bach, Beethoven, and Chopin again. This music you play, this jazz—for the young Chinese music student of today, it would be learning about a new branch of music."

When it was time to say goodbye in New Haven, Professor Tan invoked the universal formality of the parting guest: "If you two ever get to Shanghai, please visit us at the conservatory and play for us. You don't have to worry about bringing a bass to China. We have a program of teaching students to make string instruments right there in the conservatory. You must play one of our basses!"

Sooner than Professor Tan expected, at the end of the semester of his Yale visit, Mitchell and I turned up on his Shanghai doorstep unannounced. I'd written a letter to Coca-Cola, asking for a travel grant, and was surprised to get a check within a month. Mitchell and I took that as a good omen and booked passage. When the secretary at the Shanghai Conservatory asked us to wait outside Professor Tan's office while she told him we were there, we could hear exuberant surprise in his laughter. Without missing a beat, Professor Tan asked if we could play a concert the very next afternoon. "Certainly," said Mitchell, oblivious to jet lag. Now for one of those Chinese basses I'd heard about back in New Haven. Professor Tan scribbled and dispatched a note to the bass instructor saying an American bassist had arrived with jazz on his mind. Moments later the outer office rang with the high-pitched giggles of young boys, and a smiling middle-aged man strode into the room leading three bass pupils from the conservatory's junior high school program. One of the bright-eyed youngsters, the liveliest of the gigglers, stretched out his hand and said, "Good morning, my name is Wu Fu Wen." The other boys marveled at their thirteen-year-old classmate's English, then added in Mandarin, "He has just said all the English he knows," and we all giggled. The instructor led the way to a storeroom of stringed instruments and paraded out five or six basses crafted from well-seasoned and highly polished old wood. I plucked and bowed them all until I came to one that felt close to my own Luigi DiLeone back home. It even fit my hand comfortably. In no time, my fingers found one of Walter Page's old-fashioned lilting blues bass lines, and big notes seemed to lope out through the old Chinese wooden room to mix their bluesy weight with the smell of varnish, gut strings, and bow resin.

The instructor became serious and asked me to slow the notes down and show him and the boys how I made the plucking sounds. I did, explaining the twelve-measure blues pattern as I went along. The professor asked to try it himself. I showed him how to rest the thumb of his right hand along the side of the fingerboard as he pulled on the strings with his forefinger and enjoyed the added volume and tone that startled them all. After a moment the professor was playing a fairly good approximation of the blues. The three boys, with characteristic adolescent enthusiasm, grabbed basses from around the room and moments later we were all in a circle making a booming room full of blues on Chinese basses thousands of miles from the American South. After about twenty minutes, my new bass colleagues had the form and the basic notes of the blues committed to memory, even if their interpretation and rhythm did need work. I put away the instrument I would use the next day with the promise of another lesson to check their progress an hour before the Duo's performance they would be attending the following day.

There were about three hundred students and their teachers sitting in the informal concert space the next day. Electric fans on stands whirred silently in every corner, and some of the aged professors sat in large stuffed chairs. Mitchell looked around at our surroundings and said to me as we waited, "I like the feeling of this room. It's relaxing."

Then Professor Tan stood before the audience and said they were about to hear what he'd heard with great pleasure on his trip to America, and that I would talk to them in Chinese. The audience smiled and murmured at that news.

My first words were an apology and a plea for their patience with the poor Chinese of a foreigner who wanted passionately for them to know his people's music. Their friendly applause relaxed me, and I went to work.

"In the last three hundred and fifty years," I began, "black people in America have created a music that is a rich contribution to Western culture. Of course, three hundred and fifty years, compared to the long and distinguished history of Chinese music, seems like only a moment. But please remember that the music of American black people is an amalgam whose roots are deep in African history, and also that it has taken many characteristics from the music of Europe.

"The drum is the most important instrument in West African music. But to me the intriguing thing is that the people use their drums to talk. Please imagine that the drum method of speech is so exquisite that Africans can, without recourse to words, recite proverbs, record history, and send long messages. The drum is to West African society what the book is to literate society."

I waited for questions from these inheritors of one of the oldest of literate societies. There were none; perhaps they were waiting for me to unlock mysteries for them. I went on.

"In the seventeenth century, when Africans were captured and brought to America as slaves, they brought their drums with them. But laws were soon written that prohibited the African talking drum, for the slave owners feared its awesome power; its secret language might be used to incite the slaves to revolt. This very shrewd law had a tremendous effect on the development of our people's culture and our music.

"But laws have never strangled humankind's need to make music; and a long line of original musical expressions sprang up in America in the drum's absence: musical expressions that nobody else in the world invented but us. While no instrument can replace the drum, we developed musical devices that can be thought of as drum substitutes. These have come to have enormous appeal around the world." I named a few, using the English words "spirituals," "ragtime," and "blues"— words that have no equivalents in Chinese. Then I mentioned a drum substitute that had at one time been popular enough in China to deserve its own Chinese name: *Ti Ta' Wu*, or tap dancing. A few older professors nodded at the half-forgotten relic of Shirley Temple and Bill "Bojangles" Robinson movies.

After that I sat down and played rhythm on my chest, thighs, and loud-popping mouth, and said, "This surrogate of the drum is called 'hambone.'" Students around the room, like my Pygmy friends in Africa, slapped gingerly at their own thighs and mouths and laughed at the fun of it.

Sensing the need to move on to more familiar harmonic material, Mitchell struck up a few introductory chords, which turned into a hymn he'd learned as a child in his Baptist church back in Dunedin. The old hymn and what it symbolized of Protestant Europe sounded strange to my ear there, so far from its sacred purpose. But it was the very music African slaves first found in America when they arrived in captivity. The point made, Mitchell and I then sang and played a famous spiritual, "My Lord, What a Morning." The students' faces began to relax as the connections were made between what slaves found and what they invented in America. As congenially as we could, we then tried to lead the Chinese through early ragtime; we played examples of the blues, with an explanation of its form, saving the discussion of improvisation for last.

Professor Tan had said earlier, "The students will need for you to explore improvisation in great detail." "Improvisation," as it is used in jazz, is a word that has no exact Chinese translation; "something created during the process of performance" was as close as my best Yale Chinese sources could get.

I began by saying that as a young musician I worried that my people had not developed from our experience in America a written tradition of opera, like Chinese opera, which chronicled great or romantic events. "But later," I said, "I stopped worrying, because I saw that the masters of our musical story—Louis Armstrong, Duke Ellington, Charlie Parker, Billie Holiday, and so many others—have enriched our culture with the beauty of what they created spontaneously. Improvisation is the lifeblood of jazz music."

Mitchell whispered, "Let's make up one. You start on the horn." I didn't even tell the audience what was coming. I just played the first theme that popped into my head: nothing grand, no virtuoso flash or dazzle. Any student there could have thought up its simple four- or five-note design and played it on his own instrument. As I blew on, Mitchell played a countermelody to match the horn's. I caught it and turned it around, and we exchanged parts, supported one another, and entered into the nip and tuck, the call and response, the pauses and the breaks, of the improviser's game.

Improvising is interesting and exhilarating. It is art so thoroughly complex and difficult that it engages all your instincts and intelligence. Doing it before an audience always heightens the stakes; if you play to teach, the stakes automatically double. Putting forth a new musical thought means putting something personal on the line. It is the ultimate gamble; you stick your neck out, push the limits, pace yourself, and learn what to leave out. The overworked myth that improvising jazz means "going wild" and "letting it all hang out" is just that, myth. It's no cinch to make musical sense spontaneously. There is discipline, and there are rules. Sorry. When the number ended, I told the audience, "That is the newest music you have ever heard. I can be very sure of that, because we just made it up right here, right now. We call it 'Shanghai Blues.' "

Bedlam.

Roaring applause, cheers, and approval.

But Mitchell looked somber. "Man," he said, "listen here. Don't let all that clapping fool you. Those kids don't really understand what's happening yet. You'd better take some questions." I've learned to trust his nose. If he smells a rat, I sniff the air. Professor Tan's antennae picked up our edginess, and he stood up to direct the heavy traffic in questions.

One came from an older Chinese teacher. "When you created 'Shanghai Blues' just now," he asked, "did you have a form for it, or a logical plan?"

I said, "I just started tapping my foot, then a theme suggested itself, which I played on the horn, and Mitchell heard it. And he answered. And after that we heard and answered, heard and answered, heard and answered."

"But can you play it again?" the professor asked.

"We never can."

He would not accept my answer. "But that is beyond our imagination. Our students here play a piece a hundred times, or two hundred times, to get it exactly right. You play something once—something that has great value—and then you throw it away."

I said that if we played the same music twice in an improvisation, the second time would be no improvisation at all. "We call improvisation the lifeblood of jazz because the performer is challenged to do it better each time."

The old teacher as much as threw up his hands. The mystery persisted.

Students around the room unloaded their questions: "Could two or more total strangers improvise together?" and "Do you give each other signals?" and "Could a Chinese person improvise?"

I felt Mitchell's mounting anxiety. It was time to shoot the works, risk the whole wad, and lay his neck on the line. I said to the audience, "Perhaps some of you know a traditional Chinese piece that Mr. Mitchell and I don't know. Or someone might have written an original piece that we certainly would not know. We invite you to play either of these choices for us on the piano, and we will try to make jazz of it."

All hell broke loose. A name was called out, and a young man of about twenty streaked for the side door. When apprehended, he got down flat on the floor and lay there rigor-mortis stiff. Professor Tan talked him back to his feet. Then, smoothing the jacket of his Mao suit, the student collected himself and went to the piano. What we heard might have been his own composition. There were shades of early-twentieth-century French influences in the opening—Ravel and Debussy—but the overriding flavor of the piece's elegant melody and the chords surrounding it was definitely rooted in China. I sensed Mitchell fastening his concentration on that flavor, his emotional radar homing in on the music's essence and telling him the secrets of its "Chineseness" and its spirit. And then, after about a dozen bars, the perfectly constructed little piece came to its pleasant and unexpected conclusion. The audience went berserk.

It was the moment I'd waited years for. If the game were golf, smart money would be on the kid from Dunedin. Mine was on a hole in one. I just stood there holding the bass, waiting. I saw Mitchell's eyes surveying the keyboard as he sat down. He took a moment to map his course. Nothing stirred on the stage, or anywhere in the hall.

Suddenly the Steinway rang out with the *exact* notes the student had played. No one-finger pick-out-the-tune. There, in full cry, were the composer's big two-fisted chords, complete with his melody and, more important, with all his original expression. A youthful Chinese voice in the audience cried out, "That American is a human tape recorder!" Professor Tan beamed. Students slapped their thighs and doubled up in the laughter of disbelief. When Mitchell entered the second variation, he was already broadening the theme, and its weight and flavor grew regal and became a grand march. Now it had the chest-swelling quality of a prideful anthem. I leaned on the bass and enjoyed the buzzing crowd. In due course, what had been prideful eased down to soulful: not jazz soulful but human soulful, optimistic, yet always the young student's composition, its integrity intact. The moment finally arrived for the added gravity and pulse of a bass line. I closed my eyes and started plucking rhythm and let the deep, fat bottom notes on the Chinese bass sing out, warm as a mother's love. I was in the paradise of improvisers, where I stayed through chorus after chorus of Mitchell's fabulous lead. When I finally opened my eyes, still playing, they went to the faces of those boys out in the audience. They too seemed transported. They were pantomime-bass-plucking in their seats with the precise movements I'd shown them in the blues lesson they'd had an hour before the concert. Mitchell spotted their antics and the smile on his face said he was just where he wanted to be, way off in an alien land, giving proof that the lifeblood of the music that rules him and me is endlessly transfusable.

CHAPTER FORTY-FOUR

Playing on
Holy Ground

IN THE SUMMER OF 1984, I realized that thirty years had passed since
I'd learned to love the music of the Venetian School, centered at St.
Mark's basilica. Now, with time on my hands for a summer, I thought
I heard a familiar little voice urging me, "Do something nice for your
ears."

I was packing my horn for a trip to Venice when the writer Bill
Zinsser called me. I knew Bill from Yale, where he'd taught writing
and been master of Branford College. He had moved from Yale to the
Book-of-the-Month Club and was hard at work writing a book about
Mitchell and me. When I told him I was on my way to Venice, he
asked if I had work there; a concert perhaps. I said, "No, I'm going to
play Gregorian chants and spirituals on my horn in St. Mark's cathedral
at night, when nobody else is there. And I'm going to tape it."

"Can I come along?" Bill asked, all seriousness. He'd come with us
to Shanghai for his book, and now he felt another fresh, hard look at
the eccentric Mr. Ruff couldn't hurt. I said I was flying by the seat of
my pants; nobody at St. Mark's expected me. He said he would take
his chances, and we agreed to meet in Venice.

This trip that seemed so hastily thrown together was probably the
culmination of Hindemith's old lingering influences on me; it felt as if

his ghost were peering over my shoulder, urging me to explore the Byzantine richness of St. Mark's, where so much important music had first sounded. The Venetian School was actually a sixteenth-century mixture of Flemish and, later, Italian composers. Inaugurated by Adrian Willaert of the Netherlands, it included, among others, Andrea Gabrieli, Cipriano de Rore, Claudio Merulo, Giovanni Gabrieli, and Claudio Monteverdi. Two of its composers, Nicola Vicentino and Gioseffo Zarlino, were among the most progressive theorists of the time. When I first laid lip to the instrumental music of that period, under Hindemith's direction, it was the two Gabrielis—uncle and nephew—that captured my attention with their broad masses of sound. Giovanni Gabrieli's polychoral treatment, echo effects, and extensive use of voices with instruments made me wonder how such textures and invigorating rhythms could be performed in the basilica five hundred years ago and be heard clearly. Now, after thirty years, I was asking myself: Why did the sound of all this just run together like heavy molasses and not emerge a garbled echoey blotch with dead spots, as in many of the newer halls around the world today?

Since St. Mark's musicians were so daring for their time, I suspected that its builders might have known something about acoustics that was not widely known in Europe, then or now. Certainly, the builders could not have had Gabrieli in mind when they laid out the plan for the church hundreds of years earlier. The music used for church services at that time was monophonic—a single sung melody—with no harmony and not even the accompaniment of an organ until much later. By the early 1400s, six players of silver trumpets had been hired to play in St. Mark's by the doge himself. During the last two decades of that century, the church got a second organ and gradually began to assume its place as a vital center in the development of European music.

A new slant on the Byzantine world had found its way into my thinking since those student days. I had heard a record of a Paul Robeson concert at Carnegie Hall, made in 1958, on which he sang an American Negro spiritual, a thirteenth-century plainchant from Czechoslovakia, an East African tribal chant, and an old Near Eastern Jewish chant. Their melodies were nearly the same. Robeson's point was that there was a connection. And why? "Because," he said, "the Abyssinian

Church and the Church of the Sudan were part of the Eastern Church of Byzantium. Therefore, music from many parts of Africa and the Near East found its way into the liturgy of the early Byzantine Church and from there it spread out into Europe."

Robeson made me realize the connection between my spirituals, the first music I can remember hearing in my childhood household in Alabama, and other musics of the world. The notion of playing some of the interconnected music on my horn in an architecturally significant space began to excite me. And then it was clear. I had to go to Venice and find a way to play the horn inside St. Mark's. I'd play my spirituals and the plainchant from the *Liber Usualis*, the "Book of Use," containing the hymns and chants most used in the Catholic liturgy.

For weeks, my daily practice centered around the hymns, graduals, glorias, and kyries of the mass. I tried to keep track of the best of the melodies, but choices were so numerous I decided to memorize as many as possible and let the spirit inside the church guide me after I got there. Then I started to recall some of the spirituals I was brought up on. Many of these are cast in modalities similar to the church modes of the Middle Ages, and I saw their connection with the music of the *Liber Usualis* even more clearly.

When I arrived in Venice, darkness was less than an hour away. Since St. Mark's is open to the public only during the day, I planned my first visit there for the early hours next morning. My plan was simply to go there empty-handed and get a feel for the space. But I decided to beat the darkness and go and look at the outside of the church right away.

I headed for St. Mark's Square and walked around it several times, keeping my eyes glued to the locked cathedral on the square's eastern end. I was already projecting my imagination into the next morning's work. Just to get myself warmed up, it occurred to me to pace off the approach to the main door of the cathedral from several directions and hope that my sneakers would fall into the faded footsteps of Gabrieli, Monteverdi, Zarlino, and perhaps a sackbut man or two. I walked there for a very long time before jet lag said it was bedtime. That first night's sleep in the shadows of St. Mark's was filled with dreams in which old Italian musicians blowing six silver trumpets spoke rapidly to me between phrases.

The following morning, still with the sound of the silver trumpets in my ear, I scurried back to the square, arriving just in time to find tourists from around the world lined up in front of the church.

I suddenly recalled all the polite Italian expressions I'd ever heard that might smooth the way of a man needing to get into church in a big hurry. "*Scusi, permesso, prego . . . scusi, prego,*" I pleaded, and made a tight-end run around the Swedes, nudged cautiously past the Germans—and through the door. I must have given the impression of a man on a mission, for not a soul protested as I hit my stride, eyes fixed purposefully in the direction of the main altar. About midway down the aisle, still striding, I sensed an old but familiar discomfort coming over me; I never know what to do with my hands when I approach an altar in a Catholic church. I've always been confounded, too, by the neat dipping at the knee that trained Catholics negotiate so expertly. As an Alabama Baptist, I nurse a high reverence for all religious symbols and houses of worship; so to make peace with the saints, I said a few more silent *scusi, permessos,* and *pregos* and hoped that my Baptist presence would not offend.

At last I was standing in the space where something important in music had first sounded five hundred years ago. I closed my eyes and tried to imagine the sound of the old singers and players. I breathed in great drafts of the incense-laden air, shuffled my shoe soles on the geometric patterns of the marble floors, and tried to sense in all my skin pores and in the inner recesses of my ears the essence and echo of St. Mark's distant sound. I turned all the way around after several minutes and opened my eyes. I was standing directly under the center dome of the configuration of five domes in the ceiling.

One of the oldest and best methods musicians use to test resonance and echo duration is to clap the hands slowly and loudly. One cannot be inconspicuous clapping loudly in St. Mark's. I just closed my eyes again, gave two resounding claps under the central dome, and listened to *Whhhhaaaaacccckkk* . . . The first blow lasted undiminished in intensity for what seemed a very long time, hanging in the air to linger through the second clap. The slight difference between the two was clearly distinguishable, and the two beats merged and slowly decayed. I repeated the test just to make sure I was hearing what I thought I had heard. The sound came back to me with all the sharpness of the blows mellowed out of it, sounding as smooth as an organ note. I then moved all over the church, repeating my clap tests, and ignored the dirty looks of the other tourists when my whacks drowned out their tour guides' talk.

After a while, I sat down to think about it all. I needed a plan. I had to get permission to play at night, when the place was closed up and quiet. I'd not used the usual official channels for written permission to play in the church before leaving home. I was trusting that the good luck that usually went with me on musical quests would carry me through.

From the cool, comfortable stone bench where I sat, I saw a man, dressed in what looked like a doorman's uniform, standing reverently by the altar. I approached him and asked when I might hear music in St. Mark's. "Only on Sundays, for the morning mass," he said. I then asked if Sunday was the only day during the whole week that music sounded in that magnificent acoustical wonder. "*Sì*," he said. I asked him what music, and he told me that it was the sung mass, with choir and organ. I said that many things had changed since Monteverdi and Gabrieli had been at St. Mark's. Raising both shoulders high and tilting his head while turning out both palms, he said, "You speak of the time of the masters, *signore*." Then it hit me that if St. Mark's had fallen back to only one day a week for music, I might have a tough time getting permission to do what I had come for.

I was back there in the church that afternoon to make contact with the official who could authorize my playing there. The guard at the altar remembered me and said I must speak to Monsignor Semenzato. He was the business manager in charge of all such transactions as mine. I had brought with me a letter of introduction from Yale's president, Bart Giamatti, which solicited hospitality for me and attested that I was a scholar doing acoustical research in Venice. Giamatti's letter was in

English. I had also neatly folded a fifty-thousand-lire note in my shirt pocket to be presented as an offering, which, legend has indicated, often opens church doors. But not right away. I waited. And waited.

Two days later, Bill Zinsser arrived. We headed for the church together. I had my Yale letter and the fifty-thousand-lire note in my pocket. We were met at the door by Monsignor Semenzato, whose aristocratic good looks would not have been out of place in the Olivetti boardroom. Handing him my letter from Yale, I asked if he spoke English. He said he spoke a little French and handed the letter back. I said I would try to state my business in Italian. His look said: You'd better make it good, buster. I took a deep breath and started at the beginning. I was careful to take my time and sound out the long vowels in the names—Zarlino, Gabrieli, Merulo, and Monteverdi—and try to make it sound as if they were my friends. His expression told me that my subject interested him about as much as a recitation of a recipe for bean salad. I paused to ask if my Italian was decipherable. "Sì, capito," he insisted. Then, in a voice quite civil but with no charity, he asked, "What do you want to do?" I said I'd come to play and to make acoustical measurements in the church.

The reverend father said, "The basilica is open. Go ahead. Play." I told him it couldn't be done with tourists there—I needed to come at night, when the building was closed and silent.

His face changed, and his speech quickened as he shifted to the local dialect. I caught practically nothing he said, but his body language spoke volumes. Out of it all I kept hearing the word *arcidiacono*. Did it mean archdiocese? Must I go there? Was it in Venice, the Vatican? The interview was over, and Zinsser and I left. It wasn't a good beginning. But instead of just stewing, I decided to seek out a musical diversion while thinking about how to get into St. Mark's at night.

I knew that Igor Stravinsky was buried in Venice. And I remembered that I'd read somewhere that his grave was on the cemetery island of San Michele. Hindemith and Stravinsky had enjoyed a long friendship. They had great respect for each other's work.

It had been Stravinsky's wish to be buried in the Russian Orthodox section of San Michele, near Serge Diaghilev and several other compatriots. I said to Zinsser, "I know where I can play my horn." I found the island of San Michele on my map, fetched my horn from the *pensione*, and we went back to the Grand Canal for the vaporetto.

On the boat ride to the cemetery, I told Zinsser that the same Charlie Parker who had inadvertently led me to Hindemith had also been a great admirer of the Russian genius. Stravinsky had no equal as a hero to those young black musicians who'd pioneered the modern movement in jazz. I felt very good about going to his grave to pay homage. To blow a chorus or two of the *Pange Lingua*, one of the most beautiful hymns in the *Liber Usualis*, for him would be an honor. Zinsser asked, "What made Stravinsky such a favorite of Charlie Parker and all those young modern jazz masters?" I said that it was his harmonic and rhythmic daring, and the imaginative use he made of folk material, especially in his ballets.

A custodian at the cemetery gave us a map of the grounds. Seeing that we were Americans, he pointed out Ezra Pound's grave to us. We threaded our way past old graves of Venetians, stopped a moment where Pound rested, and, at last, came to the considerable Russian Orthodox area, where we found Stravinsky's grave. Off in the distance, we could hear diggers singing as they worked. That gave me courage. I ran far less risk of ejection if the workers were already amusing themselves with song. Still, to be on the safe side, I put the mute in the horn before playing the *Pange Lingua* there by Stravinsky.

With the mute in the horn, *Pange Lingua* sounded like Stravinsky's own brass writing in his orchestral works. I played through several versions of the hymn, each in a different mood. While I blew on, Zinsser moved from one gravestone to another, writing in his notepad and observing the names of celebrities resting in Stravinsky's vicinity: the as yet unmarked grave of Mrs. Stravinsky, next to Igor; to the right, Aspacia, widow of H. M. Alexander I, king of the Hellenes; nearby, Diaghilev, Stravinsky's collaborator for *Petrouchka*, *Rite of Spring*, and *Firebird*.

Later that day, while Bill and I sat at an outdoor café close to St. Mark's, I saw posters on a nearby wall advertising a concert of choral music by the Amherst College glee club, to take place the next night in St. Mark's. I said to Bill, "Somebody at St. Mark's had to make arrangements for that concert. I'm going back in there and find whoever it was." We pushed our way through the crowd at the church's front door. This time I thought to find a janitor for information. Perhaps I'd started too high up in the front office with Monsignor Semenzato. I studied three or four sweepers and dusters, looking for one with a face that smiled easily. Just such a man stood near the nave, leaning on his broom. I approached him and told him my story. He said, "Surely; sounds interesting. Speak to my *capo*—he's right over there." I went to the boss man my friend pointed out, and he, too, smiled easily. He stretched out his hand, and as we shook I started telling him in Italian that I needed his help. He seemed impressed with my willingness to try to speak his language, and asked with a smile, "What can I do for you?" After I told him I was from an American university, all his answers to my questions were: "*Sì, Professore*"; "*No, Professore.*" When I asked, "Whom must I see to get permission to play here at night when the basilica is quiet?" he said, "*Arcidiacono Spavento, Professore.* No problem. You can speak to him here. He is always around here." He called out to one of his janitors. "*Luigi, Spavento a scappato?*" "*Sì, Capo, a scappato due minuti fa.*" Then to me he said, "Professor, as you heard my man say, Monsignor Spavento has left for the day, but he will be here tomorrow evening to hear confessions. Come to this side door at six o'clock tomorrow, and I will introduce you. He's a nice guy." The *arcidiacono*, it appeared, was simply the man in charge of the church— the archdeacon. I was exhausted but happy, and Zinsser and I said goodnight.

The next evening at six o'clock, we were back at the side door. Bill said he'd wait for me out in the square, over a drink. I went inside and found the *capo*. He was expecting me and led me directly to a confession booth in a side chapel. Pulling back the curtain, he whispered something. I heard a slight movement inside behind the curtain—a soft shuffle of feet, the rustle of cloth. The *capo* whispered that an American professor was there to speak to Monsignor, and when he pulled the curtain all the way back, I saw a very old priest, slumped down in his chair; apparently, he had been asleep. He had very white hair; his face looked old and tired.

When I saw that his tongue was working in the side of his mouth in the rhythmical way of a person who's had a stroke, I thought: That does it. I'm dead. But I started my speech from the beginning, noting Willaert the Netherlander and emphasizing his Italian successors. I could see that the names of Gabrieli, Monteverdi, Zarlino, and the others were having an effect. The more of those names I called off, the more the priest sat up in his chair. I talked on, and he became tall and straight, the years seeming to fall from his tired old face; his tongue stopped working, and his eyes brightened. When I mentioned the near perfection of St. Mark's acoustics, he held up his index finger and wagged it before his face, interrupting me:

"Scusi, Professore. St. Mark's acoustics are per-fet-to! Per-fet-to!"

I could see an almost puzzled bemusement in the monsignor's face. I imagined he had been waiting, perhaps for years, for someone to come to talk to him of the past musical greatness of his beloved church. He looked up at me and said softly, "What do you want to do here?" I told him I needed time in the church at night, alone—in silence—and that I wanted to bring a recording machine and play the horn there as the musicians in Gabrieli's time had done. That was the only way I knew to explore the sound qualities that have mystified musicians through the centuries.

"How much time?" he asked.

I told him two hours would be enough. He paused a moment, rubbing the stubble on his chin, then called to the capo, who had been listening nearby. They discussed my problem in the rapid Venetian dialect, then the arcidiacono asked me, "Is tomorrow night soon enough for you?" I said it was per-fet-to.

When he told me to come to the side door at seven-thirty after mass the next night—the church would be mine—I was prepared to thank him and leave. But he took my hands in his again and asked, "Tell me, are you a Latin American?"

I had felt his eyes examining my face and head; guessing he'd not seen many who looked as I do, I said, "No, sir, I am from North America, a mix of African and American."

He squeezed harder on my hand and asked, "You are an Afro-American?"

I said, "Yes, sir, I am."

"Well, this is the first time I have met an Afro-American. It has long been one of my convictions that the Mediterranean world, with its rich cultural mixes, has shaped much of what is intriguing in Western civilization. From there came the cultural influences that are at work in the best of Europe. That is why St. Mark's is so unique. This basilica itself is such a mixture." He chuckled wistfully for a moment and then went on: "What an idea! Wouldn't it be fantastic if the glorious musical story of this church were to be brought back to the attention of the world through the interest and deep appreciation of an Afro-American!"

Finally, he let go of my hand. I felt the loss. But I left the church smiling, as I thought of the English translation of the old priest's name: Spavento means "fright."

At seven-thirty the next evening, Zinsser and I were at the side door. The *capo* had left for the day. His assistant waited by the door to lead us into the empty church. Alone there at that hour, with the fading twilight streaming through the colored windows, one felt in the church an atmosphere that was almost eerie in its majesty and beauty.

I went to work immediately, according to a plan I'd begun hatching the first day I came to the church. I turned on the tape recorder, took my horn, and stood under the center dome. Even empty, the church was not silent. There were minute creaks and shivers—the sound of groaning stone—evidence of a marble edifice cooling off and settling down for the night. I took a long moment, even with the tape rolling, to listen to the near silence.

I blew my first note, a C, neither long nor short, just barely breathing the wind into the instrument, yet the note went on flying and ringing long after I'd quit pushing the wind. It felt clear and easy. There was the expected echo, but I also heard a tone quality far richer and warmer than any I'd heard from my horn before. My note had gone searching out all of St. Mark's surfaces and returned to my ears culled of dross, with only the purest overtones remaining. The echo seemed to come from everywhere.

Zinsser had taken off his shoes and was silently padding about in his socks, examining the church's features in the fading light. "What a rich and resonant sound," he said.

"What a pleasure," I said.

Staying with the same note, I moved from dome to dome and all around the nave and alcoves. By the time I'd finished my test, I had gained some understanding of the sound characteristics of St. Mark's and why they were special. It was clear that music-making there had to be a transaction of restraint and soft-pedaling. Above all, tempos, volume, and dynamics must be allowed to set themselves. The basilica *itself* was an instrument to be played—not just played *in*.

Now I was ready. My first station would be the main choir loft, high up over the front entrance. I had already marked my selections in the *Liber Usualis*. I had also decided on four spirituals to play; these I knew by heart.

I played first an *Agnus Dei* I'd heard at the Vatican. From up high, the horn sound was even more enveloping. Since the microphone was so far away from me, down where Zinsser stayed, I thought to slightly project the horn's tone. When I later listened back to what I'd played, I discovered that I need not have made allowances for the distance. I should have remembered to trust St. Mark's to play itself.

Darkness was falling as I left the high choir loft. Down in the nave, the sacristan brought candles to light my station at a small altar at the side of the church. When the church's tower clock struck nine, I had finished playing from the book. I still had a half hour to try out my spirituals.

I began with the old song "Were You There When They Crucified My Lord." I cannot describe the ways that this song was different from the masses I'd read from the book. I can only say that I recognized that I stood on holy ground, a mere thirty feet from the remains of Mark, and that my thoughts were in my family's Baptist church in Sheffield, Alabama. My horn was the rich contralto voice of Miss Celie Appleton, our town's best singer, and the sound I had made was as close as I've ever come to Miss Celie's.

When I'd played the last note of "Were You There," the sacristan reappeared, with a friend in tow. He said, *"Bene, com'è bella!"*—"How beautiful!" He and his friend wanted to know what the music was. That the song was Afro-American and that its origins shared something with St. Mark's surprised and delighted them. He asked me to play more, and the two of them sat on a marble bench to listen. As I played the next song, both of my auditors jerked their heads in the changing directions of the sound, as if trying to follow the flying echo with their eyes.

After I'd played "Go Down, Moses" and "Give Me Jesus," my energies were spent. I had ten more minutes on the clock, so I played through a few melodies of a Bach cello suite, then packed away my horn and recording gear.

The sacristan offered to let me go on playing. I thanked him but declined. It would have been meaningless to stay. I had already done my best. And I was satisfied, finally, that my old horn—the one I'd bought from Kniaz in Columbus and the same one I'd played when Hindemith first made us play Gabrieli—had turned the silence of St. Mark's into music. I also knew that the music the tape recorder had captured would be The Kepler Label's second offering.

EPILOGUE

Coming Full Circle

O NE NIGHT DURING THE 1988 SCHOOL YEAR, I went to hear the Yale historian Howard Lamar give a talk on the paintings of Frederic Remington. About midway through his lecture, Lamar projected a slide of a bombastic picture by Remington that was so full of dash and splashing colors I could almost hear the sound of cannon, charging horses, and martial music.

"This painting," Howard said, "depicts Teddy Roosevelt's famous charge and capture of San Juan Hill in Cuba during the Spanish-American War. It is a very interesting painting, but it is bogus history. Teddy Roosevelt commissioned the work by Remington, but it was not Roosevelt who took San Juan Hill. That victory belongs to the Tenth U.S. Cavalry, a black regiment fighting on foot." I daresay I was the only other person in the room who knew this bit of history, but still I was stunned that the old story I'd first learned from salty old Sergeant Display back in basic training had at last become "legitimate" history. I asked Howard whether his "revisionist" history indicated a trend, a search now for the truth, especially as it affected black American fighting men.

"Oh, there is a new and tremendous interest in military history now, Willie," Howard said, "and much of its excitement is uncovering stories of blacks in the military, like this one. As a matter of fact, one of my students has just written an excellent paper on the subject, with a bibliography that I'll be happy to send you if you like."

Howard was as good as his word. A few days later, a list of eight books showed up in my mailbox. I headed for the university library and checked out all but two of them. Those two, I was told, were in the library, but they were so old and fragile they'd been transferred to microfilm for preservation. One of them I really wanted to see: *Under Fire with the U.S. Tenth Cavalry,* a narrative published in 1902 by a team of five black authors. The microfilm section is down in the basement, and at that moment I wasn't in the mood for a basement search. Still, I took a deep breath and slouched reluctantly down the stairs.

I don't like reading books on microfilm. I enjoy the feel of the paper in old books, and the smell of musty old ink and rag. But I set my jaw and threaded the film through the projector's sprockets, cranked the reel forward—and was borne away. I lost myself in dozens of clear old photographs of dashingly handsome black men in old-style uniforms, holding long rifles and flags. Turning the crank past troop after troop of the Tenth Cavalry, I felt transported back in history. Suddenly a picture of a band flashed up at me and froze my hand on the crank. I thought my heart had stopped. I lost all my library decorum, forgot where I was, and misbehaved: I hollered like a banshee. It was the *same* picture Pete Lewis had laid in my lap when I was fifteen years old and learning to play the horn back in the boiler room of the band's barracks in Cheyenne, Wyoming. I'd never known the book's title, seen its cover, or even known who wrote it; old Pete had simply made me wash my hands until I could prove to him they were clean enough to hold his prized volume, before he pointed out his old friends and music teachers in the picture. I still remembered the words he had me read out loud on the pages that followed, words that made me proud of the band's special bravery under fire, and proud of the way Pete said they could "tell a story." Now I cranked past the picture and read the story again, my hands sweating, even though the basement was cool. Mumbling to myself, I thought of gentle old Pete and rolled the film forward slowly, stopping several times along the way to marvel at the power in the writing and the clarity of the nearly ninety-year-old photographs. When I came to the end of the film, I rewound it to the beginning to read the preface:

> *Under Fire with the Tenth U.S. Cavalry*, a purely military narrative, was written for the purpose of telling the Negro's story of the Cuban campaign. It is, therefore, made up of testimony which has come directly from the lips of those Negro soldiers who actually participated in the struggle for humanity in the Island of Cuba.
>
> General Joseph Wheeler was invited to furnish the introduction for this work [surely, I told myself, this couldn't be the same "Fightin' Joe Wheeler," the north Alabama ex–Confederate general my stepfather, Mr. Pruitt, had talked so much about], because of his close identification with the campaign, his manly attitude toward the Negro soldier, and because the reading public has an abiding faith in his nobility of heart and integrity of character and will properly regard what he has to say as the whole truth.
>
> —The authors

I rolled on to the following page, and the next thing I saw shining up at me was the first full-page portrait in the whole book: it was indeed Mr. Pruitt's main man, General Joe, the old ex-rebel decked out in the imposing regalia of the Spanish-American War. On the next page was his introduction.

> *Under Fire with the Tenth U.S. Cavalry* needs no words of introduction or commendation from me. The title page speaks for itself and sets forth a most inviting narrative, giving an epitome of the history of the Negro in this country and a thrilling account of his courage and heroism on the field of battle.
>
> Beginning with the introduction of the blacks into America, the book mentions the Negro patriots who fought with our forefathers in their great struggle for liberty in 1776. Continuing the military history of the race in America, it notes the formation of regiments which did good service in some of the bloodiest battles of the great

Civil War, later in the Indian outbreaks in the Western territories; and leading the reader on to the hostilities between Spain and America in the spring of 1898, it describes the enthusiasm with which the troops hurried to the mobilizing centers, their embarkation at Tampa, their momentous voyage, their landing in Cuba, and their participation in the bloody fights at Las Guasimas and San Juan.

With unfaltering courage and devotion they took part in the heroic charge of the cavalry at Las Guasimas, and after that gallant fight moved steadily forward with the cavalry division, forded the San Juan River, and under a murderous fire gained the crest of San Juan Hill and captured the formidable intrenchments of the Spaniards, driving back the astonished enemy, fighting by day and working by night until glorious victory crowned their efforts and peace once more dawned upon our beloved country.

The reports of their commanders [white] unite in commending the Negro soldier. Captains Watson, Beck, and Ayers, Major Norvell and others, all speak of their brave and good conduct, their obedience, efficiency and coolness under a galling fire. A detachment of Troop B under Captain Watson were for a time in charge of a Hotchkiss gun with which they did good service, and although the gun was a special target for the enemy, the men of the troop stood by it with steady coolness and heroism.

Lieutenant-Colonel Baldwin, in his report of the battle of San Juan, says: "They exhibited great bravery, obeying orders with unflinching alacrity," and he recommends a number of the men for special bravery.

Those who see in the future of the colored race in America a difficult and perplexing problem will find encouragement in this book, the product of Negro intelligence and the record of Negro patriotism, and be brought to the conclusion that the more enlightened men of the race are solving the problem by teaching their disciples, both by precept and example, to elevate themselves through the only safe and sure method, that of education. In the unchanging natural law of growth and development will be found the answer to the problem. By education, discipline, and judicious training, the characteristics and virtues of the race will be developed;

and with enlightened judgement they will learn the great truth that a man is worthy of respect in proportion to his intrinsic mental and moral worth. . . .

Joseph Wheeler
Major-General Commanding Cavalry Division,
Santiago Campaign

I sat there unable to move. A tear fell, and memories rushed me. Against my will I had come to the basement, and I had learned from cold microfilm what no book ever taught me. This old Southerner, with his "nobility of heart and integrity of character," as cited by the book's authors, was the first American white general officer ever to write a published testimony in praise of black patriots and salute them for valiant service to the nation in *all* her wars. But as happy as I was to learn it, I still had questions.

Wheeler had, in his day, been one of the most highly regarded figures in my part of Alabama. He'd gone to Congress from my home district, and until his death, in 1906, practiced law and made his home a few miles upriver from my birthplace. We've named one of the finest state parks in America for him, as well as a vital Tennessee River dam, navigation lock, and hydroelectric plant and highway. How, then, could his moving and eloquent testimony have so completely eluded those fiercely dedicated black teachers who'd taught me back in Baptist Bottom? With access to Wheeler's words, parents and teachers everywhere could have begun using his message long generations ago to instruct and inspire young black children who should have learned of the glory of our legacy at a time when such knowledge was otherwise systematically denied us. Echoes of Mama's "Read between the lines, boy!" enlivened my senses. I didn't like what I was thinking; I had to pursue my gut instincts.

I went to the head of the Yale library's preservation department and was given permission to check out the actual old book, *Under Fire*, from which the microfilm was made. But I gasped when I was handed a folder of hundreds of crumbling, crinkly leaves. Such dismemberment, the technician said, is necessary in order to preserve the document on microfilm. I thought: Ashes to ashes, dust to dust, and took the loose-leaf treasure home and tied it with a soft cloth ribbon. That package would be my constant companion as I began my search, honor-bound and hell-bent on tracking down more of the story, finding out who in Alabama would know it today and hoping to do what I could to make it better known at last.

Classes were winding down for the summer, and in a few days I would be heading back to Muscle Shoals, Alabama, where I've kept a home since 1974.

I enjoyed a cordial relationship with the staff and management of the excellent Florence and Sheffield public libraries. Once, a few years earlier, Jo Jones had invited himself and his drums to be my Alabama houseguests for a week. Until then, I hadn't known that he was Alabama born, was a native of Birmingham, and had attended A & M College, up the road in Huntsville.

He'd asked to come and talk an oral history of his life in jazz into my tape recorder. We'd known each other a long time by then. But after the Ellington convocation at Yale in 1972, at which "Papa Jo" was honored and presented with a medal, he had gone out of his way to share many little-known but important historical accounts and stories of jazz music with me. He'd years before stopped calling me by name; I'd become "Young Talent," a term he kept in reserve for fledgling drummers with promise.

"I want you to write a book; not just a book, but a *good* book." He'd been saying that for years. "You're like a fertile garden, Young Talent!" he said when I fetched him at the airport. "That's why I came all the way down here to plant some of these rare seeds in your head. Maybe some of them will sprout and take root." We weren't in the door good before he started up again. "Is the tape rolling yet? Don't you miss any of this, boy. Have you got plenty tape?" The old master drummer spread out, made himself at home in my house, and talked into the machine practically nonstop for days. And I didn't miss a word.

Then one Sunday afternoon, several reels later, he, with his drum set, and I, with my bass, gave a free concert for children at the Florence library. We made friends and reestablished old friendships. Mutt McCord, my boyhood drumming idol and first music teacher, brought Kristi, his granddaughter, to our concert to see and hear Papa Jo, the man who'd pioneered sock-cymbal playing and propelled Count Basie's orchestra through all those recorded performances Mutt and I had marveled at together on his mama's front lawn. How can I ever forget the happiness and pride I saw shining in Mutt's face as he sat among the children that day, watching Papa Jo and me playing together?

The reference librarian in Florence, Mr. Turner, a friendly man, has always been helpful whenever I've needed help locating books there. Something of a Joe Wheeler aficionado himself, Mr. Turner helped me search for *Under Fire* in the catalogue. Nothing there. I showed him my Yale copy. The Wheeler introduction floored him, and he hurriedly copied the name of the publisher and said he'd order a copy for the library. The libraries of Sheffield and Tuscumbia were similarly unaware of the book, and nobody I asked, black or white, had any knowledge of it or knew that General Wheeler had written such an introduction. Then one day, as I remembered a picture in *Under Fire* showing the whole regiment living in a temporary tent encampment in nearby Huntsville after their return from Cuba, and recalled that Cashin was the name of one of the book's authors, something clicked. Back in 1982, I felt Alabama should celebrate the legacy of W. C. Handy with a world-class music festival. My ears were still buzzing from the exhilarating sound of the orchestra and chorus I had assembled and conducted for the 1974 Handy centennial in New Haven. Then one day as I waited in the Muscle Shoals airport for a flight back to Yale, a congenial local veterinarian, Dr. David Musselman, showed unusual curiosity about the horn I always carry with me aboard airplanes. I introduced myself and a warm friendship developed. Two years later, David and I co-founded the annual W. C. Handy Music Festival. Mitchell and I brought the 1974 repertoire south, including the spirituals, trained a singing consortium of local choirs and in August 1982 began a series of historic concerts. To cap a week-long festival with a gala concert, Dizzy Gillespie, yet again, joined the duo. Dizzy brought his friend, Dr. John Cashin, a Huntsville dentist, backstage for an introduction.

Wondering if the doctor would remember me, I called him, told him of finding the book at Yale, and asked if Herschel Cashin was kin to him.

"Hell, yes. He was my grandfather, man! Herschel Cashin was the first black lawyer in the state of Alabama. He told us, when I was a small boy, that he'd seen that black regiment camped on Cavalry Hill here in Huntsville, out of sight and away from publicity, while Teddy Roosevelt hogged it all. Roosevelt stumped the damned country taking credit for San Juan Hill and getting elected President as a result of it. My grandfather initiated the interviews that led to the book. He took what you might actually call depositions from those black soldiers camped here in Huntsville. Then, together with Mr. Anderson, a professional newspaperman, and Dr. Brown, a Birmingham surgeon who was the regiment's doctor, and two other men, they wrote the book and paid a small, now defunct, publishing house in Chicago to print a few hundred copies."

I said I was surprised by the eloquent introduction Wheeler had written. I also told him how smart I thought it had been of the authors to enlist his testimony.

"Wheeler," said Dr. Cashin, "was a lawyer too, you know. He knew and admired my grandfather. It was my grandfather's idea to invite him to write that introduction. Copies went to colleges all around the country; perhaps that's how it got to Yale."

For years I'd driven past the old Wheeler plantation and museum. But until now, Confederate generals who'd fought for the perpetual enslavement of my forebears hadn't interested me even a little.

I called a friend who'd seen the book I'd brought from New Haven, and we drove out to the old Wheeler estate, which had once been an imposing seventeen-thousand-acre plantation. I was surprised to find that the house, which serves as the museum, unlike the well-kept and manicured-to-the-teeth Helen Keller and W. C. Handy museums nearby, is not supported or maintained by the State of Alabama. Limbs from a month-old storm lay withering in the yard. My friend and I joined a small group, paid a modest few dollars entrance fee to an elderly live-in attendant, and were led into the dilapidated old house, crammed with the general's dusty effects. I examined glass-covered bookcases of his papers, books he'd written, documents he'd authored in Congress. We were shown pictures of the ex–army nurse "Miss Annie," Wheeler's famously eccentric spinster daughter. We peered into closets and at wall displays of military memorabilia, saw photos of the general as a student at West Point when Robert E. Lee was superintendent there. But no trace at all of *Under Fire* or the introduction Wheeler had written for it.

The next day I was back at the Florence library, checking all the biographical sources for details of Wheeler's life. Mr. Turner sat me at a large table and began hauling out stacks of heavy books: Wheeler's own writings; the Congressional Record; several editions of the Encyclopaedia Britannica, including the eleventh; Who's Who; and two exhaustive biographies of Wheeler, one written in the 1930s.

As I read my way through the books, the similarities in the life of the young Joseph Wheeler and my own life astounded me. The major differences were: (1) he was not from Alabama but had been born in Georgia; and (2) he was white. His mother, like mine, had died when he was young; his father, too, had never been able to keep his head above water. Young Joseph had to be sent north to be raised in the home of a relative, a judge who gave him an education. Where did the boy go to school? I hollered again when I read that it had been in New Haven! So little Joe and I had both come by a right smart of our book learning in that same up-north Yankee town.

I liked being back home where I started from, rooting out some of the paradoxes, connections, relationships, and passions that thunder through my South.

I sat there buried under Mr. Turner's pile with the feeling of having come full circle with this life in music, a life that has become inseparable from that bizarre life of mine in the military and all I got from it. I kept thinking—and I felt my spirit shine—that when I was a boy, trying to learn my craft, a fatherly soldier-musician had laid *Under Fire with the U.S. Tenth Cavalry* in my lap. And from that musician and his stories I began learning to tell my own story with music.

I kept thinking, too, that my home was bordered not just by the twin icons of my childhood in Alabama—W. C. Handy and Helen Keller—but also by an ex–Confederate general who had just laid a gentle hand on me and given me more pride and understanding.

Sitting in that library, I felt the years roll back and the memories roll in—that day in Wyoming when Mr. Ruffin gave me my first GI horn and Pete Lewis helped me learn it; when at Lockbourne, Mitchell and I decided we'd work together; when Abe Kniaz started teaching me what I needed to know, then went to bat for me in Washington; what I had gotten as a student from the towering musical presence of Paul Hindemith; years later, when Strayhorn taught the duo his music; when Mingus insisted I call back that joyous tear there in Joe Wheeler's and my New Haven . . . And now the journey was beginning to make sense. And the fire still burns.

Papa Jo Jones wanted me to write a book, and though this isn't exactly the one he had in mind, it will have to do for now. My daughter is a woman. Sister, Mama's chief surrogate, still sits as the reigning matriarch at the head of our New Haven clan. My ninety-five-year-old Uncle Grover is the last World War I veteran using VA services in Evansville, Indiana. The duo goes on its way around the world, as it has for thirty-five years, not even counting the Lockbourne days, which has to be some kind of record. I'm still at Yale. I don't know what will become of me when I grow up, but musical ambitions still crowd my inner agenda: to learn new things; to pass them on; to keep making discoveries that make me holler out loud in libraries; to be more like Mr. Brice as a musician and teacher; to conduct more large orchestras, bands, and choruses; to write more music and make more records with Mitchell at the piano, of course; to keep on playing my heart out as I go on pursuing a life in which the music—America's own unique and powerful music—still speaks and inspires. That's my story.

Index

on *Ed Sullivan Show*, 227–28
at Moulin Rouge, 243, 246, 247–58
orchestra of, 106, 227–58, 372
recordings by, 243, 247
on road, 240–58
Ruff auditioned by, 228–31
vibes played by, 229, 237, 241
Handy, W. C.:
   birthplace of, 15, 80
   as "Father of the Blues," 15, 16, 19, 31, 80, 307
   influence of, 38, 39, 68, 127, 210–11, 283, 417
   museum for, 418
   at Ruff's school, 31–32, 34, 37, 48, 420
   spirituals arranged by, 380–81
Handy, Wyer, 381
Harden, Velma Lucille "Sister" (sister), 30–31, 35,
      57, 100, 124, 153, 183, 238
   education of, 30–31, 36, 51–52, 106
   mother's death and, 84, 85–87, 90–92, 93–94
   Ruff's relationship with, 93–94, 106, 189, 191–
      192, 193, 198, 203, 214, 420
Harlem:
   black community in, 69
   rent parties in, 56
   soul food restaurants in, 239
Harmonice Mundi, 208
harmony, in jazz music, 274
"Harmony of the World, The" (Hindemith), 208,
   385
Harris, Art, 261
Hart, George, 240, 242, 244, 246, 253, 254, 258
Hawkins, Coleman, 314, 377
Haydn, Joseph, 226
Hayes, Roland, 369, 370, 371, 372, 378
Henry, Brent, 374
Herbert, Victor, 133
Hickory House nightclub, 3–5, 288, 321
Hill, Sam, 67, 68, 69, 71
Hill, Wonderful C., 59
Hillhouse High School, 197, 217
Hindemith, Paul:
   as composer, 181, 195, 197, 202, 203, 329–30,
      402
   Parker's admiration for, 181, 206, 207, 209, 210
   Ruff as student of, 206–11, 223, 384, 385, 397–
      398, 408, 420
Hines, Earl, 252
Hines, Gregory, 234, 238
Hines, Maurice, 234, 238
Hinton, Milt, 261, 369, 371, 374, 376, 377
Hitler, Adolf, 24, 74, 79, 206
Hodges, Johnny, 5, 377
Hodgson, Peter, 202, 223, 264, 290, 318
Hodgson, Peter, Jr., 290–91, 294–95
Holder, Geoffrey, 8, 9, 383
Holiday, Billie, 190, 260, 279, 393
Hollander, John, 383, 384
Holtzmann, Marvin, 261
Holy Rollers, 43, 233
Horne, Lena, 8, 9, 68, 247, 249, 255, 256, 370
hotels, segregated, 243–46, 256–57, 280, 282
housing, segregated, 214–15
Howard, Eddie (brother), 18, 31, 57, 85, 92, 153,
   189
Howard University, 158

"How High the Moon," 374
"How We Know Universals" (McCulloch), 382
Hughes, Langston, 311–12
Hunter, Ivory Joe, 172
Hurok, Sol, 288
Hutchinson, G. Evelyn, 384
huudi huudi song, 356, 358, 362

"I Got It Bad and That Ain't Good," 377
"In a Sentimental Mood," 377
Indianapolis Recorder, 145–46
Indians, American, 61, 62
International Society for the Study of Time, 383
Ironside (TV show), 327
"I've Got Rhythm," 315

Jackson, Mahalia, 344
Jackson, Milt, 349
Jacoby, Lou, 251, 259
James, Daniel "Chappy," 178, 338
jazz:
   children introduced to, 272–77
   Chinese audience for, 387–96
   critics of, 262–63
   drums for, 37, 349–50, 358, 377
   history of, 31–32, 273–77, 330, 364, 365
   improvisation in, 276–77, 389
   lingo of, 191, 239, 287, 304
   lyrics as important to, 279
   modern, 127–28, 349, 358
   modulation in, 278–79
   as musical heritage, 270–71
   "outside," 305, 306, 307
   progressive, 170–71
   Russian audience for, 295–301
Jenkins, Buddy, 45, 79, 143
"Jersey Bounce, The," 229
Jesus Christ, 61, 66
"Jitterbug Marching," 115–17
John, Mr., 87–90
Johnson, J. J., 265, 327
Johnson, James Weldon, 383
Johnson, Little Mutt, 73
Jones, Bessie, 346, 372, 378
Jones, Elvin, 160, 309, 348
Jones, Jo:
   as drummer, 37, 70, 127, 261, 307, 309, 347,
      383, 416–17, 420
   at Ruff's Yale concert, 371, 372, 373, 377
Jones, Lester, 106
Jones, Quincy, 233, 327
Jones, Rufus, 372, 382
Jones, Spike, 247, 249
Joplin, Scott, 282
Jordan, Louis, 151
Juilliard School of Music, 8, 154–55, 181

Kansas City Clowns, 68
Keller, Helen, 15, 16, 80, 418
   Ruff's interest in, 63–64, 420
Kennedy, Robert F., 343
Kenton, Stan, 230, 267
Kepler, Johannes, 208, 384, 385–86
Kepler Label, 385, 408
Khrushchev, Nikita, 302, 303